WE BELIEVE IN PRAYER

WE BELIEVE IN PRAYER

A Compilation of Personal Statements by American and World Leaders About the Value and Efficacy of Prayer

by

LAWRENCE M. BRINGS

Publishers

T. S. DENISON & COMPANY

Minneapolis

TO MY WIFE

For thirty-seven years
my faithful associate and
source of inspiration.

Brings, Lawrence Martin, 1897-   comp.
    We believe in prayer; a compilation of personal state-
ments by American and world leaders about the value and
efficacy of prayer. Minneapolis, T. S. Denison [1958]
    616 p.   23 cm.

1. Prayer   I. Title.

BV205.B7   264.1   58—13126 ‡

Library of Congress

ACKNOWLEDGEMENTS

I wish to acknowledge the splendid spirit of cooperation shown me by all the contributors of statements contained in this book. This is doubly appreciated since I realize that all the authors of these articles are busy people and it was only because of their belief in prayer that they were willing to share their experiences with the readers of this book. This fact alone proves the point that prayer holds a dominant place in the thinking of our people.

Special acknowledgement is given to publishers who gave their permission for a reprint of their copyrighted material. Among these are: The Readers' Digest, Guideposts, Little, Brown & Company, The National Council of Churches, Association Press, The Instructor, Doubleday & Company, Seabury Press, Harper & Brothers, and Abingdon Press.

LAWRENCE M. BRINGS

INTRODUCTION

Civilized man has always engaged in the practice of prayer. Practically every religion of the world recognizes the existence of a Supreme Being to whom its adherents pay homage and offer prayers of thankfulness and supplication. For man realizes that he is a finite being and that he needs the guidance and help of God if he is to live his earthly existence "in the sight and glory of God." That this attitude of prayer has become engrained in his very nature is evidenced by the utterance of such simple expressions in daily conversation as "I wish" or "I hope." These phrases are little prayers and indicate how dependent we are upon a Power beyond ourselves.

With advances made in scientific and industrial development, with an emphasis being placed on material things, with a guarantee given by Government to every citizen for a security "from the cradle to the grave," is it necessary any longer for man to feel dependent upon God? Since it is apparent in many instances that he has forgotten the fact that God still rules the universe, I became curious to discover to what extent people believe in prayer today.

I decided to poll certain leaders of America and of the world, asking them to express their views about the value and efficacy of prayer based upon their own experience and observation. No attempt was made to ascertain their religious or denominational background, or even to select individuals from whom I might expect a favorable reply. Frankly, I informed them that I had nothing to offer them except their personal satisfaction in contributing an article to this book, "We Believe in Prayer."

Letters were sent to hundreds of topflight people in many diversified areas of human endeavor. The response was overwhelming. I was surprised that so many persons occupying positions of achievement and responsibility would take the time to write a special statement for this book, giving their personal testimony about the power of prayer as experienced by them. In this book you will find proof that prayer is a potent force in the lives of thousands of our leaders.

I hope that the readers of this book will derive inspiration and encouragement as they read these personal statements of our leaders about the effect of prayer in their lives. It should convince us that there is something worth-while about the practice of prayer.

LAWRENCE M. BRINGS

The Contributors

9

11

13

15

16

19

22

23

25

26

27

29

33

37

AMERICA ON ITS KNEES

By Conrad N. Hilton

President of Hilton Hotels

❦

After I had delivered an address on "The Battle for Freedom," I received a letter from a boy of 12, Daniel Paolucci, in which he wrote: "You are very right, and I think if everyone would fall down and pray we would have real peace."

It dawned on me that something had been left out of that speech. Something that had been in Daniel's letter. Funny that I, who had known prayer and trusted the power of prayer all my life, should not have mentioned it. Prayer was the answer!

It was on a train to Chicago, thinking about Daniel's letter, that I first saw a mental image of Uncle Sam on his knees, praying. Praying for what? Certainly not that "God be on my side." Through two ghastly wars both sides made that prayer and it didn't get much peace even for the victor. Obviously that hadn't worked. Daniel himself must have learned how foolish it would be to explain to his algebra teacher how he'd like mathematics to work.

"That I be on God's side." That would be Uncle Sam's peace prayer.

Still fired with this concept when the train pulled into Chicago, I was amazed when I bought a daily paper. The first thing that caught my eye was a cartoon entitled "When Problems Overwhelm." Before a littered desk sat the figure of Uncle Sam harassed by troubles. But he didn't look like the Uncle Sam I had visualized on the train: strong, earnest, grounded on a rock of faith. Here sat a harassed old fellow. And from the wall opposite him an infinitely compassionate portrait of Abraham Lincoln spoke: "Have you tried prayer, Sam?"

To me that was confirmation of my vision. In the spirit of humility and with loving advice, a prayer took form.

OUR FATHER IN HEAVEN:

We pray that you save us from ourselves.

The world that You have made for us, to live in peace, we have made into an armed camp.

We live in fear of war to come.

We are afraid of "the terror that flies by night, and the arrow that flies by day, the pestilence that walks in darkness and the destruction that wastes at noon-day."

We have turned from You to go our selfish way.

We have broken Your commandments and denied Your truth.

We have left Your altars to serve the false gods of money and pleasure and power.

Forgive us and Help us.

Now, darkness gathers around us and we are confused in all our counsels.

Losing faith in You, we lost faith in ourselves.

Inspire us with wisdom, all of us of every color, race and creed, to use our wealth, our strength to help our brother, instead of destroying him.

Help us to do Your will as it is done in heaven and to be worthy of Your promise of peace on earth.

Fill us with new faith, new strength and new courage, that we may win the Battle for Peace.

Be swift to save us, dear God, before the darkness falls.

I visualized the portrait of Uncle Sam as I had seen him on the train, not weak, not knocked to his knees, but. freely and confidently kneeling, knowing how to do battle for peace, and by his side this prayer.

Because I felt the need of re-expressing the belief of America's founders in prayer as a vital force in national life, on July 4, 1952, I published in some magazines a full color pictorial presentation of "America On Its Knees," the portrait and the prayer. It was my present to Daniel Paolucci and my fellow Americans on Uncle Sam's birthday.

* * *

The place was the South Pacific. The time — June, 1945. Virginia Company was lost. The brush was so thick they could not see ten feet in front of them. There had been a path but they had lost it miles back. The woods in front of them was alive with the enemy and the snarl of bullets whipped through the trees. Suddenly the bullets increased; the aim began to get better; men began to fall.

"Call headquarters," shouted the leader, "and find out if we can get some help!"

A few minutes later reserves were on their way to support the company. If Napoleon had been around, he never would have been able to understand. It would have been a mystery to Caesar and to Bismarck, even to General Foch. But every youngster in America today could have told them that it was a "walkie-talkie" that got them out of trouble.

Walkie-talkie is as old as Adam and Eve. We have all had one since the day we were able to talk. We did not have to wait for the improvements brought on by years of research in the world of radio communications. What I mean is that we have always had prayer. We have always been able to talk to general headquarters any time we wished. And we never had to worry that our Commanding Officer might think our call unimportant, or that we were lacking courage for consulting Him too frequently, or that asking advice too often.

What I like about prayer is that it is a means of communication with God. You can speak to Him any time, night or day, and you can know with certainty that He is listening to you.

What I like about prayer is that there is no set formula for calling general headquarters on our private walkie-talkie. There are no call letters. You are free to send any message you want. You can just say "hello"; you can ask for something. You can tell Him that things are going rough and you need reinforcements — as those boys in the jungle did. You can call to thank Him for the things He has done for you. You can tell Him you are baffled, bewildered, discouraged or that you are the happiest person in the world.

In over forty years I had never, without good reason, missed a Sunday Mass. To me there is nothing shameful about praying when you're in trouble. If prayer has been the habit of a lifetime, it's the natural thing to do. If you have never prayed before, it's a good time to start. Either way there can be times when you are overwhelmed and there is no place else to turn.

For me, in personal living, in fulfilling our place in the world, in faithful use of our talents, each of these is a spoke in the circle of successful living. Prayer is the hub that holds the wheel together. Without our contact with God we are nothing. With it we are "a little lower than the angels, crowned with glory and honor."

WHAT PRAYER MEANS TO ME

By David C. Cook III

President, David C. Cook Publishing Company

Prayer is one of the most important things in the world to me. I could no more get along without prayer than I could get along without God.

My own mother let me know long ago about my personal need for Christ and a daily prayer period. One morning she said to me, "I have just discovered the most wonderful truth. If I just spend the first hour of each day in prayer, it changes my whole day into one of happiness and joy."

"Why, Mother," I replied. "I never heard of such a waste of time in all my life!"

Then she went on to say, "God means everything in the world to me." I answered, "I believe in God, but He doesn't mean that much to me."

Even after hearing these discouraging replies, my mother gave me a book to read. I took her book home. I don't know exactly why I read it because I really didn't intend to. It was a devotional book with a page to read each day. The book told me how to pray. Furthermore, it said that I just wasn't good enough to face life on my own. It said that I wasn't that wise or that talented or that strong. I guess I had gone through just about enough sad experiences to realize that this was true. I was forced to admit that I needed the help of Jesus Christ.

Then one morning after I hadn't slept a wink all night, I decided to have a period of prayer — like my mother and her book said. I told the Lord about my many shortcomings. I spread them all out before Him for Him and me to see. I

43

asked for his forgiveness. And then He gave it to me. He filled my heart with huge waves of forgiveness that cleansed my whole soul. Jesus Christ washed me clean. He washed out all the resentments, all the discouragements, and all the fears. He cut through all the memories of failure in my life. He forgave them. And then He saved me in a bath of tears. Jesus Christ came into my heart that day and has been there ever since.

All the way along the pathway of spiritual discovery, I have been guided by my Lord in prayer. I found out that the way to start the day off right is through the practice of daily prayer. I found out that my hour of prayer is never a waste of time. It saves time. I spend the first hour of each morning in prayer and save hours during the day in improved attitudes which work toward increased efficiency. I continue to pray that God will make the many improvements in my life that are necessary if I am to serve Him effectively.

There are many truths that God wants every one of us to know. He teaches us through His Word and through the many experiences we have each day. He teaches us through circumstances of difficulty as well as through circumstances of joy. But we really learn the lessons that the Lord wants to teach us in life as we pray through these circumstances during our daily periods of prayer. When we pray, we have the opportunity to concentrate on the lessons that He wants us to learn.

But prayer is more than this. During our prayer times we have the opportunity to listen. We listen for the still, small voice of God speaking to our souls. We listen for the experience of love that He brings to us. We are uplifted by His Presence entering into our hearts, enriching and inspiring us to go out and walk upon higher and more loving pathways. Through prayer, He leads us to step above the stumbling blocks which have tripped us in the past. He leads us to accept responsibilities and to face challenges that we never would have faced before. He leads us to dream dreams and to filter them through his prayer screen of divine approval. Then He helps his plans for us to find their spiritual fulfillment.

That's what prayer can mean to us if we practice it faithfully each and every day. It is a way to let God fulfill his desires for us. He teaches us during our prayer times. First He leads us to know what to do with our lives and next He inspires us with the strength to follow his leading. Then as we pray about his plans for us, He brings them to fulfillment. Our prayer times can be a source of wisdom, divine encouragement, and spiritual blessing in our lives each and every day.

AMERICA — AN ANSWER TO PRAYER

By T. Colman Andrews
President, American Fidelity & Casualty Company

Those who pray speak the language of humility and faith, and the rewards for these virtues are great.

Consider, for example, what a nation was to rise in response to the supplications of the Early Settlers at Jamestown and the Pilgrims at Plymouth Rock, and from the prayerful dedication of George Washington and the humility of Benjamin Franklin, no less a man of prayer than Washington.

No battle was begun, and no victory won, but what Washington sought to make God his partner in action and his guide in triumph. And but for Franklin's faith in the power of prayer the Constitutional Convention might well have blown up in acrimonious disagreement.

The Convention had been in relatively indecisive session

45

for nearly two months and the patience of the delegates seemed to be getting ominously short as the oppressive humidity of July in Philadelphia mounted. Perceiving this, Franklin asked and was granted permission to address the delegates.

Van Doren tells us in "The Great Rehearsal," his inspiring account of the proceedings of the Convention, that Franklin started off by reminding the delegates that in the beginning of the "Contest with Great Britain" prayers for the success of the Revolution were offered daily there in that same room — prayers in which some of the delegates themselves had participated — and that those prayers were answered.

"All of us who were engaged in that struggle," Franklin said, "must have observed frequent instances of a Superintending Providence in our favor. To that kind of Providence we owe this happy opportunity of consulting in peace on the means of establishing our future national felicity." But there had been no prayers for the success of the Convention! "Have we now forgotten that powerful friend," he asked, "or do we imagine that we no longer need this assistance?"

By this time the delegates were listening with rapt attention, and Franklin reminded them of the Biblical admonition that "except the Lord build the House they labor in vain that build it." And, declaring his unshakable conviction that "God governs in the affairs of men," he asked: "If a sparrow cannot fall to the ground without His notice, is it probable that an empire can rise without His aid?"

The rest is history. From then on there was daily prayer, and the Convention took on new life and new spirit and went on to agreement in September. Two years later the United States of America was born and by God's grace became the land of hope and the haven of refuge for oppressed people everywhere. And so it will remain if we constantly realize that it is not probable that a nation that was established in God's

46

name can survive without His continuing aid. "Except the Lord keep the city, the watchman waketh in vain."

"If a sparrow cannot fall to earth without his notice, is it probable that an empire can rise without his aid?" Never did any man express more convincingly the assurance that God never ceases from watching over his own, even those who forget him. Nor was there ever a more glorious answer to prayer than our country has become.

The men who assembled in Philadelphia in 1787 to write the charter of a new nation were chosen because they were learned, able and wise, and so they were. But they were human beings, and Franklin, one of the wisest among them, knowing man's limitations, and seeing these limitations becoming manifest as the debate wore on without agreement, knew that the delegates needed help from the one Source that could raise them to the utmost of the capabilities with which He had endowed them.

Franklin admonished the delegates to seek that help, and they did. And America became an answer to prayer!

Those who pray speak the language of humility and faith, and the rewards for these virtues are great.

PRAYER IS A PURELY SPIRITUAL PERFORMANCE

By Gamal Abdel Nasser
President of the United Arab Republic

Prayer constitutes one of the cardinals of Islamic religion, being the nearest approach to God and Divine Presence. That is why it is performed five times daily. That it is a purely spiritual performance is attested by the sense of ourselves in prayers when we are in direct communion with the Almighty.

MORE THINGS ARE WROUGHT
BY PRAYER

By Beatrice Plumb

Author and Teacher

❦

Through our checkered lives of joy and grief, each finds some "treasure of darkness." One such treasure I have surely found! It is wrapped up in two lines of a poem. I have written them on the fly-leaf of my Bible. God has written them on my soul. They are:

> I know not by what methods rare,
> But this I know. God answers prayer.

Not every prayer of mine has been answered at once, or in the way I expected. Sometimes He sent an answer "far more blessed," or said an all-wise "No."

But in every great crisis in my life, God has heard my prayer, so that I have been able to cry joyfully, as did the praying Daniel of old, miraculously saved in his dark dungeon from the hungry lions. "My God hath sent His angel!"

My God sent His angel during one black year of death, despair and desolation. I had lost by death a dear friend who had shared my home for twenty-five happy, productive years. She was my all—mother, sister, companion, secretary, typist, critic. When she died, it seemed as if everything ended for me.

A few months later, I discovered two alarming growths on my body. I had them removed. They were non-malignant, but when the stitches were removed, the incision on my leg had not healed.

There was no apparent reason for this. The other wound, far more serious, had healed in record time.

There followed weeks of lost days and sleepless nights, of constant pain which seemed to reach an unbearable peak after each treatment and dressing. In vain, the doctor tried every remedy, new and old. The ugly gash refused to heal. Finally, she decided that unless there was some sign of healing by the end of the week, I must go into the hospital for skin-grafting.

Back home I threw myself down on the lounge and prayed as I had never prayed before. Back of my mind, there lurked the ghastly fear of amputation. If the doctor could do nothing, Jesus could. In the anguished intensity of my prayers, my spirit seemed to actually leave my body, and limp along a dusty Palestine road after the Great Physician ahead, who had healing even in the hem of His garment, in His very shadow.

"Jesus," I entreated, "cure me! I want to be whole—to be able to walk again. Dr. Jesus, heal me—**now!**"

I seemed to see Jesus stop, turn, and look at me. **God had sent His angel!** For at that instant, there flashed into my mind the mental picture of a book, so real that I put out my hand to take it. It was a book that had deeply interested my dear friend whose death I mourned. She had read bits of it aloud to me. But that was twenty years ago! I had never read the book, and could not remember its title or author.

Yet now there leaped into my mind one particular incident in that book which had thrilled her, and which she had insisted upon reading to me in full.

It told of a man who, for no reason medical science could find, had lost the use of his right arm. Asked if he had suffered any great loss recently, he replied, "Yes, I lost my only son."

"Do you recollect what you first said when told of his sudden death?"

"Yes," replied the man, "I said, 'I have lost my good right arm!' "

As soon as he was shown what this deep, searing thought had done to him, he found, the book recorded, that he could move his arm again!

What had I first said when told that my beloved friend had just died? The memory was like the deep thrust of a knife. I had said—what I had continued to say through all these black weeks—"There is nothing left now to hold my life together. It will fall apart. Everything has come to a standstill without her."

That was it! Months of that sort of thinking had defeated the doctor. The wound had come to a standstill, for it would not knit. I had wept so many times, "I shall never get anywhere without her" that the leg that had helped me get to places was fast becoming helpless.

I could almost see God's angel! I had no previous experience of the healing power of prayer. Indeed, in times past, I had been skeptical when I read of such cures. Yet now I knew positively that in some miraculous way the healing had started!

When the doctor, at the end of the week, inspected that stubborn wound, she called to her nurse, and spoke in a low, excited voice. Together they busied themselves with lights and instruments. Then with a rare smile lighting up her face, she said, "It has started to heal!"

The day she discharged me, cured, I told of the miracle—that the wound had been healed by prayer. She agreed.

"Most doctors know of such cases," she said. "The great Dr. Carrel, winner of the Nobel prize, said that he once saw prayer shrivel a cancerous sore to a scar before his eyes. He considered prayer a force as real as terrestrial gravity! He said it is the greatest form of energy we can generate."

She reminded me of what Steinmetz, the great wizard of electricity, had said before he died: "The scientists of the world will one day turn their laboratories over to the study of God, prayer and the spiritual forces which as yet have been scarcely touched."

Meanwhile, humble Christians the world over are touching those spiritual forces through prayer. We cannot explain or understand them. Awed by the miracles wrought by them, we can only say, with Daniel of old, "God hath sent His angel!"

PRAYER IS COMMUNION WITH GOD

By John Warren Hill

Presiding Justice, Domestic Relations Court, City of New York

When pure reason convinces you that there is an omnipotence behind the creation of this universe and of man, you can fasten on to that fact with your mind and rationalize that power as emanating from a divine entity. You recognize its existence with awe. It bears a somewhat vague, personal relationship to you sufficient perhaps to cause you to appeal to it in time of need. But when, through the revelation of the Scriptures, this Supreme Being is interpreted to you as a personal God and when you hear Jesus Christ, whom you know to be the incarnation of truth, speak to you as the avowed Son of God, saying to you: "God is your loving Father, lift up your hearts to Him in prayer," then indeed, in your need, will your heart in full faith cry out to God praying for help and guidance that will sustain.

COMMUNION WITH OUR CREATOR

By Lily Pons

Concert and Opera Singer

❦

Prayer is part of the daily bread of the soul. I do not believe that it has to be something which should be limited to the strict forms of religious services, or even to the so-called morning and evening times of prayer. It should, instead, be a living thing which is a constant companion.

Actually, I see prayer as a combination of hope and faith. If you have faith in an Almighty Being, regardless of what you call Him, you will know that, when your prayers are based on worthy hopes, they will be heard.

During the war, when I toured Army and Navy hospitals all over the world, I saw constant re-affirmations of how much spontaneous prayer can do. A warm thought or word for a sick boy, I found, is like a prayer. And it is answered immediately by the joy and gratitude in the young man's eyes.

I also noticed, during my visits to these hospitals, that those of the boys who seemed least emotionally upset by their injuries almost invariably showed themselves, in conversation, to be fairly religious. They seemed more engrossed in their blessing . . . in offering prayers of thanks for what they were spared, than in that which they had lost.

I feel that this ability to overcome tragedy without really seeing it in a tragic light . . . to appreciate what is left rather than bemoan what is gone, is one of the great rewards of prayer. I have had many occasions in my own life, where, by thinking my prayers for guidance through the day, I have found pleasure and comfort in events which would otherwise have been very upsetting.

Since prayer is and can be so much a part of our daily lives, and music is so much a part of my life, even in music, I find that one can find nearness to God. What a constant source of hope and inspiration there is in the swelling sound of music as the tone seems to reach, as it were, up to Heaven! Music accompanies some of our most sacred ceremonies. Music can inspire us, soothe us, and lift us up. Who can not react to the pure beauty of Handel's "Messiah" or Bach's "St. Matthew Passion?" Song is a symbol of joy, and music can reflect the spirit of the highest.

For all of us, there can be in everything in our daily lives a communion with our Creator. We can and must look for it in all ways, and our own prayers can lead the way.

PRAYER IS AUTOMATIC WITH MEN

By John Temple Graves
Editor and Author

❦

I believe that men of science and reason can pray today as they never prayed before we came to this era when physics is turned to metaphysics and mathematics touches God.

Einstein could take his E equals Mc2 formula billions of light years into space, but he hadn't the faintest idea, as he would tell you himself, what's behind the next billion, what's behind the "baths of all the Western stars." He could project us backwards and forwards through the ages and aeons, but he hadn't the faintest idea what time it is in eternity.

It is this confirmation of the fact of things inconfirmable that makes prayer automatic with men of sentience now.

THE WIDENING CIRCLE OF PRAYER

By Wilfred Kitching

General, The Salvation Army, International Headquarters in London

Prayer has ever been for me like a widening circle. Its influence began in the home, where parents folded the hand of the infant and early in life taught the child to whisper the fond name of Jesus. The place of prayer at the family altar became another circle and the child went to school having taken its own part in prayer with its parents. In the home can be taught the naturalness of prayer, as the relationship is strengthened between a Heavenly Father and His children. These, the first imprints on the mind, are all-important.

I speak from personal experience as one who can say, "the lines have fallen about me in pleasant places and I have a goodly heritage!" I can never get away from those first influences of prayer. But the prayers of childhood, whilst building a foundation for the life of prayer, must not be taken as the final pattern. Prayer must be developed from the "cry in the hour of need" to a realization that by this means is to be found the one and only reliable medium in the discovery of God.

It is true that prayer so often begins with asking for what we want, like little children running to their parents with seemingly trivial requests, and if we become displeased because our puny desires are not granted, it is evident that we have little understanding of a God of Love. God has a plan for our lives and even when He says "no" to our requests, great is the peace in the human heart when we recognize the wealth of love in that answer.

In prayer there must be growth and it is by the constant communion of the soul with its Maker that new revelations are received of His purity and power. Sooner or later there comes

54

not a problem nor a profit to me, but one who exists in the mystery of his life with God, his fellows, and himself, and who has my prayers for his good in the goodness of God.

To experience prayer is to be knit together in love. For prayer is love's inner life. Every person I meet is either a potential threat to my confidence and self-esteem, whom I must criticize and knock down to competible size—OR—he is a brother for whom Christ died, for whose best good I pray, and wish him the riches of Christ in confident, glad living and the peace of life everlasting. Through prayer my ego joins up with the human race and becomes part of the Son of Man's intercession for all men. I am made a man as, haunted by the face of Christ in the face of every man, I pray.

PRAYER HELPS US "TO SEE THE RIGHT"

By Francis Case

U.S. Senator from South Dakota

❦

To pause for prayer is to give one's inner self a chance to get himself in tune with God.

From the calm of reflection and meditation there comes a confidence that what one should do, he can do and will have God's help in doing.

If anyone wants to know how much faith in prayer has meant at a critical hour, let him read Abraham Lincoln's Second Inaugural Address "With malice toward none, with charity toward all—and with Faith in the Right as God gives us to see the right—." We "see" when we pray.

OBEDIENCE TO THE UNATTAINABLE

By Dr. Joseph Simonson

Former U.S. Ambassador to Ethiopia

"You must be perfect, as your heavenly Father is perfect" is the way Jesus once put His standard of life before us. Reading it in St. Matthew's Gospel I suppose we are tempted to think Christ was exaggerating this all-inclusive demand for emphasis and effect upon His hearers. But we cannot accuse our Lord of playing with words; He meant what He said.

God's demand **is** that we be perfect. But immediately we despair and say that if that is what He requires of us we just do not see any point in even trying. If we choose that response (not all do), we shall miss the joy and power of obedience to the unattainable.

No Christian should desire less than perfection. He should want to be the best he can, not only better than he was yesterday. The "better" is too often a deceiving half-way house on the road to the "best." The Christian wishes to attain the summit, not only pitch his tent on the slopes leading up to the top crest.

What if a Christian does not realize perfection? Is that any excuse for not trying? He will have immense power and lift in his life because of the effort he makes and because he keeps perfection ever before him. This must be so because Christ deliberately placed perfection before us as the ideal and because I know in my own life and that of others I know it has worked out that way.

That which is important for us to practice in our obeying the unattainable is disciplined and earnest prayer. Do you recall that one time when His disciples wondered why they could not do what their Master could do, He replied that only by prayer could it be done? If any task is difficult, if a problem seems impossible to solve, if we try and try and still fail, try prayer. It will not fail! Prayer specializes in the impossible, the unattainable. Prayer recognizes that with man there are many impossibilities, but at the same time rejoices that praying opens for weak man a channel to God's limitless love and power, with Whom nothing is impossible.

CALM FOLLOWS PRAYERS

By Dr. Jim Dan Hill

President, Wisconsin State College and Major General, USA, Retired

❀

I have long harbored a suspicion that prayers are sometimes made of which the supplicant himself is hardly aware, and, conversely, there are formal utterances of prayer that hardly fall within the true definition of the term.

One grim day during the Battle of the Bulge, as a National Guard Colonel Commanding the 190th Field Artillery Group, I happened to ask a soldier if he ever prayed. He said he didn't know for sure, but there were times when he couldn't tell whether he was praying or merely expressing mixed emotions of fear and hope. I asked him if he felt better after such prayers, and he said it gave him a calm, peaceful feeling.

We can leave the logic and rationalization to the psychologists or to whomsoever else may apply themselves to explaining it in their own way, but in my scheme of things, the soldier had been praying, and his prayers had been answered.

PRAYER: GOD'S WIRELESS

By Dr. C. Sverre Norborg

Philosopher and Pastor

❧

During World War II it was my privilege to serve in our American intelligence. It was a demanding but fascinating experience to be thrown out of the quietude of a professor's study into the life-and-death unit of this world-wide struggle for freedom.

To most of us there was no physical danger involved in our intelligence assignment. To some of our co-workers, however, the work meant an existential gamble, by day and by night. Those were the volunteer agents, who manned our secret senders in enemy lands. They lived dangerously. Many of them died heroically. All of them have remained anonymous to the nation they served so well.

I can still sense the drama-filled silence of the wireless control rooms established to receive the nocturnal messages from the secret senders behind the enemy lines: The calling signal, the contact, the crackling tones of the coded messages, and the sign-offs. To me the wireless station seemed like a sanctuary of freedom, where we listened to brave men's significant messages.

One chilly dawn, as we walked out into the morning mist, the whole experience suddenly became a symbolic analogy to God's personal contact with us — in prayer.

Prayer is personal communication. The Magna Charta of prayer is the Bible with its Divine Call, its promises and its personal challenge.

Prayer is a community experience, which we participate in together, when we worship with the living congregation of fellow believers, who are citizens of that vast, invisible Kingdom of God through all ages, all races and all nations. In fact, the worship hour is the green pastures of our soul's busy week. The worship fellowship is the edge of eternity in a world of that confusion, which we call time. Keeping the Sabbath holy, we receive the keys to spiritual and mental health.

The rest of the week we are in the midst of an existence filled with speed and greed, self and pride, competition and exhaustion, worries and temptations. It is in this daily routine that we need the wireless of personal prayer.

The Mohammedans kneel and bow in prayer towards Mecca, each day, at regulated hours. The Christians are invited to pray always, without ceasing, in the Divine Intelligence System, which gives his heart its homing radar and his faith the assurance of God's personal presence.

As the children of God, we carry our secret sender along with us, even behind the enemy lines, always knowing that the Divine Receiving Station is open for contact, as soon as we call.

Prayer communications are of many kinds: Supplication, calls in need, calls of praise and thanksgiving, interspersed with moments of the wordless communication of adoration of our Father which art in heaven.

In conclusion, two observations — the one practical, the other scientific.

To a scientific mind, in our day and age faith in prayer has become an almost natural thing. In our era of IBM machines, mathematical magic, space conquest, and astrophysics, it would be almost stupid to believe that the Creative Intelligence of God should be blocked by time or space.

From the point of view of practice: If you are a skeptic or a faltering novice in the practice of personal prayer, the classical textbook is the Book of Psalms. Read the psalms, pray the psalms. Suddenly, one day, you will experience the Copernican revolution called Divine Contact.

THE SEARCH FOR GOD

By Edward Martin

U.S. Senator from Pennsylvania

❀

The longer I observe the course of American advance toward higher spiritual levels the more I am convinced that faith and prayer have been powerful factors in building the strength of our nation.

It seems to me that greatest influence in our leadership for world peace and human freedom is the strong religious foundation upon which God-fearing men and women established and have maintained the American way of life.

Going back to the earliest settlements on the North American Continent we find the spirit of religion as the dominant force that guided the pioneers in their daily struggle with the perils and hardships of the savage wilderness. In humble prayer they acknowledged the presence of God and their submission to the Divine will. They turned to the Holy Bible for spiritual comfort and guidance. From those early beginnings every advance in the progress and development of our country can be traced by the golden thread of deep religious conviction.

In every crisis our great leaders have placed their faith in God and have prayed for Divine help and guidance.

The spirit of religion guided the Pilgrims to the New England coast. Firm reliance on the protection of Divine Providence is set forth in the Declaration of Independence. When the Constitution of the United States was being written and little progress was being made, Benjamin Franklin reminded his colleagues that "God governs in the affairs of men." He proposed that daily prayers be held "imploring the assistance of Heaven upon our deliberations." That practice continues today in our legislative halls. Our trust in God is expressed in our State papers and on our coins.

Every American can gain renewed inspiration from the immortal example of George Washington kneeling in prayer on the frozen ground of Valley Forge to ask Divine guidance in the dark and discouraging days of the struggle for independence.

Prayer has been in the heart and on the lips of every President in all our history as a nation. After his first inauguration President Washington implored Almighty God "to keep the United States in Thy holy protection."

In the tragic time of crisis, when brother fought against brother in the War between the States, the faith of Abraham Lincoln in the power of prayer never wavered. That faith was voiced when he said:

"I have been driven to my knees over and over again by the overwhelming conviction that I had nowhere else to go. My own wisdom, and that of all about me, seemed insufficient for that day."

Coming down to our own day we can all recall the eloquent and reverent prayer uttered by President Eisenhower as a prelude to his inaugural address.

"Give us, we pray, the power to discern clearly right from wrong and allow all our works and actions to be governed thereby . . . so that all may work for the good of our beloved country and for Thy glory."

The United States will live and prosper so long as we continue the search for God in our daily lives.

HOW TO PRAY

By Dr. Samuel M. Shoemaker

Calvary Episcopal Church, Pittsburgh

❊

We are to think together now about how to pray. Once Jesus was praying, and when He stopped, one of His disciples said, "Lord, teach us to pray. . ." That disciple saw that prayer was a habit of Jesus', and one which brought power into His life. He wanted and needed that same power; so he said, "Lord, teach us to pray. . ." We begin with that prayer now.

Immature Prayer

We always begin praying by asking for what we want. Later on we see that this is selfish and childish, and move out of it to a more mature kind of prayer. But while we are spiritually immature, we are concerned with what we want. I talked with a very intelligent man about a problem in his life, and asked him if he ever prayed. "Yes," he said, "I pray every day." I asked what he did when he prayed, and he said, "I just keep telling God over and over again what I want." And I said to him, "Did it ever occur to you that God might some time ask you, 'Which of us is God, anyway?' Are you telling God in prayer,—or is God telling you?"

Mature Prayer

Now the difference between our telling God in prayer, and our wanting God to tell us, is the difference between childish prayer and mature prayer, between selfish prayer and unselfish prayer, between the kind of prayer that will not weather the storms of experience and the kind of prayer that will carry us through those storms, between unconverted prayer and converted prayer. Until we want God's will more than we want our own, prayer for us is contending with God, not cooperating with Him. It is trying to change His will, and not trying to find His will. Prayer is for many people only the intensification of self-will, the projection of self-love.

Prayer Changes The Pray-er

The first change that prayer accomplishes, therefore, is in the person who prays. The first objective of prayer is the alignment of ourselves with the will of God. We are not there to tell God what He does not know, nor to persuade Him to do something He might not have thought of, or been willing to do, without being asked. God is perfection—perfection of love and perfection of holiness; therefore His will is always loving and holy, always kind in its intention, and always holy in its purpose. Some prayer assumes that we are better than God, or know more than He; and therefore it is false prayer. And so we need a great initial surrender of ourselves to His will, once and for all, if we would pray aright. And we also need to bend ourselves anew to the will of God each time we pray. "Thy will, not mine, be done" must be shot all through our prayers for specific objects. When our wills have been brought into line with the will of God, then we are praying "in the Spirit," then the mighty, energizing force of prayer is released, because we are truly cooperating with God, and God is using the power of human prayer to release His will in us and through us.

Praying In Christ's Name

All this puts a point on prayer in the Name of Christ. Jesus told us to pray this way, "Hitherto have ye asked nothing in my name: ask, and ye shall receive, that your joy may be full." Most of our formal, and many of our informal, prayers close with the words "through Jesus Christ our Lord." This is not a talisman attached to the end of a prayer to ensure its arrival at the throne of God, and His attention to be given to it; this is our pledge that we have compared this prayer with the Spirit of Christ, strained it through the sieve of Christian

63

standards, and brought it to God because it is the truest prayer we can pray, and so we bring it and offer it at the feet of God.

Praying For Yourself

Does this mean, then, that we can never pray for ourselves, or for things'? By no means! Someone told me the other day that he never prays for himself. I told him that I frequently needed to pray for myself—not to get what I want, but to be told what I ought to do, and to re-align myself with God's will. I need forgiveness, I need grace, I need direction. But the objective is not my pleasure, but the quality of my service. Anything that heightens our service for God is a legitimate object of prayer. To pray for a comfortable home may be a selfish prayer if you want it all for yourself; but if you want a home where, through entertainment and friendship you can work for Christ, your prayer may be unselfish.

The great personal prayer of a Christian is always, "Thy will be done," and the great public prayer of a Christian is always, "Thy Kingdom come." When we have thought through any course of action, or the acquiring of anything, and it honestly seems right to us, as a contribution to the Kingdom of God, we certainly have a right to bring that prayer before God, and ask Him to answer it, if it is His will.

God Always Answers

Such praying will teach us that there is no such thing as unanswered prayer. God always answers. It has been truly said that sometimes His answer is "yes," and sometimes His answer is "no," and sometimes His answer is "not yet." If our great object in prayer is not to get our own way, but to find the will of God, then we can never come away from that kind of prayer unsatisfied.

Praying For Others

The prayer of intercession means prayer for others. It is our faint echo of Christ's everlasting intercession for us before

64

the throne of God. It is love and concern for people lifted to the highest point, as we bring them before the throne of God in prayer. I do not know why God should need our prayers, or why He gives us the unspeakable privilege of helping Him in His world; but I am sure He does. I am sure that human intercession adds something to the creative and redemptive energy even of God Himself. I am sure that the people He can most depend on are the pray-ers who lift up other people before Him, and hold them there in prayer.

Prayer For Healing

Prayer for healing is a great subject, and must be dealt with, remembering that so great a soul as St. Paul prayed for healing which was never given, though grace to bear his affliction was given. Nevertheless, one has seen some astonishing healings that have taken place where many prayers were concentrated upon a person who was ill, where he was kept constantly before God. Serious illness means also great weakness, so that one cannot pray for himself as he would. It almost seems as if, in a believing person, this made him all the more open to the power of the prayers of others. I wish that we all might go deeper in this kind of prayer. This is a day when all want to serve, when many will need prayer when they are in action, and when all of us who can should pray often and pray deeply for them.

Divine Guidance

Another kind of prayer is the prayer of illumination. You have sometimes knelt down with your soul in a whirl, and gotten up feeling quiet and steady inside. You have also sometimes knelt down with your mind perplexed, in doubt about what you should think or believe or do, and gotten up with the course clear, so that you knew what you should think or believe or do. For people who have prayed, in all ages, it is unmistakable and beyond question that God gives us luminous thoughts when we pray. Sometimes these come to us suddenly and without long preparation. Sometimes they come after a considerable period of prayer. Sometimes they only come after a night's sleep, or even several days of waiting. God deals differently with different souls; but He can hardly deal at all with a soul that limits Him at the outset by prescribing what He can or cannot do. Let us shut off our eager petitions, and still our bodies into repose, and wait for the word of comfort, or the clear conviction of sin, or the flash of insight, which God may choose to send to us. Do not think so much of your own unworthiness as you think of God's wonder, nor of your own spiritual incapacity as of His infinite desire and power to make Himself known to His children.

Practical Suggestions:

1. **Form A Habit Of Prayer.** It takes time and discipline to form a habit, but a time for prayer in your life can become as natural a necessity as breakfast, and it should. Pray often briefly—in your office, as you go to keep appointments, on the train—asking God's help and guidance for yourself or others. But allow a regular space in your day for longer prayer—not two minutes or five, but fifteen or thirty minutes, so that you forget time. Carve that period out of your early morning, and make the adjustments necessary.

2. **Read Before You Pray.** Read the Bible systematically. You may find helpful the serial books of devotion called Forward Day by Day, or the Upper Room or E. Stanley Jones' "Abundant Living." Use any devotional book that helps you. This draws your mind towards God, and makes you ready to pray.

3. **Let Great Prayers Help You To Pray.** Make frequent use of books of prayer. Let us really know the treasure-

houses of inspired devotional utterance. There comes a time in private prayer when we want to talk to God out of our hearts, and in our own words. But the prayers of others will help us to do this. As we fill those ancient and modern and universal prayers with our own needs, they will live for us, and help us to lift up our hearts to God.

4. **Pray Aloud Sometimes As An Aid To Concentration.** One of the worst enemies of prayer is just wandering of mind. We are accustomed to finish a sentence or conversation when we speak; it helps to talk aloud to God. Shut yourself in a quiet place, and pray aloud.

5. **Pray With Others Sometimes As An Aid To Fellowship In Prayer.** I well remember the first time I ever prayed with another person, and it marked a milestone in my life. It banished self-consciousness, and included another in the serious work of prayer. "If two of you shall agree on earth as touching anything that they shall ask, it shall be done for them of my Father which is in heaven."

6. **Fix The Results Of Your Praying By Writing Down What Comes To You.** Many thoughts pass through your mind as you wait listening before God. Some are more important, some less; but writing them down will help you remember them, so that you can carry them out.

I give you these suggestions which have helped me. Nothing yields fruit like experiment, and each of us must find what helps him most in the glorious enterprise of prayer.

Lord, teach us to pray!

THE LIGHT WITHIN

By Frederic Babcock

Editor, Magazine of Books, Chicago Tribune

❧

When I was a boy and a member of one of the respectable religious sects I was taught that unless we confessed our sins and prayed to God for forgiveness we would be doomed to eternal hellfire and damnation. Our God was a wrathful God, a God of vengeance, looking down at us from somewhere in the sky and ready to pounce on us and punish us whenever we were guilty of the slightest indiscretion. There was nothing benign or merciful about Him.

The war came, and, like four million other young Americans, I was seduced into it. The preachers and the professional patriots did their best to spread more hatred. They told us it was our Christian duty to fly at the throats of other Christians whom we didn't know and against whom we held no grudge. When we found ourselves allied with non-Christians we were to instruct them how to fight and kill in the Christian manner. And all this was in the name of the Prince of Peace, whose greatest teaching was that we can attain our goals through spiritual rather than physical force.

Our preachers led us in prayers to God to help us kill the Germans. The German preachers led their youngsters in prayers to God to help them kill the Americans. God helped. Ten million Christians were slain, and God must have been mightily pleased by the slaughter of His people. Ah, yes.

I came home disillusioned. Somehow, the lessons I had learned from the clerics didn't seem to make much sense. That was when I left the church.

Years later, after a great deal of reading and listening and observing, I joined the Religious Society of Friends. I had learned that for three hundred years the Quakers had refused to have anything to do with warfare, had declined to bow to despotic authority, and had suffered in silence when they were persecuted for standing by their principles.

I was inspired by Thoreau and his doctrine of civil diso·bedience, and by Gandhi and his doctrine of passive resistance—the latter borrowed, as Gandhi readily admitted, from Thoreau's writings. These appeared to me to fit in with the preachments and practices of the Quakers.

I learned that the Society of Friends has no formal creed. Every member is free to believe what he wants to believe. As Carl Sandburg once remarked to me, "Every Quaker is his own pope." No ecclesiastical authority dictates what we Friends have to think or do.

We acknowledge the existence of a Supreme Being, but we don't pretend to know exactly what He is or where He is. We follow what we call the Light Within. Most of us believe there is a spark of the divine in all of us, Friends and non-Friends alike, and that by listening to our conscience, and following the light of that inner spark, we can achieve true simplicity and serenity and spirituality.

Except when the spirit moves one of us to talk, we sit silently in our modest meeting houses. We erect no spires or cathedrals for the glory of God. Unlike that preacher in one of Sinclair Lewis' novels, we don't presume to "tell God that God is God." We have no quarrel with the pomp and circumstance of rival religious groups; we recognize the right of everybody to worship God as he pleases. We meditate and we pray—mostly without speaking or sermonizing. We realize that we are "standing in the need of prayer."

If our form of worship doesn't appeal to other people, we are not concerned. For us, at least, it has proved efficacious, and that's all that matters.

THERE'S MORE TO LIFE THAN LIVING

By Keith Wegeman

American Olympic Ski Jumper

❧

"This is the greatest thrill life has to offer," I said to myself as I stood poised at the top of the world's highest ski jump at Oberstdorf, Germany. It is an electrifying experience just to see men make that jump, let alone to be part of the spectacle!

For a moment I paused, all alone, 650 feet above the outrun of the jump. Below, 80,000 people seemed no bigger than ants.

Then the signal was given.

Suddenly the crowd was silent as I plummeted down, crouched for the take-off. My speed was picked up by a system of electric eyes at over 80 miles per hour. The world careened madly past. My senses couldn't keep pace with the scream of the wind and the blur of trees, snow and sky.

And suddenly I was in the air, hanging motionless over the white knoll below—lost in the mystery of another world altogether. After what seemed an eternity, I landed 16 feet beyond the 400-foot mark, the longest jump an American skier had ever made. But mere statistics could never describe what I had just experienced.

Two months later I was aboard a plane bound back to the United States. The engines droned endlessly, I knew no one aboard—it was a good time for thinking.

Thinking! There had been so little of it in my life. Always, energies had been spent **doing** things. From the time I strapped on my first pair of skis at the age of three, until the moment I stepped on that plane, I'd been living from one moment of high adventure to the next. Boxing, pole-vaulting, high diving, mountain climbing in the summer, football in the fall, and in the winter—most thrilling of all—skiing.

I don't remember when I first began to want to make the Olympic ski team; as long as I can remember it had been the chief goal of my life. The college ski championship, state, national—all of them were just getting ready.

And at last, in 1952, I was picked for the Olympic team. The months of practice, the trip to Europe, the Olympic Games in Oslo— they were the high points in my life.

And then the Olympics were over. For the rest of that winter I bummed restlessly from tournament to tournament: Norway, Yugoslavia, Germany and the record-making jump at Oberstdorf. Always a new challenge, a new jump, one more skier I wanted to beat, a new thrill ahead.

The ski season over, I went to Paris and made the rounds of bistros, music halls, night spots, but even the thrills of Paris wear thin after awhile. I boarded the plane for New York.

Up there over the Atlantic, I tried to summon up the excitement of the winter behind me. It didn't come, I was forced to sit still, and as the engines droned on I half-admitted that my "triumphs" in Europe had been trying desperately to recapture the tremendous elation of the Olympics, trying to make it last.

And suddenly I said aloud, "What then, does last? What's important? What's the answer?" I was as startled by the question as my seat mate. I was 23 years old, and never before had such questions even occurred to me. I turned red, apologized, and tried to push the stubborn questions away.

When the plane landed in New York, I all but ran down the steps, so happy was I to be out in the world of **doing** things once more. I'd had enough of thinking. I looked up a buddy, and for a month we "did the town." I discovered that I was something of a celebrity. In the daytime there were appearances, speeches, endorsements; at night we went to the race tracks or the night clubs. I never stopped moving.

But the thrills of New York soon wore thin too. It was May—the tennis season! I went home to Colorado and threw myself into tennis as though my life depended on it. My draft call was coming up, and I was almost glad. Maybe I'd be sent to Korea. Dodging bullets—there'd be excitement that didn't wear thin!

One warm afternoon on the tennis court, I was conscious of a pain in my side. After dinner, I went for a long walk under the stars, trying to make the pain go away. By the time I returned home the appendix had ruptured; I was on the operating table for three hours, and in the hospital for a month and a half.

For the second time that year I was forced to lie quietly where my thoughts could reach me. "What's important? What's the answer?" Why did these questions nag me? I was a athlete, not a philosopher—questions like this had no place in my life. Anyway, I **had** the answer: live for the thrills life has to offer. What other answer was there?

Out of the hospital I was more restless than before. I went to visit my brother in California. Laurie sensed right away that something was wrong. "You seem at loose ends, Keith," he said. "Why don't you come up to the Conference with me?" The young adult group at Laurie's church was planning to spend a week at a camp up in the San Bernardino mountains with young people from other churches.

I looked at Laurie blankly. It didn't sound like my kind of fun.

"We'll be right up in the mountains," he went on, knowing I had never been able to say "no" to a mountain. "Maybe you can get in some climbing." I went with him.

I attended a couple of lectures and a Bible study class or two, but mostly I climbed and hiked and swam. The final night of the Conference came, and I decided I'd better put in an appearance at the closing lecture. The big hall was packed. I sat back, not listening much, drowsy in the warmth of the room. The speaker was winding up his talk. ". . . because pleasures like these are not lasting" he was saying. "What then, does last? What's important in the long run? What's the answer?"

I sat up straight in my chair. Those were **my** questions? The very words I had said aloud on the plane! The questions that had never quite let me alone since then.

"Do you want to know the answers?" the speaker continued.

I leaned forward, waiting for the answer like a tennis player waiting for the serve. It was very short. "Try Jesus," he said.

To this day, I don't know whether the speaker was finished, or whether I got up and walked out in front of him and all those people. I only remember that suddenly I was outside, running, racing toward the comforting bulk of the mountain, away from the lecture hall. An hour later I lay on my back on a steep slope, and let the words I'd been running from catch up with me.

I'd known about Jesus all my life, believed in Him too— as an idea or a principle. But there on that mountainside for the first time, I spoke to Him as a Person.

"Show me," I whispered. "Show me how to try."

It was almost dawn when I started down the mountain, happier than I had ever been in my life.

A few days later my draft notice came through: I was assigned as an instructor in the newly formed Mountain and Cold Weather Command. With it, came my first opportunity to try Him.

Everyone has a weak spot in his make-up. With me it has been honesty. I wasn't exactly a liar, but on occasions when my performance hadn't been quite so good, I described it later in the most favorable light I could find.

Now, with the men in my Command, I tried the experiment of plain, undecorated truth.

I remember one soldier in particular, who was in big trouble. The Army had developed some highly specialized equipment for our Command, Arctic sleeping bags, light-weight skis, climbing tools. Jack had taken a few of these things for his own use and been caught at it.

Awkwardly, I tried to "open up" to this boy, to tell him what Christ had meant to me, what He could do for him. It seemed to mean something to Jack; together we prayed that this experience of being caught would work for good in his life. When his court-martial came up, they threw the book at him. He came into my quarters that night and called me and my prayers every name he knew and a few he made up just for the occasion.

It was like a bad spill on the slopes, a meet where I'd come in last. But strangely enough, the defeat didn't panic me. I wasn't running away anymore.

It's not the end of the story, either. A few months ago I saw Jack again at a friend's wedding and he caught my arm.

"I've been looking for you, Keith," he said, "I thought you'd like to know. I'm going into the ministry."

As for me, I've decided that my life can best be spent telling young people the "good news" that I've found. Sports can help me do this.

I haven't changed much, in one respect. I'm still living for thrills. But I'm living now for the big ones, the ones that don't wear thin.

—Reprinted from **Guideposts** with permission. **Guideposts** is an inspirational monthly magazine for all faiths published at Carmel, N. Y. Subscription price, $2 a year.

PRAYER STRENGTHENS THE SOUL

By Robert Paterson

Editor, Author, and Lecturer

Prayer, uttered or silent, general or personal, public or private, is strengthening. It strengthens the soul as nothing else can do. Everybody prays in crucial moments, sinners as well as saints. No one becomes too hardened in this life to spurn any means of relief in serious emergencies. Praying instills a feeling of confidence even in depraved minds, as well as in those in the sinking depths of despair, as seen in Kipling's famous line that if damned of body and soul "I know whose prayers would make me whole."

Prayer is the main stimulant that carries us through crises, spurs us to attain objectives, and eases physical pain. It drives nations to victory in war and speeds them to happiness and ameliorative achievements in peace. Prayer undoubtedly is the most beneficial thing mankind knows.

75

PRAYER IS SPIRITUAL
COMMUNICATION WITH GOD
By *Angelo Patri*
Educator and Author

❋

I believe in prayer as I believe in the sunshine and the rain, in the certainty of sunrise and sunset, in the sureness of the eternal laws.

The power of prayer was granted us that we might communicate with a benevolent Power beyond our understanding. It was granted us as a refuge in time of trouble, that time when we all turn for help that can come from no other source. The soldiers said there were no atheists in the trenches. They learned the power of prayer in their emergency, in the hard way of personal experience. There is no other way.

Prayer is a sustaining force as we go about our daily duties. It is a way of merging our mind with the Infinite Mind of God and, relying on that, of casting out fear, denying weakness, affirming power through contact with Infinite Power. It can be but an instant of thought winged in faith or it can be a season of prayerful communication with God. As long as it is breathed in faith it will bring strength and peace and direction.

Prayer, at times, should be a thought of gratitude for what has been received. Often that prayer is forgotten. One prays in anguish of spirit for help, but how many times has one remembered the prayer of thanksgiving for relief? That, too, brings strength and the peace the soul craves.

I believe, and firmly, that we are spiritual beings and that prayer is a means of spiritual communication with God, the Infinite Spirit. I believe that this communication allows us to conquer fear, distress, weakness, and enjoy power and sound minds. I believe this because I, like the soldiers in the trenches, have proved it.

GOD IS WITH US IN PRAYER

By Judge Francis O. Clarkson
The Superior Court of North Carolina

❦

The more we try to learn about prayer the more it can mean to us. I used to think of prayer as mostly asking God for something I wanted. Gradually, I realized by study and being taught that there are many kinds of prayer and that God is with us in all kinds of sincere prayers. Also that the Bible contains many examples of the different kinds of prayer if we will only study and seek to find them.

For example, prayers usually fit into one of the following: confession, intercession, thanksgiving, petition, and adoration. In the Bible we have examples of all of these.

God was with David in prayer in his confession of sin and humble prayer for forgiveness. "For I acknowledge my transgressions: and my sin is ever before me." Psalms 51:3.

God was with Jesus in prayer in His intercession for the disciples. "Holy Father, keep through thine own name those whom thou hast given me, that they may be one, as we are." "I pray not that thou shouldest take them out of the world, but that thou shouldest keep them from the evil." "Neither pray I for these alone, but for them also which shall believe on me through their word." St. John 17: 11,15,20.

Again we find that God was with David in his superb psalms of thanksgiving: "It is a good thing to give thanks unto the Lord, and to sing praises unto thy name, O Most

High. . ." "Make a joyful noise unto the Lord, all ye lands. Serve the Lord with gladness: Come before his presence with singing. . . " Psalms 92 and 100.

There are many examples of petitions in the Bible. For example, God was with David in his prayer that his child might be spared, II Samuel 12: 16.

So in the Acts of the Apostles we find that God was with St. Stephen in his Christ-like prayer for his persecutors when be was being stoned, Acts 7: 60. Many more examples of such petitions are found throughout the Bible.

Many of the psalms are prayers of adoration of God, but the most beautiful and sublime prayer of adoration in the Bible is the Magnificat, St. Luke 1: 46, the Virgin Mary's hymn of praise, "My soul doth magnify the Lord. And my spirit hath rejoiced in God my Savior. For he hath regarded the low estate of his handmaiden: for behold, from henceforth all generations shall call me blessed. . . . ."

So from the Bible and the writings of saints and prophets and from the liturgy and literature of the Church we learn that God is with us in our prayers, when we confess, give thanks and adore His Holy Name. So can we also out of our own experience give testimony that God is with us in prayer.

Prayer is not easy, nor is it easy for one to write about so sacred a subject. But to sum it all up, we can say with assurance that God is with us in prayer, that prayer is power, and that prayer works. It is the human soul's connection with God Almighty and a means of fellowship which he has provided for Christian believers of all ages, and the only true source of strength, joy and help.

PRAYER IS REAL TO ME

By The Rev. James Payson Martin

Minister of The First Presbyterian Church, Jackson, Michigan

❦

When I look back, I cannot remember life without prayer. In the preacher's family into which I was born, talks on prayer and the results of prayer were just as natural as eating and sleeping. During my high school days, I was a part of a discipleship group that met in my home church at 7:30 one morning each week, and we, as young people, sought guidance and tried to deepen our discipleship to Christ.

Upon graduation from high school, I went to college in Tennessee, some 800 miles from home. My first night on the train en route to college was a lonesome one, but through prayer, which by then was so natural to me, I discovered that "The Lord was my Shepherd," and never again did any feeling of homesickness come over me. I am thoroughly convinced that prayer gave me that sense of calm.

But it was not until some years later that the power of prayer came to me with its fullest meaning. I was in my first parish in Minneapolis, and I had, of course, prayed for many people and had preached sermons on prayer. And then came a crisis in our own family.

My wife had taken our son to the pediatrician for his one-year check-up. The appointment was in the morning, and my wife had promised to stop for me at the church at noon so we could go home for lunch. I waited long after the appointed hour, and when she finally arrived her face was tense with concern. In not too gentle a way I chided her for being late, and then she told me why.

The doctor had checked Billy's weight and height, and then began to feel his abdomen, and after a few minutes of silence he had said: "Something is in there that should not be there. It seems to be a growth near his liver. It could be a cyst or a tumor." My wife was sent with our son to the X-ray department, for a series of pictures. Later in the day, the doctor called and said that the X-rays had confirmed his suspicions, and that a large tumor was located near his right kidney.

The next day, with heavy hearts we took our son to the hospital, for our minds were filled with thoughts of tragic possibilities. I remember we went home and spent much time in prayer and Bible reading.

I called my parents in Illinois, and since my father was about to leave for a speaking appointment in Detroit, we urged him to go there by way of Minneapolis, which he did. Although we, as Billy's parents were not allowed in his hospital room, his grandfather was allowed in, and he prayed for him, laying his hands on Billy as Jesus had done to people during His ministry. My father, also a strong believer in prayer, told us that we should thank God in advance for healing Billy. His presence and the power of his prayers did much to bolster us in our faith.

When the day for the surgery came, we waited what seemed a life-time for the surgeon's report, and when he came down, he said: "Well, God has certainly answered your prayers." He explained that the tumor was encased in a capsule-like material. Since it came out in one piece, it lessened the likelihood of any further spead. We thanked God for this, knowing that He was working along with the surgeon.

Within a few days the reports of the operation came back from the laboratory, and we heard those inevitable words: "The growth is definitely malignant." It was a neuroblastoma, weighing two pounds and attached to Billy's adrenal gland on the right side. This gland, along with the tumor and right kidney were all removed. Following this verdict, a series of deep X-ray therapy was given, which made him very weak. But finally he began to show signs of improvement and strength. The doctors were not too encouraging, for they told us that they could not pronounce him cured until he lived for five years after the operation.

During the entire time of Billy's extreme illness, we were overwhelmed by the tremendous response on the part of our family and friends, and the continual prayers which were offered all over the world by our friends on his behalf. Even though the hour seemed dark, we never lost faith that God was working in this situation.

Truly our experiences made us realize that prayer **is** real, and its power became especially real to me. And now, when people come to me as their pastor with their problems, I always point them to prayer as the greatest source of strength and fountain of wisdom for every person and difficulty. I can do this, for I speak out my own deep experience that prayer **does** sustain us—it **does** change things— that it **does** work. Always I give them the assurance of hope, for I know that God cares for us as individuals.

The glorious and fullest answer to prayer came to us in Billy's perfect healing, and just last November he celebrated his sixth birthday, and is today a healthy, active, growing boy —a child of God to whom the power of prayer has been released, and through whom God will continue to work. Thanks be to God for His power which is released through prayer, and for making this power available to every person.

A HANDCLASP WITH GOD

By Garfield G. Duncan, M.D.

Professor of Medicine, University of Pennsylvania

❦

Prayer is a means of contact—a channel of communication which makes possible a personal relationship with the Infinite. It is an access to the powers of the Almighty—". . . unto whom all hearts are open, all desires known and from whom no secrets are hid."

In times of crisis, great anxiety, illness and bereavement the power of prayer is most discernible. It is then that, through a feeling of inadequacy, we reach out to establish personal contact with God.

In the mind's eye I think of prayer as a means of grasping the hand of the Almighty. A tighter grip in times of distress brings increased courage and wisdom to meet one's need. This is a simple concept but none the less comforting.

In quiet, prayerful meditation thoughts are stripped of extraneous inconsequential matters. A feeling of tranquillity develops with a welling up of new strength and inspiration within one. The immediate effects of such an experience do not subside with the return to the complexities of every day. They remain as threads running through the fabric of one's life and may, quite unknown to the individual, exert a far-reaching effect upon those with whom he comes in contact.

The power of prayer is intangible. It is difficult to define, but those who have gained access to this power know of its force for good. The results of prayer are not intangible. They are very practical experiences which can be measured in terms of peace of mind, of increased well-being, and of the joy of living.

The wise physician never discounts the healing power of faith—the handmaiden of prayer. Often he has felt the inward calm and courage of a patient about to undergo a serious operation. He has observed the lack of fear and the abiding faith in the patient who has learned that his survival time is short. He has seen the remarkable convalescence affected favorably by the faith and prayers of the patient, his friends and relatives who visit him, and of his clergyman. All is well with the man who has established this means of grace and source of inspiration and strength, this hand clasp with God in his daily living.

PRAYER BRINGS PEACE OF MIND

By Joe Foss

Former Governor of South Dakota

If a person can pray, he is never alone.

A prayer brings comfort, peace of mind, and proper perspective to all our problems. Worries and fears are lessened in the light of a Greater Being who shares with us as we pray.

Regardless of our walk in life, to learn to pray is to learn to love and understand. The basic of all human frailties is the lack of Christ in our daily living. Nothing in the world is simpler or more rewarding than a prayer, as it needs no special time, no special place and no special effort. Yet it brings a knowledge of oneself in relationship to God, which cannot be attained through another means.

Prayer is a personal thing. Without it in our lives, we are not quite a person.

INTO HARMONIOUS TOUCH WITH GOD

By Judge Ben Moore

Former Judge, U.S. District Court, Southern District, West Virginia

❦

When Jesus' disciples asked him to teach them to pray, the Master complied by suggesting a form of prayer. It did not consist merely of asking for something. It was composed of elements of praise, adoration, worship, submission, and only incidentally of supplication.

Anyone who would enter into communion with his Creator ought to study The Lord's Prayer. While doing so, it must be remembered that the God to whom we pray is a Spirit. He is no long-bearded autocrat, sitting on a throne "far beyond the starry sky." He is not merely "Somebody up there who likes me." He is not even the Jehovah of the Old Testament whose face Moses was not permitted to see, but who granted him a fleeting glimpse of his "back parts." Not even is He the magnificent figure depicted by Michelangelo on the ceiling of the Sistine Chapel, whose electrifying finger calls into being the first man. Such personifications may be useful as symbols, but even as such they are dangerous. They encourage one to think of God as a sort of **deus ex machina,** or at best as a puppeteer who stands behind the scenes and pulls the strings while his marionettes move about on life's stage.

No; God in His spiritual essence is all-pervasive, all-powerful and all-knowing. If He were a person, as we apply that term to a created being, He could not possess all these qualities.

If He lacked any one of them, He could not be God. Because the finite cannot comprehend the infinite, He will always remain a mystery. We cannot hope to understand the nature of the power, the knowledge or the presence of God, nor can we remotely conceive of His mercy in giving ear to our voices. We can, however, come into harmony with the Divine Spirit which is God.

Prayer, as I understand it, is the process of bringing myself into harmonious touch with God. To do so is not easy. So many conflicting, always emotional and sometimes inherently selfish motives and desires exist at once that it is hard to find the spiritual plane on which alone I can meet Him.

This is the point at which the several steps suggested in The Lord's Prayer become significant. I must first acknowledge the holiness, that is, the spiritual purity and sanctity, of God. I must then be willing that all people may share in His blessings. I must acknowledge His will to be supreme and my own will subordinate. Only then may I confidently ask for a personal blessing. Even then, it is proper only to the extent of necessity or protection. If I go further and ask for favor, it must be on condition that I am willing to grant the same favor to another. "Forgive - - - as we forgive - - -."

Effective prayer does not require God to perform miracles. Spiritual and mental laws exist as truly as do physical laws. When harmonious communion with God produces, by whatever agency, a result that would not otherwise have occurred, I do not call it a miracle. I call it the answer to prayer.

Prayer can "remove mountains." It has done so again and again in my own experience.

PRAYER KINDLES THE DIVINE SPIRIT

By Dr. Morris Silverman

Rabbi, Emanuel Synagogue, Hartford, Conn.

We do not discover God through prayer. God discovers us —our hopes, fears, dreams—our true selves. One can feel lonely, downcast and forsaken, even in a teeming city, but God is always there. Through prayer, we are able to reach Him, to feel His presence, and thus we know we are not alone.

"Cast your burdens upon the Lord and He will sustain you." That admonition is as psychiatrically beneficial today as it was in the days of the Psalmist. Some people stop praying when their petitions are unfulfilled. The purpose of prayer is not to induce God to do our will but that we do God's will.

All prayers are not answered. However, there are some that are: the prayers for comfort, strength, courage to do the right, to resist evil, to uphold justice. Surgeons tell us that, all things being equal, the patient who has faith and who prays is more likely to recover after a serious operation than is the unbeliever.

It does not follow that the man of prayer and faith will be spared frustration, pain and tragedy; but, when confronted with such trials, he will have the stamina to cope with his obstacles, rise above misfortune, and bravely continue life's tasks and responsibilities.

In a civilization of so many gadgets, push-buttons and conveniences, we are apt to take life and its blessings for granted. Prayer makes us aware of the beauties of nature, the goodness in man, the mystery of creation, and the miracles which are daily taking place. Prayer makes us humble. It makes us realize that every day we live is a gift from God, and as such we should consider it: "This is the day that God has made; be glad and rejoice thereon."

Prayer kindles the divine spirit within us. It links our soul to the eternal God. It enables us to rise above pettiness, greed, envy, and hatred. It turns our thoughts away from our little selves and widens our horizons so that we can see in true perspective life and its problems. As a part of humanity, we are concerned not only with our own well-being; we are concerned with the well-being of our fellowmen. That is why all Hebrew prayers are expressed in the plural: "Heal **us**, O Lord, save **us**, grant **us** peace." We pray not only for ourselves but as members of the community, as citizens of the world.

Prayer is neither an escape from reality nor a substitute for action. It challenges us to remove the evil about us, to distinguish between the good and the false, to choose justice and love mercy. Prayer develops the best within us. It humanizes, spiritualizes, democratizes, socializes and internationalizes us. In short, it makes good and useful human beings out of ordinary human beings.

Prayer is at its highest and noblest when its purpose is not to **get something** but to **get close to Someone**—the eternal Lord. He it is who understands and who cares, to whom we can turn at any time, in all our joys and sorrows; who heals and sustains, uplifts and inspires; who assures us that each one of us is a unique personality, that each one counts, that each one has his place and function, that each one can be a co-worker with Him in re-fashioning the world into a better world. Thus prayer enables us to approach the Almighty Father who gives meaning and purpose to our lives, with whom and in whom we can find peace throughout life and when life's work is ended.

"THANK YOU VERY MUCH, GOD"

By *Edward D. Kuekes*

Chief Editorial Cartoonist, Cleveland Plain Dealer

❦

I have never started the day with a prayer. Not that I don't believe in it, but I have always been under the impression that the man upstairs is far too busy with more important things than listening to me. With all the intricate problems of the world there probably are many more supplications to attend to than my feeble effort to ask for His divine guidance.

Don't get me wrong. I believe in prayer.

My business is trying to analyze the woes of the world, then try to find a graphic analogy that will interpret these woes to the newspaper reader so that he might instantly grasp the situation without wading through columns of printed matter. There is no set chronological sequence of events that will guarantee the evolving of a cartoon idea.

Soon you find out that when an idea does strike, you alone were not responsible for it. You sense that there was help and that help probably came from your faith and knowledge that the night before you thanked the Man upstairs for the power that saw you through the day.

Yes, that is the time I pray. Without Him I couldn't get along. So, at the tag end of the day when I have retired, I figure that is the best time to give thanks for all the blessings I have received and to show appreciation for what he has done for others and to ask guidance in one's problems.

To me, it has always been more comfortable to give thanks than to ask for favors. I do not like to liken Him to Santa Claus and expect, childlike, that He will grant all wishes. I am just grateful for those He has seen fit to bestow.

WE MUST LOOK INWARD
By Peggy Wood
Actress

❀

What I have to say about prayer is very likely to be far from the accepted pattern.

One is so often met with the words on a page telling us that prayer is a powerful thing, that we should put ourselves into the stream of that power that we may benefit by it. When I encounter this reasoning or this suggestion I stiffen. It's the implication that we are to **benefit** from it that irks me. As if we were not to be captured by any suggestion that didn't hold out a profit for us. Constantly I read and I hear that if we will just take our troubles to God He will take care of them, if we will just shift the burden over to Him we will be relieved and can go about our worldly businesses.

A tycoon of international fame once told on a radio program how be became successful: he said that in the depression he was near bankruptcy and was about to go under when he went into a church and prayed for all his might. Sure enough, not long after that things began to improve for him and today he is so rich he can't count his millions. Well, that sort of thing puts me off the kind of thinking too often surrounding the phrases about the power of prayer. I cannot think of prayer as a sort of Horn & Hardart Automat where you put in a prayer like a dime in the slot and get out a blessing like a cup of coffee.

Of course, it is not always that our requests are trivial. We can ask for guidance, or understanding, or hope, even a blessing. But these are also intensely personal desires. "That Thou wilt grant their requests," says St. Chrystostom's prayer at the end of the morning service in the Episcopal Church and I don't know that I am very comfortable with that phrase. I am moved by the first sentences of his prayer, "that when two or three are gathered together in Thy name," for these words fill me with the sense of the early beginnings of the Christian meetings: how dangerous it was for them to be seen together, those early believers, how near was the word of God in those tiny gatherings. But I don't find it inspiring that the Lord should be pressured into granting requests just because two or three make known their special needs. Or that He should be pressured at all, ever.

However, the more one resorts to a Higher Thought the more one sets in motion thoughts higher than the material world about us and the human race could do with endless amounts of higher thoughts in the course of its wrestling with the lower ones which have never seemed more flourishing. When I read year after year of corruption in high places, of venal and evil practices employed by men in responsible positions, or organized vice and its invisible government, the murder of children by other children, I sometimes wonder if we may not have come the full circle to the time just before Noah when the Lord God got to such a state of exasperation with the human race that he was about to wipe us out, write us off as an experiment which hadn't come up to His expectations.

What monumental folly it is to pray to be saved from extermination while at the same time we improve the very methods by which extermination may be accomplished! Let us pray to **ourselves,** really, let us face the lack of values within us and reason with the promptings of evil, deny them, beat them down and rise above them to live by the good that is within us, the spirit of God which is breathed into man. We don't have to look up to the skies, we know better than that now, for the skies are no longer a comfortable residence; we must look inward and instead of asking, **promise.**

PRAYER WITH GRATITUDE

By Frank S. Land

Founder and Secretary General, The International Supreme Council,

Order of DeMolay

Prayer ushers us into the presence of God. By faith we know that He will hear us. It is never a wish for material things that we seek, but rather a sincere desire to be shown the way and correct our thinking. It is a mental approach that ostracizes materialism.

My life has been spent in helping young men to think rightly. They now number nearly three million. Thus far I am told that not one of them has ever been charged with a major crime. Today the greater portion of these men are leaders in all walks of life, throughout this Nation and the World. To me, this attests the efficacy of prayer.

Emerson once said, "We see young people who owe us a new world—so bravely do they promise, but they either die young or else they dodge the account and are lost in the crowd." The temptation and apathy to lose one's self in the crowd is very great. I am thinking of what Paul told us: "A great door and effectual is opened unto me, and there are many adversaries."

There are great opportunities for service if we take God into our thinking. For me, prayer with gratitude has been the path that I have attempted to follow. To God, and his Son be the Kingdom and the Power and the Glory Forever and Ever. Amen.

TRUE PRAYER

By Henry A. Wallace

Former Vice-President of the United States

There is false prayer and true prayer. False prayer is asking for material blessings, which if granted, might bring harm to others. Many people have engaged in false prayer and have thought their petitions were answered. True prayer is a very great responsibility and entails the complete re-orientation of the inner being toward God. An electrical contact must be made between all that is good in a particular individual and all that God wills for man through that individual. In other words the Lord's Prayer must be brought to a particular time and place without losing either its depth or simplicity.

I do not care to cite specific instances of the efficacy of prayer because such instances seem so often to violate the greatness of God and the dignity of man. All I can say is that true prayer made by a man in great need can make God's power available for the well-being of all of us. A man who is convinced of the service of his daily work can make that day-by-day work a continuous prayer. You remember that poem of E. R. Sill written about sixty years ago:

"Forenoon, and afternoon and night; Forenoon
    and afternoon, and night; Forenoon; and — what?
The empty song repeats itself. No more?
    Yea, that is life; make this forenoon sublime,
This afternoon a psalm, this night a prayer,
    And time is conquered, and thy crown is won."

All I wish to say is that prayer is important but that there are many ways of praying and that day-by-day work in the spirit of the Lord is one of them.

I KNOW THE POWER OF PRAYER

By *Lyndon B. Johnson*

Majority Leader, United States Senate

The efficacy of prayer is not simply a matter of belief with me. I **know** the value of prayer. I have learned what prayerful hearts can do.

After I was stricken down by a heart attack in July of 1955, thousands of men and women from throughout the Nation wrote me that they were praying for my recovery.

Some of these communications came from lifelong friends. Some came from people I had met casually over a period of years. Many were written by individuals I had never known and who, I would have thought, could not have known of me.

As my wife read these messages to me, and later as I became able to read them for myself, I could literally feel myself gaining strength of spirit and body.

"We are praying for you to get well," these wonderful people would write me—and I did get well.

I have hoped a thousand times since then that all of them knew what they did for me—and for members of my family as well, for they, too, benefited from the prayers of these friends, acquaintances and strangers.

A belief in prayer may be accounted by some a matter of faith. So it is. But, so far as I am concerned, it also is a matter of sure and certain knowledge.

I know what the prayers of others did for me. There is no more powerful force than prayer. There is no greater source of new strength and new courage for the individual than daily communion with the Supreme Being.

GOD TAKES THE INITIATIVE

By Dr. Clifford M. Drury

Professor of Church History, San Francisco Theological Seminary

One of the greatest and most challenging conceptions embodied in the Christian faith is that God takes the initiative. Even as an earthly parent loves the child long before the child ever begins to love the parent, so our heavenly Father loves us before we loved him. As the Apostle Paul stated—he loved us while we were yet sinners, unworthy of that love.

A second great Christian conviction is the unchangeable nature of God, the Father. There is no wavering in his love for us. What a tragedy it would have been if the Prodigal Son in the hour of his repentance felt that he had sinned away every chance of reconciliation and that his father would **not** welcome him back! But there was never a doubt on that score. "I will arise and go to my Father."

Faith in the efficacy of prayer rests upon these basic convictions. God has taken the initiative in establishing fellowship with man, the height of his creation. Because of that love for man, he sent Jesus into the world. The birth of Jesus at Bethlehem was evidence of God breaking through the time-barrier. The initiative was with God. When this is true—how logical, therefore, it is to believe in prayer. He who so loved the world that he gave his only begotten Son also so loved the world that he hears and answers prayer. The love of God is a continuing love. Without doing violence to personality by forcing itself upon man, the love of God is constantly ready to bless whenever and wherever the individual becomes aware of his need and asks.

God waits for man to pray. Of course prayer is more than just asking God for something. Prayer is fellowship. Prayer can be a dialogue when God speaks to man and man speaks to God. Prayer should include moments of quietness when we feel the spirit moving within us. Often in our sinfulness and ignorance, we don't know what to ask for. But God is patient and waits until we come to that stage of our spiritual development when we become aware of our needs and enlarge our petitions.

I know of a father who was helping his son build a collection of United States stamps. The father had a big supply of duplicates and could have filled every space in his son's stamp album, but he wisely refrained. The son acquired the full set of a certain issue only to discover that the one-cent stamp existed in several varieties of perforations. The lad then went to his father and asked for these additional stamps. In a real sense this request was a prayer. It was based upon a knowledge of an existing need. Whereas the father could have supplied these stamps in advance, the wiser course had been adopted of letting the boy discover for himself what was needed to perfect his collection.

So it is with God and us. It is the love of God for mankind that restrains the initiative of God. We must discover for ourselves our greatest need. Then when we go to God in prayer, as a son to an earthly father, we will find our heavenly Father eager to bestow to the fullest of our ability to receive.

PRAYER PROMOTES PROSPERITY

By Dr. R. H. Gerberding

Former Executive Secretary, Board of American Missions,
The United Lutheran Church in America

❀

Prayer, to me, is a continuing outgoing expression of confidence and dependence in response to God's revelation in Christ to the believer. Forms for both public and private worship are excellent and helpful disciplines in promoting a prayerful life in private. If one really enters into all such valid forms their spirit will more and more permeate all one's thinking, one's deliberation and one's planning. In other words, one's whole life will be lived in conscious relationship to God's will and to His loving purposes.

Such confidence and the resulting prayer life effects in the believer joy, confidence and optimism, not to mention strength against temptation. There result from it innumerable instances of direct interposition of divine aid in both spiritual and temporal ways. This is a valid form of faith healing. It also promotes prosperity. For example, in my home mission ministry I have found hundreds of cases in which people who were poor in worldly goods before the church found them and they the church, attained not only comfort in material things but even affluence. In all such cases that I have observed the result has been a spirit of love and benevolence which is proof of the Source of their prosperity.

Such a life is always humble and self-effacing because it realizes that the center of its power is the cross of our Lord Jesus Christ.

CREATIVE PRAYER

By *Alex F. Osborn*

Co-founder of Batten, Barton, Durstine and Osborn, Inc.

President of the Creative Education Foundation

❧

Imagination can do much to empower our prayers.

We can get a lot of good out of silent prayers—not only the longer ones we say before going to sleep, but the kind which Lee Bristol Jr. has called "flash" prayers.

A friend of mine who does a lot of cross-country motoring in connection with his business revealed to me that, while speeding along the road alone in his car, he often takes off his hat and expresses a few words of thanks for his own blessings, together with a brief supplication for others.

Our prayers do us more good when vitalized through conscious application of imagination.

All of us possess the power consciously to visualize. As Harry Emerson Fosdick has said, "We can run movies through our minds at will—we can even change the reels."

Yes, we can cause ourselves to see what we **will** to see, even if we are blind.

Try making some mental slides to visualize your thoughts. Take the 23rd Psalm, for instance . . . "The Lord is my Shepherd." (Surely you can see that bearded herder with his sheep.) "He maketh me to lie down in green pastures." (You can even put flowers into your visualization of that field.) "He leadeth me beside the still waters." (Surely your mind's eye can picture that placid pool, with lacy clouds mirrored on its surface.)

According to a psychiatrist, that Psalm—as thus consciously visualized—can serve as an aid to mental health. Even more surely—by thus using our power of imagination—we can do much to tone up our spiritual health.

As to the benefits of prayer, we have no right to expect that our supplications should be answered according to our specifications. Divine wisdom may often veto, and rightly so, the wishes we express.

Above all else, the selfish benefit from prayer mainly consists of re-inforcement of our faith—the "feed-back", in the form of spiritual strength. And such self-invigoration depends upon how intensely we **concentrate** while praying.

We can do most to exclude the extraneous by deliberately conjuring up the pictures which should go with the words we run through our heads. Thus we can intensify our concentration. Thus we can induce maximum "feed-back."

By coupling creative thinking with our faith, we can build up our belief—we can better live up to our religion in our relations to others and to ourselves.

As my minister, Dr. Albert Butzer, has said, "Imagination is essentially spiritual. Therefore, let us use and develop this most wonderful gift—to make the Bible more interesting and inspiring—to make prayer more vitally effective and transforming—especially our prayers for others, as we hold their faces before us, and hold them up to God on the wings of prayer."

THERE IS ALWAYS THE POWER OF PRAYER

By *Emmet Lavery*
Author and Playwright

❧

Prayer inevitably means different things for different people. For some, it is true communication between friends, regardless of the usual barriers of time and space. For others, it is a fleeting hope—something seldom put into words, yet deeply felt and long remembered. But one thing is certain—most people would like to believe if they could. And so a short scene from **Monsignor's Hour** may be in order at this point:

Monsignor

There is always the power of prayer. Do you believe in it, Gabriel?

Gabriel

(gallery guide)

It depends on what I'm praying for. There's no use in making it too hard for the good Lord.

Monsignor

Think how many millions would learn to pray if they believed prayers were answered. All most of us have against praying is the fear that it won't work. . . Come let us stand here a moment before this painting . . . it was for this that I stopped off in Rome . . . can't you hear what is being said . . . "My peace I leave with you, my peace I give unto you . . . let not your heart be troubled nor let it be afraid."

* * *

Monsignor's Hour, one of Mr. Lavery's early plays, was first produced at the Josefstadt in Vienna in 1936 with Albert Basserman in the leading role, and is still in the repertory of many European theatres. It is published in this country by Samuel French, Inc. (All rights reserved)

I BELIEVE

By John D. Rockefeller, Jr.
Philanthropist

❁

I believe in the supreme worth of the individual and in his right to life, liberty, and the pursuit of happiness.

I believe that every right implies a responsibility; every opportunity, an obligation; every possession, a duty.

I believe that the law was made for man and not man for the law; that government is the servant of the people and not their master.

I believe in the dignity of labor, whether with head or hand; that the world owes no man a living but that it owes every man an opportunity to make a living.

I believe that thrift is essential to well ordered living and that economy is a prime requisite of a sound financial structure, whether in government, business or personal affairs.

I believe that truth and justice are fundamental to an enduring social order.

I believe in the sacredness of a promise, that a man's word should be as good as his bond; that character—not wealth or power or position—is of supreme worth.

I believe that the rendering of useful service is the common duty of mankind and that only in the purifying fire of sacrifice is the dross of selfishness consumed and the greatness of the human soul set free.

I believe in an all-wise and all-loving God, named by whatever name, and that the individual's highest fulfillment, greatest happiness, and widest usefulness are to be found in living in harmony with His will.

I believe that love is the greatest thing in the world; that it alone can overcome hate; that right can and will triumph over might.

THE MINISTRY OF PRAYER

By Dr. Thomas J. Pitts, Lawyer
Former President, Baptist Brotherhood Convention of Texas,
Odessa, Texas

All Christians should believe in prayer and should pray in obedience to the teachings of the Master. Christ's followers today are taught to pray even as the disciples were instructed in that day. Our Christian laymen, and all other Christians, should come to depend more and more upon prayer, not only in their daily devotions, but also in resolving problems that seem almost insurmountable in one's own strength. Prayer is an imperative ministry of the Christian faith and we should always return to prayer in our greatest difficulties. Faith in prayer should be primary and fundamental in the life of the Christian.

On becoming a new person in the Christian faith, one also comes into new areas of service in the plan to send the gospel to the ends of the earth. Many times faith in the ministry of prayer needs encouragement and assurance to give a feeling of support in the living of the Christian life to which one has been called. The belief in prayer may be clearly evident in this situation. Perhaps, more often than we think, prayers are answered in relation to Christian duties. Too often, I believe, we are hesitant to accept or declare our belief in prayer and prayers of thanksgiving for blessings already received are delayed or neglected altogether.

The writer is definitely aware that prayers have been answered under many circumstances as a result of faith, but it is one thing to profess faith in the ministry of prayer and quite another matter to lean heavily and confidently on that faith in seeking divine guidance through the proper channels. In the plan of the scriptures, the power of prayer has been made evident over and over again and is still available for all who bring themselves within the implications of this ministry. The efficacy of prayer in so many situations and interrelations in our contacts in life and in several different directions and segments of society and among other races of people, has been so abundantly manifested to me as to be beyond all question. This ministry has been fully established.

Primarily, the ministry of the Christian religion is based upon prayer and the Master would achieve his purposes through human means. The personal witness is important. The teachings of the Christian faith are delivered to the people through personal witnessing of the Lord's servants. More attention should be given to prayer in the days ahead.

While the pastors as the chief officers of our churches have always been and will, of course, continue to be our leaders and advisers, we are pleased to know that so many of our laymen from all walks of life are taking an active part in witnessing to the power of prayer in the Christian ministry. The laymen have made, and are making, significant contributions to the spread of the gospel message. They have greatly strengthened the influence of the churches. They have extended the Christian efforts and attitudes in making leaders of Christian laymen in all parts of the country and in other lands. Certainly we believe in prayer as the dominant force in every aspect of the Christian's spiritual life.

We believe in prayer because its potency is demonstrated almost constantly. The practical aspects of prayer should always be a stabilizing thought in the life of the Christian. We believe in prayer because of its infinite and sustaining assurances in the activities of life. My convictions shall always be aligned with the proponents of the power of prayer. Many of life's consequences are overcome or lessened through prayer to God.

PRAYER IS CONVERSATION WITH GOD

By Dr. Paul H. Heisey

Formerly Professor of Religious Education, Newberry College

❈

Among the many definitions and explanations of prayer the one that appeals to me is "prayer is conversation with God." This relieves me of thinking of prayer as a command. Prayer receives its power not by our commanding God. In general I do not like to think of prayer as an attempt to change the will of God. His will is perfect, hence why should I seek to change it? Rather prayer is the effort to change my will in order to bring it into harmony with the will of God. By conversation with God, through prayer, I can change my will. Through prayer I seek to change myself.

Prayer brings my will into conformity with God's will. My attitudes, actions, and hopes change through fellowship with God. Through prayer I do not change God but I change myself. Prayer does change things. It changes me. It changes my attitude toward God, my attitude toward my fellowmen, toward institutions, toward causes and agencies. Prayer changes my attitude toward myself and my own problems. From a very practical point of view prayer restrains me from evil, prayer inspires me to do good, prayer comforts me in difficulties and problems.

But prayer is not inaction but action. All of the above thoughts lead me to believe that prayer should lead to the dedication of self. Prayer demands co-operation with what we believe to be the will of God. One must work for that for which he prays. We cannot ask things of God without doing all in our power to realize our request. Prayer requires action, co-operation, and dedication.

START BY PRAYING

By Dr. Edgar M. Carlson

President, Gustavus Adolphus College

❧

I cannot speak as one who has earned any spurs on the field of prayer, but rather as one who must acknowledge that it is for him too largely an untapped resource. It is like a uranium mine that has been discovered and whose value has been verified by a few samples in the discoverer's possession. But these samples give evidence of the riches to which he has a claim if he will but work the mine.

Actually, we all do pray if things get bad enough. When there doesn't seem to be any other place to go than on our knees we are willing to try that too. But for mature, adult people, it seems to me, prayer ought to come at the beginning rather than at the end. It should be the first step, not the last stand. It is this kind of praying that has seemed most helpful to me.

Let me illustrate what I mean. If there is someone that you don't like, try praying for him. I dare you to try to go on hating someone that you are praying for. You won't long be able even to snub him or say nasty things about him. You can go on justifying yourself and nursing your grievances until you die and the barrier between you will grow ever more formidable and impenetrable. But it cannot survive your praying. Or on the other hand, if there is someone that you really want to help, the way to start is by praying for him. See how your understanding and your friendship grow in the intimacy of that communion which is possible only between man and God. See, too, how your imagination quickens and you become alert to opportunities to prove yourself the friend.

If there is something that one really wants to achieve in the world, he should start praying for it. Regardless of what it is! Unless I am mistaken, two things are almost certain to happen. One is that the ambition will be clarified and purified. You can't hold up an unholy, self-centered ambition to God day after day without its character changing so that it becomes something for which you can honestly and respectably seek His endorsement and support.

The other thing that will happen is that praying for the goal you seek to achieve will harness your energies, focus your efforts, and organize your activities, so that you really devote yourself to the goal of which God has approved.

If one is really sincere in his desire for peace and freedom in the world, one can do no better than to start by praying. He doesn't have to wait until he is in a foxhole. The President of the United States must be credited with both sincerity and insight when he appeals to the people of the world to join in praying for peace. The climate of a world is one that slips easily into the holocaust of war. Even if the enemy does not pray with us, we can still pray for them. Any shortage in the number of people to pray with can always be made up by an increase in the number of people to pray for.

I suppose there are problems connected with praying. There have been times when they seemed important to me. I do not know either that very many of them have been solved, at least not in any fashion which would permit the solutions to be transferred to others. But I do know that wherever my life has touched the life and power of God, it has become clear that He is able to do exceeding abundantly, far above all that we ask or think, according to the power that is at work within us. The biggest problem for me is not prayer, but the pray-er — and how to keep him praying.

EQUALITY BEFORE GOD

By Dr. Howard E. Kershner

President, Christian Freedom Foundation, Inc.

❀

From a distance of not over ten feet we watched the face of a great musician, as he translated something of the harmony, perfection and beauty of God, on the keyboard of a piano. It was a marvelous coordination of brain, nerves, hands, fingers and muscles. During the performance his face expressed the exultation and serenity which one feels in the presence of something that is altogether just the way it should be, leaving nothing to be desired in the degree of its perfection.

For two hours the problems of the world were below the surface of consciousness while everything seemed to be harmonious and beautiful, just the way God would have it, unmarred by the sins, shortcomings and imperfections of men.

The master had reached the very pinnacle of his profession and he drew the rest of us up to the clouds with him. We thought how wonderful the world would be if all of us could attain a high degree of excellence in our capacity to express some of the beauty of God's world.

But we can, all of us, do just that!

We cannot all be great artists, musicians, poets or philosophers, but we all have some unique talent or capacity which no one else possesses. Each of us has a certain sparkle, a way of being helpful to others, and an ability to do certain things as no other person can do them. This gives every man, woman and child the value of uniqueness. The world would be less, my friend, if you had not been born. You have added something to it, that was not here before you came. That something is from God and it is precious beyond all price. If you fail to use it to the best of your ability and to seek diligently to nurture and cultivate your talents, you are depriving the revelation of the personality of God, of one outlet which He needs; and sent you into the world to supply. No one can take your place, and if you fail the loss will be irreparable.

No two flowers are alike. No two snowflakes in all the vast snowstorms that have swept this world are exactly alike. No two leaves on a tree are alike. Eyes, voices, personalities all differ. Each person being different from every other person is of infinite importance in the plan of God for developing man in His own Image. Your contribution to that process can be of priceless value. Don't depreciate yourself. Think not that you don't matter. God has entrusted you with something He gave to no other person, and the way you use it is just as important to Him as the way our most gifted men and women use the talents they possess.

A man is tallest on his knees. In that position he stretches clear up into heaven itself. The man who most nearly brings his life into complete harmony with God, is the one who excels, as the servant of God. We are all equal before that test. No one has any advantage over any other and we may be sure that the humblest among us may avail as much as any other in our efforts to tap the power of God and apply it to the redemption and salvation of the world.

CULTIVATING THE HABIT OF PRAYER

By Dr. Preston Bradley

Pastor, The People's Church of Chicago

❦

Man has always prayed from his earliest beginnings, whether it was to the sun, a peculiar stone, a crooked stick, or a grotesque wooden face. There has never been a moment when he did not feel the necessity of prayer. As the centuries have passed and he became more deeply sensitive to the reality of the God we know and love, his technique in prayer has evolved until now, from the depth of his heart he can commune with the ultimate reality.

True prayer to me is not asking God to be my errand runner. It is not merely petition or request. Neither is it necessarily spoken by the lips. Most public prayers, either by clergy or layman, create the impression that words and phrases are being used for the ears of man and not for the ears of God.

The highest and most effective example of prayer was given by the Master himself, when he said: "But thou, when thou prayest, enter into thy closet, and when thou hast shut thy door, pray to thy Father which is in secret; and thy Father which seeth in secret shall reward thee openly."

Has it ever occurred to you that prayer is a two-way communication: not only are we asking for the ears of God to hear us, but we should be waiting to hear the voice of God for us. Prayer is not only man speaking to God, but it is God speaking to man. That is the great power and strength of silent prayer — an attitude in which I deeply believe and which is a part of the worship service of our church.

Cultivating the habit of prayer is the most efficacious manner in which to fortify one's self against materialism.

THE PINNACLE OF PRAYER

By Dr. Frank H. Caldwell

President, Presbyterian Theological Seminary,
Louisville, Ky.

❦

There are lower and higher levels of prayer. At the elementary level, prayer is chiefly concerned with the self as center—my desires, my needs, my ambitions, my prosperity, my happiness.

At a more advanced level, prayer is concerned with the needs of others. The pronouns of prayer become plural and extend from the first to the second and third persons—"we," "you," "they." This is the higher level of intercessory prayer.

But prayer reaches its pinnacle only when we actually recognize in our praying that God's will for us, for our fellow-man, for the whole world, is the greatest good for which anyone can pray. At its highest and best, therefore, prayer seeks less to accommodate God's will to our desires than to conform our desires—our whole lives— to God's will. When we can really pray "Thy will be done"—not in a mood of reluctant submission to life's inevitables, but in a mood of confident trust in God's wisdom, love, and mercy—we have reached the pinnacle of prayer.

At the climax of a memorable talk on prayer, which I heard many years ago, the speaker said, "When God can reach out His hand and do what He wills with your life, then you can reach out the hand of prayer and do what you will with God—because then your will and God's will are one will."

But such reaching can only be done from the pinnacle of prayer.

PRAYER IS A SPIRITUAL LIFELINE

By Morris Hursh

Commissioner, Department of Public Welfare, State of Minnesota

❦

Actually, prayer is worth nothing unless it is based on the absolute conviction that your prayer is being heard. If there is first this firm conviction, this soundly based faith, then prayer provides the ever-present strength, the support, the hope, the tender mercy, the understanding, the help we need.

With this basic faith comes the knowledge that our specific and individual prayers are answered many times in ways which we cannot immediately understand. With this faith we achieve the efficacy of prayer and in a sense this means the "practical value" of prayer and there is no question of its practicality in the minds of those who have experienced it. It is a crutch when we are weak, it is an inspiration when we are strong. There should be no need for explanations—but one explanation of the efficacy of prayer is that in praying we admit the existence of a Being superior to ourselves. This admission of a supreme being does not weaken, it strengthens.

I do not agree with those who call prayer "talking with God." In my view, one does not converse with God. He communicates with God through prayer and both in content and in form of prayer indicates his subservience to God. Prayer cannot be dissected, tabulated and analyzed. The rope one uses as a lifeline cannot be tested for its maximum strength without destroying it. Prayer is our spiritual lifeline. It need not be tested. It need only be used, often, regularly, to ask for help and to give thanks.

PRAYER MAKES THE MAN

By Rev. Carroll L. Hinderlie

Youth Director, Young People's Luther League

❂

Not even the most pagan among our beachcombers who shared a Japanese prison camp with us could call it "Coincidence" when our camp was moved from the mountains of Baguio to Manila. Those few days were the only days the American planes were grounded. We thought there had been some agreement, but were told later, it was due to a shortage of gas. Otherwise our movement would have been strafed or bombed as a troop manuever around Lingayen gulf now that we had control of the air over Luzon from Leyte.

The most blase among us said of those final days of imprisonment: "Must be the whole world is praying for us with all these missionaries here. Like a wall of prayer surrounding us." That was it—a wall of prayer which one could almost feel. One could multiply such incidents but it might deepen the despair . . . of some. For there were many who never returned.

We saw our fellows fall as flaming torches from an exploding B-20 . . . for our freedom. They died all around us later. Every day in our own Bilibid at least one, often two or more of the remnant from Bataan were put to their last rest. Where were **their** prayers?

They were answered wherever men died in the faith with confidence in the goodness of God. For prayer is not a skill game to pry favors from God, but the rest of the soul in the goodness of God. It transforms the man who lives in prayer. People become persons to be encouraged and built up even in one's hidden attitude. Each individual remains exactly that,

111

the experience in which the soul gives itself in utter and complete abandon, willing no longer to retain anything that hinders.

Prayer in its development brings the soul to a state of complete trust. No longer is there any attempt at self-direction—it is God who guides. No longer is there doubt concerning personal safety—it is God who protects. No longer is there anxiety for personal needs—either physical or spiritual—all are met by the God who answers prayer.

Despite the most adverse circumstances the way is not all darkness, for the God of light illumines our path. No longer is there loneliness, for there is the consciousness of His nearness.

No longer need one be bereft or poor in spirit— for the prayer that is real and earnest appropriates the riches of God's grace.

Prayer that brings with it the realization that God is ours and we are His does much to solve the problems of life. There comes the experience in prayer when in child-like trust we are prepared to commit ourselves entirely to Him, being unconcerned whether we receive the things for which we have asked or not. When we possess Him the gifts are comparatively unimportant, for the Giver is always greater than His gifts.

Real prayer is as a diamond in the sun. When it catches the light it constantly reveals new aspects of its nature.

The widening circle of prayer is never fulfilled until we have begun to bear in our hearts the needs of the whole world. Prayer changes hearts—it will change the world. Prayer works miracles, and the man who prays constantly sees them performed by the hand of God.

To pray compels us to love and to love compels us to pray.

I am able so to write, because this is my belief and experience.

EFFECTIVE PRAYER

By Robert G. Le Tourneau
President, R. G. Le Tourneau, Inc.

❀

There is much power in prayer, but I look at prayer a little differently than some others. We are told to come boldly to the Throne of Grace and find help in time of need, and I believe we can do just that. But, I do not believe we can pray for and get everything we want and think we ought to have. I have discovered that God knows better what I need than I do.

The Lord Jesus Christ prayed, "Lord, not my will, but thine be done." I have found that kind of prayer to be far more beneficial than just asking for something I would like to have. The Psalmist prayed, "Lord, search me and try me and see if there be any wicked way in me, and renew a right spirit within me." My experience with God is that He wants to open the windows of Heaven and pour out a blessing upon us, but many times He cannot do it because He knows we would take the credit to ourselves. He loves us so much He wants us to return His love, so the most effective prayer I know is "To help me to love Him as I ought to." I think many times we are trying to use God instead of asking Him to use us. I remember one time I started to pray, "Lord, don't let me down now," and then I said, "No, Lord, that is not what I wanted to say, help me not to let you down." God has never let me down.

Christianity is a cooperation with God. In prayer we talk things over about what God wants done and what we need to do it with. The marvelous thing is that the Maker of the Universe is willing to cooperate with anyone who will recognize his need of a Saviour first and then take a little time to talk it over.

THE SPIRIT OF PRAYER

By Philip H. Nason

President, First National Bank, St. Paul, Minnesota

❦

I believe that prayer is a many-sided concept and far more inclusive than many people realize. In today's society it is not uncommon to hear your neighbor, your business associate, your fishing companion, even a member of your own family say, rather apologetically, "I'm not a religious person and I'm afraid I haven't really prayed since I was a child."

In most of these cases nothing could have been further from the truth. Your friend need not have had that little nagging feeling of inadequacy. What he should have said was that he no longer prays in a formal way by articulating words, either aloud or to himself.

I believe this person prays every time he acknowledges to himself that man did not create the world, that he did not himself alone produce his own native talents, abilities, family, friends, opportunities, successes and failures. He knows there must be some outside, all-powerful force, but since he has less definite conviction than his neighbor as to its nature, form and character, he believes he does not pray and somewhat wistfully admits that he is irreligious.

I believe this man prays each time he sits in church—away from the distractions of every-day living—and listens to the music exalting God. He prays when he opens his mind to the thoughts expressed by the leader of the congregation. He prays every time he marvels at the beauty and mystery of nature, of immortal music, art or poetry. He knows that man could not develop this genius by will alone. He prays when, in a reflective mood, he puts himself in proper perspective to the rest of the world, for to do this he must acquire a considerable measure of humility.

The words of formal prayer simply help attain an attitude of reverence, but it is the spirit, not the words, which is important. I believe that attitude rather than education or form is the essential ingredient of prayer.

A couple of weeks ago one of our janitors came into my office to say goodbye. It was his last day prior to retirement after thirty-five years of service. He is a man of strong religious conviction, a man who praises God daily as he goes about his work, and a man who is greatly beloved by all of our employees. As a little farewell token he handed me a copy of the following prayer which he had composed himself. What it lacks in meter, it far more than makes up in spirit and sincerity.

> Master, as I begin my work today
> Give me strength, faith, hope and charity.
> Let me walk in the spirit of humility,
> And if pride should cause me to stumble or fall,
> Lift me up, let me stand.
> And when I come to the end of the day,
> Let me not grumble nor complain,
> But give me grace to thank Thee, Master,
> For the countless blessings Thou has given me today.

My friend, though almost entirely lacking in formal education, is doubly blessed—he has both an attitude of reverence and the words to express it. Some of us are self-conscious and inarticulate when trying to put our thoughts into words. I believe that a feeling of inadequacy in this regard is harmful both to our own well-being and to the world at large. Let us all have the wisdom to recognize the spirit of prayer even when it doesn't have the form.

THE MYSTERIOUS POWER OF PRAYER

By Dr. Ferdinand M. Isserman

Rabbi of Temple Israel, St. Louis, Missouri

❧

Prayer is the soul of man, questing for God, and sensitively attuned to recieve and to respond to His message. It is not man influencing God, but God influencing man. It is "Thy will be done." It does not transform the world, but it does the individual who prays. Prayer cannot repair a broken bridge, but it can heal a broken heart. Its harvest is spiritual, not material. A regenerated individual will be moved to work for the kingdom of God on earth and bend his sacrificial energies for the creation of a just society. I frequently have witnessed the effect of prayer.

Prayer can heal when the ailment is caused by inner disturbances, by conflicts, anxieties, frustration and disappointments. It can dissipate resentments, hostilities, grudges, desires for vengeance, these cancers of the soul.

At the close of the services on the Day of Atonement in my Temple, an elderly lady came to tell me how deeply she was stirred by the religious experiences of that day's liturgy. Then she turned to her son and said, "Charles, get my cane from our pew where I left it, please." For the first time in many years she had walked without a cane. The exaltation, even the ecstasy of worship, had led her momentarily to overcome her infirmity.

A woman suffering from a deep sense of inferiority caused by having lost the affection of her husband had not been able to eat, and was starving herself to death. Standing by her bed

116

in the hospital, I voiced the priestly blessing, "The Lord bless thee and keep thee; the Lord cause the light of His countenance to shine upon thee, and be gracious unto thee; the Lord lift up His countenance upon thee, and give thee peace." When I concluded this blessing, she proceeded to eat from the tray of food which was before her. The blessing had stilled the turmoil of her soul which had prevented her from eating.

A Dutch Jewess in a concentration camp, embittered by the cruelties to which she had been subjected, turned away from God, and hoped quickly to die. In a bunk beneath her lay a pious woman who regularly voiced the traditional prayers of Judaism. The Dutch woman resented her neighbor's worship, her praise of God, but after some days, out of the habit of her youth, she joined in the prayers, regained the will to live, and survived the terror of her oppressors until liberated.

A British soldier in North Africa who had served in the Eighth Army and had been wounded in Tunisia feared to return to his outfit after his convalescence. He attended a Sabbath Eve service. By joining with others in the praise of God, he regained his faith and his courage. Thereafter he felt God to be with him, and therefore was unafraid of the hazards of battle. In a mood of confidence he returned to his regiment.

Daily prayers, when we confront not the dramatic but the routine challenges of life, make us aware of our indebtedness to God, the Creator, Who causes the sun to rise and to set, thus humbling us. In such humility there is healing for the hurts of life. It brings many blessings. It dwarfs our frustrations. To call upon God is to be answered by Him. He responds to the hungers of the soul, and strengthens it with the nourishment of re-invigorated faith. Such is the mysterious power of prayer.

117

LEARNING TO PRAY

By Faith Baldwin
Author and Novelist

For many years I used prayer conventionally and sporadically—the formal prayers or a sudden plea for help—when things went wrong. Looking back, I know all prayers are answered, though often not in the way we might wish.

During the last four years I have learned to pray—in the way most helpful to me. I literally think aloud as I have never been able to concentrate except through words. Now and then the desire for direct communication with God is so intense that words do fail and it is a voiceless cry.

The most passionate prayers I ever voiced were during seven terrible weeks some years ago; they weren't, I then believed, answered. Now I know they were if not according to **my** will. But when my husband died and I turned for strength and comfort to the Unseen there wasn't anything there at all. So my trust and belief had been mere lip service after all.

Since then my prayers for **other people** have been unmistakably answered and this makes me happy and confident. For myself, perhaps I ask too much. I think I ask little, but I daresay I am wrong.

One of the things I have worked for in prayer is an inner quietude which can manifest outwardly, no matter what the circumstances of my life are nor how deep my anxieties. Little by little I have achieved something of this.

Prayer is trust in operation; answered prayer is love in operation. All God's ways are mysterious but His spiritual laws are as plain as print; and His plan is Order, Justice and Balance.

Without help, without recovered belief, I would not now be alive in this material world. Why I am, must be part of a purpose.

I often forget to say Grace at mealtime; and before a working day; yet in my heart is the sense that without asking, I am being blessed.

I wish I had come into this path half a century ago, yet in retrospect I see how many of my frantic prayers were answered, even though, once answered, I forgot the Source to which they were directed.

All prayer is good—the formal, the informal, the talking aloud, the silent, the prayer at desk or table, watching a sunset or storm; the prayers in church together with one's fellow men, the prayers in the dark night and the lonely dawn.

The spirits of men struggle to mainfest themselves through the erring stubborn, density of the flesh and physical mind. Almost always the link between is corroded or walled off. I believe that our spirits—or if you will, souls—are part of the Divine Spirit and that if we could learn to know our higher selves and allow the knowledge to come through us, we would be happier and better people.

Prayer is a reaching for a Hand; prayer is sometimes a spontaneous and selfless petition; prayer is, in secret, a secret. And it always reaches its destination.

PRAY FOR ME

By The Rev. Frank Lissenden Eversull, Ph.D., D.D., LL.D.

Pastor Emeritus, First Presbyterian Church, Belleville, Illinois

❦

She was burdened with the weight of uncontrolled fear and silent rage. We had just come through a long and tearful discussion of personal problems and intimations of inadequacies. All of the suggestions that came from religion, psychology and experience seemed to no avail. Reluctantly and slowly she rose to go. There was a halting pause at the door, a half-hearted hand clasp, the wiping away of tears, then a turn to reach for the door knob. With a faltering voice that trailed off into the indiscernable she looked through tears and softly pleaded, "Pray for me."

This was the turning point. She had, at last, moved across that line which always separates the visible, the tangible, the coldly reasoned patterns of life. She stood there falteringly as she acknowledged the inner yearning for that power which she had vehemently denied throughout her outpouring of vituperation and contempt.

Now she recognized her need for some power that would come from without herself. In that instant she had placed herself in the attitude of a suppliant asking for mercy and understanding, both of which she tacitly admitted could come only from God. The cycle of training, experience, belief was completed. Personal incompetence was admitted. Dependence upon others, and above all upon God, was confessed. The road opened upon new vistas. She turned back into the room and waited. Then there followed a torrential outpouring of a soul that, at long last, had found the calm peace of an assurance. Ahead was a new direction.

Prayer is the natural channel that leads to re-orientation. It is the pathway that each must take when the problems of life overwhelm and the bitternesses of life overtake. It is the total admission of personal inadequacy. It is the acknowledgement of the reality of God. It tears down the prejudices of the past. It allays the fears of a lifetime.

To those who have participated in such struggles there come proofs and arguments that put to shame the cold logic of alien philosophies and the rote answers culled from outmoded texts. The simple request alone can open new vistas of human need and point unerringly to destiny. The soul of man craves participation with God. To get His active enlistment against the causes which annoy, perplex, and create fear, prayer is the only answer. It soothes the mind of the little child as he finds a great security in the simple words, "Now I lay me down to sleep." It becomes the answer to the turbulence of adolescence. It gives meaning to the unsolved questions of the mature mind. It serves as the anchor to the sick, the distressed, the fearful, the wavering and the anxious. It is the sweet benediction that is the crowning assurance of age.

"Pray for me," is the first great single step in the search for a vibrant faith. It means that others are needed and are ready to help. It brings that assurance of belonging to a company of those who know and love the same Lord. Above all, it gives nurture and nourishment to an embryo faith that can blossom into a life of dedication and devotion. It stands at the foot of the great mountain peaks of all time, the Mount of Temptation, the Mount of the Transfiguration, the Mount of Olives, and the Mount of Calvary. "Pray for me" are the simple words that give meaning to life and affirm the reality of eternity. "Pray for me" is the golden key that opens the great doors of Faith, Hope and Love.

MAN'S HIGHEST ASPIRATION

By Dr. Olaf C. Christiansen
Director, St. Olaf College Choir

❧

"What we master is not as important as that which masters us." Man is given a free will, but unless he recognizes and subjects his will to a greater power he lives unto himself. If we recognize God as our Creator and submit to Him as our Master we can be guided toward fulfilling His purpose. A desire to make contact with God and the willingness to serve Him gives us incentive to do greater things for others. Those who are mastered by the spirit of God are apt to respond to ideas which relate to the making of a better world.

We need to know that God is concerned and willing to guide us. Like children we often attempt to govern ourselves until our mistakes catch up with us. Then we turn to our Father for guidance. How childish we are! Eager to be free but unable to cope with freedom!

Through communion with God we receive the gift of faith, and the assurance that God has a plan for each of us and that this plan includes the welfare of all of His Creation. "What is man that thou art mindful of him?"

We need reminders at every turn to keep us aware of God's nearness and availability. Beauty in nature, creations of art, man's search for truth, a kindly deed, an act of love, patience and forgiveness, can all serve as reminders, if we are observant and sensitive. Response to all forms of beauty will often lead us to prayer.

With understanding of our relatedness to God, to nature, and to our fellow creatures, comes the urgent desire for more frequent contacts with our Master.

Surely, man's highest aspiration is to be in constant communion with God.

"GOD IS ONLY A PRAYER AWAY"

By Dr. Fred Pierce Corson

Bishop of the Methodist Church

❁

My earliest remembered experience with prayer goes back to my thirteenth year. I was away from home and lonely for my loved ones even though I was in the home of friends. The activities of the daytime diverted my thoughts from this feeling of separation but the nights alone in my room made this sense of separation very poignant. One night especially stands out in that first visit away from home. Awaking from a dream in the still and darkness of the night a sense of utter desolation took hold of me. What to do I did not know. Pride kept me from calling to the others in the house whom I know now would have gladly come. Then the thought came to me—"Talk to God. He is near." So I did and I wasn't lonely or fearful anymore.

Now the reality of this experience was its real value. What as a boy, reared in a godly home, I had been taught about God came true for me that night.

Since then I have had to travel much in far away and lonely places, separated from my loved ones, away from friends and the familiar scenes of my life and at times in some danger, but the reality of that experience has never left me. As a boy I discovered the truth of God's promises! I learned for myself that "God is only a prayer away." I knew then what Christ meant when He said, "I will not leave you comfortless." Even when I neglected to use this means of grace I still knew that it was real. It has quieted me when I have been in the throes of an inward panic and it has sustained and lifted my spirits when "the nights have been dark and I have been far from home."

PRAYER FOR THOSE IN PUBLIC LIFE

By Hubert H. Humphrey

U.S. Senator from Minnesota

❋

For men and women holding public office today, time has become a premium commodity, as the pressures of an ever-more complex society focus themselves in and on government. The tension and strains of public life are heightened by the enormous number of decisions which are required of a public servant—decisions which must be made daily, hourly—frequently with too little time for careful study and analysis.

Decisions of great moment, made under the pressure of deadlines, with precious little time for reflection, demand that strength and confidence be drawn from a source far greater than the man himself. Prayer, in which we seek guidance and strength, and in which we earnestly seek to bring our own actions into harmony with God's purpose, is of vital importance. Yes, the value of prayer is incalculable.

Prayer is the pause that truly refreshes the spirit, the mind and the body. It is the means of receiving that extra source of strength and understanding that is needed to carry us through in times of difficulty, challenge and uncertainty. Prayer makes it possible for us to synchronize our lives with spiritual power.

It would be rash and presumptive for a public servant to claim Divine sanction for a decision or policy which he espouses, but certainly the man who seeks earnestly, privately, and humbly for Divine guidance may be expected to make wiser and more just decisions in his daily work.

THE COMFORT OF PRAYER

By Irving M. Ives

United States Senator from New York

🎖

I pray each night—and through all of my lifetime, prayer has strengthened me. I cannot conceive of retiring without first falling upon my knees and drawing close to Him. I pity the man who has not learned to know the powerful force of prayer.

For the man who does not pray is naked and alone—alone with his doubts, his inadequacies, his fears of what may lie ahead. Where has he to turn when, as all humans must, he fails himself or fails others? Who can guide him, comfort him, show him the way if he denies himself access to the Lord by ignoring prayer?

Not to pray is to burden oneself with the arrogant assumption that God's creatures do not need Him, can live without His daily presence in their lives. It is a false and corrosive assumption. To lack the comfort of prayer, to deny oneself its opportunities for self-knowledge, is to live most barrenly indeed.

Prayers are answered. We do not always get what we ask for, do not always receive what we want. But God knows where we are, God knows what we need. As we pray for others, as we pray to be made worthier of reward, and as we pray for fulfillment of needs in the light of our worthiness to have those needs met, the Lord will respond. Those words in the old hymn, "Take It to the Lord in Prayer," constitute as fine a piece of advice as any man will ever encounter in his lifetime.

125

GOD'S PERFECT PATTERN

By Arthur G. Linkletter
Radio and Television Star

❦

For twenty-five years I have been engaged in building a career in a field wherein the only unchanging thing is change itself. Insecurity is the norm. Frustration is commonplace. The stars worry about the fickle public. The supporting players are striving to win marquee space for their names. "What I believe" has kept me relaxed, and (my friends tell me) normal, in spite of these dizzy-daffodil surroundings.

First, I believe a man can do no more than he can. It seems almost stupid to parrot such ancient advice, but everywhere around me I see smart operators disregarding it. Instead of worrying about what might happen during a performance, or what critics might say after a show, I spend my time getting ready to do the very best I can; and I believe if that isn't good enough they should get another boy.

Instead of going over and over a blunder committed during a program, I give myself one good hard mental kick in the pants, make a careful note of what led up to the boner and go on to the next production challenge. This kind of a belief cannot be blithely acquired like a new necktie. You must live it to believe it. And perhaps I can believe it and live it because of the way I began my career. As the only, adopted son of an itinerant evangelist who never knew what it was like to have the rent paid in advance, or a five-dollar bill in the bank, I had to make my start from zero altitude. And as my old friend, stuttering Joe Frisco said, "When you ain't got nothin' to start with, the worst that can happen is you'll break even!"

Well, next, I believe that every human being must have a goal in life that is a constant challenge. As fast as a temporary goal is reached I must move the boundaries and take a fresh start. I, personally, have never chosen goals so far distant as to be discouraging in their unattainability. When I was a studio staff announcer, I dreamt of starring in my own show with a real, live, local sponsor who could afford to pay me $300 a month. At each turn, I promptly discovered that my life's ambition had its limitations and something more was needed to make me satisfied. And so today, my pattern for the future is bound up in a desire to use my talents for the good of mankind. Lest you think this grandiose, consider my principal belief.

I believe in people. I have always been more interested in people than in ideas or things. As a youngster I remember being teased by older friends about my persistent questions concerning why other folks loved, hated, laughed and cried.

In college I took many subjects devoted to the study of human psychology. Unlike Will Rogers, I cannot say that "I have never met a man I did not like." However, I can truthfully say that I have never met a person in whom I was not interested. I believe that people are innately good and that they want to be loved, respected, and remembered. They are often otherwise because of where they must live, and how, and with whom. But my faith in their need for one another and in their basic good is such that I want always to be doing something wherein I can underscore the good and diminish the evil. Whether I continue as a broadcaster, or use my abilities in social work, politics, or teaching, my goal is to help people know that they are a part of a perfect pattern first traced by God and that in the return to this ideal, we must all do our share.

I BELIEVE IN PRAYER

By Dr. G. Bromley Oxnam

Bishop of the Methodist Church in the Washington Area

❧

Prayer is first of all an affirmation of faith in God. The God who carries in his mind the whirling spheres and the unfolding flowers, knows me. This is the faith upon which prayer is based. I cannot pray unless I believe.

Prayer is more than affirmation of theism. It is encounter. The Eternal who is being sought by me is ever seeking me. We meet in prayer. It is like meeting a friend upon a busy thoroughfare. Thousands are rushing by. They do not know my name, but my friend does. There is the flash of recognition, the word of greeting. I count in the crowd. I am an individual known and knowing. Prayer is like that. I can meet Him in crowded street, in quiet garden, in the soft lights of the chapel. Trysts at twilight transform encounter into an enchanted evening.

In such encounter I learn to know God better. I discover His will. I resolve to put myself at His disposal in a new and dedicated sense. Not my will, but thine be done.

Jesus taught us to pray and in so doing put his stamp of approval upon the practice of prayer. He indicated that attitude of mind and heart requisite to prayer. He said, "When ye pray, say Our Father." This is first an affirmation of faith, but it is more. He said, "Hallowed be thy name." The approach is one of reverence.

Like an athlete, the man who would pray must train. He must keep in condition. Occasionally an athlete of a generation gone will attempt today to throw a baseball or punt a football. Usually the attempt is a dismal performance. Men who pray only when the ship is sinking or the aircraft is on fire can expect little to happen to themselves or to the situation.

Prayer sounds the death knell of totalitarian tyranny. No state is really totalitarian as long as there are those who hold there is a power greater than the state, and this is done whenever grace is said. The cross may not be visible, or it may still surmount the spire or stand in sacred beauty upon the altar, but visible or invisible, it is present in the hearts of those who pray. Even in the darkest days of tyranny, the cross "towers o'er the wrecks of time." When the swastika and the hammer and sickle are but reminders of historical night-mare, the cross lives on in the power of an endless life.

Prayer is encounter; it is also enrichment. It is the testimony of great souls who have learned to pray that the experience enriches life. Such persons have learned that prayer is not begging. It is fellowship.

In prayer the mind and heart are made ready for the mind of God. Prayer is spiritual intercourse. Prayer is communication. Truth so communicated does make us free.

Prayer is commitment. "Come clean," we say to the accused who sits at an interrogation table in the police station. "Come clean" is a proper order when we pray.

Prayer strengthens, not every time but cumulatively. We move from strength to strength. The courage so often revealed by men who have faced the mob, dared gibbet, and victoriously withstood brain washing, is a courage born of prayer.

Jesus came to do the will of his Father. That will is best learned in prayer. So I pray.

—Excerpts reprinted by permission from the chapter entitled "I Believe in Prayer" from the book "A Testament of Faith," published by Little, Brown & Company.

WHY PRAYER IS OUR BEST MEDICINE

By George W. Crane, Ph.D., M.D.

Psychologist and Lecturer

❧

Prayer is the unique "tuning-in" process by which we children of God can make personal contact with the invigorating power of our Heavenly Father.

Psychologically, it permits us to touch God, much as the woman of the bloody issue touched Christ's garment and immediately felt curative forces surge through her.

Prayer also has wonderful psychiatric value. For when we pray, we face our problem and state it in words, which is the first step in psychiatric therapy.

It also halves our load, for when we share our dilemma with our Heavenly Father, that very act immediately divides the weight.

Meanwhile, prayer promotes wider perspective out of which we often obtain an inner answer to our own entreaties, without needing an outside miracle in Nature.

It is also an empirical fact in medicine that people who attend church regularly and who talk over their problems with their Senior Partner via prayer, do not become sleeping pill addicts. Nor do they require tranquilizer drugs.

They are not likely to be troubled by insomnia. Their blood pressure drops farther at night and their tendency to peptic ulcer and spastic colitis is much less.

Prayer thus makes us Junior Partners of God.

If nervous and distraught at bedtime, just talk to God and say: "Lord, I have a heavy day tomorrow and need eight hours of sound slumber. Will you please take over the night shift for me, since I am trying to be your Junior Partner?"

God **never** refuses to take over your night shift under such circumstances!

THE COMFORT OF PRAYER

By Allan Price Kirby

Chairman of the Board and President, Alleghany Corporation

It makes no difference whether one is in the solitude of home, in the confusion which frequently exists in his office, at a business meeting, driving an automobile, riding in a public conveyance—no matter where—if he will take the time to meditate, even though it may be for only a few minutes, he can receive great solace and much comfort if he directs his thoughts to God. When I am in the midst of trying to solve a difficult problem and take the time to ask for Divine Guidance, if I am heart sick and physically ill and pray for help or if, as I have at times, feel that I am in great danger and pray for help, I have found on many occasions that it gives me comfort and peace.

The joy of giving has its compensations, too. It is difficult to give wisely and well. None of us can give to as many worthwhile things as we would like but when I am struggling with what I should do in a given situation I sometimes find that when I ask for guidance it comes clearly to me as to what I should do—not always at first but finally, in time.

Yes, the power of prayer is great. I would feel lost without it. If more people practiced it, this could be a much better world for all of us to live in. The best way to start is by going to church. When we are young we go to school to learn how to read and to write. It is even more important that we first go to church school and then to church to learn how to worship God. It cannot help but give one a sense of comfort and well being if practiced soberly, seriously and religiously throughout one's life. It becomes as important as the other necessities of life. I know from experience.

I BELIEVE PRAYER
CREATES DYNAMIC SERENITY

By Dr. E. Preston Sharp

Executive Director, Youth Study Center, Philadelphia

It takes little imagination to realize the many problems faced by one who deals with 12,000 delinquent children each year as Executive Director of the Philadelphia Youth Study Center. These children are brought to the Youth Study Center which serves as a detention and study facility for the Juvenile Division of the Municipal Court of Philadelphia. There are few "pat" answers in working with delinquent children because each child represents a different problem and a challenge.

During the organizational stages of the Center when the majority of the staff was without experience there were numerous crises in controlling the children. Many delinquent children are similar to psychotic patients. They must be protected from themselves because they act first and think second. Unless properly supervised, there is the danger of serious or fatal injury. There were some injuries but, fortunately, there were no fatalities.

Long ago I learned that administrative responsibility carries many pressures. The ability to remain calm in critical and trying conditions is essential for intelligent problem solving and to maintain the confidence and respect of the staff. Worry prevents constructive thinking, undermines one's health, and definitely affects one's disposition. The only source of dynamic serenity is a sincere belief in God and constant communication with Him through prayer.

During the times of extreme tension, my greatest help has been the habit of talking with God as I drive to work. I discuss my problems with Him and when I start my duties I am not working alone. I am part of a team; the most important member is God. As a result of one of my early morning discussions, I decided to ask the administrative staff what they thought about beginning our administrative meetings with a prayer. They agreed and this procedure has been followed ever since. It creates an awareness of our Unseen Partner. On one occasion I almost overlooked the opening prayer and I was quickly reminded of the omission. All agreed that starting a meeting without prayer would be incomplete.

There are about 175 boys and girls in residence at all times. We have a complete religious program for the three major faiths. It is not unusual in our cafeterias to observe boys or girls voluntarily saying blessings for their food. Never has a child been "jeered" for this practice. To the contrary, it is not unusual for others to follow the example. The tone of the Center has, undoubtedly, influenced this practice.

Experience has proved that mal-adjusted adults cannot help disturbed children. It is, therefore, important for every employee, from the director down, in an organization dealing with delinquent children to be at peace with himself. All of us are faced with tribulations in our private lives, in addition to the pressures of our business responsibilities. We cannot face these issues nor perform our work efficiently without the help of God through prayer.

THE PRACTICE OF PRAYER

By Dr. Ralph S. Cushman
Bishop of The Methodist Church

❦

I can sum up my theory and practice of prayer in three or four propositions. And in saying my theory of practice of prayer, I believe this is likewise the teaching of the Scriptures.

First—I can do more than pray after I have prayed, but I cannot do more than pray until I have prayed. I heard Dr. Robert E. Speer speak words like these years ago, and I have found them true. Prayer changes things!

Second—More things are wrought by prayer than this world dreams of. Of course, this is the poet Tennyson's proposition; but it is more than poetry, it is profound truth for all of us. And Jesus practiced it while in the flesh. If He needed prayer, we certainly do. "I have prayed for you," He said to Simon Peter, "that your faith may not fail." And the self-confident disciple proved soon how he needed prayers. So do all of us, for, as Saint Paul witnessed, "we have this treasure in earthen vessels!" Prayer connects one with power from on high, and enables one to live victoriously even when living earthen vessels.

Third—Prayer is not mere telephoning to God with some request; it is communion with God; it is talking with God; it is fellowship with Jesus Christ; it is commitment to the guidance of the Holy Spirit. Without this communion with God, there can be no developing life and character; we remain spiritual dwarfs.

Finally—Jesus commanded His disciples to pray: "Watch and pray" was His final word in Gethsemane. Indeed, during his last hours before Calvary, more than a dozen times, He exhorted the disciples to pray, pray, pray! And His promise was that prayers, in His Name, would be heard and answered. I have found this to be the truth.

134

PRAYER IS A TWO-WAY CONVERSATION

By Paul F. Douglass

Lawyer and Advisor to Foreign Governments

❦

In the companionship of a Swiss professor as a student, I came to experience prayer long ago as a two-way conversation with God. When I speak to Him, I know that he listens. When he speaks to me, I hear. Over the years I have found vivid guidance from a conversation with God recorded in 2 Ezekiel 1. In the presence of the glory of God, the Hebrew prophet had fallen to his face. Then God spoke and Ezekiel listened: "Son of man, **stand** upon thine own feet and I will speak unto thee." Because God makes use of instruments, He wanted Ezekiel to be up and about his mission with a concrete plan for the future of his people.

Moses experienced the same voice when God suggested: "Put off thy shoes from off thy feet; for the place whereon thou standest is holy ground." In the conversation God awakened Moses to his mission and set him to work on the major task of his life. From the splendor of God revealed in the beauty of a rainbow Ezekiel, like Moses who had talked with God at a commonplace rendezvous by a commonplace bush in a commonplace desert sheep pasture in Midian, saw with his eyes and heard with his ears God's expectation of man: to be about life's constructive business.

Over my desk hangs a portrait of Hugo Grotius, the father of international law. He was a lawyers' lawyer and a Christians' Christian. One of my pleasures is sitting down with the original text of **The Law of War and Peace** (1625). Here is a book written by a Dutchman, in Latin as the international

135

language of the age, in a Paris flat where he was living as a refugee, and first exposed for sale at the fair in Frankfort. Exiled from his own country, Hugh Grotius became a first citizen of the world. Denied the practice of his profession in his native country, he spoke to mankind with the only instrument allowed to him in exile: his pen.

To Grotius the major mission of his life lay in the establishment of the law of nations. He dedicated his treatise to Louis XIII of France, who gave him sanctuary, by the assertion of three down-to-earth propositions of counsel:

1. "Hard the task is; but no task except one fraught with difficulty, one that all others have given up on despair, is meet for so great a king."

2. "This is to be in very truth most Christian, not merely by a right inherent in your lineage but **by a right inherent in yourself.**"

3. "May the God of Justice, O Peace-Making King, heap upon Your Majesty, not only all other blessings, but with them also **the distinction of having accomplished this task.**"

The great jurist concluded his epochal treatise with a prayer of petition that God might grant to leaders a "mind possessed of knowledge of divine and human law," holding ever before them the reflection that God hath chosen them, living things most dear to Him, as His plenipotentiaries in the cause of establishing peace through law among men.

In life I have found most helpful the belief that God makes use of instruments to achieve his purposes; and that he makes his goals clear to us as we talk and listen in conversations with Him—which process to me is prayer.

136

PRAYER BUILDS A PATHWAY

By Dr. Maris M. Proffitt

Writer and Educator

❦

Prayer is the natural consequence of the recognition by man of the self-evident truth that there is a superior power to himself. He looks upon this power, this authority, this spirit, this being—his God—as the giver and the protector of his life. And just as it is natural for a child to want to make known to his parents his happiness, his troubles, and his desires, so it is inherent in man's nature to commune with his God, expressing gratitude for his blessings, asking protection from evil, and seeking guidance for his actions. This communing with God may be in the form of thought only or it may be in the form of thought expressed in words or in actions. But in whichever form it occurs, if carried on in true sincerity and adoration, it is prayer.

In order that man may make contact with God for holding communion with Him, he must first show his good intentions by a sincere effort to do so. God places upon him the responsibility for initiating action for communion and fellowship with Him. This is made clear by the conditions underlying the promises: "Behold I stand at the door and knock: if any man hear my voice, and open the door, I will come in to him." "Ask, and it shall be given you; seek, and ye shall find; knock, and it shall be opened unto you."

God, who is a spirit, is available to each and all of us at any place we may be, and at any and all times. He stands on the outside of our door and knocks for admission, and if we will listen to His summons and open the door He will come in. But He will not force an entrance. We must show by some act our sincerity of purpose to have Him come into our hearts.

Prayer creates an attitude of mind favorable to the development of a good way of life. As one communes with God, who is love and who is good, he tends to bring his spirit into harmony with God's spirit and thus to attain more and more unto God's ways. It is the old story of, ". . . as he thinketh in his heart, so is he." The more one thinks about any worthwhile subject, the more he is convinced of its worthwhileness; and such conviction tends to lead first to a desire and then to a corresponding action to secure the thing deemed desirable.

Thinking with God—communing with Him—about any vital problem or subject brings about a state of mind that better enables him to consider the problem in a sound and rational manner. Such action helps one to help himself, which is the best possible answer to a prayer of importunity. Self-attainment gives one pride and courage and spurs one on to other noble efforts. Faith in the efficacy of prayer is exemplified by the acts of great leaders, such as Washington and Lincoln, who did not hesitate to pray and who in times of crisis urged the general public to concerted action in prayer.

Prayer builds a pathway to the throne of God, which improves with continuous use and makes for ever-increasing fellowship with God. King Arthur, in Tennyson's Idylls of the King, expresses this thought beautifully in his plea to lift hands high in prayer,

> "For so the whole round earth is every way
> Bound by gold chains about the feet of God."

HOW DO I PRAY?

By Dr. James V. Claypool

Trinity Methodist Church, New Bedford, Mass.

Growth of the modern scientific spirit and the increased reliance which we now place on "things of the earth, earthy" has done something to people. To me in particular it has caused much and long reflection on just how far to place my faith on the things which moth and rust do not corrupt and where thieves do not break through and steal.

In my life prayer has steadily grown more effective and useful. My Heavenly Father is personal enough to hear my prayers, patient enough to listen to them, and kind enough to answer them. That which really constitutes my inner life is in reality my prayer life.

I am a minister. Were I a layman and member of a committee seeking to secure a new pastor for my church I think I would judge and evaluate him more by his prayers than his sermons. The kind of a man he is, his knowledge of God, and his friendship with Christ would all be more evident through prayer than homiletics.

For both public and private prayer I want to be prepared and ready. I don't jump into it like a diver into a swimming pool. I like to be physically composed, emotionally calm, at least when I commence. Quietness helps but is not essential.

Prayer to me is a matter more of cultivation of the Spirit rather than communion with the Spirit. It is an attitude of perception rather than framing thoughts into words.

And I like to kneel. Standing is all right, but kneeling is better. Staying seated is poor. I just can't get into the spirit of prayer sitting comfortably in a rocking chair wih my legs crossed. God is too high and mighty for me to get chummy with Him like that.

I like to read prayers of others over and over again. The prayers of the Bible are among the best. In praying I easily and customarily use Jesus' name. By that I mean that my prayer is to Him, in His name. The person I am praying to is closer that way, just as my mother wrote after my preacher father's sudden death:—

"I pray to father, my lost lover; think of him always when I should look into Jesus' face and worship Him."

Jesus is the picture and presence of the Father to me.

I like to pray out loud, or at least let my lips move when praying alone. Sometimes the same thoughts are expressed over and over in different word forms and thought imagery. There is almost never any trouble, any place or any time, in being able to create the intimate sense of God's spiritual presence and response.

Reading the Bible is an exercise in prayer which is par excellence for me. I pray what I am reading in Scripture as I am reading it. The sacred words lead and guide to prayers. I know no vehicle superior to the Bible for keeping one's prayers from becoming hackneyed, trite and sterile. When using the Bible as a prayer guide one's petitions, intercessions, confessions and gratitude are saved from becoming narrow, restricted and repetitious.

To a degree the same can be said for the hymn book. I have read every line in the Methodist hymnal prayerfully, and many of the hymns over and over again. Perhaps the best religious poetry in print may be found there. At least some of the best prayers and aids and leads for prayer are the stanzas of Christian hymns.

It is pleasure to pray. I don't pray because I feel I have to do so. I pray because I like to, and miss it when I don't.

PRAYER IS WONDERFUL

By Dr. Charles B. Foelsch

President, Pacific Lutheran Theological Seminary

❀

"More things are wrought by prayer . . . . "

How true! Even if I had not myself experienced the power of prayer, I could not honestly deny the testimony of the millions who say and have said with joy "I sought the Lord and He heard me." But I have found it out for myself that prayer is wonderful. Let no one doubt this confession of mine. When I really pray, in faith, God hears my prayer, and blessing is wrought for me.

Why then are there periods of prayer drouth in my life? Times when my words fly up, and then bounce right back like burned-out sky-rockets on a long-ago Fourth of July? Times when the Amen sticks in my throat (though unlike Macbeth I have no brutal murder on my conscience)? Times when my prayers, I fear, are just a form of godliness, without the power of it?

Why? Let me look again at what King Arthur was saying, "More things are **wrought** . . . ." The word **wrought** gives me my clue. That word has faith in it . . . and sweat . . . and tears . . . and patience.

It has in it what James is thinking about in his epistle when he testifies that when a Christian prays vigorously, faithfully, enthusiastically much good is **wrought.**

The word fits that very human Jacob of long ago, there at the Ford of Jabbok, and his praying. What a weight he had on his heart! What woe the next day threatened for him. That

141

night he prayed, all the night through, with such penitent intensity of soul, that he felt he was wrestling with God's angel; or was it with the Lord Himself? So fierce was his soul agony that the token of it lingered on in his body. In the morning when his prayer was done, and he went on his way, there was a hurt in his thigh that made him limp every step of his way. His prayer, however, **wrought** something worthy. The record says, God blessed him there.

Let me look at Another, in His anguish in the Garden praying intensely . . . in an agony . . . great drops of blood falling to the ground. His frail human companions wrought nothing in Gethsemane. They slept while He prayed . . . not my will . . . not my will . . . not my will. **Thy** will be done. Thy will be **done.** An angel came and strengthened Him. He prayed on . . . He **wrought** . . . .

> "O the worm-wood and the gall!
> O the pangs His soul sustained . . . .
> Turn not from His griefs away,
> Learn of Jesus Christ to pray."

He **wrought** . . . . .

One thing is now plain to me. I must let God's Spirit **energize** my praying. I must let Him take me firmly in hand, and put me **to work** at my praying, morning, noon, and night. Praying so, in Jesus' name, I shall find my own voice of experience singing the good news daily in my soul:

> "More things are wrought by prayer
> Than this world dreams of."

AN ANSWER TO PRAYER

By Dr. William R. Cannon

Dean, Candler School of Theology, Emory University

My life, at least the genuinely good part of it, is altogether an answer to prayer.

It illustrates, I feel certain, the force and efficacy of intercessory prayer. Before I was born my mother, like Hannah of old, dedicated me to the Lord. My parents had been married a dozen years with no children to bless their home. They felt they would not have any; so when they realized what they had always wanted was about to happen, my mother looked on that event as a peculiar favor of Providence. When I was a tiny boy, she would say to me, "Bill, I do not think of you as being really mine. You are something God has lent to me. You belong entirely to Him."

Consequently I can never remember a day when I did not know what I was to do in life. I never had the struggle most youngsters have in reaching a decision as to my vocation. God had called me, so I firmly believed, to be His minister. I gave myself to Him in Christian baptism when I was seven years old. That act of faith was at the same time an act of life dedication. My parents accepted the choice as I did. They gave themselves and their resources completely to my education for the Christian ministry.

"If thine eye be single," Jesus said, "thy whole body shall to full of light." Since I knew what I wanted, I did not dissipate my energies in unnecessary and extraneous activities. Though I participated fully in the program of the school and local community, I was always happiest when I was studying to improve my mind and spirit or busy sharing what God was doing for me with other people. Though my health was not robust and I was subjected to many illnesses as a child, I managed to do creditable work in school, to secure a good education, finally attaining the Ph. D. degree in Historical Theology from Yale University.

I had planned all along to give myself to the pastoral ministry. Though I was invited to teach in a northern university on my graduation from Yale, I returned to my native state, Georgia, and was assigned to a small pastoral appointment in the Methodist Church.

I had been there scarcely one year when I was asked to join the faculty of Emory University. At first I felt a reluctance to accept; but, when my Bishop indicated his willingness to appoint me to that assignment, I accepted this as an act of God.

I have been at Emory University thirteen years, nine as a classroom teacher and four as Dean of the Candler School of Theology. I feel that it is great to be a preacher of God's Word but greater still to be a teacher or maker of preachers.

My personal creed is simple enough. I believe in the deity of Jesus Christ and in the personal guidance of the Holy Spirit, Who together with the Father constitute the Godhead. I believe in the revelation of God through the ideas and the events of the Holy Scripture, culminating in Jesus Christ, the incarnated Word of God made man, perfect, therefore, in both His divinity and His humanity. I believe in a real atonement for sin on the cross, that Christ forgives me my sins and gives me day by day the power to live a good life, and that what He has ordained for me by His grace He desires to give to the whole world if men will freely accept Him by faith. The Church should be the temporal replica of the Eternal Kingdom, which someday will exist in its fullness when time is no more and Christ is all in all.

My Christian life began through the intercessory prayers of my mother. It is continued through my own prayers and my love of God and neighbors.

PERSONAL COMMUNICATION THROUGH PRAYER

By Erle Cocke, Jr.

Vice President of Delta Air Lines

Past National Commander of the American Legion

❀

I believe in a Supreme Being. I have received tangible evidence of the results of prayer, and have never failed to express my innermost thoughts to God Almighty, for He has been "my rod and my staff" on many occasions.

I believe in people, for people have meant much to me. Their individual and collective personalities have been the guiding light, the distributor of messages coming from above. The personal communication through prayer, and the daily devotion to living each day as if it were the last day, I believe prepares one mentally and physically for the life beyond.

Life by the Ten Commandments coupled with the Golden Rule still offers us the greatest chance for a peaceful survival of the world in the age of space.

The Holy Bible has taught us the importance of a design for living, and I was so nurtured from my mother's knee. Personal meditation and constant Christian re-evaluation offers much in tolerance of others and strength of self. The prayerful encouragement of others to spread the Gospel has been the underlying theme of civilization for the last two thousand years, and I believe that the teachings of the past are still a prologue of the future.

I believe in prayer.

PRAYING FOR GUIDANCE
By Vera Connolly
Writer and Journalist
❦

I am humbly grateful for answered prayer. I have known the quiet joy of it in small daily occurrences. Sometimes it has guided me in major crises. I have witnessed the beauty of it in others' lives.

I believe that every selfless prayer we offer is answered. First, as inflowing peace; then as fresh light on the immediate problem. Courage and wisdom are renewed. Once more we can go forward.

I was an American Army child, reared in isolated corners of the world where often there were no church facilities. So my Protestant parents taught me to love the Bible, turn to it in trouble, and trust its eternal promises. Years later I was to be profoundly grateful for this. I was by then a young journalist in New York, being sent out across the country to investigate flagrant evils, write the facts, and try to obtain corrective legislation. Always my small Bible was tucked into my suitcase. And many a night at my hotel, when things were going wrong and guidance was urgently needed, I searched its pages earnestly.

Countless times since then—through more than thirty years of crusading journalism—I have opened my Bible at night, in a hotel somewhere, after a day of ugly threats and concealment of the facts. And I have prayed: "Lead me to the truth." Usually I have found my answer quickly. One such night, I recall, I opened to the glorious promise: "Behold I send an Angel before thee, to keep thee in the way, and to bring thee into the place which I have prepared." (Ex 23:20). Thankfully I closed the book and went off to sleep. And the following day I was led to go directly to the only possible source of the real facts—a spot I had not even thought of visiting.

My prayer, when starting to write an article, is often: "Let the words of my mouth, and the meditation of my heart, be acceptable in thy sight, O Lord, my strength, and my redeemer." (Ps 19:14). Different answers to this prayer have come to me down the years. Usually the article has unfolded without difficulty, and gone to press, and all has been well. But now and then I have felt impelled to stop writing, go out into the field, investigate further. Each time this guidance has proved an incalculable blessing and protection to all.

I do, indeed, believe in prayer. And so, I think, do all human beings—harassed as many of us may outwardly appear today in this tumultuous world. Always, in the big crisis, when the great blow comes, we find we really do believe. A few years ago, in a one-story hotel lounge in the tropics, during an earthquake, when the walls were rocking and the tiled roof was threatening to crash in, I beheld an impressive sight. The frightened, milling throng of white tourists and dark-skinned natives suddenly ceased to panic and began to pray. The cause of it? A young native school teacher with face alight and arm upflung, who pleaded, now in English, now in dialects: "We must pray! Each must pray . . . not for himself. Each must pray for **all present!**" The earthquake shocks went on. Two walls and part of the roof fell. We were enveloped in dust and powdered lime. But when it was over, no one in the room had even been scratched.

I often think of that roomful of men, women and children, of many nations, races and creeds, who, in dire peril, were willing to pray for one another. Surely, what is possible for a dedicated roomful is possible for a dedicated worldful!

If the terrified persons in that shaking room could pray for the common good, and be saved—can not we, the frightened peoples of this shaking world, begin praying together for the common good, and be saved?

THE HEART OF PRAYER

By D. Campbell Wyckoff

Professor of Christian Education, Princeton Theological Seminary

One summer during my early high school days I joined a group that was talking about philosophies of life. The discussion went deeply and seriously into many religious questions, belief in God in particular. At a crucial point the leader broke in to say that she had the feeling that we were talking about God without having experienced him. Then she led us quietly into the living presence of God, and I learned what prayer is. Ever since that day the words of prayer have been something added to the unspoken prayer that is a sense of relationship to God.

Is this too simple and naive? I am willing to let it seem so. In my personal experience this sense of the living presence of God has made my prayer real, and has safeguarded me against the sentimental prayer that listens to itself and not to God. It has made my prayer intimate, but has safeguarded me against its becoming chummy.

Later on, during college, I heard of Brother Lawrence, who practiced the presence of God as he went about the ordinary tasks of life. This struck me as being the key to realizing the living presence at every moment of life. There have been many and long periods of forgetfulness, but once I have come to myself again and remembered whose I am, it has been possible quickly to recover the awareness of God's presence. To me the heart of prayer is to live one's life and to do one's work conscious of the reality and presence of God.

The life of prayer was what enabled me to weather the blows of doubt and agnosticism that were so severely dealt by the intellectual world in which I lived and was trained. But there was the assurance of the reality of the living God, and there were teachers, friends, and members of the family who shared the sense of God's presence and who helped me to grow and to forge a strong faith rather than to become defensive and to retreat into a closed world of small experience and brittle ideas. Thus I came to know the power of shared prayer—spoken and silent.

During the war my witness to the way of peace was directed and steadied by God's living presence. It was at that time that I began to think in a definite and more penetrating way about the Christian faith, and realized that God's presence is that of the living and redeeming word, Jesus Christ, and that of the Holy Spirit. My participation in public worship, whether liturgical or not, gradually took on new meaning as I began to know what it means to offer up prayer to God together with the whole company of those who are in Christ.

New discoveries in the life of prayer continue, but in no grandiose or spectacular way. Undergirding them, one finds, must be a life of faithfulness and work. But one listens more and speaks less. There is a growing sense of being on the borderlands of the realm of prayer, with untold possibilities ahead, and the secure faith that one will not only be permitted but led deeper into the living presence.

"LET US PRAY"

By *Major General Charles I. Carpenter*
Chief of Chaplains, United States Air Force

❀

The occasions on which we have heard the words, "Let us pray," are numerous. What the suggestion means is varied according to the intent of the one who makes such suggestion, or even the feeling of the hearer at the moment of suggestion. Whatever our reaction to the words, it is not possible to escape the realization that the admonition, "Let us pray," opens the door to a personal, enriching experience between the individual and his God.

Prayer is the line of communication to God available to all. Through prayer, conversation with the Divine God is consummated. The individual devoutly enters the presence of the Almighty and presents his petition of adoration, his words of thanksgiving, his plea for forgiveness. From the experience come the realization that the period of prayer is not a one way means of communication, for God is heard speaking to the one praying. The moment becomes rich in communion with the Divine. The Father "who heareth in secret" answers, and the individual is blessed and strengthened through the experience.

A Christian must pray. Prayers are vital to the developing of faith, to the sharpening of vision, and to the enriching of life. Yet the opportunity to pray is of no value unless used by the individual. "Let us pray" is an admonition and the presentation of such an opportunity.

RECOVERY FROM SPIRITUAL FATIGUE

By Dr. Luther A. Weigle

Dean Emeritus of Yale Divinity School

❀

The Christian faith affords the abiding motive and stimulus to prayer. The man whose mind is set on low and immediate ends has little to pray about. He gets the things he wants easily enough. The Pharisees prayed to be seen by men, said Jesus; and they received their reward. They were seen. That was all they wanted, and they got it. So the man who lives for food and drink and clothes, gets these things. He has his reward. He feels no especial need for prayer. If he tries to pray, he begins to use vain repetitions. It is the man, on the other hand, who has caught the vision of the new social order for which Christ lived and died, and who is seeking to follow him in devotion to the Kingdom of God, who finds himself moved to prayer. He is living for ends that lie beyond immediate attainment; he is undertaking tasks that are too big for him alone; he comes to barriers that look impassible, and meets disappointments that are heart-breaking. Such a man comes to God in prayer; it is the most natural thing for him to do. There is no strain about it, no searching for things to say. He has common interests with God.

What is the use of praying? That prayer has certain subjective values, is generally granted. It brings insight and vision; it opens the mind to fresh truth and to a new understanding of familiar things. It begets wholeness and sanity. It mobilizes one's resources and gives strength and power. Just as sleep refreshes the body, prayer recreates the spirit and brings recovery from spiritual fatigue.

151

But has prayer objective value? Does prayer actually count in the determination of the course of events? Yes, it does. Prayer must count if human minds and wills count at all in this world.

The denial of prayer's objective value has sometimes been cast into the form of a dilemma. There is no use in praying, it is said, for either one will pray for what is not best for him, and God will not grant that; or he will pray for what is best for him, and God will do that anyhow. Like most dilemmas, this is based upon a fallacy—the fallacy of assuming that what is best for a man remains the same, whether he prays or not. A father has two sons, for both of whom he desires to do the best that he can. Suppose that one of them answers his love with trust and confidence; while the other ignores him, will have no speech with him, and is even inclined to deny that he exists. Can it be imagined that the father's course of action will be the same in both cases? Or that the two sons will be equally esteemed in the community in which they live, or will meet like cooperation as they enter into the activities of the world?

There is a paradox in Jesus' teaching concerning prayer. He kept encouraging his followers to ask God freely for whatever they desired; but at the same time assured them that "your Father knoweth what things ye have need of, before ye ask him." What can it mean but that man's prayer is of value to the accomplishment of God's purpose. God does not need our information; He does seek our trust and cooperation. Our prayers may constitute that right adjustment to the great spiritual forces of the universe which is necessary if His will is to be done in us and through us. God will do the best He can for us; we can depend upon that. But what that best will be, depends in part upon how we pray.

DIVINE GUIDANCE THROUGH PRAYER

By Dr. Allen E. Claxton

Pastor, Broadway Temple Methodist Church, New York City

❦

Getting Divine guidance and developing the capacity to hear the voice of God is for me one of the most challenging and stimulating aspects of the life of prayer. It is also one of the most difficult.

There are many ways in which I sense the leadership of God and feel the urgency of His spirit. He speaks to me through my intelligence, my common sense. God expects me to use my powers of reason and judgment and He expects me to act in harmony with what I know to be right according to the best information I can get. As James says, "He that knoweth to do and doeth it not, for him it is sin."

God talks to me through the accumulated spiritual wisdom of the ages, most of which I find in the Holy Scriptures. When I am in need of special counsel, I can go to specific parts of the Bible for light on my problems, but I find it much better to approach my decisions under the influence of the total teaching of the Scriptures. I am under obligation to saturate myself with the Law and the Prophets, to flood my soul with the words of Jesus and to make His life so familiar to me that I am influenced by it. A knowledge of all of Paul's writings gives me better direction than relying upon some isolated verse for specific guidance.

God talks to me through expert advice. Just as I go to a physician for medical treatment and to a lawyer for legal counsel, so I go to informed consecrated clergymen and devout, well-instructed laymen for help in checking my conclusions to be sure that what I consider guidance is not merely wishful thinking.

The most important way God directs me is through His Holy Spirit. I need one hour a day in prayer and meditation to keep myself, my mind and my will, open to God. During the first twenty minutes, I read the Scriptures and other devotional literature to cleanse the mind and set up spiritual motivation and spiritual momentum in my consciousness. I take the second twenty minutes to talk to God about my life, my joys, my problems, my work, my loved ones and everything that is important to me. During the last twenty minutes, I sit quietly in meditation, listening for the urging of the Holy Spirit. Some times I take notes, but not always. God does not dictate directions to me, rather He clarifies, convicts, and urges me. Sometimes the guidance is direct and forceful, sometimes almost imperceptible, but always it is consistent. It is amazing how my problems filter through and are affected by the ideas in my devotional material. The solutions are different from those which I would have had, if I had not first sought God's presence through meditation and reading.

It is important to check what I believe to be Divine Guidance, to discover if it really is the leading of the Holy Spirit. I check it with my common sense, with the total impact of the Holy Scriptures, and with expert advice. My own ignorance, or lack of information and prejudices, will distort what God is seeking to say to me, but by a consistent obedience to the best I know and a continual re-consecration of my life to my Lord, He gradually increases my sensitivity to His will and my ability to obey.

AN ADVENTURE OF THE MIND AND THE SPIRIT

By *Rear Admiral Richard E. Byrd, USN (rtd)*

Former Officer-in-Charge United States Antarctic Programs, and

Honorary Chairman, International Rescue Committee

❦

Once upon a time on one of my expeditions to the bottom of the world, I found myself, through a combination of unforeseen circumstances, alone during the long polar night living in the shadow of the South Pole. The inland weather of an area in the clutches of an ice age had never been studied, so I had established a meteorological station for this purpose. And also I was taking observations of the Aurora Australis. My tiny shack was buried under the snow and there were 800 feet of ice under the shack.

Thus, I was at the world's end near the axis of the earth and cut off by the darkness and the cold and ice from any physical contact with the rest of the world.

There was no dust at the Advance Base, so that the celestial bodies took on a brightness and a beauty—yes, and even a meaning—unknown in civilization. I was living under the Aurora Australis, which was most brilliant and awe-inspiring when the great spots appeared on the sun 90,000,000 miles away. And every second when it was clear I could see a meteorite flashing brilliantly across the sky. Often there were ice crystals, created by the bitter cold, that scintillated the celestial bodies until they resembled myriads of diamonds floating through the air. The stars did not rise and set but made a circle of their course in the sky.

I had the strange feeling that somehow I had gotten onto another planet and that I was witnessing the imponderable processes and forces of the cosmos, harmonious and soundless. But out of the silence I felt a gentle rhythm—the music of the spheres perhaps. The conviction came to me that the rhythm was too orderly, too harmonious, too perfect, to be a product of blind chance. I realized that there must be purpose in the whole and that man was part of that whole and not an accidental offshoot—that therefore in the creation of man there must have been a design. Thus, there at the end of the earth I had found a confirmation of man's faith.

As the weeks of the long night wore on the temperature got lower and lower. The barrier ice contracted and began cracking as if with the sound of cannons. Bottomless crevasses opened up around my shack. My meteorological records began to show that probably I had come upon the world's coldest area.

Suddenly, disaster struck me. I was poisoned in the middle of the polar night by carbon monoxide from the faulty burner of my oil stove. To cut down the poison I had to keep my stove out twelve hours out of the twenty-four. The ice started crawling up the walls of my small shack and then across the ceiling and did not melt. Soon the poison affected my eyes so that the flickering candles no longer afforded enough light to read the books I had on my shelf.

Thus, most of the time I found myself lying in my sleeping-bag in the darkness, with nothing to do but think. I was living, in effect, precariously on the edge of an abyss. My thoughts, naturally enough, were on the gloomy side and they soon began to take charge of me.

And so I found that I must somehow take charge of my thoughts and completely control them. So I began to explore my mind to see what I could find there in the realm of imagination and thought that might help me.

The cold, the silence, the darkness, the "evenness of things", were rude and persistent companions. Difficult though they were to ignore, it was either deny their effect on me "or else."

Gradually I was able to control my thoughts more and more. In the field of imagination there semed no time-space limitations. I found that I could throw my thoughts backward or forward in the stream of time to any place I chose. It was as if my mind were a motion picture screen and I could run through it whatever picture I selected from an unlimited list. You may be sure that most of my scenarios took me to places as different as possible from my very gloomy surroundings, such as warm sunny lands.

Thus, there were moments when my predicament was forgotten; when I was conscious only of a peaceful mind adrift upon the adventurous tides of imagination.

But these adventures of the imagination were in the physical field and they were not enough. It was not so simple as that. I had to find other assets within myself if I hoped to survive. To substitute pleasant thoughts for gloomy ones was good but something more was needed.

So I explored as best I could into the uncharted and unknown areas of the mind; and slowly, as the days passed, I came on to some things. I discovered how much a man's world can be a world of the mind. And that a man himself determines or makes his world, which thus, to a degree, is the reflection of his own inner self wherein dwells the universal spirit of good.

It seemed to me that if a man could bring about the domination of his spiritual self over his worser self he could dry up the springs of fear and could then be captain of his ship and

157

invulnerable to any fate, even to the sting of death.

And so went my battle at the Advance Base. It was an adventure of the mind and the spirit.

And now, many years later I have been asked to pass along some of the observations I made during the long night in the shadow of the South Pole.

Much has happened in those years. Probably relatively few people today find it necessary to look within their spiritual selves for help. And they do not have to depend upon their imagination for entertainment. They are literally flooded with entertainment by the radio, television, and the movies. And now there is the new age of atom bombs, rockets, faster-than-sound planes, and so forth.

All of that seems quite wonderful. But in the meantime there is universal confusion. Freedom is in danger the world over, and there are threats of a third world war.

The trouble started in the twentieth century; the technological century. There have been more technical advances in the first half of the twentieth century than were made in the entire previous history of the world.

Man has been making for the past fifty years the very costly mistake of believing that real human progress consists in the development of ever more powerful weapons of destruction and in the development, more particularly, of all sorts of mechanical appliances and apparatus to bring him greater comforts and ease, diversions and entertainment, and all manner of pleasures.

Thus, most of the genius that man possesses has been used in the field of the material sciences. Man has shrunk the world with lightning-like rapidity and has thereby created among human beings a great interdependence with which

158

man is not ready to cope. In other words, he has created an extremely complicated environment into which he cannot adequately fit himself; thus making people everywhere easy prey to the "isms" taught by the false prophets. Man is too selfish to change his environment to fit himself. Therefore he must change himself to fit his environment.

A man beset by evil within and from without can mobilize his spiritual self to conquer that evil. Just so can the human race mobilize its moral and spiritual power to defeat the material power of evil that threatens it.

As I see it, the absolute essential for a peaceful and free world is a human race united—I repeat united—against the onward march of evil.

Here is how I believe man can achieve a united world if he so wills. We know that in the affairs of men it is essential to have a common purpose in order to achieve unity. As I see it, man has for long had that common purpose. All decent men and women the world over, of whatever creed or race or color, desire for themselves and their loved ones **a chance for the pursuit of happiness and liberty and freedom of worship.** This is our common global purpose.

And to achieve this purpose there is a workable method— the Golden Rule, which men and women of all religions can understand. It is the idea of consideration, ordinary everyday kindliness and decency, good will and friendliness, justice, mercy, and human sympathy. In short it is the brotherhood-of-man idea. It is the realization that the well-being of one man depends upon the well-being of his neighbor, the well-being of one group depends upon the well-being of its neighbor group, and the well-being of a nation depends upon the well-being of its neighbor nation. And all nations are now neighbors.

But we must not make the mistake of considering what the Great Teacher told us 2,000 years ago as a teaching based on weakness. Above all things, it is important for man to base his fight for brotherhood and unity upon firmness, strength and fortitude behind what is right and just.

But we know it will take time to mobilize the moral and spiritual force of man so as to unite the world behind this common global purpose. And we also know that until the world is so united the war-like leaders and false prophets must be held in leash by physical force.

PRAYER, AN ETERNAL VERITY
By Robert St. Clair
Playwright, Motion Picture and Television Writer

I believe that prayer is faith in God and in oneself as a child of God. My prayer time has become a vital part of my life. I come away from a "session" with God feeling relaxed and at peace with myself and the world. I have found prayer to be the perfect instrument of spiritual growth.

However, I have learned not to pray for things that are un-Christian, for I do not believe that our heavenly Father will listen—let alone answer—if the thing we ask for is not in accord with the teachings of Christ.

Stanley E. Jones has given us three steps in the art of prayer which I have found seems to bring me closer to Him. They are, "Listen, Learn and Obey." When I have sincerely tried to follow this advice, it has been amazing how many positive answers I have received.

WORTHY WITH PRAYER

By J. Irving Crump

Author and Editor, *Boys' Life*

❦

I really don't know when I learned how to pray. Of course, I grew up with childhood prayers. There were family prayers, ritualistic prayers, and later selfish, adolescent prayers through which I asked for the impossible and unnecessary and felt a sense of disappointment when there was no material answer. But it was not until I became a newspaperman following up police reports of accidents, crime and human tragedy that I began to get some understanding of the place prayer should occupy in my life, and, I am sure, in the lives of others.

The Reverend S. Parks Cadman helped me to form the pattern of my prayer. Dr. Cadman, then gaining a national reputation as a minister, was well liked by all of the New York reporters. The light in his study burned all hours of the night and it was a pleasant place for lonesome, nighthawking news-papermen to stop for a bit of copy and for a sociable cup of coffee. On one occasion Dr. Cadman, standing in the doorway of his home as I was about to leave, put his hand on my shoulder and said:

"My son, you are constantly seeing the seamy side of life. Don't let it make you lose your faith in God or cease your prayers."

From that time on I began to think of my prayers with much more objectivity. It dawned upon me that God had been very, very good to me and that my prayers should be first peans of gratitude and thanksgiving. I was sure that God was just as good to everyone of my fellowmen too, but some of them through selfishness, greed or other forms of sinfulness negated His beneficence and thus were responsible for the seamy side of life Dr. Cadman spoke of. They were really standing in the need of prayer. So gradually my prayers have become first prayers of appreciation for my good fortune, and prayers for the other people who have not had the happiness I have had. For myself I pray that God will help me to do my best and the result will find favor in His sight. Thus do I try to make myself worthy of His love with prayer, and in this way I have found complete contentment.

A TRUE SOURCE OF STRENGTH

By George Fielding Eliot
Writer and Military Analyst

I cannot pretend that I have believed in prayer all my life. In earlier years, I am afraid I turned to prayer only when in desperate trouble, through my own fault.

As time passed, I made a discovery. My prayers brought help and comfort only when I was doing my best to help myself. There is logic in this discovery which is infinitely reassuring, and a true source of strength.

To me it is proof that I have a Friend Who knows all my weaknesses, Who understands and forgives them but Who knows also that mere supplication is no substitute for "try, try again."

Thus through my own experience—which is the only lamp to guide one's feet along paths spiritual—I have come to believe in God's mercy and wisdom; mercy because I have been forgiven for wrong doing, wisdom because I have not been encouraged in it.

THE TREMENDOUS POWER OF PRAYER WITH FAITH

By Henry L. Scott

Concert Pianist and Humorist

First of all, I believe that all our prayers are answered even if sometimes the answer is "no." The power of prayer with faith is so enormous that we should pray only after serious thought. Prayer should not be a constant asking for something, for God already knows what we want and what we need. We always have His love, and if we can show our love for Him in our own lives by reflecting that love toward our family and toward our fellowman the tremendous power of prayer is ours.

I believe our prayers should usually be prayers of gratitude and thankfulness for the constant blessings which God has freely given us. I believe that most of our "asking" prayers should be the kind which ask God to make us better fathers and mothers, better husbands and wives, better sisters and brothers, better friends and neighbors. I believe that most of our other "asking" prayers should be the prayers which ask God to show us what His will for us is.

I do not think it is wrong to pray for specific things occasionally, but I do think that when we pray for help and guidance toward our hopes and dreams we should always let God know that we only want them if they are in accordance with His will for us.

Finally, I believe that prayer with faith is the greatest power on earth and ever available. It is this great power to which we must constantly strive to tune our lives.

FEELING IN THE NEED OF PRAYER

By George Meany

President, American Federation of Labor

Strongly impressed upon my mind is a scene of some years ago. We were in the midst of one of those crises that have recurred since the end of World War II. An American Secretary of State was about to board a plane for a conference in Europe. I can never forget his pausing at the foot of the steps to the plane and saying that he was leaving "feeling in the need of prayer."

Many of us many times feel in the need of prayer. Weighted down with problems, disturbed by conflicting advice, anxious to make the right decision, we realize the need for divine guidance. We know the necessity of a helping hand from the One Who has set our course.

Prayer is not easy for all of us. We know what it is—talking with God, with the Creator. We know the formal prayers. We realize they help us to get in touch with God, but to many of us the step to an informal communion with Him is wide and difficult. The years have made it hard to be again like little children, to kneel down, and with the faith and confidence of a youngster, pray to our Father Who art in Heaven.

To me it is good to be told that the will to pray is the essence of prayer, that it is a means of bridging the chasm beyond voicing worn words. As I see it—I am not a theologian—an earnest effort to work out the will of God is in itself a kind of prayer and I would say it is thus communion with God. One is recognizing God as our Father Who art in Heaven.

HOW TO PRAY

By Deane Edwards
President, The Hymn Society of America

Ten Simple Rules

I

Pray where you are. God is present everywhere and ready to listen.

II

Pray when possible in a quiet spot where you can be alone. It is well to fix your mind deliberately on God, apart from confusing distractions.

III

Pray to God simply and naturally, as to a friend. Tell him what is on your mind. Get help from the prayers of others.

IV

Pray remembering the good things God has done for you. Reckon up your blessings from time to time and give thanks for them.

V

Pray for God's forgiveness for the unworthy things that you may have done. He is near to a humble and contrite heart.

VI

Pray for the things that you need, especially those that will make your life finer and more Christlike.

VII

Pray for others, remembering the situations they confront and the help they need.

VIII

Pray for the world in its need, asking God to bring better things and offering your help to him.

IX

Pray above everything else that God's will may be done in you and in the world. His purposes are deeper and wiser than anything we can imagine.

X

Pray, and then start answering your prayer.

PRAYER IS MY GYROSCOPE

By Mildred Buchanan Flagg

Author, Editor, and Lecturer

Prayer is the gyroscope by which I check the accuracy of my decisions. It is a steering apparatus which helps make me big enough for my job. Through prayer I find the renewal of hope, the strengthening of purpose and the means by which I am able to hold my loved ones up to the "throne of grace." Prayer, for me, is not only talking with God but it is waiting and listening for His answer. Sometimes my prayer isn't answered but I always am.

Prayer is also the weapon by which I ward off the blows of the greatest heavyweight champion in the world—life itself. It is never reserved for a special day or hour. It is voiced in quick little moments of special gratitude or joy or need. Prayer is work-for-others, even when the going is tough. It is as necessary for me as sunshine or rain or food or clothing.

Without prayer and the belief in a personal God, I could not live.

PRAYER SHOULD NOT BE A LAST RESORT

By George Witten

Writer, Explorer and Aviator

❧

In books, movies and television when disaster has struck, and those concerned have tried every human means to get out of their trouble, they say: "Now there is nothing left to do, but pray."

This looks like they had the cart before the horse. If they had always prayed, disaster might not have struck. Or, if when it struck, they had resorted to prayer first, and asked God's guidance in their human efforts, He would have shown them the way out.

One of the greatest messages Kipling gave us are his lines:
"When war is threatening and danger is nigh.
For God and the soldier the people cry.
But, when war is over and things are righted,
God is forgotten, and the soldier slighted."

How sadly true these lines are, not only of war, but so many disasters. People are prone to think of God as a convenient trouble-shooter, someone who sits and waits, like a fireman, until you are in trouble. Then, all one needs to do is to cry out: "Come, God, and help me!" When the trouble is over God, the trouble-shooter, can go back to his post, and wait until He is needed again. In the meantime, when things are running smoothly, one doesn't need to give him any thought.

When President Eisenhower had his attack of illness people all over the world prayed for his recovery. This was mighty fine. But, after his recovery, and he was able to take up the burdens of his office, how many people thanked God?

167

In the early days of World War I the German armies swept across France, pushing the Allies back, and destroying everything in their way. Thousands of French families crowded into the uninvaded areas, and were taken care of by other more fortunate French families. One French woman, whose house was just behind the British lines, but out of range of German artillery, refused to open her doors to refugees. If any Allied soldier dared to step on her property, she would call the authorities, and complain. She gave so much trouble the authorities put her place out of bounds to all troops. New troops, coming into the area, were given special warning to never, under any circumstances, enter her property.

When the Russian army collapsed in 1917 Germany brought most of her troops from the Eastern front to the Western front — and started another push. This time the woman's house came under shell fire. A direct hit started her house burning. She ran to the local British Headquarters, and begged for help. "Your place is out of bounds," the Commander said. "My men dare not go near it!" She appealed to her French neighbors. But they paid no attention to her. Finally she was seen down on her knees in the mud, praying, while the flames consumed her barn and outhouses.

In a recent issue of Reader's Digest there is a story of a boy, who noticed that his friend's grandmother was always reading the Bible. " Why is she always reading the Bible?" he asked. "She's cramming for her final exams," his friend replied.

A good student doesn't have to cram for his final exams. We in the United States have more than most people in the world. Why not thank God for our prosperity, and make a friend of Him now? Don't treat Him as a last resort trouble-shooter.

PRAYING TOGETHER

By Rev. Deane Edwards

President, The Hymn Society of America

❀

The lines of John Oxenham express beautifully the nature
of private prayer:

> "'Mid all the traffic of the ways,
> Turmoils without, within,
> Make in my heart a quiet place,
> And come and dwell therein.
>
> A little place of mystic grace,
> Of sin and self swept bare,
> Where I may look into thy face,
> And talk with thee in prayer."

Christ Himself bids us "enter into thine inner chamber,
and . . . pray to thy Father who is in secret."

Yet private prayer can be greatly enriched by prayer **together.** This may be in public worship; but I refer particularly
to small groups gathered together solely for prayer. Here in
the intimacy of such a company a fresh undergirding is given
to the spiritual life. The expressed faith of one quickens the
faith of others. The voicing of inner problems causes each one
present to search his own soul more deeply. The intercessions
that are lifted to the throne of God stimulate the imagination
of the group, and lead to a broader horizon of spiritual concern. God speaks to the soul of each through the souls of others,
and thus a community of faith is created. In this manner the
private prayer of each is quickened and the effectiveness of
the devotional life strengthened for all.

169

PRAYER WILL TURN
THE TIDE FOR PEACE

By Justin J. Cline

Executive Director, American Youth Hostels, Inc.

❁

Men of good will have always had one major hope—a world at peace. Most men are people of good will. Very few in any country really want war. Why then do we not have peace?

I believe it is because men do not pray enough—pray in earnest and follow prayer with action. If we did we would have peace, because prayer sets men thinking earnestly, correctly and wisely. Prayer turns one away from mistrust, selfishness, revengeful thinking, narrow-mindedness and greed which cause wars.

Prayer is a recognition of God's infinite love and almighty power—the power which moves mountains. Prayer means asking for divine guidance. It means atoning for one's sins. It means humbling one's self—freeing one's self from fear— getting into proper relationship with God and your fellow man—all this is pre-requisite if man is to achieve peace.

Prayer helps us to understand life in the proper light. It helps us realize the sacredness of human personality. We are all children of God, no matter what our color, race or language. What matters is not how rich we are or what power we wield but how much we love our fellowman—how willing we are to share the good things of life with them.

It is my belief that most of us, unconsciously and unthinkingly, take too much from life and give too little. The problem is to get people to spend more time contemplating whether their actions are leading to love and friendship and peace or to hate and enmity and war. More time spent in prayer would bring us all to a realization of what we are really like.

Life is very complex and full of problems—we all have them. Unfortunately, there is no easy way to avoid them. Achieving peace is a problem because peace first must be forged in the mind of the individual before we can reach collective peace. Unless each one of us realizes we are not the only pebble on the beach we cannot forge peace in our own minds or in the minds of others. The lust for material wealth and power has built a great tide for war in this world. I believe that communion with God through prayer and appropriate followup actions as indicated by God's answer to our prayers is the means by which the tide will be turned away from war to peace.

GOD IS IN CHARGE

By Dr. Nels F. S. Ferre

Andover Newton Theological School

Without prayer I cannot now conceive of life. We are real and right as we pray correctly, for we are real and right in relation to God, and prayer, at its deepest, is our relating ourselves to God's will.

For me prayer is, more and more, adoration and acceptance. God is in charge. And when He is in charge the whole world is included in concern and work. All of life becomes different as we thank God for His universal love, as lived in Jesus Christ, through which alone we and the world can find the freedom and fellowship of forgiveness and fulfillment.

Thank God for prayer, but more for Himself who "lavishes" His grace on us as we are willing to receive Him.

171

PRAYER AS NECESSARY AS BREATHING

By *Albert B. Chandler*

Governor of Kentucky

❦

Life teaches a lot of lessons, but none so certain as the need for a faith in a higher power when the going gets tough. Anyone can meet life with a smile when all is going his way. Life is not all roses and the person who tries to serve the public is going to find that handshakes always do not mean friendship and backslapping can sometimes be with dagger in hand.

At times like these, if a man cannot turn to a friend that is higher, life can turn sour. I have had some pretty hard knocks in my life, but I have learned that prayer can make a man spring back with power to change a disappointment into an opportunity. It is a great comfort to know that when the winds of life's storms threaten us, we can always reach up and anchor ourselves to the hands of the unchanging Christ.

Prayer is as necessary as breathing. The man who laughs about prayer is the man who has never been in a really hard situation. Eventually, one learns there is only one thing to do, and that is to look up to God.

What a man needs more than anything else is a lasting friend. When a man knows God is by his side, he can stand for the right and let the chips fall where they may. I have gone a great many places and have been given some trying assignments in my life, but one thought has always kept me going:

> He leadeth me! Oh, Blessed Thought.
> Oh Word with Heavenly comfort brought,
> What ere I do, where ere I be,
> Still 'tis God's hand that leadeth me.

They say there is a famous statue of Jesus Christ in Our Lady's Church in Denmark that looks all ugly and out of proportion until one gets down on his knees and looks up and then the statue is seen in its beauty and strength. Our world is chaotic today and nothing can save it except the good old-fashioned use of our knees.

PRAYER HAS A FAVORABLE INFLUENCE

By Paul Dudley White, M.D.

Physician and Heart Specialist

❁

My experience with patients and other individuals through the years has convinced me that in many instances prayer has a favorable psychosomatic influence. It tends to counteract the physiological effects of anxiety, it favors better sleep, and stimulates one to better efforts. In fact, devotion to one's work can itself serve as a form of prayer. This effect of prayer is personal for the individual himself or herself.

As a part of a church service in which the congregation takes part, prayer is a form of religious motivation for better ways of life, ethical behaviour, and spiritual uplift. What is good for the spirit is good for the body, too, and however one may view life after death one can assuredly agree with the motto which appears on one of the illustrations in Vesalius' great Anatomy, namely "The spirit lives, all else is mortal."

Finally, a brief quotation from Sir William Osler who wrote many helpful essays during his important lifetime is worth presenting: "In all ages the prayer of faith has healed the sick, and the mental attitude of the suppliant seems to be of more consequence than the powers to which the prayer is addressed."

EXPLORATION THROUGH PRAYER

By Edward J. Thye

Former U.S. Senator from Minnesota

❦

Could there have been any time in history when the full need for prayer was as obvious as it is today? Today we speak in terms of breaking the sound barrier, launching satellites, and planning for full exploration of space.

What we in effect have done is to dramatize man's explorations and utilization of God's universe. This fact alone is not disturbing because God created the universe and placed man within it. The question before us today is whether man can be trusted with the task which lies before him. To me it is obvious that without Divine Guidance—man is due to fail in his quest. The only real security and peace of mind and soul which we can hope to enjoy is that which comes through a close and real relationship with God, the Creator. This every person must establish for himself.

Prayer is a vital and fundamental part of this relationship between man and his God. Prayer undoubtedly is many things to many persons. It is most surely a source of strength and power—it is serene and comforting—it is penetrating and powerful—it is simple and yet profound—it is an instrument of giving and of receiving.

Prayer is the richest kind of communion. Through prayer man has the challenging opportunity to visit personally with God. He has the time to resolve questions which are burdensome, he has an opportunity to petition and request God's grace and understanding, and most important of all he, through prayer, can spend wonderful moments with God in building a faith which transcends time and life itself.

For anyone in public life—prayer is an absolute necessity. The longer one serves in public office—the more he realizes the inadequacies of man and the necessity for God's help. Great men in history have never been reluctant to go to their knees in prayer. Through prayer they have learned how to make right decisions and how to bring forth courage in moments of travail.

Whether it be in a quiet place of worship, in the family circle, in the office—prayer with God gives me courage, understanding, and faith.

I have come to realize many times in my personal life as husband, father, soldier, farmer, citizen, public office-holder, and as a man the deep meaning found in the Sermon on the Mount where it is said:

> "Ask, and it shall be given you;
> seek, and ye shall find;
> knock, and it shall be opened unto you:
> For everyone that asketh receiveth;
> and he that seeketh findeth; and to him
> that knocketh it shall be opened.

If peace and progress are to be found in an age of space and universe explorations, they must be on God's terms. They will be found in the Divine hand of God which can in turn be found and felt through prayer.

I BELIEVE IN
THE POWER OF PRAYER

By Dr. D. Stanley Coors

Bishop of the Methodist Church in Minnesota

❦

It was my great privilege to be brought up in a Christian home where family worship was a regular daily practice and where prayer was recognized as having importance for a person's life. However, it required maturity in years and experience of crises in personal and family life to develop a conviction within me that there really is power in prayer. I fully realize that one exposes himself to misunderstanding and even ridicule if he describes certain events which he simply cannot explain adequately except in a frame of reference where prayer is acknowledged as a powerful factor in what happened. Among several significant experiences permit me to cite only one, which made a profound impression upon me and which no cynical comments or critical questions about the effectiveness of prayer can efface.

About thirty years ago I had my first serious illness. After a short time in the hospital my physical condition became so critical that a consultation of six physicians one evening arrived at a consensus that I could not be expected to live through the night. That medical report quickly spread throughout the city, with the result that special services of prayer were held in my behalf in various churches and homes that very evening. I can only say that to the surprise of the physicians I was alive the next morning, and from that time on I began to make a steady recovery of health.

Competent physicians were attending me. One of them, the President of the State Medical Society, said to me shortly after my release from the hospital, "I cannot account for your surviving that illness except on the basis of prayer in your behalf." Another physician used to call upon me occasionally when I had moved to another city, and always invariably would comment, "I cannot see how you can be alive except that God worked with us in answer to prayer in a way we do not understand." I can only humbly say that in a mysterious way science and religion complemented each other and I was restored to health to carry on the work to which I had committed my life under God.

One refers to such experiences in a spirit of humility and gratitude. There is no disposition to discount everything medical science was doing to prolong my life, but when the physicians speak reverently concerning what prayer had apparently done to supplement their medical and surgical skill, one who has been the beneficiary of such scientific ability and of faith in prayer is bound to be a witness bearing affirmative testimony concerning "This I believe concerning the power of prayer."

My experience was similar to that of a well-known columnist on the staff of the Detroit Free Press, who survived a most serious operation in Grace Hospital in Detroit a few years ago. The surgeon who operated for three hours said quietly to him, "It was a miracle. I deserve no credit. When I first saw you that night I thought it was hopeless, but I asked God to guide my hands. He must have answered my prayer, mine and all the others."

I conclude such evidences of the power of prayer in the words of that columnist: "It makes you humble and full of awe. It makes you feel like a little child walking in the dark unafraid because a firm and gentle hand is holding yours and guiding you."

PRAYER IS INTENSELY INDIVIDUAL

By Richard Eberhart

Poet

❦

In religion, faith begins where reason leaves off. Prayer has to do with unreason, with faith, although it is a reasonable mode of behavior. One learned prayers as a child, ancient and simple prayers, and said them beside the bed. But I never could get over the dichotomy between the rational, which may preclude prayer, and the irrational, where prayer is perhaps most profound.

Perhaps one should not let the mind know what the spirit does. Reason is a protester and intelligence is a goad. It may be that there is an insoluble dichotomy. But, then, reason in some sense is a prayer itself, a long petition for a high order. We say Episcopal prayers around the table now, sometimes have a silent Quaker grace, but these are outward forms. I think of prayer as intensely individual and spiritual. If I say I do not believe in it, this is a paradox and a compliment to prayer.

It is some vast reservoir into which one would go by submitting the personality, by negating the will, by overcoming the human condition, which is another paradox. For prayer is most human. Prayers may be answered in mysterious and subtle ways a quarter of a century later. Maybe they are answered if they are never asked. Maybe prayer is action itself, the actions of our days as we move from birth to death.

If you pray for an end to the sufferings of mankind you still do not believe it for without suffering man would not be man. The Fall is evident every day.

One of my poems, not published in a book, begins:

Prayer, itself an endlessness,
Never made peace with the New England mind.*

Another, entitled "God and Man" (**Undercliff,** p. 25) ends

And God has the deep justice,
And God has the last laugh.
To be God God needs man
And man needs God to be man.

*from "The Truth Hurt Worse Than a Thought Bullet"

YOU AND PRAYER

By George H. Olmsted

Major General, USAR, and Insurance Executive

❧

You stand alone. And about you surge the pressures and the problems of life, joy and sorrow, success and failure, love and hate, health and sickness.

You know them all. What are you to do?

Alone you seek the strength of wisdom and understanding, tolerance and humility. But alone you are so inadequate.

And then you pray. You are no longer alone. Beside you now are the faith of others who pray, and their strength. You have now the strength of many. You have now the faith of many.

You have now the right to believe that Almighty God will hear and understand.

This is the Power of Prayer.

PRAYER IS AN ATTITUDE

By Dr. Randolph Crump Miller

Professor of Christian Education, Yale Divinity School

❀

Prayer is primarily an attitude toward God, expressing our yearning for his presence and our concern at our separation from him. Even when it is wordless, as it often is, it takes the form of a dialogue, in which we are responding to all the signals which come from the presence of God. It is, then, an attitude expressing a personal relationship, an encounter, a communion with God.

Prayer is an attitude which grounds us in the reality of God. A radio without a ground wire suffers from static, uneven reception, and outside interference. A person not grounded in God is swayed by unexpected suffering, is "tossed to and fro and carried about with every wind of doctrine, by the cunning of men, by their craftiness in deceitful wiles," and is unable to stand in the face of temptation. Prayer provides stability and steadfastness, so that we may "grow up in every way into him who is the head, into Christ" (Eph. 4:14,15,RSV).

The habit of prayer is a corrective to other habits. Important as habits are for the efficiency of daily living, they may become such a deadly routine that we cease to grow. Prayer keeps open the channels of appreciation, so that we can form new habits and can bring out the hidden potentialities residing in all of us.

Prayer is a source of strength in the face of life's obstacles. Through prayer, we find ways to overcome our anxieties, our confusions, and our defeats. The gift of God's grace is something which we cannot earn; we can only ask for it. Prayer is one of the channels by which his grace is made available to us as we face illness, as we confess our sins, as we seek to become transformed into a "new man," or as we strive for a right answer to a complex moral question in business or home.

Prayer is a source of comfort in the face of inevitable occurrences. Through prayer we learn how to face death with confidence and hope, we learn how to live with the limitations of being crippled or of adapting to the routine of making a bad heart last, and we find ways of helping others who have not learned to accept the inevitable. Prayer provides a creativity in the face of such experiences which causes the more fortunate to marvel. But the God who brought victory out of a crucifixion is not going to be mocked by the things which happen to us.

Prayer is a means of insight. Because prayer takes us away from routine and habitual responses, it provides the stimuli which open our minds to new truth. Through the finding of these new data, we may come to new conclusions as we see life in a new perspective. We are changed through prayer, because our awareness is opened to a new level of existence.

Prayer should always be in the spirit of **"Thy** will be done." This is often the hardest part for many of us. There is a prayer for those who are dear to us, which says that we entrust them to "thy never-failing love and care, for this life and the life to come; knowing that thou are doing for them better things than we can desire or pray for." In this spirit, of course, we may pray for anything. "Anything large enough for a wish to light upon, is large enough to hang a prayer upon," said George Macdonald.

Prayer is an expression of the joy of faith. "Throw all your anxiety upon him, for he cares for you" (I Peter, 5:7,G).

We are freed to be obedient to God's will, and we are strengthened not only by the person-to-person relationship of prayer but also by the person-to-person relationship of corporate worship in the Church. Our prayers become more than an individual's aspirations when they draw us into the fellowship of believers where we lift up our common prayers in adoration of the God who came in Jesus Christ.

Finally, we must be clear that prayer really does nothing. It is an attitude. It is a channel whereby **God** does things in us and for us, enabling us therefore to say, "Amen," or so be it; and then, uplifted and transformed by the Holy Spirit, we are able to apply the demands of the Gospel to our personal and social life, to the life of our community and our nation, and ultimately to the whole of mankind for whom Christ died. Prayer does not do this; God does all these things because prayer opens up the channels of communication and power enabling us to do them. We are, then, to "pray without ceasing" (I Thes. 5:16,KJ).

GREAT PEACE OF MIND

By Bill Stern

Sports Director, National Broadcasting Company

I pray every night of my life, repeating the Lord's Prayer, and asking him to bless my family and to help me. He never fails me.

I have found great peace of mind through my faith in prayer and the Lord.

TRUE PRAYER

By Dr. Alfred P. Haake

Economist, Consultant and Lecturer

❈

Prayer is vital to anyone who recognizes the fact of a Creator whose Will is implemented in the laws that govern life and hold the universe in harmonious and continuing purpose.

The key to happiness and fulfillment lies in obedience and harmony, born of love. Whatever may be the ultimate purpose, it must be clear that growth and evolution are realized in harmony with and obedience to the laws that govern life and implement the Will of God.

The greatest good of which I can conceive is ultimate fulfillment in at-one-ment with God.

It is through prayer that we reach God. It is so that we can acquire understanding of His Will, renew strength and sustain fortitude in holding ourselves to the path that understanding reveals to us.

I have learned that prayer is much more than the mere voicing of hopes and needs in petition. Mere asking is not prayer.

I have never seen God, nor have I been able to make Him real to my senses in terms comprehensible to a human being. If that is necessary to prayer, then I am still in the inarticulate void of an empty cavern. There have been times, many of them, when it has seemed to me that words tumbled from my lips and failed to rise to heaven, like the earth-bound vapors of an unacceptable sacrifice. In the very earnestness of my efforts to reach God in prayer, I have come to appreciate Paul's confession that now we see through a glass but darkly. I think I understand what the Master meant when he said: " . . . if any man will do his will he shall know of the doctrine."

I have not been able to clothe God in habiliments discernible to my mind's eye, nor been conscious of His presence as I can be conscious of a pulsating human body somewhere near me. But within me has grown and is still growing an awareness that makes God very near and real to me. It is as though I were enveloped in an aura of serenity and mutual understanding, out of which comes an apprehension of what I should be and do. In terms I cannot articulate, I feel His presence, the pulse of His Will, the ineffable ecstasy of His love. And I feel myself moving toward at-one-ment with Him.

It becomes true prayer when, asking nothing for myself, I yield in utter obedience to Him and find myself, as it were, in tune with the Infinite. Each of us must find his own way in framing his prayer, but for me the words are these: "Take me, Father, as I am and make of me what You will. Let me have understanding that I may use the stewardship entrusted to me in helping to build Thy kingdom on earth and Thy righteousness in the hearts of men. Thy Will, O God my Father, Thy Will be done."

THE PATTERN OF PRAYER

By James E. Van Zandt

Representative in U.S. Congress from Pennsylvania

❈

Prayer is the opening of the channels of communication between ourselves and God. Christ has said: "Ask, and it shall be given you; seek, and ye shall find; knock, and it shall be opened unto you: For every one that asketh receiveth; and he that seeketh findeth; and to him that knocketh it shall be opened." I believe this is one of the central truths of the Christian religion, and the foundation of Christian life in the world.

The source of all wisdom and virtue waits only for our asking; the goal of our life is to be found, with certainty, by all who seek; the door of the treasury of truth and love will open to the knocking of any one of us. In this situation, let us not be such fools as to make our requests petty and selfish. When we ask favors for ourselves, let them be the spiritual favors that will assist us in the service of God and our fellow men; aid in the elimination of defects and the cultivation of virtues; wisdom in making decisions and courage in acting on them. But let us, in our asking, never forget the needs of our friends and relatives.

The pattern of prayer usually set in early childhood, calling down blessings upon those dear to us, should never be abandoned. And the larger interests, civic and national and world, can be solved rightly only in that atmosphere of justice and charity which belongs to prayer.

But too often we think of prayer only as a means of obtaining favors. It is so much more than that! It is with the divine grace of Christ Himself that we speak in any form of prayer. Even the simple morning prayer may be no more than a morning greeting to God, or the evening prayer may be no more than a simple prayer of gratitude for the blessings of the day.

By prayer we worship God, and recognize His transcendent majesty. By prayer we express our love for Him, and our gratitude for His gift of all we have and are, and of all the future, of time and eternity, that lies before us.

By prayer we open our minds to God's teachings of truth, and offer our wills to His guidance and commands. Truly, the power of prayer is no less than the infinite power of God Himself.

PRAYER HELPS IN A CRISIS

By Gene Tunney

Former Heavyweight Boxing Champion of the World

❀

I believe in the power of prayer. To me, it is vital, true and permanent . . . permanent when prayer becomes a daily practice.

The reaction I have received from prayer has helped me in many crises in my life. As a matter of fact, I pray to avoid crises and when they come, I am all the more armed to face them. There is definitely no psychological thought more powerful than the reaction to fervent prayer.

All our great American leaders believed in prayer in times of trouble and frustration. It benefited them and this nation. Prayer fortified them against spiritual defeat and every kind of assault.

"THY WILL BE DONE"

By Dr. William Jansen

Superintendent of Schools, New York City

❀

I have always enjoyed the story of the captain who found himself alone at the wheel of his ship in a raging night storm —all hands below manning pumps against the battering sea. One surging wave towered to the bridge itself, forcing the captain to his knees. Finding himself in this unaccustomed position of piety, he raised his voice to the black sky: "Please, God, knowing how busy You always are, I never bothered You before; if You get me out of this mess tonight, I promise I'll never bother You again!"

I suspect that the Good Lord Himself had to chuckle over that one because He knew that when the captain again found himself in some situation completely beyond himself, he'd be back with a similar plea.

All men pray at times; most pray with some regularity; some few lead a life of prayer. These last make up for the slack in some of us.

The truth is that no man of prayer is ever alone, for prayer leads to that lofty, eternal companionship which can never be severed.

Because of the nature of my work, I have been invited to many functions held by the Catholic, Protestant or Jewish teachers, and I have been permitted to share some blessings with all of them. Such experiences are invariably inspiring and heartwarming for, even though the words may vary, the intentions are the same.

187

Personally, I believe that the best verbal prayer is one of the simplest: "Thy Will be Done"—a prayer to be uttered often during the turmoil and tensions of each day's work. If it doesn't become mechanical and meaningless through repetition, and if it doesn't lead to a fatalistic, do-nothing philosophy, it can be a powerful prayer of daily dedication. Then again, it helps to know you're on the right side.

STRENGTH THROUGH PRAYER

By H. W. Prentis, Jr.

Chairman of the Board, Armstrong Cork Company

We are finite. Time and the universe in which we live are infinite. We look up at the stars at night; we face the mysteries of birth and death, and a sense of our own inadequacy to face the facts of our existence well-nigh overwhelms us. We intuitively know that we need help from without to sustain us.

This realization brings us to our knees in prayer, and as we pour out our supplications for strength and guidance, the Holy Spirit descends into our hearts, heals our troubled souls, clarifies our minds and gives us that peace which the vexing world about us cannot give.

Thus we are enabled to mount up on wings like eagles, to run life's race again with courage and renewed purpose. Prayer has healing in its wings for all who truly put their trust in a benign, everloving God and Saviour.

PRAYER IS AT WORK

By Judge Luther W. Youngdahl

United States District Court for the District of Columbia

Today's biggest religious story is that prayer is at work in our nation. It is at work in the home, at the work bench, in the office, in the factory, in our nation's capital. In this hydrogen bomb, missile and satellite age, American hardheaded business men and politicians are asking God's help to solve our problems. They are becoming partners with God, realizing they cannot succeed without Him. Thousands are starting each day in the office with prayer—they are making religion work in their everyday lives.

It is significant that not long ago a resolution was adopted by the Congress of the United States establishing a Prayer Room in the Capitol building. It was approved quickly and quietly. Members of Congress deliberately tried to avoid publicity. The room is non-denominational with no religious symbols except the Bible. It affords a place to which our distinguished leaders may go for a moment of silent meditation and personal communion with their God for help in resolving the many difficult problems with which we are faced.

More and more successful business men are speaking out as to the efficacy of prayer in their lives. Witness, for example, Lem T. Jones of Kansas City, Missouri, who starts his day with his head bowed in his chief executive's office of a ten million dollar a year candy firm. Mr. Jones states he starts each day with the prayer: "My God, make me adequate in Thy sight for this day." I would not feel that my day was started properly without the family devotion at the breakfast hour

and the silent meditation at my desk in the United States
Court House as I start my work.

A great number of business and governmental leaders have
come to see that the real world crisis has a lot to do with
human relations, and when you get to human relations you
are on the threshhold of religion. Only a dedicated spirit of
prayer and religious conviction in the lives of individual people
will save this country and the world.

STRENGTH THROUGH PRAYER

By Allen S. King

President, Northern States Power Company

Prayer is an instinctive reaction shared by all men in all
times. It is the unconscious acknowledgement of the existence
of a higher power outside and beyond one's self, to Whom one
instinctively turns in cases of trouble or frustration.

The frequent use of prayer is often inhibited under the
disciplines of civilization, and comes into being only under
conditions of great stress and strain. Prayer then becomes the
last hope of a troubled soul.

Prayer can be a source of continuing strength through good
times and bad. The frequent disciplined practice of prayer
can, in effect, bring God into close contact with every facet
of life, and give a feeling of confidence and strength to the
individual.

The practice of subjecting one's self to God's will through
prayer elevates one's life to a nobler plane and gives an individual added strength to meet the issues of life.

Prayer, consistently practiced, will give a person new
strength and confidence, and will give real meaning to life.

GROWTH THROUGH PRAYER

By Dr. James DeForest Murch
Managing Editor, *Christianity Today*

🏵

Prayer does something to us which is evident to ourselves and others. When our Lord took Peter, James and John with Him into the mountain to pray on the occasion of His Transfiguration, the divine record tells us that "as he prayed the fashion of his countenance was changed." As Jesus talked to the heavenly Father something took place in His own spirit and His shining face reflected that new joy and strength which were His. So apparent was this change that His disciples marveled.

The greatest and best thing that happens when we pray is that we are changed and transformed; maybe not in one prayer experience, but certainly through the days and the years. It is unfortunate that most of us have a narrow, childish concept of prayer. We think of it as asking some special favor and getting it; as something that does not involve a spiritual relationship of man with God and God with man. Thus we miss the touch of God's spirit upon our own that is like the touch of the potter on the clay. Blessed is the man who can pray—

> Have Thine own way, Lord! Have Thine own way!
> Thou art the Potter; I am the clay
> Mould me and make me after Thy will
> While I am waiting, yielded and still.
>
> Have Thine own way, Lord! Have Thine own way!
> Search me and try me, Master, today!
> Whiter than snow, Lord, wash me just now
> While in Thy presence humbly I bow.
>
> Have Thine own way, Lord! Have Thine own way!
> Hold o'er my being absolute sway!
> Fill with Thy spirit till all shall see
> Christ only, always, living in me!

If through prayer God is doing something in our lives it will be evident to others in many ways. If we have been selfish, prayer will make us unselfish. The life that seeks only its own good and is motivated by a desire to get and hoard and gloat can be changed into a life empowered of God to live like the selfless Christ, esteeming the welfare of others of prime importance and giving freely to supply their needs.

If we have been proud, prayer will make us humble. Man by nature is proud, adoring himself more than he adores God. But when we come to know God we realize that by comparison we are nothing. All our sin, our suffering, our inadequacy combine to make us humble in His presence, and soon we are able to see ourselves in true perspective in our relationships with others.

If we have been contentious, prayer will give us the spirit of meekness. God somehow teaches us to be like Christ, who stood like a rock for His convictions and was not to be moved from His purposes, yet when He was oppressed and afflicted He opened not His mouth.

If we have been a seeker after the flesh-pots of this world, prayer will cause us to hunger and thirst after righteousness. Our appetite for pleasure may remain but it is no longer satisfied in the capricious, the wanton, the lustful things of this world, but in the things of the spirit of God. We may go on buying, possessing and accumulating, but with the love of God paramount in our lives.

If we have been "hard" and "tough", prayer will give us a heart of compassion. Love, grace and mercy flow into our lives from the heart of God, and to some degree at least, we express those attributes toward others. To those in trouble we show benevolence and pity in every way we can. We learn that we cannot be great and generous until we are tender and compassionate.

These are only a few of the changes that may come into our lives as a result of prayer. Christ's Sermon on the Mount (Matt. 5-7) reveals the ultimate in human conduct which God expects of His children. It is an entrancing picture. If we could be like that we would be like Christ. A world with any appreciable number of people in it who exemplified the characteristics enumerated would be a better world in which to live— a paradise compared with its present state. When we think we have attained perfection, we should sit down and read this remarkable document. It will keep us humble and cause us to realize our constant need of prayer and the fellowship of the heavenly Helper. We ought to memorize the Sermon on the Mount and keep its life goals ever before us when we pray. We need to cherish its idealism as we would some earthly ambition and strive with all our hearts to rise to its sublimity. We may never attain it perfectly in this life, but the adventure will add new zest to living and its splendor will leave its divine mark upon us.

I BELIEVE IN PRAYER

By Roy E. Dickerson

Executive Secretary, Cincinnati Social Hygiene Society

❧

I believe in prayer because I believe that I can communicate with God not in the same way, but just as certainly, as I can communicate with my human friends. I believe that the ideas, sometimes put in words or silently marshalled in one's thoughts, become known by God. This is not less credible and no more remarkable than that the sound waves set up by my vocal cords, or the variously shaped lines called writing, can convey my ideas through the hammer and anvil of the ear or the rods and cones of the eye.

I believe in prayer because I believe it is a two-way process. God can and does communicate his thoughts to me, not by the ordinary means by which a human friend conveys his thinking, but in many other ways. There is, for example, the conviction which takes shape in my mind, the certitude I have not felt before, the new insight into, or a new way of looking at, some problem which might prompt me to exclaim: "Aha, I never thought of that before."

I believe in prayer because I am sure that the good gift which my Father is eager to give me is often wisely withheld until I prove, by seeking it sincerely, whole-heartedly and with fineness of purpose, that I am ready to use it aright.

I believe in prayer because I believe it has a unique place in God's plan for man's helpfulness to man. It is one way in which man may work with God to awaken some worthy purpose in a fellow man, to move him to some fine deed, to quicken his understanding of truth, to comfort him in a time of trial, or otherwise lift his life to a higher level of thought and action.

PRAYER OF THE HANDICAPPED

By Howard A. Rusk, M.D.

Associate Editor, New York Times,

Chairman, Department of Rehabilitation, N.Y. Univ. College of Medicine

❧

One could not practice "Rehabilitation" if he did not believe in God and prayer. To those who have suffered severe physical handicaps the question is always, "Why? Why did this happen to me?" An answer from one human being to another is not easily forthcoming. It can only be interpreted as a part of God's Master Plan for us all, the testing of us here on earth, as Christ was tested, for a greater life to come. Possibly the answer comes in the work of the potter. Great ceramics are not made by putting clay in the sun; they come only from the white heat of the kiln. In the firing process some pieces are broken just as life breaks some people who do not have faith. However, those that survive the heat are transformed from clay into porcelain and are ever so.

So it is with sick, suffering and crippled people. Those who, through medical skill, opportunity, work and courage, survive their illness or overcome their handicap and take their places back in the world have a depth of spirit that you and I can hardly measure. They haven't wasted their pain. That is why it is such a great privilege to serve those who are going through the fire of the kiln. They have a closeness to God that few of us so-called "normal" people have experienced.

How and when the ability to pray comes, how the prayer is offered and how the individual attains a oneness with God differs in each and everyone, like the sunrise—sometimes it is a soft blending of pale tints on scattered clouds and on occasion comes like a bright shining light of spiritual rebirth. To those in travail it is usually not a matter of teaching but of deep spiritual experience born from within.

The most appropos and universally accepted prayer of the handicapped is that of an unknown Confederate soldier. It was first read by one of our patients who said to his fellow-patients, "This man is talking about us. He is talking about us! This is our creed." And they titled the prayer "A Creed for Those Who Have Suffered."

"I asked God for strength, that I might achieve
I was made weak, that I might learn humbly to obey . . .

I asked for health, that I might do greater things
I was given infirmity, that I might do better things . . .

I asked for riches, that I might be happy
I was given poverty that I might be wise . . .

I asked for power, that I might have the praise of men
I was given weakness, that I might feel the need of God . . .

I asked for all things, that I might enjoy life
I was given life, that I might enjoy all things . . .

I got nothing that I asked for—but everything I had hoped for

Almost despite myself, my unspoken prayers were answered.
I am among all men, most richly blessed!"

This is their creed. It could well be the creed of all of us.

THE BEST KIND OF PRAYER

By Steve Allen

Television Star, National Broadcasting Company

It has always been a difficult thing to determine the true value of prayer. One philosopher has gone so far as to suggest that saying prayers is equivalent to believing that the universe is governed by a Being who changes his mind if you ask Him to. The religious mentality, of course, recoils at this analysis but those of us who pray would seem to have brought the indictment down on our own heads by praying in the wrong manner.

Some people, for example, are so naive as to believe that all prayers are answered. Then, when a particular prayer elicits no response from heaven, they rush to the other extreme of unbelief.

Common sense, that most uncommon commodity, would indicate that on a simple logical basis much prayer is doomed to reap no material benefit. When two men, for example, pray for the same thing—when Notre Dame prays to beat Southern Methodist on the football field while Southern Methodist is praying for just the opposite result—it is obvious that God is going to please only one group of supplicants, and very probably the one that is the better trained. The same thing will be true of much prayer that is only entreaty—begging for a handout from heaven. There are young girls praying for jobs as actresses who would be better off staying home, young men praying for help in passing tests for which they have not had the foresight to technically equip themselves; these and mil-

197

lions like them are in breach of religious etiquette. If God were the old man with the long white beard that we pictured when we were very small children we would not think of asking Him, to His face, to satisfy our desires at the cost of depriving someone else, or to grant us something that was not truly essential to our welfare.

Skeptics are fond of pointing out that there has never been a scientific test made of the efficacy of prayer in the same sort of sense that there are experiments made to determine the power of medicines.

A fair testing method, for example, would be to check two groups of people, one group praying for certain types of things over a certain specified period, the other not praying for these same particular things. It might very well turn out that the group that did not pray subsequently found just as many lost articles, got just as many desired jobs, won just as many football games, and had just as much rain fall on its farms. All of which would be by way of proving what many people already suppose: that the most meaningful form of prayer is the prayer of thanksgiving, the prayer for grace, the prayer that we might be given strength to improve our spiritual selves. If Christ came to preach the spiritual values and to de-emphasize our involvement with the tangible, why should we constantly pray for material things? God, it has been said, helps those who help themselves. We usually can, if our wills are strong enough, secure our material needs for ourselves. We should pray to God then for wisdom, for a love of peace, for an increase in charity. This is the sort of prayer that is answered in the very moment of its utterance. This is the sort of prayer, indeed, that would be answered even if there were no God. This is the sort of prayer that is unselfish, because it makes us better able to love one another.

PRAYER . . . THE GREATEST GIFT

By Nora Lynch Kearns

Clubwoman

❦

I like to think of prayer as the touchstone God gave us when Christ admonished, "Ask and it shall be given you; seek, and ye shall find; knock, and it shall be opened unto you." (Luke 11:9)

For eventually each of us, in his own way, and in his own time, must turn to God. We come to Him in humility; we come in fear; we come in joy. We come for myriad reasons, seeking: why we are here; a code we can live by; comfort in our sorrow; and to praise and give thanks for our joys. Slowly, sometimes painfully, as we come, we learn to pray.

To me, the wondrous miracle of prayer is that it is instantly available to everyone. Prayer is not restricted to a privileged group or a chosen race. Prayer requires no special place, no certain time, no brilliant mind, not even words. For prayer is of the heart. Solomon in his great wisdom noted, "Keep thy heart with all diligence; for out of it are the issues of life." (Proverbs 4:23)

Prayer is man's lifeline to God. Spoken or unspoken, when we turn to God in prayer, we are at once, one with Him. We can, at that moment, draw on his universal wisdom and strength—for God's storehouse is always overflowing. Before His mighty resources, worldly problems diminish to pygmy statures and we begin to find God's answers.

Answers to our prayers come in many guises. Praying for grace, I have felt the hand of God reach out and touch me. Praying for faith, I have known unexpected illumination of a familiar parable or of God's written word. Praying for healing,

199

I have been witness to the fact that, "With men this is impossible; but with God all things are possible." (Matthew 19:26)

Each of us may learn a favorite prayer. Mine was written by my finest teacher:

MY PRAYER

Christ of Bethlehem teach us to love,
Christ of Nazareth teach us to obey,
Christ of Galilee teach us to serve,
Christ in the Temple teach us to learn,
Christ on the mountain teach us to pray,
Christ in Gethsemane teach us to suffer,
Christ on the cross teach us to die,
Christ on Easter teach us to live.
So that loving, obeying, serving, learning, praying,
suffering, and dying, we may be fit to live with
Thee in Paradise.

Amen

Though we may learn a favorite prayer, each of us, through trial and error, and through practice, must find his own best way to pray. I have found, just as the greatest teacher of all of us —Jesus—taught at Gethsemane, the hardest but wisest of all prayers comes with learning to pray, "Father, not as I will, but as Thou wilt." (Matthew 26:30) Amen.

TO PRAY AT ALL TIMES

By Charles E. Dunbar, Jr.

Lawyer

In my opinion there is no greater or more profound consolation, comfort and inspiration in life than to be able to have direct contact with and to talk privately with Almighty God and our Divine Savior and pour out and confess with humility and in a spirit of abject unworthiness our many grievous sins, including the soul-killing sins of indifference and selfishness; to pray for forgiveness, divine grace, redemption and everlasting life, and at the same time solemnly and earnestly to ask for aid, assistance and inspiration to lead a more unselfish, dedicated and Christian life.

While we may also make requests for personal things for ourselves, we should be fully aware and willing that they should and will only be granted if they serve the Divine Purpose and Will. However, I feel, and we should feel, that if we are willing to make greater and greater efforts and sacrifices ourselves, if we pray for help, ability, grace, divine guidance, inspiration and effectiveness in serving and advancing Christian ideals and God's kingdom, our prayers will be granted.

We should never forget in our prayers that Jesus taught and requires a very practical religion and vigorous activity by His followers and servants in advancing and implementing religious principles and ideals during their lives. The Sermon on the Mount and Christian ideals as taught by our Savior make crystal clear that our lives and activities on earth must never cease to be self-sacrificing and consecrated and that we must make constant efforts to foster and advance these ideals and principles both by precept, example and service. At all times we should beseech our Divine Father to grant and give to us the determination, energy, courage, ability, wisdom, inspiration and leadership to be useful and effective servants in His service.

I feel that in all of our plans and hopes for humanity and posterity we must realize that good government, economic and social justice and lofty and peaceable international relations all depend, in the final analysis, upon the unselfish service and fundamental morals and Christian character of the individual citizen. A lofty Christian character, born of a deep and abiding love for the Golden Rule and inspired with a love of God and country and one's fellowmen everywhere and a devoted and effective Christian service, I believe, can only be granted to us with the aid of and through prayer. Christian character and service are the sole solution and hope of America and civilization. It is public and Christian service and Christian character, above selfishness, above material gain and higher than the triumph of brute force, which alone can lead our Church, our nation and the world to those high places that become sacred in history.

FOR INSPIRATION AND GUIDANCE

By Chester W. Nimitz

Fleet Admiral, U. S. Navy

❦

Since the beginning of time, men who have been close to the sea have been close to God. Men who go down to the sea in ships have a doubly rich understanding of God as Pilot, Chart and Compass. Sailormen, whose lives are continually jeopardized by the forces of Nature, realize how insignificant they are in relation to God, and turn to God for inspiration and guidance.

NO PRAYER GOES UNANSWERED

By *Kathleen Norris*

Author and Novelist

❦

I base my whole life on prayer. A hundred times a day my thoughts go to the one human life that so supremely influenced the world; the life that gave us our titles of "Christian" and "Christendom," and I renew my personal faith in my relationship with the Savior of mankind.

I prayed differently as a child. Through mature years my prayers were different too . . . demanding, desperate, despairing, defiant. To cling to prayer through two bloody and ineffectual wars was a hard thing. But even in the darkest moments of doubt and weariness light came through prayer. I have silently prayed during great battles, during crises in the nursery, and sometimes at glittering dinner tables, and often as a speaker on flag-draped platforms.

And gradually the miracle has been forced on me. The miracle that no prayer goes unanswered. It may be answered by seeming disappointment, even humiliation. It often is answered in a totally unexpected way, or when it is forgotten even by the suppliant. The insufferable has disappeared, the unbearable has become precious and right, the heartbreak has become heartsease.

And so the day's constant aspiration: "Give me wisdom— make what I say right—let me have a chance to eradicate the injury I caused" is like a clear fresh river running under the heat and dust of life. Praying folk have conquered fear. With her hand in that of an all-strong, all-wise, all-loving Brother, what woman can fear either life or death?

SINCERITY IN PRAYER

By Dr. Harry Emerson Fosdick

Pastor Emeritus, Riverside Church, New York City

❦

The Master laid reiterated emphasis upon sincerity in prayer. He meant that the petition offered must be the genuine overflow of inward desire. The fault of the Pharisees who prayed on the corners was not that they were asking for unworthy things. Their petitions were doubtless excellent, springing out of scriptural ideas and couched in spiritual language. But the prayers did not represent the inward and determining wishes of the men. The petitions were not sincere. The lives of the Pharisees blatantly advertised that their habitual ambitions did not tally with their occasional supplications.

When the Master bids us make prayer private, to think of God when we pray as "the Father who seeth in secret," to use no futile and repetitious formulas but to go at once to the pith of our want, he is making a plea for sincerity. Prayer to him is the heart, with all its most genuine and worthy desires aflame, rising up to lay hold on God. It is no affair of hasty words at the fag-end of a day, no form observed in deference to custom, no sop to conscience to ease us from the sense of religious obligations unfulfilled. Prayer is the central and determining force of a man's life. Prayer is dominant desire, calling God into alliance.

The fact that we do not stand on street corners to perform our devotions ought not to blind us to the subtle temptations by which, even in private, we are led into theatrical, insincere praying. We pray as we think we ought to. We ask for blessings that we feel are properly to be asked for, graces that we should want, whether we do or not. We mask ourselves behind an imaginary personage—ourselves disguised in court clothes and asking from God the things which we presume God would like to be asked to give. We cry as St. Augustine did, "O Lord, make me pure;" and then we hear our real self add as his did, "but not now!" How much such praying there is and how utterly ineffective! It is not real. We have not at the center of our lives controlling desires so worthy that we can ask God to further them and so earnest that our prayers are the spontaneous utterance of their urgency.

Economists describe what they call "effective demand." It is the demand of those who not only need commodities, but who are willing and able to pay the price. Only when a petition becomes an "effective demand" is it real prayer. When a man rehearses all the blessings he has prayed for himself and the world, he may well go on to ask whether he really wishes the prayers granted. Is he willing to pay the price? The great servants of the Kingdom in history always have been men of prayer and the implication is sometimes suggested that praying would make us similiarly serviceable. But this essential element should never be forgotten. These servants were men of powerful prayer because they were men of dominant desires for whose fulfillment they were willing to sacrifice anything. Paul, Carey, Livingstone, and all their spiritual kin praying for the triumph of Christ with all their hearts and hurling their lives after their prayers. These are examples of costly praying which achieves results. This is not prayer called in to eke out what is lacking in an otherwise contented life; this is life centering in and swung round prayer like planets round the sun. Prayer becomes serious business when it becomes dominant desire. We stand there at life's center, at the springs of its motive and the sources of its power.

—Reprinted by permission of the copyright owners, Association Press, from "The Meaning of Prayer" by Harry Emerson Fosdick.

STRENGTH-GIVING POWER OF PRAYER

By W. G. Wyman

General, United States Army

❦

Throughout the recent great war our servicemen all over the world placed greater and greater dependence on the Divine Authority of life. He sought God and found strength and courage to continue his task in the face of all extremities, favorable or unfavorable, in his travels on land, by sea, or through the air, all over the surface of the globe, by day or by night, in storm and in sunshine, and in the agonies and horrors of war, whether in victory, or in temporary defeat. God gave him strength through prayer.

I, myself, remember on the green frond couches of the jungle in Burma, in the shallow sleeping trenches of Africa, Sicily, France, Germany and Austria, God was always in His Heaven and in my effort to give Him praise or seek His guidance, I found myself constantly with the beautiful 23rd Psalm—a prayer of comfort and of inspiration. After the rigors of the day, or the night spent with troops in the field, or in travels through the battle area, or in my field command post the intensity of living and the intensity of life itself amongst the men left one so often with a sense of complete exhaustion. But with God close by in His Heaven, with Whom one could commune and find solace, rest came and renewed strength to insure that His Will would be done.

THIS I PRAY FOR

By Dr. Amandus Johnson

Historian and Founder of American-Swedish

Historical Museum, Philadelphia

❊

I believe that man is fundamentally the architect of his own success or failure and of the material world in which we live, as this is modified and influenced by nature and its laws, but "there is a Divinity that (partly) shapes our lives, rough-hew them as we may."

The spiritual and the material are dependent upon each other. One cannot exist on this earth without the other. In fact, the spiritual is based on the material. Man has a tendency at times to stress the one above the other and go to extremes in certain directions. In the Middle Ages, man stressed the spiritual to the extreme, preparing man mainly for citizenship in Heaven. Today we stress the material to the extreme and we are so busy preparing man for citizenship on earth that we forget his spiritual nature. We forget that man has a soul that needs nourishment and attention. We neglect the higher values of life, values far more important for our survival than bombs and deadly weapons. Communism with its related isms is a by-product of this material tendency that dominates the world today.

I make a distinct difference between culture and civilization. By civilization I mean material progress, electric lights, automobiles, automatic machinery, etc., ad finitum. By culture I mean the products of the spiritual part of man, religion, literature, the fine arts, etc., etc.

In civilization, we have achieved what the Greek and

Roman philosophers did not even dare to dream of in their wildest flights of imagination. The Greeks believed that their gods could pass from one mountain top to another; that they could communicate with one another from a distance. We on wings of our own making can circumnavigate the earth in a few hours. We can communicate through the air with the pilot of a plane that travels faster than sound. We can pick up a receiver and talk to a person in London, Paris or Stockholm, thousands of miles away, and hear him as plainly as if he were standing by our side. Yet in culture we are probably much inferior to the Greeks and the Romans at the peak of their power.

The pathways of history are littered with the ruins of nations that once flourished and were great. The peoples that have survived down the centuries have done so by preserving their spiritual heritage and by retaining their spiritual power, not mainly by material might and material advancement.

Greece is still with us, and no other nation on earth had, in the early days, a richer spiritual life, nor left to the Western world a more important heritage in art and literature than she. Rome, although no longer the dominating power she was at the height of her glory, is still, under the name of Italy, a great nation, whose cultural influence in some ways surpasses that of other nations of the West. Her achievements in art, literature and music and her dominating place in religion have sustained her through all her vicissitudes. Why have the Jews survived as a people for countless generations, in spite of persecutions, in spite of pogroms, in spite of attempts at their total annihilation from the days of Pharaoh until the present? I believe we all agree that it is due to their spiritual heritage and religious stability. No sputnicks and no atom bombs have preserved this people from destruction.

The world is growing smaller almost by the hour, and before long China and India will, so to speak, be at our front porch. Therefore, what the world needs today, far more than at any other period in history, is a re-appraisal of our spiritual and material values, and a new approach to other peoples of the world, friends and potential enemies alike, not with a sword in one hand and a pistol in the other, but on a spiritual and moral plane in an atmosphere of friendship. Where is the statesman big enough to achieve this? The prayers of a million Americans for this noble end would bring results.

At present our chief aim seems to be to outdo our potential enemies by making bigger and deadlier weapons than they. It is time we stop dead in our tracks and ask ourselves: Where are we going, where will it end? This I believe we must do to survive, and this I pray for.

FREEDOM OF RELIGION

By Charles Coburn

Actor and Motion Picture Star

❦

I subscribe to the principle of freedom of religion and firmly believe that every man should be allowed, without criticism from others, to worship his God in his own way.

I believe in a Supreme Power which is beyond the understanding of man. I know not from whence I came or whither I shall go. I am content with the knowledge that I have lived and that all living things must die.

Therefore, I have come to the realization that death, being inevitable, should not be looked upon in sadness by one's relatives and friends.

STRENGTH THROUGH PRAYER

By E. W. Rawlings

General, U.S.A.F.

Commander, Air Materiel Command

❦

The men who fly, whether they pilot supersonic jet air-craft or the less-glamorous propeller-driven types, know the value of prayer. This has certainly been true in my 30-year career as a rated officer, which began in 1929 when I was graduated from the old Advanced Flying School at Kelly Field, Texas, and I know that I am not an exception.

When a man purposely takes leave of his natural element, the earth, and climbs to great heights in the sky, he cannot escape the realization that man and his works are, after all, small and ephemeral when viewed in relation to time and the cosmos. He remembers that the normal span of a human life is all too short at best and is constantly threatened by numerous perils that could bring it quickly to an unnatural end.

Yet there is an orderly and infinite pattern that governs all things: the pathways of the stars; the renewal of the seasons; birth, growth and death. And although man can see but a small portion of the pattern, it serves as convincing evidence that only a Supreme Being could so order a universe that extends far beyond man's ability to comprehend. That God exists, there can be no doubt. Only the most irresponsible arrogance could deny it.

It follows then, that just as surely as God exists, He is mindful of man, for man is a part of His pattern. Man, there-fore, must attune himself to God before he can hope to play the role intended for him. A ready means of achieving this is provided through the avenue of prayer, and this I have found to be an inexhaustible source of strength, courage and solace during a career that has had its full share of rewards as well as problems and crises. A person who has experienced the true efficacy of prayer, however, does not resort to it only in time of need or danger. There is, for example, the prayer of thanksgiving that should be said perhaps more often than any other. For what day has passed in any of our lives that we were not given at least one blessing for which we should be grateful?

Man, by nature, is self-centered. Most of our personal troubles, the troubles of groups and nations, can usually be traced to some form of selfishness—that of ourselves, an individual or a group powerful enough to impose its will on others. Destructive wars between nations are too often the tragic results of the selfishness of a single person or small group. To me, selfishness is probably the basic weakness of mankind. It is an insidious weakness because it is so seldom recognized, particularly when it goes under the guise of a thoughtless ambition.

The best remedy I know for selfishness is prayer. A person in the act of prayer cannot be very selfish. At such a time, one is attempting to harmonize his heart and mind with the will of God. He may petition for a personal benefit, but he does so with a humility which enables him to say: "Thy will be done, not mine."

Although my faith in prayer is unshakable, I am confident that it imposes a full share of personal responsibility. To say a prayer, then sit back and wait for something good, or perhaps miraculous,to come our way is not enough. Instead, the individual must take positive action of his own.

I believe that God answers prayers, but I also believe that "The Lord helps those who help themselves."

DO I BELIEVE IN PRAYER?

By Dr. Andrew C. Ivy

Distinguished Professor of Physiology and
Head, Department of Clinical Science, University of Illinois

❦

Do I believe in prayer? Yes, because I pray.

Why do I pray? I pray for several reasons.

First, the more I learn about the machinery and reactions of living things, and the more I learn about the Universe and everything in it, and the more I learn about the infinite extent of the law and order which characterizes the structure and manifestations of all things, the more firmly I believe in God, and the more I am **awed** by His infinite power and wisdom, and the more I am compelled to thoughtfully and reverently in some form of prayer and in my daily conduct hallow His name and worship Him.

Second, the longer I live, the more sincerely and frequently I pray for guidance, wisdom, and courage to do that which is right in the sight of God so that I may contribute all that I can toward bringing about His Kingdom and Will on Earth as it is in Heaven.

Third, I pray to express thanks and appreciation for the good things which I may have enjoyed or am enjoying, and for the lessons, which bad things of my own and not of my own making have taught me.

Fourth, I pray for forgiveness for those things which I may have done knowingly or unknowingly by precept or example which may have injured my body, mind and soul or the body, mind or soul of others.

Fifth, I pray in order to produce and maintain a sensitive conscience so that I may be alert to temptations and avoid evil and may live so as to leave the World a better place in which to live because of my having lived in it.

GOD'S PROMISES IN PRAYER

By Dr. Lawrence M. Stavig

President, Augustana College in South Dakota

A young woman lay seriously ill of typhoid fever. This was a day when modern remedies for this disease were not yet known and available. The doctor pronounced the case incurable and warned the family that death was the certain outcome of the illness. This time the doctor was mistaken. After several days of unconsciousness, the patient rallied and began the slow climb back that resulted in complete recovery. To her this was not at all unexpected, but simple and natural. For in the darkest hour she was convinced that a heavenly visitor had brought her a message of life and hope and promise: "You will not die, as those about you believe, for I have for you a special mission. You are to sow this seed." The messenger held out to her view a pan filled with seed.

Some years later the young woman married. In due course of time she became the mother of a little son. At the time of his birth she became convinced that through him the heavenly seed would be sown.

Twenty years later the boy lay ill with an infected ankle. A baseball injury had resulted in a poisonous infection that threatened his life. Again the doctors, including a consulting specialist, gave their verdict. There was every indication the youth would not recover. If by a miracle his life should be spared, he would certainly remain an invalid, for his heart tissue was too seriously injured to ever permit a normal life.

At night, alone with his God, the young man faced the future. Through his mind flowed remembrance of God's promises in prayer. Decision was made and a prayer went up for healing, if that might be within the plan of God. So certain was he of a response that he wakened his nurse and asked that the heart be checked. A few weeks later the specialist in wonder pronounced the heart completely recovered.

I was the young man in the story. This experience brought dramatic realization of how slender is the cord that sustains life. Out of it ultimately came the call to the gospel ministry. Only when the mother heard from her son concerning his decision for his life work did she tell him the story of her own heavenly visitation. Then too she told the reason for her confidence when he lay seriously ill; the heavenly mission must be accomplished.

The years since have brought other experiences of answered prayer. One feels very guilty when he realizes how poorly he has used this privilege of seeking divine guidance and assistance. But when he has turned to God, then the Heavenly Father has never failed to respond.

UNSELFISH PRAYER

By Basil L. Walters

Executive Editor, Knight Newspapers, Inc.

Too many of us try to unload on God all our problems and burdens.

Many of our prayers are selfish, asking some special favor, even sometimes to the disadvantage of some fellowman.

Prayers should start with the giving of thanks, followed by a meditative and prayerful search of our own souls for ways in which we can be really worthy of our blessings.

PRAYER IS PERSONAL

By Dr. Robert P. Daniel

President, Virginia State College

From the very beginning of his existence on earth, man has sought help from some source outside himself for deliverance from bonds of the flesh or from bonds of the spirit. Whether he has called upon gods of vengeance or upon a God of Love, upon gods whom he has created in his own image or upon a God in whose image he has been created, his supplications have been evidence of the recognition of his impotence, and of his need for help from a power greater than he. At no time in history has prayer had greater significance, however, than it has today when man is faced by crises such as his forefathers never dreamed of experiencing, and when each discovery seems fraught with a new and more terrible means of ultimately destroying himself. Plagued by nameless fears of an uncertain future, man prays—alone and in groups—for himself and for others—as he seeks to satisfy his needs.

The prayer experience may vary with individuals because each one approaches God always as he interprets within himself the needs which he feels. One person may think of God as "high and lifted up," while another thinks of God as his companion. One thanks God that he is not as other men, while another thanks God for being merciful to him, a transgressor. Whatever may be the attitude of the individual, prayer is for him a very personal experience. It is this personal element which gives to prayer its appeal to people of all faiths and in all walks of life. Perhaps the most eloquent prayers are those which cannot find expression in words, but which are, rather, a feeling of nearness to God.

The prayer relationship between the individual and God has a distinctively intimate quality. God bids anyone who will, to come to Him in prayer, and all people have a common opportunity to turn to this well-spring of life and strength. But, on the other hand, every individual feels that his needs are peculiarly his own, and only God knows the extent of his innermost thoughts and feelings. Although he is conscious of the fact that when he prays, he is on an open circuit of communication with the Holy Spirit, at the same time, he feels that he is on a private line which connects him directly with the Infinite. "And He walks with **me**, and He talks with **me**..." This is the sort of experience that makes prayer for me an intensely personal relationship with God, sufficient for my every need. Through such communion, I find strength; I find peace.

There are three personal elements in my prayer experience: grace, guidance, and gratitude.

I believe that the quality of grace is the special trust which God has placed in us to help bring about His kingdom on earth. It is this belief which keeps me ever near Him in prayer. My hands must do His work; my heart must understand the needs of my fellowmen; my voice must bring comfort and courage to those in need. Through me His grace must flow out to all with whom I come into contact, and it is only by staying close to Him in prayer that I am able to grow in sufficient grace and power to become worthy of this great trust.

I have found that the more we grow in grace, the broader become the reaches of mind and spirit that we can attain. "We are the sons of God, and it does not yet appear what we shall be." No matter what we have achieved, no matter how dedicated our lives may be at any one time, there is still perfection beyond our comprehension. Our influence extends in ever increasing force as we grow in grace nearer to the Source of all power. And so I return in prayer to this source of my strength and trust, not just every day, but many times a day.

The quality of guidance in prayer has been the mainstay of my life. As an administrator, it has been my responsibility to make decisions which affect the lives of thousands of individuals, and I have found that when I pray, I am aware of a strength and a clarity of vision over and beyond any personal ability that I may possess. Through prayer, it is both a wonder and a great joy to make the impossible become possible, to turn apparent defeat into victory, to use the forces that push backwards as the basis for a surer forward start. Difficult situations need not be alarming because there is in prayer the wisdom that guides me. Relieved of nameless fears and apprehensions, I am free to think through the intricacies of the various problems which I must face. Though I may seem to be alone at the very moment of crisis, I am not dismayed because prayer, even without uttered words, is the source of my strength.

The quality of gratitude is the third most compelling element in prayer for me. In any life, there are moments when one feels a sense of uncertainty and of inadequacy. A weariness of spirit may come over an individual because of disappointments and disillusionments, when his best seems not to be good enough, when even those closest to him turn away in bewilderment and misunderstanding. How natural it is, then, for a person to turn to prayer for the assurance and the life-giving strength to carry on!

But to me adversity is not so compelling a drive to prayer as is gratitude for prosperity and triumph. Prayer is easy when we are experiencing anguish and calamity. Its real challenge comes at times of joy and success. It saves us from self-conceit and arrogance; it fosters modesty and a spirit of thankfulness.

When I am at the peak of success, surrounded by family and friends who love me, acclaimed by those who admire me—at that moment I am filled, and I must be filled, with an overpowering need to pray. I feel that God is not only "the ever present Help in time of trouble," but He is also the undergirding influence which sustains within us the sobering spirit of humility and of dedication.

Through these three elements—grace, guidance and gratitude—prayer has become the strength of my life.

A LAYMAN'S PRAYER

By Charles F. McCahill, Senior Vice President
Cleveland, Ohio, Plain Dealer and News

❦

I like to regard prayer as a conversation with God. When I converse with God, I am mindful of my relationship to Him. He is my Sovereign, supreme in His dominion over the universe. He is my Master; I am completely dependent upon Him. I know, too, that all the gifts I have ever received are His benefactions.

I am thankful to God for His gifts. I am well aware, though, that I have not always used these gifts well. My resolve is to make up for the injustice of my actions. I am confident that God in His goodness is still willing to help me.

I even feel free to discuss with Him my needs as I see them. Perhaps I do not understand my own needs clearly. But God does. He hears me. I know that I shall receive from Him the helps that are best for me. My hope is in the infinite goodness of God.

THERE IS POWER IN PRAYER

By Ezra Taft Benson

Secretary of Agriculture

In the Cabinet of President Eisenhower

❧

Prayer is direct communication with God who hears and answers, though not always at the time or in the manner that we might suppose. To hear the sweet, simple prayer of a child is to know that prayer is real. Prayer not only keeps us closer to God but in so doing it strengthens our daily actions for righteousness because of our willingness to acknowledge Him and to bring Him into partnership with us. It helps keep our thinking straight and positive. It teaches faith and helps bring understanding. It develops an attitude in which joy and love know no bounds.

> I know not by what methods rare,
>   But this I know God answers prayer.
> I know that He has given His word
>   Which tells me prayer is always heard,
> And will be answered soon or late,
>   And so I pray, and calmly wait.
>
> I know not if the blessings sought
>   Will come just in the way I thought,
> But leave my prayers with Him alone
>   Whose will is wiser than my own;
> Assured that He will grant my quest,
>   Or send some answer far more blessed.

Prayer has literally changed the development of man. It has brought him out of the morass of indecision and discouragement into the sunlight born of faith through works and love and trust.

Fervent prayer on the part of a young 15-year old boy in New York State in 1820 started a chain of events which is literally changing the lives of one and a half million people today. The direct result of this prayer has brought a positive understanding of the being of God the Father and his Son, Jesus Christ. It has caused the uncovering of ancient histories which contain divine truths that if obeyed will lead directly to the eventual exaltation of man and to a situation of happiness and joy that words cannot describe.

Prayer will bring solace and comfort. It has healed sickness, comforted those distressed and has continued the faithful in paths of righteousness. The value of a man is evidenced in part by the dust on his knees. His willingness to believe in and accept a being greater than himself as evidenced by his prayer has increased his moral stature, refined his understanding and has brought him along the road of his eternal development. Our great example in prayer is our Lord and Master Jesus Christ who knew that only through constant supplication and obedience would God the Father manifest His will and release the power for its attainment through man.

Truly there is power in prayer.

PRAYER IS A WAY OF LIFE

By Dr. Sidney A. Rand

Executive Director, Dept. of Christian Education,

The Evangelical Lutheran Church

❧

"Don't forget to say your prayers."

Such an admonition has followed many of us upstairs to bed. The trouble with it is that it tells us that mother or dad were not involved. Prayer was for the children.

But it is a good admonition nevertheless. The man or woman who has remembered to cultivate the prayer habit down through the years is richer because of it. For prayer does many things.

Have you talked with the man who was healed through prayer? At least he said he was, and who of us would say he is mistaken?

Or there is a woman whose troubles included a broken marriage, runaway children and no job. She says prayer changed things for her. Indeed, it may well have been a major factor in her changed life. She has found a way to live in spite of these unfortunate circumstances.

But is this why we pray? Is prayer only a way to get out of life's corners? Is prayer a "last resort" which we use when nothing else will do?

Often it seems so, doesn't it? The most serious error in this kind of prayer is what it does to God. It puts him at the end of our resources for living instead of at their beginning. It tells him we will use him if there is no other way.

And the glory of our God is that in his grace and love he helps even then. No-one ever turned to him in vain, even after trying everything else. He is faithful. As Christ assured us, "Whatever you ask in my name you will receive."

But if God is this loving and understanding one when we come to him as a last resort, how much more blessed life can be when we come to him first. Then life is always lived in his presence, and his power and goodness can shed all the blessings into life which he wants so much to give.

Prayer is the practice of going to God first instead of last. It means living life in full faith that he is real and present. And each one who lives that way finds God is real and God is present.

This is the good life.

PRAYER WILL MAKE A BETTER WORLD

By Goodwin J. Knight

Former Governor, State of California

❁

The stresses and uncertainty which face all of us from day to day only serve to emphasize our ultimate, absolute reliance upon the grace and mercy of Almighty God. For centuries, prayer has been the most widely accepted means of giving expression to this dependence in the solution of our problems, the realization of our hopes and the alleviation of our fears.

Devout, personal gratitude for the bounty which has been bestowed upon each of us requires unquestioning recognition of the infinite majesty and power of God. In prayer we find protection, encouragement and comfort during every day of our lives. Personally, I have implicit faith in the power of prayer to make this a progressively better world for all people everywhere.

FINALLY HE BEGAN TO THANK

By Dr. Alvin N. Rogness

President, Luther Theological Seminary

❧

He had not been too successful at wheedling things from God. He had wanted to be happy and to sleep without anxiety. He had asked to escape illness and sorrow.

One night, while parading his inventory of wants before God, he seemed to hear a voice say, "Who calls the signals in this game, you or I?" And as if a meteor had streaked across a darkened sky, he suddenly saw! He, not God, had been issuing the commands! He had been using God as some sort of celestial errand boy. He fell silent, and tried to listen.

As he listened, he heard again welling up from within his own memories all the wonderful things he had been taught about this God. This was the God who had created him for His own royal family. This was the God who had sent His only begotten Son to give him forgiveness and new title to a Kingdom. This was the God who had promised to help him walk as a citizen in this Kingdom day by day, even when this walk would entail suffering, loneliness and even death. Although never promising paths of ease, this God had promised strength for every task and deep comfort in every sorrow.

Suddenly he began to pray again, but now his prayer issued forth in a flood of thanksgiving. His catalog of needs became strangely irrelevant in the overwhelming need to praise and adore a God who already had done so much for him.

This, it seems to me, is the highest form of prayer. To be sure, a great and good heavenly Father gives ear to all our desires, even those that seem trivial and even harmful, and is anxious that like little children we come to Him with all our wants. In His own towering wisdom He may know that it is best that we be denied much of what we ask. We trust Him most if in all circumstances of life we can give Him ceaseless praise. Lifted above whining self-pity and petty complaints, we then stride through life in the strong and merry mood of the Thankful One. On this high plateau, prayer finds its richest rewards.

DIRECT ANSWER TO PRAYER

By Robert Emery Smith

Railway Financial Consultant

❧

My esteemed kinsman, the late George Albert Smith, President of the Mormon Church, was an ardent believer in the spiritural rewards which flow from prayer and had equal faith in the divine granting of pleas for physical and material aid. He has told me of many specific instances where such requests have been granted and I particularly recall the following:

His grandfather, one of the original Mormon pioneers, settled at Provost, Utah. While on a visit to Salt Lake City his grandfather had a premonition that his family was in danger. Going to the Mormon Temple he prayed for their protection and safety.

Upon his return he learned that his son, my kinsman's father, had fallen into a mountain stream so swift and turbulent that human rescue was impossible. After all hope for the boy had vanished, a huge flood unlike anything which had previously been known, came tearing down the mountain side, overflowed the stream's banks and washed the boy ashore unharmed. All agreed that it was a direct answer to the father's prayer.

CONSTANT AWARENESS OF GOD IS PRAYER

By Dr. Frank Kingdon

Columnist and News Analyst

❀

Prayer is so intimately a part of my life that I find it difficult to isolate it from the rest and look at it, so to speak, as something apart from me which I can describe. It is a constant awareness of communion with, obedience to, and dependence upon The Whole of which I am but a part, a Whole at once all-powerful and all-loving, the mystery of His Being altogether too great for my understanding to grasp or to interpret.

There is for me in this experience nothing of the concept of God at which the profane and the wicked mock. God as the informing Spirit of the Whole that links each of us to the uttermost star is not apart from me as though I could see Him, nor is He one to whom I could possibly bring petitions. I am in Him and of Him, and He already knows my follies, my weaknesses, my sins, my needs more profoundly than I myself ever can. Only one prayer can form itself into words: "Thy Will Be Done."

Vividly aware of this Power not myself investing my life, how can I be afraid? Nothing can touch me to do me harm unless it be God's will, and if it be His will, then He will turn the harm to His own purpose, and His will is my good. As I go out to do that work with which I am charged I go in the knowledge and, indeed, in the constant and unceasing communion, of God. Thus, in a sense, every act is itself a prayer, and nothing but creative good can come of it because His love and His power are in it.

225

This, I believe, is the experience to which the Apostle pointed us when he wrote **Pray without ceasing.** His was no exhortation to walk through life with closed eyes uttering rituals and liturgies, but rather a call to be every minute so aware of our unity with God that every breath and word is communion with Him. Prayer in its deepest meaning for me is not the word that my lips address to God, but that unceasing awareness in me that I am never apart from Him.

PRAYER CAN BE CONSTANT

By *Hubert Eaton*

Founder and Board Chairman,
Forest Lawn Memorial Park

❦

I believe in prayer because I have found it the best way to commune with God. I believe in prayer because I can talk to the Christ who smiles and loves you and me. I believe in prayer because several times in my life, when all earthly help had been swept away and there seemed no way to turn, I dropped to my knees and asked God's help for strength to carry on, and each time I arose from my knees strengthened and freshened.

Every time, those prayers were answered, not always in the way that I had asked or anticipated, but answered in God's way, which I ultimately found was the best way. Jesus said, "When thou prayest, enter thy closet . . . Pray to thy Father which is in secret . . ." But I have also discovered that prayer can be constant, almost as though one were entering into a conversation with Christ.

To me, a life without prayer would mean that the day's work was drudgery and that the future held neither promise nor hope. I believe in prayer.

PRAYER AS A ROAD TO PEACE

By Dr. Georgia Harkness

Professor of Applied Theology,

Pacific School of Religion, Berkeley, California

❦

The two things for which most men long for today are peace among the nations and peace in the inner life. Prayer is related to both. We shall have no reconstructed world without reconstructed individuals, and in the remaking of human life in the direction of changed attitudes and acts, prayer has a major place.

Prayer that is merely perfunctory or clamorous is not true prayer. But when prayer is humble, devout, God-centered and submissive to His will, it quickens the heart and strengthens the spirit to try to discover and do what God requires of us. Thus it enlarges horizons and increases sensitivity to the needs of others, including those in other lands we have never seen. It makes us want to share what we have, and this gives realism and support to both church and government programs of foreign aid. It increases human brotherhood, and by reducing racial tensions it reduces the appeal of Communism to our colored brothers around the world. It helps us to distinguish between evil systems, which must be rejected, and the persons under their control—sons of God like ourselves—for whom we ought to feel not hatred but sympathy. Prayer thus helps to create and cement the ties of understanding and reconciliation which, expressed politically in negotiation at the upper levels of statecraft, can abate the tensions of the cold war and lead to peace.

Prayer is the surest road to peace in the individual. This is not to overlook the many grounds of disturbance to inner peace, such as a bad family situation, a vocational misfit, economic insecurity or lack of physical health. All of these ought to be corrected when they can be, for it is not the will of God that any of His children should suffer from preventable pain or social maladjustment. Yet when these things cannot be changed, prayer in trust of God's sustaining care helps to make life not only endurable but bright with His presence. For changing what can be changed, prayer as a source of guidance and strength is an indispensable support.

Note that we have not been speaking of prayer as words only. Prayer for most of us must be expressed in words, but it is the deep devotion of the heart that matters. Prayer must never be viewed simply as a panacea, or a tool for getting what we desire; prayer is the lifting up of the soul to God in adoration and dedicated service.

Thus, in the world scene, it is the prayer that prompts us to do what our Lord called "the things that make for peace" (note the setting in Luke 19:42) which contributes so vitally to the peace of the world. Similarly in the inner life of the individual, we can affirm with the Book of James, "The prayer of a righteous man has great power in its effects," (James 5:16) but let us be sure it is the prayer of a righteous man whose life is centered in God.

It is my deep conviction that prayer is a road to peace in both senses of the word. Yet it is no easy road, for true prayer costs much. The power that comes through prayer is God's power, not our own, and in His will is our peace.

PRAYER —— AND WORK!

By Dr. Julian B. Feibelman

Rabbi, Temple Sinai of New Orleans

In the concluding paragraph of her great book, "David, the King," Gladys Schmidt pictures the aged monarch bemoaning his life and work. He has sought God, praised God in psalms and with psaltery, and now, he plaintively asks, what notice has God taken of me? Whereupon his handmaiden, with the insight and maturity one might have expected from David, calmly reassures him that it is enough that "you" sought and aspired to know God; it is not necessary that God should recognize you. This sage counsel strongly calms the old monarch.

I believe this is a good approach to prayer. For prayer is a quest, an aspiration, and an inner urge to reach unto God and to gain sufficient knowledge and strength to fulfill God's will.

God has been defined as "the unconquerable spirit in man." If our spirit seeks union, or communion with God, if our spirit strives for merger with the all-spirit, through prayer, then we have the noblest and most sublime expression of which man is capable. Prayer is as instinctive and necessary, in the spiritual sense, as is eating and sleeping in the physical. It never troubles me overmuch to ask if prayers are answered. But prayer is answered both negatively as well as positively. Often, people think prayers are unrequited unless they receive what they ask. We do not ask God for material gifts, and personal benefits, as children ask of indulgent parents. We ask God for strength to help ourselves, or to help us to evaluate the desires we are never without.

My favorite prayer is the one of Moses directing Joshua to pick up the staff of leadership. "Be strong and of good courage." I pray for strength and courage. That is what I urge others to pray for—patients in hospital beds; stricken souls in despair and loneliness; the young—to face the test and challenges of life; the old, to persevere and take heart.

God has found a counterpart, or placed a counterpart of Himself, in us, who respond to this spiritual incentive and aspiration. It is this spirit that must prompt us, with unrelenting insistence, to do the right in the earth. It is this spirit that urges upon us the necessity of doing God's work. The great objective is the establishment of the kingdom of God upon earth. A fit place for God to be.

Now who is going to do this? Man is both required and expected to do it. Peace upon earth? Who is going to determine peace upon earth? God? Certainly not! He has given us the vision of peace, the great spiritual incentive for peace, making swords into plowshares and spears into pruning hooks. God gives us the moral insight to see the virtues of peace, and the great good of decency and honor and justice and truth. God revealed to Moses and the Prophets the Moral Law and the ethical commandments and God gave us the freedom of will to work and establish these. He also allows us to turn our backs on them, deny them, forget and ignore them, and even to defile them, as witness the indescribable horror of recent wars!

We cannot do God's work upon earth without God. That is why we can and must pray to Him—for courage and strength. And for all the other needs we feel and which we cannot accomplish without assurance of confident divine fulfillment.

I feel stronger after I have asked God to give me strength. I feel encouraged—yes, with much more courage than I could give myself without God.

And then I must often thank God. This too is as instinctive and natural as I would thank a benign friend who has helped me. I thank God fervently for many blessings. My country, my family, my friends, my opportunities, my freedom, my conscience and my right to follow the dictates of it.

There are those who feel none of this. They have no tendency to prayer, toward the knowledge of God, to the force of directed destiny, nor to the good of universal peace and brotherhood. And often people give no response to good music, or good art, or good causes, or even good living.

Religion, or my religion of Judaism, is **responsibility.** This is a heavy and profound obligation of faith! It is a serious duty. Too much for me alone. But with God, I can go forward in the hope and faith that if He gives me the courage to preserve and "keep faith," I shall not utterly fail. His revealed words through the Prophets make me aware of the kind of world which would honor His name. I need a portion of His strength and His spirit to do whatever lies within my humble power to help achieve it. And I pray for that power!

I choose to think I am a co-partner with God. God depends on man to do His will, as man depends on God to believe that that will shall ultimately prevail. It is the triumph of good over evil. Prayer helps me to keep these lofty aspirations in mind, and to work for them.

Peace is God's will; making peace is man's work. Brotherhood is God's plans; being brothers is our task. Thus, God and ourselves!

We do know something of God's will and His plan. It is enough for us to know that, and it is incumbent upon us to perform His will. When God's kingdom is built upon earth, God will not build it and give it to us. We shall build it and give it to God. Pray to do that—and work as though the smile of God's favor is on the work of our hands.

231

MY PRIMER OF PRAYER

By Michael T. Kelleher

Chairman Executive Committee, National Catholic Community Service,

Vice President, Marsh & McLennan, Inc.

❦

As a Catholic, devoted to the practice of my religion, I have no doubt regarding the power of prayer or the place of prayer in my life. I pray first of all that I may afford humble recognition of my dependence upon God as one of his creatures. I pray that I may express gratitude to God, Who has blessed me with so many of the good things of this life, and Who has promised me an eternity of happiness as the reward of my efforts to obey His law here below. I pray that I may offer some measure of satisfaction and reparation for my own sins and faults and for the obvious shortcomings of the world in which we live.

Only when I have prayed in adoration, in thanksgiving and in humble contrition and satisfaction can I ask God in confidence to give me the blessings of which I seem to stand in need. I do this because I know from God's own words that He wants me to ask for the things He is willing to give me and that He knows to be for my own best interests.

I have learned from the teachings of my faith that the one thing I need more than anything else is the grace to live and die in the friendship of God. I have learned too from the life and example of those who have been close to God that health and material prosperity are not essential for the working out of my eternal destiny as God has fixed it. When I ask God to keep me in good health, or to make me successful in the work by which I gain my daily bread, I must remind myself to keep these blessings, desirable though they be, in proper subordination to the state of my soul. If I am able to work, I must work for God and not just for myself. If I enjoy any degree of material prosperity, I must not forget that I owe it to God and that I shall not be worthy of it if I enjoy it in selfish disregard for the misfortune of others whom I may be able to help.

In this spirit of humble submission to God's Will I pray day by day that God may look with favor upon me and upon those near and dear to me. I have learned another lesson about prayer, however, which I regard as of even greater significance than the necessity of praying myself. I can and must pray for others; I can and must ask others to pray for me. In the Carmelite Monastery of my native city of Boston, there are consecrated religious nuns who have dedicated their lives to prayer and who storm heaven continuously in earnest supplication for the intentions which are recommended to them. These devout religious nuns have prayed for me and for my needs. More than once, during these past few years I have sought their help, as the trials of life have besieged me and my own efforts seemed to be falling short of the spiritual power which would save me. I know now, better than I could have known before, that prayer is a cooperative venture, and that the efficacy of prayer is a function of the life of self-sacrifice and union with God which transforms human beings into saints. We must all help one another, as the Carmelite nuns have helped me and countless others, for whom their praises of God ascend daily to His heavenly throne in the sweet fragrance of their saintly lives.

Prayer is indeed successful; but it must be the right kind of prayer, and it must be joined with a sincere and honest determination to live in accordance with God's Will and to elevate the pursuit of virtue to the supreme level of love of God and love of our fellow men because they, like ourselves, are children of God.

DIVINE RESPONSE TO PRAYER

By George Romney

President, American Motors Corporation

❦

The promise made in the first chapter, fifth verse, of James probably has had a greater impact on my life than any other part of the Bible. It reads:

> "If any of you lack wisdom, let him ask of God, who giveth to all men liberally, and upbraideth not; and it shall be given him. But let him ask in faith, nothing doubting, for he that doubteth is like the surge of the sea driven by the wind and tossed."

To me, this is an unqualified promise of divine response to prayer. Acting on this promise, I have gained, through study and prayer, the most priceless possessions—a knowledge that our Father in Heaven lives and that Jesus is the Christ, having been His only earthly Son.

Also, I have found this promise of wisdom in answer to prayer the most important formula in making the most important decisions in my own life. No amount of personal effort can assemble all the facts or judgment required to make life's paramount decisions but, through such personal effort and prayer, we can receive guidance that is based on eternal and unlimited wisdom. As an old colored woman said, "When we face big problems, we need big prayers."

Frequently prayer must be coupled with fasting to demonstrate the faith required to secure the needed help of guidance. From personal experience, I know that through persistent prayer it is possible to have a burning assurance of the proper choice between carefully studied and considered alternatives.

BEFORE WE SEE THE LIGHT

By Ann Sothern

Motion Picture Actress and Singer

❦

It is a sad fact that many of us must pass through dark days before we see the light. I spent most of my life going through the motions of prayer; I thought I believed, but my faith had never been put to the test. My career had proceeded smoothly for many years, I had a lovely daughter, and no major worries. The time spent in prayer was primarily a time of quiet and rest, giving thanks for the abundance in my life.

Then eight years ago, I suffered a severe attack of infectious hepatitis. This illness left me weakened in mind and spirit as well as in physical health. Ordinary worries and fears were suddenly magnified and seemed insurmountable. Tortured with self-doubt, I felt I could not resume my career. My doctor had no prescription to assuage these fears.

A friend reminded me of a phrase we've all heard, "Replace fear with faith." I recognized the validity of the statement, but how to begin? I started with a simple prayer asking for faith and strength. There was no miracle — my problems were not immediately solved. But there was a gradual awareness that I must draw upon something within myself to give me courage. We must make our own decisions; and so often fear of making a mistake prevents us from making any decisions at all. Only God is infallible, so why be afraid of a human error? Most mistakes can be rectified. I realized that it was much worse to neglect God-given gifts. If we seek help from Him, we must utilize to the fullest degree those assets He gave us at birth. We certainly cannot expect help from God, if we have wantonly tossed aside the things He has already given us. So, I began to ask His help each morning in making plans for that day.

I was determined to resume my former activities. However, determination and actual accomplishment are sometimes far apart. My first test came one day when I decided I was well enough and should be able to drive my car to the doctor's office. There seemed to be too many cars going too fast and I became frightened and returned home after going only one block. Shaken and nervous, I almost despaired of ever leaving the house again. My emotions and nerves were preventing my body from regaining health and the joy of living.

One day my daughter, Patricia, came to me and confided her fears about an examination at school the next day in a subject which she found difficult. She was so nervous that she found it impossible to eat. She maintained she couldn't possibly go to school and face such an ordeal.

"Darling, with God's help, you have nothing to fear. Relax, spend the time you have now studying; in your prayers, ask for guidance and you'll find that you can do it," I said.

Then I realized that I was asking Patricia to do what I knew, but had failed to do. I had refused to face my problem and had doubted the talent God had given me.

Slowly, in the months that followed, I tried to cope with each new situation as it came up, with the one thought in mind that I was not alone, that I did have help from above. This extra strength made it possible to resume my work and personal life. Fear still returns from time to time; but I know now that a few moments spent asking for Divine Guidance will show me the way to banish this fear.

THREE GREAT ESSENTIALS OF PRAYER

By Dr. Herbert V. Prochnow

Vice President, The First National Bank of Chicago,

Former Deputy Under Secretary of State

If prayer is to have far-reaching power, it must come from the depths of a humble and forgiving heart.

Two men went up into the temple to pray. One in his humility smote upon his breast, saying, "God be merciful to me a sinner." His prayer was heard. This man went down to his house justified. Only the humble person has a profound sense of his own failures and shortcomings and of his dependence upon God.

Prayer must come from a heart that not only seeks forgiveness, but is also forgiving. We are told that when we pray we ought to forgive anyone against whom we have anything, so "that your Father which is in heaven may forgive you your trespasses." In the Lord's Prayer, Jesus emphasizes forgiveness by teaching men to pray, "and forgive us our debts, as we forgive our debtors." On the cross, in the agony of crucifixion, he could cry, "Father, forgive them; for they know not what they do."

Prayer also requires intense faith, as well as a humble and forgiving heart. "All things are possible to him that believeth." "Whatsoever ye shall ask in prayer, believing, ye shall receive." We say "Amen" at the end of our prayers. Translated, "Amen" means, verily, verily, it shall be so. This is faith. We entrust our prayers to the Father in His wisdom, judgment and mercy.

Speaking of his relationship to the Father, Jesus said, "I do always those things that are well pleasing to Him." Not occasionally, not frequently, but always. If one does always those things that are well pleasing to Him and according to His will, prayer is answered. Then "whatsoever thou wilt ask of God, God will give it thee." "Every one that asketh receiveth."

Sometimes in prayer we face terrible problems. In Gethsemane, Christ prayed, "O my Father, if it be possible, let this cup pass from me." Again a second time He went away and prayed, "O my Father, if this cup may not pass away from me, except I drink it, Thy will be done." And He "prayed the third time, saying the same words." Here is complete faith and trust in the Father.

Finally, prayer expresses gratitude. We have each been blessed a thousand times, but rarely does a word of thankfulness fall from our lips. We are guilty of ingratitude daily. Must we be blind before we realize the beauty of sunsets, forests and lakes? Must we be hungry before we show gratitude for countless material blessings? Must we lose our freedom before we give thanks for this priceless blessing? Does it take disaster and tragedy to open our hearts? Someone has asked whether it is necessary for Christ to be crucified in every generation for man fully to understand the blessings which are his forever.

A humble and forgiving heart, faith and gratitude—these three are great essentials of prayer.

A DAILY VISIT

By Eddie Dowling

Actor and Producer

Prayer is my daily visit with God.

MY BELIEF IN PRAYER

By Sir Hubert Wilkins
Explorer and Scientist

❦

All praying, whether individual, communal or congregational, may be egostic or aesthetic. The earliest prayer forms used by primitive man were not addressed to Diety but today the act of prayer admits the consciousness of God worship.

Prayer is the second stage in a three-stage gear shift toward happiness. The first stage in Faith, the second stage requires action and applied power; it is not equipped with automatic transmission. In regard to egostic prayer the third stage will not be achieved unless it is clearly certain that your prayer is valid and proper for your personal, beneficial and experimental development. In your prayers in regard to yourself, do not ask for a fait accompli, ask for guidance and strength; pray for values, not things, for growth not gratification. Also, you must have honestly exhausted the human capacity for human adjustment.

Material praying is destined to bring disappointment and disallusionment as advanced scientific discoveries demonstrate that man lives in a physical universe of law and order.

God is the source of cause; he has an overflowing warehouse. He is not only in the retail business; he can distribute on a wholesale scale to those who are sincere and deserving. If your desire is valid and for yourself, God will reveal the roadmap wherewith you may reach the destination. If your prayer concerns friends and loved ones you may be sure that your supplications will, through Jesus, be a supporting influence to those concerned. To merely ask is not enough. Desire must be supported by Faith. Never forget that sincere prayer of faith is a mighty force for the promotion of personal happiness, individual self control, social harmony, moral progress and spiritual attainment.

And Faith and prayer, to be free-wheeling, must be activated by Love, love of God, love of your friends, your neighbors—even your enemies, and love of yourself in-so-much as it concerns your personal dignity and self respect.

WHY I BELIEVE IN PRAYER

By Lemuel C. Shepherd, Jr.

General, U.S. Marine Corps

❀

I believe in prayer because of the great spiritual help and comfort it has afforded me throughout my life, especially during periods of physical danger and mental strain.

From boyhood, I was taught to believe that a person was sustained by two great mental stimulants, "His honor as a man and his faith as a Christian."

It is during battle that men most strongly realize that there is a Divine Providence watching over them in which they must place their trust. Each night a soldier thanks the Almighty that he was spared during the day—and prays that God's Blessing will continue to follow him on the morrow.

I have also found in later life in positions of great responsibility where vital decisions are required, that one must look to Almighty God for guidance and judgment.

In answer to my prayers, God has saved me from many false choices and given me strength and understanding to uphold that which is right in the performance of my duties in the service of my country.

240

YOUR PRAYERS WILL BE ANSWERED

By John Charles Thomas

American Baritone

An example of the power of prayer comes to my mind in connection with a property transfer in a western Maryland town where my father was sent by the presiding Bishop of the Baltimore Conference, the Methodist Church property was in a most dilapidated and run-down state and I remember very well that the membership had also suffered from the same neglected pastorate. The land upon which the church and parsonage stood was a loan from the local mining company and it had a reversible clause in the contract which stated that when the property was no longer used for church worship, the land and buildings would automatically revert to the mining company.

My father soon began covering ground and in his pastoral calls and his sermons he awakened an enthusiasm in the community which finally led to plans for a new site and new buildings to take care of the progress in the membership drive. Things really started humming. He preached a sermon on tithing and without exception the entire membership pledged a tenth of their gross earnings to the church. Then came the snag. At a meeting with the heads of the mining company, my father explained his plans for the new church and parsonage and a new site. The heads of the company were most receptive and actually enthusiastic, and even gave a financial donation to the project. But—and here was the snag—when it came to issuing a deed for the new property without a reversible clause, there was a positive refusal. My father was most discouraged, but he immediately organized a series of prayer meetings where the reversible clause was brought before the Lord and Master.

It seemed like a dream come true. But what really happened was this: After a few weeks of constant supplication at the throne of Grace by my father and the members of his congregation, the head of the company summoned my father to his office and said, "Rev. Thomas, we have changed our minds. It is my pleasure to present this deed to your church without the reversible clause. The property is yours."

No wonder that as long as he lived my father was a firm believer in the power of prayer. Our breakfast time was always followed by a word of prayer—of thanks and for guidance during the day.

Believe on the Lord Most High and your prayers will be answered.

UNLESS I AM WORTHY

By Margaret Chase Smith

United States Senator from Maine

❦

My feeling about the power of prayer is so simple and fundamental that it doesn't take many words to express it.

Like any other religious human being, prayer to me is a source of divine guidance in my daily work and not just in time of crisis. I try never to pray for anything unless I am worthy by my own actions of what I pray for.

THE PSYCHOLOGY OF PRAYER

By Dr. Clyde M. Narramore

Consulting Psychologist, Los Angeles County Schools

❦

As a psychologist, I am impressed with the fact that every human being has an innate desire to pray. This inner longing to talk to a supreme being takes many forms but it is always a **built-in part of every human being.**

It would seem unreasonable, wouldn't it, for God, who created man, to give him the amazing power of speech and yet make it impossible for man to talk with God?

As we read God's Word, the Bible, we find that one of the reasons why God made man was so that He could commune and fellowship with man. But that fellowship and prayer line was broken by the first man, Adam — because he sinned. And, of course, God, a righteous, holy God, cannot stand in the presence of sin. This was man's choice. And men today in the twentieth century space age have broken communication with God — not only because of their innate natures which stemmed from Adam, but because of their own will to sin. One time I was talking with a lady at Columbia University where I was completing work on my doctorate. During our conversation she said, "I am not a sinner because of my forefathers."

"Well," I said, "then you are a sinner by choice?"

After thinking for a moment she replied, "Yes, you're right there."

And it is true. We are sinners either by nature or by choice, but actually we are sinners by both!

But God in His mercy has dealt kindly with the human race. And in due time He sent Himself in the form of his Son,

Jesus Christ, to die on the Cross for us that through Him we might have atonement for our sins. As the hymn writer expressed it, "What a mighty gulf God did span at Calvary!"

Although God's provision has been available for many years, it meant nothing to me personally until several years ago when I experienced spiritual conversion. After reading God's Word I was convinced that it was possible for God to give me a new nature so that I could **talk** and **walk** with Him. One day I knelt down alone and asked God to forgive me of my sins. I asked Him to come into my heart and to save me. I acknowledged Christ's death on the cross as the substitute for all my sin. I asked Him to dwell in me. And I promised Him that I would serve Him as long as I lived.

When I got up off my knees I was a **new man.** The miracle had happened! God had saved my poor soul!

"What kind of a feeling did you get?" you might ask.

Actually, I didn't get any sort of a "feeling." You see, I wasn't looking for a feeling. **I was looking for Jesus.** And I found Him! Of course, I **did** have peace. And I knew definitely that if my life should be required of me, I could stand in the presence of a holy God, not on my merits but because of the intercession of God's Son, Christ Jesus, who paid the penalty for me.

Through the years I have walked and talked with Him and He has been wonderful to me. We read in the Scriptures that the "effectual fervent prayer of a righteous man availeth much." However, we also read that, "God heareth not sinners," except as they call on Him for forgiveness.

Many people go through the motions of praying but their prayers never get any higher than the ceiling because they have never been born again—they have never been born into God's family. So He can't possibly be their father. When you take

Christ as your personal Savior, God will become your father and you will become God's son. "But as many as received him, to them gave he power to become the sons of God, even to them that believe on his name: Which were born, not of blood, nor of the will of the flesh, nor of the will of man, but of God" (John 1:12,13).

Then you can really pray and He will answer your prayers.

Yes, prayer is real and it is wonderful. As a consulting psychologist I can say that the experiences of conversion and prayer are the most fundamental experiences in all of life!

AN EXPRESSION OF FAITH

By Arthur H. Motley

President, Parade Publications, Inc.

❀

I believe in the power of prayer because prayer to me expresses faith; faith not merely in a benign diety but rather in the ability of man made in the image of his maker to handle with dignity the problems of human life.

I believe in prayer that asks not for favors for one's self but a prayer that by implication assures the individual that he has been endowed with virtues and power, the power to overcome handicaps and obstacles and the virtue to premit him to live in harmony with his fellow man.

I believe in prayer, not only as a sign of religious feeling, but as an expression of faith in one's self, in one's beliefs, and in the world in which we live.

THE EXPERIENCE OF PRAYER

By Fred F. Florence

Chairman, Executive Committee, Republic National Bank of Dallas

❁

There is a human instinct to pray. This prayer instinct may be marred by sin, blinded by ignorance, encompassed by superstition and in some men may be sometimes utterly absent; yet when we take a wide view of the human race, the impulse to pray is practically universal. Whether the story goes back to the ages of the dim and unknown past or forward to the latest achievements of this scientific world, the story of humanity is interwoven with prayer and intercession.

God's providential message provides for prayer and its answer. God's eternal purpose includes the creation of free beings, capable of fellowship with Himself. True religion takes the form of Fatherhood and sonship; and this implies the utmost freedom of intercourse between God and man. God speaks to man and man speaks to God. In fact, prayer is the central and characteristic mark of religion. Religion involves communion and fellowship between the Creator and the created, between the Lord who hears in Heaven and the dependent man who cries from the earth.

A child will pray naturally; a soldier wounded in battle will unconsciously turn to Heaven for help; a man in deep agony and distress will beseech the mercies of Heaven. These cries are primitive and instinctive. When they are cultivated and directed through all of life, they produce in man the highest order of behaviour and moral character. Living the presence of God each day, communing with the Almighty and Eternal each day, takes one of the basic urges of life and sublimates it into a heavenly fellowship and a glorious experience. We really begin to live when we live in the will and Word of God; God talking to us and we talking to God. This is the experience of prayer.

PRAYER—A SYMBOL OF FAITH

By Ernest Henderson,

President, Sheraton Corporation of America

Boston, Massachusetts

❂

Prayer is usually thought of as a vehicle for the communication of hopes and aspirations between an individual and the Divine Being in whom we believe. But prayer goes much further and deeper, for it serves as a means of communication between an individual and his spiritual inner self, that subconscious area of the mind which provides us with a sense of right and wrong which we call our conscience.

Many prayers are answered, some are not. At first we are confused by our failure to understand why some prayers are not answered, and then again at times we are strangely awed by the promptness by which certain prayers are fulfilled.

I believe that such astonishment would diminish if we recognized our own spiritual inner self as a divinely created censor which determines through our own conscience what prayers should and which ones should not be answered. If our prayers fall in the former category, then our inner self —that which perhaps some of us think of as our subconscious mind—directs us with a compelling force to the achievement of those goals which we may have sought in prayer. Under such circumstances there should be little wonder that many prayers are answered.

247

PRAYER IS COMMUNION WITH GOD

By Admiral Arleigh Burke

The Chief of U.S. Naval Operations

❦

Prayer is a profoundly personal thing. Each man prays in his own way — according to his own beliefs and in the manner which he personally finds most effective in achieving communion with God. Our great United States stands as a monumental guardian of man's right to this priceless freedom.

The power of prayer is the power of hope and strength which comes from within. A man without faith has no hope. Without hope strength is lost. Prayer is the spiritual injection which restores to man his confidence, his determination, and his will.

Prayer is the power of inner motivation, the most effective inspiration to action. Americans understand this power because they have grown strong under a concept which places God above country. Americans die to preserve this system because it stands for peace on earth and good will toward all men.

Military and naval leaders down through the ages have recognized the power of prayer. General George Washington, during the dark days of the American Revolution, sought divine guidance at Valley Forge through prayer. Thus did he derive new strength and determination to see his cause through to a glorious victory.

The United States Navy is a combat organization which must meet its world-wide responsibilities practically and realistically. Just as essential as material readiness and training is the moral and spiritual strength of our men at sea. For in the final analysis it is the manhood of the nation that determines the nation's destiny. For this reason the Navy provides spiritual guidance to its sailors and marines in the conviction that the inner strength of men, renewed through prayer, is the wellspring of national power.

TO FIND PEACE OF MIND

By Gabriel Heatter

News Commentator, Mutual Broadcasting Company

❦

I stand in need of prayer every day of my life. I have never approached a microphone for a broadcast without a prayer. I have never finished a broadcast without a prayer. I believe in prayer. My prayers have been answered time and again. Whatever privilege I have had in my humble life to use words which might reach other people, have all come from the humility of prayer. If anyone were to ask me what can I do to find peace of heart, my answer would be:

"Put yourself in the hands of prayer. Regard yourself as an instrument of life to carry out some divine purpose on this earth. It will give you courage. It will give you peace of heart."

I have had my share of fear all my life. But prayer helped me to overcome fear. I have had my share of troubles. Again prayer helped me find my way out. Pity anyone who can never walk into a room alone, shut the door, stand in a corner, and open his or her heart in prayer.

A PRACTICAL APPROACH TO PRAYER

By John H. Kraft

Former President and Chairman, Kraft Foods Company

❧

The idea still persists in some quarters that it is inconsistent for a business man to be a religious man—a praying man—whereas in actual practice it is the business man who most often applies his religious beliefs to his daily life. The man who carries the responsibilities of keeping a business going, of meeting a payroll, of guarding the welfare and insuring the contentment of many employees, is the man who needs Divine help and guidance—and is often the man who prays most. In fact, all the good, happy, and successful men that I know are praying men. They pray daily and often, about many things.

I have never known or heard of anyone, in any walk of life, praying for something that would make him unsuccessful or unhappy; therefore, I think it is fair to say that everyone prays for what he thinks it will take to make him successful and happy. In this sense, we all put a "commercial" value on prayer, whether we are an individual in private life or a man in business. I believe that it is perfectly legitimate to pray for the success of a legitimate project. God has surrounded us with benefits that He wants us to have, but we have to work for them, we have to deserve them, and we have to ask Him for them. Therefore, before we pray we must weigh our request properly, decide whether **we** have done all we can before we ask for help, and particularly whether our project is worthy of God's attention. If we think it is worthy, we can pray for it. If it **is** worthy in His sight, He will help us. If it is not, He will leave it alone.

This sort of an approach leads to a constant self-analysis

of one's motives, a constant effort to keep them worthwhile, clean, and unselfish. It becomes necessary for a man to slow down, contemplate, figure out where he is going and how he stands with God. Prayer becomes much more than a Sunday observance of religious practices; it becomes an everyday part of one's life, the dynamo of energy and purpose that keeps a man going and (if he is going in the right direction) that leads to success.

This is indeed the "practical" approach to prayer, for at the same time one develops the good habits of self-examination, proper evaluation of wants and needs, and concern for others, he also moulds the kind of character and personality that makes people want to do business with him. Some may say that this is putting a definite commercial value on prayer. I believe that it is simply carrying out God's wishes and His plans for His children; that is, that we live in such a manner that we are successful, happy, and in harmony with our fellowman.

A CHALLENGE TO
RELIGIOUS THINKERS

By Abba Eban

Ambassador from Israel to the United States

❧

In the torment of two thousand years of exile my people has prayed from the depths for its redemption in the land of its fathers. The vindication of faith and prayer enshrined in the phenomenon of the renewal of Jewish independence in our generation represents a challenge to religious thinkers of every creed.

PRAYER—ITS UNIVERSALITY
AND PERPETUITY

By Dr. William B. Lipphard

Executive Secretary, The Associated Church Press

❦

Prayer has two basic characteristics, universality and perpetuity.

Ever since man appeared on earth, in adjusting to his environment he has recognized resources and forces outside himself on which he might call for guidance and stability. Throughout the centuries and across the continents, wherever man has lived, on a primitive scale or has evolved into higher forms of organization, prayer has persisted as a personal practice or as a social phenomenon. The incantations of the witch doctor of an African jungle tribe, the endless repetitive supplications of Buddhist priests, as I saw and heard them in the temples of Japan, the formal pastoral prayers in metropolitan pulpits, the silent prayer of delegate or visitor who sits in the Meditation Room at United Nations Headquarters in New York, the sustained minute of silence at the opening of every session of the United Nations Assembly, when all delegates, including the alleged atheistic Russians, all newsmen, all radio and TV broadcasters, all visitors, stand in meditative solemnity and prayer, the voiced entreaties to God of people in trouble or faced with disaster or tragedy—all evidence the universality and the perpetuity of prayer.

Sometimes this universality of prayer manifests itself in curious ways. In a restaurant on the Pacific Coast some years ago I noted a steady stream of guests, one by one, pass through a little door into a quiet recess. For a few moments each tarried there and then departed. Prompted by curiosity I did likewise when my meal was finished. I discovered the reason. In a small cubicle, like a miniature cathedral, just large enough to accommodate one person, I listened to a recorded voice offering a brief prayer. Across the continent, on the Atlantic Coast, a Protestant church has been swamped by telephone calls. People merely dial a number in order to listen to a one-minute nonsectarian recorded prayer. Until the end of time there will always be prayer.

Thus prayer is a universal and perpetually continuing phenomenon. Most people pray regularly; some occasionally; others spasmodically; still others only in times of acute need or emergency; again others pray by listening to public prayers, or by repeating prayers from a prayer book either individually or in unison in some formal worship. Of course atheists, agnostics, cynics, and skeptics deny that they pray. Their denials are meaningless because everybody prays at some time or another, even if only in the beautifully expressed words of the hymn writer,

> Prayer is the soul's sincere desire,
> Uttered or unexpressed;
> The motion of a hidden fire
> That trembles in the breast.
>
> Prayer is the burden of a sigh,
> The falling of a tear,
> The upward glancing of the eye,
> When none but God is near.

However much the atheist may deny that he prays, he cannot deny nor refute a cardinal principle of evolution that anything that persists, any phenomenon that survives, any practice that continues throughout the ages, must have abiding value. Otherwise it would long ago have been discarded.

To make prayer, whether as personal practice or as social phenomenon meaningful, helpful, and contributory to happiness and stability, requires discipline. Prayer must be freed from superstitious associations, must transcend mere devotional habit. However helpful as an adjunct to public worship, prayer must also be a private spiritual experience. Long ago it was urged upon those who pray, by one who himself knew the need and the value of prayer, "When thou prayest, enter into thine inner chamber, and having shut thy door, pray to thy Father who is in secret, and thy Father who seeth in secret shall recompense thee." Thus is the full efficacy of prayer realized. By such spiritual exercise he who prays achieves his adjustment with his environment and his universe, discovers himself to be in tune with the Infinite, and conforms himself to the will and purpose of God.

THE BEST POSSIBLE RESULT

By Dale Evans

Author and Motion Picture Star

❦

The power of prayer is in believing that God, our heavenly Father, through the mercies of our Lord Jesus Christ will grant our petitions according to his perfect will for our lives.

When we pray we are subordinating our own will to the will of the Father, thereby releasing God's power to work in and through us to accomplish the best possible result for God and ourselves. Our Lord Jesus Christ said "Your father knoweth what things ye have need of before ye ask." Therefore, when we pray our heavenly Father is pleased to give us his good and perfect gifts.

A BRIDGE OF PRAYER

By Thomas M. Johnson and Eleanore G. A. Johnson

Writers

❦

Hard necessity forces us to spend altogether too much time separated by altogether too many miles; one of us in New York, one in Minnesota. Yet in spirit we are not parted, for we have evolved what we call—reverently—a Daily Half-dozen Devotions—a bridge of prayer to span the distance. Thanks to this bridge, we can join in finding together means to meet the primary needs that are felt by everyone in this life.

For Daily Physical Needs: From the incomparable Lord's Prayer: "Give us this day our daily bread."

For Daily Health: From the 91st psalm, the "Health Psalm:" "For he shall give his angels charge over thee, to keep thee in all thy ways."

For Daily Encouragement: From the universally loved John 14: "Let not your heart be troubled, neither let it be afraid."

For Daily Relief From Worry: The 23rd psalm, to be sure: "The Lord is my shepherd; I shall not want."

For Daily Inspiration From Nature: The 121st psalm which reminds us of our country home in the hills where we are together in fact, part of the time: "I shall lift up mine eyes unto the hills whence cometh my help."

For Daily Thanksgiving: From Psalm 147: "O praise the Lord. Yea, a joyful and pleasant thing it is to be thankful."

We recite or read these inspiring words each day at the same time, the gloaming. In that mellow light the intervening miles melt away and together we find communion with God.

PRAYER INSPIRES MORAL COURAGE AND CHARACTER

By Hon. Edward R. Finch

Former Justice of the Supreme Court, State of New York;
Former Presiding Justice, Appellate Division,
Supreme Court, New York.

❦

One of the most arresting incidents in the Bible is where one of the disciples of the Lord with Him when He ceased praying, said to Him, "Lord, teach us to pray!" This disciple with the other disciples had journeyed with Jesus for a long time and had followed Him through many a long day, had frequently slept near Him at night and had observed Him turning constantly to prayer. They felt in themselves a lack of something which He possessed. It seems obvious that they had been taught to pray since their youth and probably they had used daily prayers, but apparently they felt that their prayers did not mean as much to them as the prayers of Jesus meant to Him. They desired to lay hold on this great source of strength for they had watched Him patiently, tired after a hard day of ministering, go apart by Himself and kneel in prayer. They saw Him return to them refreshed and strengthened and ready for whatever the next day might bring forth. Jesus had given to His disciples what is known as the Lord's Prayer, which is indeed a model prayer for all time. What the disciples really wanted, however, was the gift of being able to come into communion with God.

So many of us have become so occupied with other things that we have lost that great communion which means so much to the Christian. Unfortunately, as we grow older, we allow this real meaning of prayer to become spasmodic and lacking.

Some among us have stopped praying because it seemed as though our prayers are unanswered. Many of those who listen to the prayers in the church services seem to have no real sense of being an actual part of such prayers, which seem far removed from the everyday experience of the worshiper. Often, however, these persons may be brought back to the prayer life which they have neglected or have never known, by asking them to notice how often prayers are really answered. This can be done by suggesting to such disbelievers that they pray earnestly for help when at the crossroads of their lives. In my experience this will restore them to their prayer life and bring them great peace and comfort.

After all, adult human beings are children grown up—and sometimes not even fully grown. Just as a child, they crave and need guidance. So, in later life they are blessed if they substitute the Infinite for the parent. To lay a burden at the feet of God is to find comfort, which is even more precious when an individual is distraught.

It is likewise surprising to find what a powerful help prayer is in the makeup of the individuals who have lived long lives filled with peace and contentment and accomplishment.

Faith is the most satisfying solace in life. Prayer fixes and clarifies and completes faith. Prayer, furthermore, furnishes inspiration for moral power. Prayer solves problems and crosses in the life of the individual. One of the reasons for the power of the Moody and Sankey hymns is that they touch on and are based on the power of prayer. The individual who prays is not alone and finds comfort and serenity when he gives himself in prayer.

BENEDICTION

By Judge Paul W. Alexander

Court of Common Pleas, Family Court Center, Toledo, Ohio

Instead of writing over again the same thing that has already been said by far abler pens than mine, I submit a prayer which tells how I feel about prayer. This is a benediction I gave at the closing meeting of the International Association of Y's Men's Clubs at Paris, held in August 1955, in conjunction with the centennial of the World Alliance of YMCAs.

BENEDICTION

Great Love at the Heart of the Universe—
    Dwell Thou in our Hearts also.

Blind us to the Beauty of Thy World—
    When, in that Beauty, we see not Thy Face.

Deafen us to the Music of Thy Spheres—
    When, in that Music, we hear not Thy Voice.

Disturb us with continual Discontent—
    When we value: Form above Substance, Creed above Deed,
                  Doctrine above Character, Dogma above Love.

Sear us with Self-Contempt—
    When we promote Self and self-developed Concepts
    While disdaining Others and their cherished Beliefs.

Confound us with our own Inferiority—
    When we refuse to tolerate, and to cooperate,
    When we reject instead of receive.

Confute us with the Simplicity of Thy Truth—
    When we contend our Way is the only Way,
    When we arrogate to ourselves the only Key to Thy Love.

Consume us in our own Shame—
    When we contrive divisive ideological or theological Barriers,
    Then seek Thy pardon because All are not One.

Stab us with a Portion of Thine Own Anguish—
    When we permit ourselves to be used by the Forces of Evil:
    Who would divide us in order to conquer us.

Abide in us, we beseech Thee,
    As we disperse to our several Homes.

Grow within us
    Until the Holy Flame of Thy Love
        Is the only Light in our Lives;
    Until we see Others
        Only in Thy Reflection;
    Until we serve them
        Only in Thy compassionate Radiance.

As simple, as trusting, as pure, as perfect as the Love of a little Child
    Make Thou our Love:
    That we—Thy Children—Christian, Hindu, Moslem, Jew—
    That all Thy Children may truly be One;
    That in and through Thy Y's Men's Clubs, throughout Thy World,
        In and through Thy Young Men's Christian Associations,
        In and through Thy Churches, Temples, Mosques, Synagogues,
        In and through our Families and Homes, our Work and Play,

We, all Thy Children, may put into Action, may actually live
    Those universally revered and respected precepts and principles
        Voiced by Jesus of Nazareth;

That we may all walk together peacefully and joyfully in that perfect Way of Life
    Portrayed by Him as He walked this Earth;

And that All we do, evermore,
    May be as the Overflowing from our own Hearts
        Of that incomparably precious, Holy Love
            Exemplified by Him on the Cross.

—This benediction was inspired by an invocation delivered by the Rev. Frank Ricker of Columbus, Ohio, in 1946.

OPENING ONE'S HEART TO THE GREAT HEART

By Geoffrey O'Hara

Composer and Lecturer

Prayer, as I understand it, is opening one's heart to the Great Heart, the Creator. At that moment we are in tune with the Infinite, of which we are a part at all times whether we know it or not. I believe that the admonitions spoken by Jesus are true. I cannot put into words the truth and immensity of what I have just written. One must feel it for himself.

MIRACLES IN THE MAKING

By Harold R. Medina

Judge, U.S. Court of Appeals, New York

❦

If human beings are to fulfill their destiny and bear good fruit in their season, like the trees planted by the rivers of water mentioned in the First Psalm, they must develop their native capacities to the highest possible degree. This means physical development, intellectual growth, and, above all, the building up of spiritual strength and character. The first step toward spiritual strength is taken when each of us comes to realize that he or she cannot accomplish really worth while things in life all by ourselves and under our own steam. When the big I begins to fade out and we turn to the one and only true source for strength and guidance, we are on our way.

And the means by which we communicate with the High and Mighty Ruler of the Universe is prayer. When this becomes a habit, when we tell God not once but many times a day that we love Him and want Him close to us, miracles are in the making. Little by little we accustom ourselves to be obedient to God's will and to subordinate our own petty, selfish desires; and pretty soon we notice a change come over us.

I have lived a full, exciting life as a lawyer and as a judge fighting for what I thought was right. In every crisis I turned to God for help and I never called for help in vain. Prayer without faith is a meaningless gesture. And faith is not something to be turned on and off like a faucet. It is one of those deep, pervasive forces that come, not from discussion and argument, but from thoughtful reading of the Bible and meditation and the regular performance of the offices of our religion.

Prayer is the one indispensable key to spiritual strength and spiritual strength means power, power to do the things we were put on this earth to do, as Woodrow Wilson used to tell us when I was an undergraduate at Princeton.

PRAYER REQUIRES HUMILITY

By Norman Kent

Editor, *American Artist*

❧

St. John said: "If we say that we have no sin, we deceive ourselves, and the truth is not in us; but if we confess our sins, God is faithful and just to forgive us our sins, and to cleanse us from all unrighteousness."

No man is devoid of conscience but not everyone realizes that prayer is the means by which we can place its burdens on Him "who came into the world to save sinners;" that in prayer we may establish a direct communication between our conscience and our Maker, between the admission of our frailty and the wellspring of an eternal grace.

Prayer to be effective requires humility in the supplicant —a quality all too rare in the world today. We ask God for things instead of forgiveness. We neglect to thank Him for the blessings we have; instead we pray for a way out of our troubles. May God have mercy on us.

Nevertheless, the act of private prayer should be the prostration of man's spirit to that still small voice within him, until the miracle of peace pervades his being and he finds solace and direction in the reservoir of God.

"SINCERE DESIRE"

By *Palmer D. Edmunds*

Attorney

❦

I believe that our world operates under a master plan, ordained by our Creator. It is part of the design that problems, sometimes seemingly unsurmountable, should come to each individual, and it is also part of the design that in its major aspects the life.of each individual involves grappling with those problems.

Our Creator has equipped us to meet the test. He has bestowed upon each of us a free soul, and fortified that soul with powers of reason and conscience. The freedom of his individual soul and his right of private judgment are to me the most sacred things that man possesses. They attune him to the "still small voice." Through their exercise man is able to adjust himself to the life around him and thereby fulfill his destiny, at the same time finding a measure of that true happiness that comes only from such adjustment.

I like the words of the old hymn, "prayer is the soul's sincere desire, unuttered or expressed." These words imply that man does not gain insight into his problems, or strength to solve them, by formal precatory appeals, made perhaps without attempted evaluation of the considerations involved. "Sincere desire" means that he has put to use the spiritual powers with which he is endowed, and has thereby acquired, in accordance with his best lights, an inner conviction. In this world, conviction must ordinarily be manifested through deeds. The man who has acquired conviction by the process of attempting to conform himself, in his humble connection, to the master plan, finds that in the process he has been given strength to carry forward with the necessary acts.

Man's spiritual attributes being fallible, the result may not always seem fair or just. But the result in a given case is not as important as that he gains in the development of those spiritual attributes. Learning by trial and error is part of the Creator's plan. Happiness in its highest sense comes to those who persist in relating the affairs of their lives to their souls' "sincere desire," and who occupy themselves with deeds in conformity therewith. To me, this is true prayer.

PRAYER IS LISTENING

By Dr. J. Calvitt Clarke

Founder, Christian Children's Fund, Inc.

❧

Prayer to me is as much listening as speaking. I need not tell God as much as I need Him to tell me, and if I listen, He speaks in myriad ways—in the trees that climb to reach Him, in the leaves kissing each other in a summer's breeze, in the gentle sigh the rain whispers as it meets the upturned face of a flower, in the endless round sea, in the waving wheat, in the lazy falling snow and in the voice that speaks within my soul.

There are other ways, too, of course. But my problems I must solve, my work I must do, my responsibilities are my own. I cannot always kneel—the night is short, and the day's work awaits my doing. But if I pause now and then and let Him speak in His various ways, my strength is renewed, my courage is revived, and my hope is assured.

IT'S IMPOSSIBLE TO OVERESTIMATE THE VALUE OF PRAYER

By Wendell Phillips Dodge, F.R.G.S.

Explorer and Ethnologist

❦

The object of prayer is God alone, and we should supplicate the Divine Being for the blessings we stand in need of, to enjoy fellowship with God. It does not consist in the elevation of the voice, the posture of the body, the use of a form, or the extemporary use of words, nor anything of an exterior nature; but simply the offering up of our desires to God. (Matthew 15:8): "This people draweth nigh unto me with their mouth, and honoureth me with their lips; but their heart is far from me."

Secret or closet prayer is recommended by Christ (Matthew 6:6): "But thou, when thou prayest, enter into thy closet, and when thou hast shut the door, pray to thy Father which is in secret; and thy Father which seeth in secret shall reward thee openly." He, himself, set us an example of it in Luke 6:12: "And it came to pass in those days, that He went out into a mountain to pray, and continued all night in prayer to God."

Prayer in the Bible is the uplifting of the heart to God. It includes supplication, intercession, thanksgiving. As an example we have Christ's prayer in Gethsemane (Mark 14:35): "And He went forward a little, and fell on the ground, and prayed that, if it were possible the hour might pass from him," and (Mark 14:38): "Watch ye and pray, lest ye enter into temptation. The spirit is ready, but the flesh is weak." He was wont to visit the Mount of Olives.

Among the different kinds of prayer is the ejaculatory, by which the mind is directed to God. Derived from the word **ejacular,** to dart or shoot out suddenly, therefore appropriate to describe this kind of prayer which is made up of short sentences, spontaneously springing from the mind. The Scriptures give us many instances of ejaculatory prayer, which may be practiced at all times and in all places. It has a tendency to support the mind and keep it in a happy frame. It fortifies us against the temptations of the world, elevates our affections to God, and directs the mind into a spiritual channel.

In one of his celebrated lectures on "Life and Religion," Max Müller said: "What can we pray for? Not for special gifts, but only for God's mercy. We do not know what is good for us, and for others. What would become of the world if all our prayers were granted? And yet it is good to pray—that is, to live in all our joys and sorrows with God, with whom we cannot reason, but whom we can love and trust. Human misery, outward and inward, is certainly a great problem, and yet one knows from one's own life how just the heaviest burdens have been blessings. The soul must be furrowed if it is to bear fruit."

The dying words of Tennyson's Arthur, "More things are wrought by prayer than this world dreams of," clearly shows that it is not possible to overestimate the value of prayer. Prayer is efficacious. It has power with God. It brings great blessings. Nothing that men can do has so vast an influence.

> "O Lord, my God! Assist Thy loved ones
> to be firm in Thy Faith, to walk in Thy
> ways, to be steadfast in Thy Cause. Give
> them Thy grace to withstand the onslaught
> of self and passion, to follow the light of
> Divine Guidance. Thou art the Powerful,
> the Gracious, the Self-Subsisting, the Bestower,
> the Compassionate, the Almighty, the All-
> Bountiful!"

OUR POTENTIALITIES ACHIEVED BY PRAYER

By Arthur E. Summerfield

Postmaster General of the United States

❧

Man is never sufficient to himself, nor can he ever be. In everyday life all of us constantly lean upon one another, upon our mothers, our wives, our fathers, husbands, brothers and sisters, friends and associates. They support us, sustain us. For this is the way God fashioned us and our world. When we deviate from this pattern we fall into great danger.

Alone-ness is the most terrible of all situations for a man to be in while at-one-ness with our Lord and with each other is the best.

I believe our lives are a series of peaks when we rise to great heights of high faith and purpose, and valleys where we tremble in the shadows fearfully. If a man were to live on a monotone at the same level of spiritual and human strength day after day I would pity him greatly.

Dark times come into every human life; periods when in frustration, fear, pain and torment we are all too prone to cry out angrily, rebelliously, selfishly: "Why should this happen to ME?"

At such times a few unfortunate humans seek release in suicide; others may become permanently soured, trying to turn their backs on mankind and go it alone. But most of us gradually recover from our despondency and again face the tumult of living with healthy, faithful determination.

I have lived through such periods and, even as you, have recovered to join the battle once again. Our friends and relatives—all the people around us—help us in such recovery, but most of all our return to a healthy, normal outlook is the work of God.

It is His purpose that we shall live courageously, but only God can make it so. For we do not have the power of our own to accomplish this for ourselves.

It is only through prayer that we can achieve our greatest potentialities.

GOD IS MY HELPER

Rabbi Edgar F. Magnin, D.D.

Wilshire Boulevard Temple, Los Angeles, Calif.

Prayer is an integral part of my life. Every single day I turn to God, not once, but many times and thank Him for blessings received. I am sure I can never be worthy of them. I call upon Him to help me in the solution of such problems as may confront me, many of which have to do with solving other people's difficulties. I ask Him to confer upon me the light of wisdom and the heart to help.

I seek His protection for my family and friends and every night on my pillow, I pray for peace for all the world, for all nations, races and creeds, wherever they may be scattered.

Prayer is not a crutch for me. It is a part of my very tissue. It is as necessary as bread, butter and water, as the fresh air that I breathe, for God is very near; for I know that God is, and He, who created a billion worlds, is very close to me, closer than hands and feet. It is this sense of mystic communion that strengthens me and makes life sweet and wholesome and worth living.

THE POWER OF PRAYER

By Dr. Louis I. Newman

Rabbi of Congregation Rodeph Sholom, New York City

Prayer is a natural expression of the impulse to link one-self with the great, universal and eternal stream of life. Whether we pray in affirmative or negative terms, we cannot help but reach out for communion with the Supreme Intelligence and Personality Whom we call God. The religious sense arises not out of fear but out of wonderment and reverence before the majesty of the universe. The foremost utterance in religious literature is to be found in the words: "Praise ye the Lord to Whom all praise is due; Praised be the Lord to Whom all praise is due forever and ever."

It is true that in our mortal frailty we strive to draw into our being the marvelous power we behold within the Universe of God, the Creator. Our weakness prompts us to depend upon a Being, beyond ourselves, Who is the Source of ever-continuing and everlasting life. Our span of life is exceedingly brief, and even if we are arrogant for a moment, in the end we must expect that our physical structure will crumble, and, as individuals, we must take our departure from this world. We hunger for immortality, but we must be satisfied to believe that out of eternity we have come; amid eternity we live, and unto eternity we at last return. Through prayer, therefore, we strive to keep open the channels of communication between ourselves while on the earth and the Universe which the Eternal One guides.

Through prayer, we sometimes try to bend the will of the Universe into consonance with our personal wishes, for health, prosperity and happiness. We make a mistake, however, if we imagine that prayer is a magical instrument that mechanically yields us benefit. The best prayer is a formulation of our yearning to make our will the will of the Universe, and to accept the decrees of circumstance, even though we are wounded and overwhelmed. Through prayer we must always be ready to voice our thanksgiving for the benedictions of life, and to be grateful for the gifts of experience. Thus we can be spiritually prepared for the hammer-blows of fate which inevitably overtake us.

Any religious teacher who offers through prayers the attainment of specific objectives which he promises is blemishing the escutcheon of true religion. No one can guarantee a recovery from dire illness, even through supplications to God, the Healer. No one can assure an unhappy individual that he will be popular and joyous unless he adds to prayer an appreciation of the values which medical, psychological and social science can offer. Prayer must be divested of all selfish interest if it is to meet the highest standards of spiritual activity.

At the same time, we must recognize that through prayer we can remain continuously in tune with the infinite. We can capture for ourselves a glimpse of the glory of life, and an insight into the goodness of the universe. We can place our own individual nature in its universal setting, and derive from the aspiration and the searching, a comprehension of the meaning of life. The "secrets of eternity" continue to baffle us; the riddles and dilemmas of human conduct are unchangeably mysterious; the unpredictable operation of God's universe offers no key to unlock its inmost treasures. But a "man's reach should exceed his grasp, or what's a heaven for?" By the same token, a man's prayer should flow from the deepest wellsprings of his nature, and soar to the furthermost corners of the universe.

Let us turn aside from spurious prayers; from prayers that are recommended as a "crown wherewith to adorn oneself, or a spade wherewith to dig." And let us realize, that, however mighty, affluent and fortunate we may be for the moment, we have the over-arching task and duty to link our tiny self with the Universal Self; to join our feeble quest for wisdom and goodness with their Eternal Fountainhead. Thereby we can rise to our full stature as "Children of the Living God."

OMNIPOTENT

By Nick Kenny

The New York Mirror

Somebody listens to every prayer . . .
    When you are ill and burdened with care,
When your soul is bent with its weight of woe,
    Tell it to Someone who loves you so.

Someone will tell you that He understands . . .
    He'll hold your heart in His gentle hands . . .
Just like a child when the father's near,
    With God at your side, there's nothing to fear.

When days are long and nights have no end . . .
    When things go wrong, there's always one friend . . .
Just lift your eyes and you'll see Him there,
    With His gentle smile as He hears your prayer.

PRAYER AS I SEE IT

By Dr. Adam Clayton Powell, Jr.

Pastor, Abyssinian Baptist Church, New York City

❦

Prayer is direct communication with God. It is exercised in the atmosphere of devotion, consecration, belief, penitence and praise. It is the spiritual electricity that recharges the battery of the body. It is motivated by the quest of the soul. It establishes confidence in God who determines the finality of life in the realm of human destiny.

If a man prays, it is an open declaration of his belief in the Highest Power in the universe. Prayer is the resolve to the outworkings of life's situations. That's why people adhere to the theory that: "Prayer Changes Things." Of course, some skeptic or fatalist might conclude that there is a law that is inevitable which makes it impossible to change the laws of the universe without experiencing some disastrous shock by twisting it out of course into the realm of another haphazard setting. It is often argued that since the laws of nature are fixed, prayer has no power of changing the course of nature. It is asking God too much, for to change His mind would disannul His immutability and relegate Him to a sort of errand boy, rather than recognizing Him as the director and determiner of human destiny.

All of this argument springs from a natural source of reasoning without adequate knowledge of God and the totality of His operative methods. To begin with, prayer is not a natural phenomenon. It is a spiritual dynamic. It does not demand that God change His mind. True prayer lays the case in point on the altar before God and pleads:

271

"Have Thine own way, Lord! Have Thy own way!
Thou art the Potter; I am the clay
Mould me and make me, After Thy will,
While I am waiting, Yielded and still."

Prayer prepares the soul for communion with God. There is something always crying out from within man for his rightful relationship with God. The words of the Psalmist tells us this:

"As the hart longs for the flowing streams,
So longs my soul for Thee, O God.
When shall I come and behold the face of God?
(Psalm 42:1,2)

Prayer, then, is not only a conditioner for consecration, it is also a pacifier for better human relationships. I feel that we get a sense of the sovereignty of God in the words of Joyce Kilmer:

"I think that I could never see,
A poem lovely as a tree,
A tree that looks at God all day
And lifts its leafy arms to pray."

Often prayer may not only change things but what is much more important is: It changes us . . . our attitudes, behavior toward life's situations. Prayer softens the hard beds of life, changing them into cushions of resolves. Prayer is the refining fires of the soul that changes our dispositions. It becomes the symbols and declaration of the badge of true religion. When St. Paul who once was the pronounced persecutor of the Church became converted to the Christian way of life on the Damascus Highway, the first proof of his conversion was dispatched in these words: "for behold, he is praying." (Acts 9:11)

When a man prays he aligns himself with the laws of the

universe, not against them. He is in tune with the universe. Jesus established this fact in the prayer which He taught His disciples:

> "Our Father who art in heaven,
> Hallowed be they name.
> Thy kingdom come,
> Thy will be done,
> On earth as it is in heaven,
> Give us this day our daily bread;
> And forgive us our debts,
> As we also have forgiven our debtors;
> And lead us not into temptation,
> But deliver us from evil."

The adherence to prayer gives us the power to rise above narrow creeds and biased ceremonialism to the high place of the unity of all mankind in the supervised universe. We really cannot pray to God as Father and maintain a circle that is too small to include and enclose everybody. Jesus advised us to pray: "Our Father."

Then, prayer neutralizes us for the role of an open mind in our daily living. It gives God the right away: "Thy will be done, on earth as it is in heaven."

Prayer also rejects grudge by revealing that we all stand accused before the Holy Throne of God who in our penitence only have the right to join the ranks of the forgiven. And so, we pray: "And forgive us our debts, as we also have forgiven our debtors."

Since prayer seeks the protection of God, we pray: "And lead us not into temptation, but deliver us from evil."

Finally, prayer gives us what Dr. Joshua Loth Liebman called "Peace of Mind." Having established peace with God, we enter into the fellowship of prayer which removes all fears because we know that God understands and cares. This is well summed up in the Gospel Hymn written by Dr. C. Albert Tindley:

"If your body suffers pain and your health you can't regain,
And your soul is almost sinking in despair,
Jesus knows the pain you feel, He can save and He can heal;
Take your burden to the Lord and leave it there.

When your enemies assail and your heart begins to fail,
Don't forget that God in heaven answers prayer;
He will make a way for you and will lead you safely thru;
Take your burdens to the Lord and leave it there.

Leave it there . . . . leave it there,
Take your burden to the Lord and leave it there;
If you trust and never doubt, He will surely bring you out;
Take your burden to the Lord and leave it there."

WHAT CAN A MAN BELIEVE?

By Bruce Barton

Chairman of the Board, Batton, Barton, Durstine & Osborn

I believe in myself. I know that I am.

I know that I am intelligent. I know that my intelligence (and by **me** I mean, of course, mankind) is the highest and most powerful thing in the natural universe. I have intelligence.

Because I have intelligence, there must be Intelligence behind the universe. Because otherwise the universe has created something greater then itself, for it has created me, and the assumption that the lesser can produce the greater, that something can come out of nothing, does violence to my common sense. In other words, because I am, I believe God is.

"There is no unbelief;
Whoever plants a seed beneath the sod
And waits to see it push away the clod,
He trusts in God."

274

ON THE JOB AND OFF

By Lee H. Bristol, Jr.

Director of Public Relations, Bristol-Myers Products Division

A few years ago, a research study made at a steel company revealed that even the more religious employees prayed about what happened to them outside the plant—their homes, their families, etc., but seldom about what happened to them inside the factory gates on the job. It rarely occurred to them. To me, this study seemed a sad reminder of the way many of us fail to relate our Sunday faith to on-the-job situations the rest of the week. Isn't it true that we all too often fail to see the sacred side of seemingly secular situations—on the job as well as off? After all, does "Religion in Business" mean psalm-singing in the Board Room? Or does it mean, perhaps more importantly, the sacred act which a personnel manager performs when he reminds his colleagues at a meeting how human beings will be affected by some new policy change?

With all the distractions of modern business life, prayer seems to me to be one "must" for the Christian who wants to keep on the track and come closer to God's highest expectation for his life. As I see it, it is important for me periodically to shut out the telephones, the office clamor, the interruptions— if only for a minute; otherwise, how else can I hope to hear the One Voice which can call the true signals for my life?

To develop your prayer life you may find it helpful like one friend of mine to begin by actually writing a few prayers. Some find it helpful to try just reading over the words to some hymns. Family prayer can help, too, because it can give you the encouraging sense of participation with others. It helps me to get more out of church services when I pray about those services ahead of time.

At the office, of course, my prayers oftentimes may only be little "spot" prayers said hurriedly as I hurry off to some luncheon meeting or hang up the phone. But prayers, however brief, can give us the kind of through-the-day contact with God which can help us grow. And by praying about "specifics" and by praying for trouble-makers and even those I do not like, I have over and over again seen proof of how prayer can condition the atmosphere in which one works, how prayer can change even the seemingly impossible, awkward situations of life. Prayer can work miracles. Prayer can work the miracle of helping us to "forgive the unforgivable and love the unlovable." What's more, developing a prayer life can be for us the same kind of adventure it has been for an old friend who called me Friday afternoon. He has many problems in his current job, but he told me "They're nothing, Lee! The big news is what I've discovered about prayer!"

Certainly prayer has been the mark of the Christian from the start. Look at the early Christians. We are told "they continued steadfastly in the apostles' doctrine and fellowship, and in breaking of bread, and in **prayers**." (Acts 2:42)

In prayer you and I in **this** world can be with Our Lord in His Kingdom. We can come back at our lives and see the same places and the same faces but we can see them all differently —because we have been with Jesus.

Brother Lawrence, several centuries ago, washing pots and pans in the monastery kitchen said he learned to feel the presence of God in his work. And even today, there are men of faith who tell us they can sense God's presence in even their busiest days.

My own first steps at prayer have been faulty, erratic, perhaps naive, but in just what little progress I have made I have had a glimmer of what I once saw in the deep-lined face of a very old bishop. His very eyes told me of his faith, that he had taken Our Lord at His word and found that it works!

HOW SHOULD I PRAY?

By Dr. Norman Vincent Peale

Minister, Marble Collegiate Church, New York City

❦

How should I pray? Day after day the letters come in asking this question—which is, after all, the very heart of religion. One of the answers I give has to do with the prayer of experiencing. To my way of thinking this is the highest order of prayer.

How can you experience the presence of God?

Across the street from my office in New York City is the Metropolitan Museum of Art. One day not long ago, I went over there during my lunch hour and there I was taught a great lesson on How to Pray. The first mistake I made was to visit the museum when I was pushed for time. I walked quickly from room to room, glancing at the pictures and thinking, "I'm certainly not much of a highbrow. These just don't say anything to me."

Then, suddenly, I came upon one of the museum guards, standing before the El Greco **View of Toledo.** He was absorbed by it, yet to me the picture was little more than dramatic painting of some buildings sitting on a green hill under a wild blue sky.

The guard turned and saw me looking at him. "Never has there been such a landscape," he said. "And to think when I first came here, it didn't speak to me at all."

I asked him what he meant. "Well," he said, "at that time I didn't know how to experience a picture. But as I saw it day after day, I began to brood over it and wait for it. And after a while, it began to speak. Try it yourself. Wait for it. It's worth the time."

This was the finest lesson in art appreciation I have ever had. But it was also a lesson in prayer. Wait! Waiting is not one of the fine arts of this century, but if you want to learn how to experience the presence of God, you must first learn how to wait.

And you can't wait comfortably if you're under the pressure of time. That's why it's so important to choose a prayer-hour which you can guarantee. I personally prefer the late night hours, because I know they won't be disturbed. I get all ready for bed; then, for a while, I read. My reading may include some inspirational pamphlet or book; but it always includes the Bible. I read until I sense that I have slowed down from the rapid pace of the day. And then . . . I wait!

I simply relax and am quiet. I begin to thank God for all that has come my way. Even when I have worries that weigh me down, I start my prayers by thanking God, one by one, for His gifts to me this day. I pay no attention to time, but I pray prayers of thanksgiving until I get a wonderful feeling of well-being. I feel that after all, this world is governed by the divine plan. . .

And again I wait. If I sense that there is something blocking my contact with God, I try to discover what it is, and ask for forgiveness. Then I wait again.

What am I waiting for? I am hoping to experience the presence of God. And sometimes if I wait long enough, there comes a wonderful moment when I **know** that God is close.

"It's worth your time to wait," the museum guard said.

Indeed it is! For when we let Him come, we received joy, peace, and life in great abundance.

—Reprinted from **Guideposts Magazine**, June, 1958, issue, with the permission of the author.

FAITH CAN CARRY YOU ON

By Henry J. Kaiser

Industrialist

❦

Faith, it is my conviction, is the key to unlocking limitless powers of the mind, the heart, the soul . . . Faith in God . . . Faith and belief that right triumphs over wrong . . . Faith and belief that you can win out over disasters and setbacks . . . Faith and belief that smash fear . . . Faith and belief in the ultimate realization of your hopes that are right.

Again and again I have seen the tremendous power of faith.

What faith can mean to your own future is summed up in a brief quotation from an author whose name I regret I do not know. He declared:

"All things are possible to him who has faith.

Because faith sees and recognizes the power that means accomplishment.

Faith looks beyond all boundaries. It transcends all limitations. It penetrates all obstacles. And it sees the goal. Faith never fails. It is a miracle worker."

I believe that with all my heart.

You surely will feel the need of some sustaining Power beyond and above yourself.

It is the tragedy of this age that whole races of man seem to have sunk into a faithless surrender to fatalism and a confused despair. They feel that they have lost control over their own destiny — that war, tyranny, and personal bewilderment have swallowed them up and tossed them about like hopeless robots. They follow false prophets of Godlessness and materialism. You must battle the ideologies and philosophies of imposed destiny and disbelief, in order to save and utilize your immortal soul and the Power we call God.

You may have to search hard, in this disbelieving time, to discover religious belief that can sustain you throughout life. You may find it in prayer and in silent meditation; you may find it in the quiet of a church and the understanding of a minister; you may find it in the teachings of the Bible and the philosophers whose secrets of the good life stand the test of modern psychology and today's problems.

Only you can work out a code to live by and a faith that means you need never be defeated. See if you cannot find for yourself the faith that says, as does Philippians 4:13—"I can do all things through Christ which strengtheneth me."

I have seen demonstrated beyond possibility of doubt, the words of Christ—written in the 9th chapter, 23rd verse of Mark: "If thou canst believe, all things are possible to him that believeth."

Will you join me now in a prayer for a *living* faith?

O God, help us find the spark of soul
Thou hast dropped in every human being,
Help us live each day by faith—
Faith in our fellow men and our highest aspirations,
Faith that brings us fellowship with Thee
And gives us eyes to see
God in everything.

Amen.

ESSENTIAL VIRTUES
IN EFFECTIVE PRAYER

By David O. McKay

President, Church of Jesus Christ of Latter-day Saints

❦

Prayer is the pulsation of a yearning, loving heart in tune with the Infinite. It is a message of the soul sent directly to a loving Father. The language is not mere words but spirit vibration.

If parents and teachers would teach their children to live upright lives, they themselves must live uprightly. If they would teach children to pray, they must first have prayer in their own hearts. Jesus Christ, the great Teacher, was Himself the embodiment of all that He taught.

Let us consider the essential virtues in effective prayer.

The first and most fundamental virtue is **Faith.** It is the height of folly, if not deep hypocrisy, to pretend to pray to a being in whom one does not believe. ". . . He that cometh to God must believe that he is, and that he is a rewarder of them that diligently seek him." (Hebrews 11:6.) A disbeliever in the efficacy of prayer implies atheism; a belief in God brings peace to the soul. An assurance that God is our Father, into whose presence we can go for comfort and guidance, is a never failing source of comfort.

The greatest need of the world today is a sincere faith in an overruling providence. Too many men have forgotten God and eliminated Him from their lives; they have transgressed His laws; they have broken the everlasting covenant. That is one reason why there is strife, unrest and suffering in the world.

You cannot imagine an effective prayer without visualizing

and feeling a personal God. Think as you will, you cannot conceive of a power beyond personality. Electricity, the atom, all the mighty forces that man has discovered are inferior to God's greatest creation— man. Go to Him in faith, believing.

Reverence is another essential virtue in effective prayer. This virtue is exemplified in the model prayer given by the Savior in the words "Hallowed be thy name." You can imagine an irreverent man sneering at things holy, but you cannot imagine him praying.

Reverence is a principle which needs emphasis throughout the Church; it needs to be taught by example by priesthood officers and the auxiliary teachers. It should be exemplified in classrooms, and particularly in our houses of worship.

A third essential element in effective prayer is **Sincerity.** Prayer is the yearning of the spirit. The Savior said:
". . . When thou prayest, thou shalt not be as the hypocrites are: for they love to pray standing in the synagogues and in the corners of the streets, that they may be seen of men. Verily I say unto you, They have their reward.

"But thou, when thou prayest, enter into thy closet, and when thou hast shut thy door, pray to thy Father which is in secret; and thy Father which seeth in secret shall reward thee openly." (Matthew 6:5-6.)

The wicked king in **Hamlet** sensed the futility of insincere praying when he cried, "My words fly up; my thoughts remain below. Words without thoughts never to Heaven go."

Sincere praying implies that when we ask for any virtue or blessing we should work for the blessing and cultivate the virtue. A good and striking example of the effectiveness of this kind of praying is George Washington Carver, a venerable Negro.

On one occasion some students and others who were on the campus at Harvard saw an old colored man, rather plainly dressed, walking along, passing by unnoticed. As he walked up the steps to one of the buildings he was met by a group of men who were waiting for him, and they ushered him into the presence of some of the leading doctors of that institution. He was George Washington Carver, who was born a nameless slave. He never knew his mother, and was bought back by his owner in exchange for an old, broken-down race horse.

When men look at his accomplishments today they declare he was a genius, and undoubtedly they are right. The basis of that genius, however, was a prayerful soul.

When a section of our country was suffering terribly from a diseased crop, people sent Dr. Carver some specimens of their diseased plants. He told them what was wrong and how to cure it. After his treatment had proved correct, they sent him a check for $100, promising the same amount monthly. He sent back the check telling them that as God did not charge anything for growing the peanuts, he should not charge anything for curing them.

One day he was asked how he found time for all his accomplishments. He answered, "Chiefly because I have made it a rule to get up every morning at four o'clock. I go out into the woods. Alone there with the things I love most, I gather specimens and study the great lessons that Nature is so eager to teach me. In the woods each morning, while most other persons are sleeping, I best hear and understand God's plan for me." And he continued, as he bent over his microscope, "God has been mighty good to this poor, old negro."

A newspaper man who interviewed him later said it sounded like a benediction when he said, "God bless you."

A reverent, sincere heart! God will answer that heart, and

He is no respecter of persons. Sincerity of soul brought to Joseph Smith his glorious vision in the spring of 1820.

Another essential virtue I shall name is **Loyalty.** Why pray for the Kingdom of God to come unless we have in our hearts a desire and a willingness to aid in its establishment? Praying for His will to be done and then not trying to live it, gives one a negative answer at once.

If we pray for the success of some cause or enterprise, manifestly we are in sympathy with it. When, therefore, we pray for the Kingdom of God to come on earth, we should work for its establishment, or our prayers are mockeries. It is the height of disloyalty to pray for God's will to be done, and then fail to conform our lives to that will.

A final essential virtue is **Humility.** Not the outward, hypocritical pretense of a Uriah Heap, but a humility that springs from the heart, from an absence of self-righteousness. Self-respect is a virtue, but self-conceit is an inhibition.

The principle of humility and prayer leads one to feel a need of divine guidance. Self-reliance is a virtue, but with it should go a consciousness of the need of superior help. A consciousness that as you walk firmly in the pathway of duty, there is a possibility of your making a misstep, and with that consciousness is a prayer, a pleading that God will inspire you to avoid that false step. Students would find great help in their studies if they would just grasp that truth.

They can learn their lessons, but with the inspiration and the intelligence they have inherited from their parents, their native ability, there should always be associated a consciousness that there is something greater to accomplish than that which their own native ability will give them power to accomplish. A consciousness that God can inspire them just at the right moment. You do not have to kneel down to get that if it is in your heart. Remember, prayer is a soul vibration.

Students, pray for divine guidance and you will find that you will have greater success in your studies.

Teachers, when you are downhearted and discouraged because you cannot get some boys and girls to heed your teachings, or even remain quiet in the class, just pray to God to give you power to touch their hearts. Yearn for it, and you will see some plan, there will be a flash which will come to your mind to aid you in winning those children.

True humility is a consciousness that here, in this old physical world, one may be in harmony with an infinite power, a source of strength and guidance; and I testify to you that this is true. "Humility is not a weak quality; it must be carefully distinguished from a groveling spirit. There is such a thing as honest pride and self-respect. Though we may be servants of all, we should be servile to none."

These virtues—faith, reverence, sincerity, loyalty, and humility—you will find exemplified in the Lord's prayer, which was given in answer to the question of the disciples: "Lord, teach us how to pray."

"Our Father which art in heaven, . . ." is an acknowledgment of His existence. He that cometh to God must believe that He is.

". . . Hallowed by thy name," expresses reverence.

"Thy kingdom come. Thy will be done, . . ." is at once a plea for its establishment on earth, and an implied promise loyally to cooperate in bringing peace on earth, good will to men.

"Give us this day our daily bread," is an acknowledgment of our dependence upon God for our very subsistence—at least that we are in need of His help and guidance in all our constant strivings.

". . . Forgive us our debts (or trespasses), as we forgive our debtors," (or those who trespass against us) makes our forgiveness entirely dependent upon the sincerity of our hearts in forgiving others, and upon the extent to which we render forgiveness. That is a wonderful principle—we shall get forgiveness in proportion to our forgiveness of those who have offended us. That goes into the very soul, the very center of our being, and that is the source of effective prayer.

". . . Lead us not into temptation, but deliver us from evil: . . ." is the yearning plea of a humble heart for strength and guidance of an acknowledged Superior Power.

What a glorious world this would be if in our homes, in our business offices, in our classrooms, in all phases of daily life we could feel the presence of God—at least be conscious that we can go to Him, and have Him guide us and keep us throughout the day!

God gave us power to pray sincerely, to live worthily, and thus be better prepared to teach effectively, I humbly pray in the name of Jesus Christ, Amen.

—Reprinted from "The Instructor" with the permission of the author.

PRAYER IS POWER

By Floyd Starr

Founder and President, Starr Commonwealth for Boys

In my childhood home the Bible was read aloud daily. The positive march of the words made me feel safe and strong long before I understood their meaning. So I repeated them to myself whenever things went wrong. And I always felt better because of it. Unknowingly, I was praying. Later when I ran into a blank wall in establishing the work of redirecting confused boys I turned to my Heavenly Father, and in the wall I found an opening.

In 1936 our schoolhouse burned to the ground. It happened at night. Only a third of the cost was covered by insurance. The next morning one of my boys came up to me as I stood looking down on the blackened foundation and said, "Don't be discouraged, Uncle Floyd. Here's two cents, all I have in my account. It isn't much but if we pray folks will send us the rest." How could I have forgotten the promise "Faith is the substance of things hoped for, the evidence of things not seen?" Rebuilding began at once and when completed our school was debt free.

There are times when it is difficult to have faith enough. This is where prayer comes in. As Franklin's kite led him to the discovery of electricity, so prayer puts us in communication with God and the reassurance of his love and power. If we pursued prayer as diligently and perfected our approach as constantly as we have the use of electricity, nothing could prevent our winning the best God has planned for us. I found that once the wires were strung and I learned how to plug into that source of power, I gained courage. This worked best when I had put forth my entire effort for the good of the whole.

A chapel for the campus had been a longtime hope, but daily needs kept pressing. Rising prices sent us to the architect. When our little church was in process of construction the unexpected caused us some bad moments but before the day of dedication all bills had been met. I believe this came about because we all continued with one accord in prayer and supplication.

Suddenly a friend of many years was desperately ill. A man of quality and performance, unable to accept the verdict, his family telegraphed us to pray for him. The quality of the man was so high, the need of the world for his kind so great that, as our habit was, word went to all the cottages. The tide turned and he was restored to health.

A former Starr boy, on furlough to be with his young wife at the birth of their first child, found the lives of both in jeopardy, so he wired us. Word went out and prayers went up to add our prayers to his. I guess God couldn't refuse the sincere petitions of teen-aged boys for a fine young family that seemed close because the soldier-father had once been a Starr boy. For when the happy letter telling us that all was well came to us I heard them calling to each other along the walks, "Hey, fellows, Andy's folks are O.K." There was a special lilt in their voices that struck an answering note in my heart. That boy had conquered much and is now taking his place among men of quality and position.

I have had repeated letters from my old boys telling me how prayer had helped them over many a hump. The knowledge that they are in league with their heavenly Father enriches their lives and multiplies their courage, gives them a sort of "My Father's business," incentive. This means something very special to our boys. Most of them haven't had much reason to love and respect fathers. One of them once wrote me, "I love you as I would like to have loved my own father." A vivid interpretation of boyish suffering by one who had been denied his birthright.

During the war many of my boys were under fire in Korea. Their letters seldom failed to mention the beauty of the campus, the peace in the chapel, the moments of quiet counsel, the friends they had made and the feeling of worth they came to know.

In a moment of respite from dirt, discomfort, din and danger they felt safe and strong remembering these things. My good friend, Mrs. Edith Rhetts Tilton, used to tell the stories of great music to the grade children of that city as a prelude to hearing their musical interpretations by the Detroit Symphony Orchestra. She once said that after World War II a young veteran told her he was able to keep his sanity under the demands of war by recalling loved passages of Beethoven's Fifth, his shield and buckler. This, too, is prayer.

Prayer is Power. Blessed power!

DO SOMETHING YOURSELF FOR GOD'S HELP

By David W. Armstrong

Retired National Director, Boys' Clubs of America

The most important thing I can say about prayer is that I believe in it. However, I also believe that if you ask God for help that you have to do something yourself. You cannot just put the matter in His hands and wait for results.

"GREATER THAN THE H-BOMB"

By *Eddie Cantor*

Radio and Television Comedian

❦

The most overworked word in America today is "security." Economic "security," psychological "security," national "security." It has become a frightening word. Its mere mention panics us into insecurity—sends us frantically searching for new ways to win the coveted key to happiness.

Every day headlines shriek news of "security" developments: the jet plane, the guided missile, the atom bomb, the even more devastating H-bomb.

But more powerful than all of them put together is prayer. It may not make headlines, but it's the only real security for the life lines of the world.

I've always known about the power of prayer—from the days on New York's lower East Side when my very orthodox grandmother prayed that this skinny, popeyed kid would somehow survive without adequate food, clothes, fresh air, medical care. I'm convinced my early battle for life was won by Grandma Esther and her only weapon against poverty: prayer.

In show business I'm known as a "single" act. That's not true. I was never alone; my partner was prayer. Every step of the way, we walked hand in hand. With the years came security in all its forms—fame, a family, prestige, money.

I recall the morning of the Normandy invasion in 1944. Leaving my New York hotel to go to a rehearsal, I was almost stampeded by a swarm of people making their way to St. Patrick's Cathedral. Some compelling force swept me along with them. Inside the Cathedral it was easy to pick out the hundreds of other non-Catholics. They didn't know the ritual, but they all felt at home in this house of God. We prayed together. A great calm came over the crowd. Despite the terrible battles that lay ahead, we felt a sense of peace—and security. We knew we'd win. We had the power of prayer on our side.

Whenever I think of that morning, I think of Father Peyton of Los Angeles. He created the slogan, "The family that prays together stays together." It became the theme for the fine radio program "Family Theater." It would make a good theme for the entire nation: "People who pray together stay together."

My latest proof-positive of the power of prayer was last September when I was taken to the hospital with a heart attack. At first, my doctors weren't sure. For a little while, I wasn't sure.

Then the letters and phone calls started pouring in. A hundred and forty-three people in a Pennsylvania town donated blood to the Red Cross in my name; every pint was like a direct transfusion to my battered heart. A priest in Ohio telephoned that candles were being burned for me and prayers were being said. A family in Boston contributed money to Brandeis University in my name. Every message was a prayer. The thousands of others who wrote or telephoned the hospital ended with: "We're praying for you, Eddie."

Each time I heard a new message, new strength surged through me. Fear left me. Security returned. I knew I was going to be all right. The power of prayer was at work.

Prayer is the only foolproof system. President Eisenhower, a man trained in warfare, is the first to proclaim this truth. The overwhelming force of a nation united in prayer would result in a security that no man-made weapon could destroy.

Stop searching for false "security." Real security is yours for the asking—if only you "pray as you go."

A CONTINUING REASSURANCE
OF HIS PRESENCE

By Maud Hart Lovelace

Author and Novelist

❦

I believe in praying as I believe in breathing. An involuntary procedure, prayer runs along with the day, following the convolutions of work and play, duties, problems and delights.

Of course, I pray in more formal fashion at stated times —before going to sleep at night, before starting work in the morning. And I certainly would not relinquish the fellowship of praying with others in church. But it is my way to turn to God at any hour, with a small joy as well as with a sorrow, with plans, hopes, thanks—even wishes.

Not that I expect Him to stay the course of the planets while He grants my often misguided petitions. But since He is love and is everywhere, "nearer than hands and feet," one may share everything with Him, and there is a blessed release in doing so. What He gives, I earnestly believe, in response to such spontaneous prayers, is strength, insight, appreciation, serenity, but above all a continuing reassurance of His presence.

As for formal prayers, they differ, naturally according to one's faith. But I love to say upon awaking the opening verses of the greater doxology. They include the whole world and sweep away pettiness as the sun is sweeping away shadows, focussing one's thoughts on the glory of the unseen creator, the One who gives us the gift of life.

"Glory be to God on high, and on earth peace, good will towards men. We praise thee, we bless thee, we worship thee, we glorify thee, we give thanks to thee for thy great glory, O Lord God, heavenly King, God the Father Almighty. . ."

WE NEED THE POWER OF PRAYER

By Dr. Wernher Von Braun

Scientist and Engineer, Director of Development Operations,
Army Ballistic Missile Agency,
Redstone Arsenal

❦

Belonging to the group of scientists and engineers who need sober facts for their studies and hardware for their work, I find it difficult to express feelings and irrational incidents. I am more at ease when reporting about the thrust of missiles or the feasibility of space travel than in revealing inner feelings. To me prayers are sublime and I would rather leave it to a minister or a great philosopher to lecture on the power of praying. However, being asked to supply a contribution to the inspiring and valuable statements compiled in this book, I consider the honor too great and the objectives of the book too worthy to decline this offer.

I do not think I have experienced one of the striking cases where your prayers come true the moment you say them, and the number of less significant events in my life, when prayers did help me, might be too great and their results not striking and convincing enough to be mentioned here. But I do know from experience that prayers bring actual and immediate relief from worries and I personally believe that today's mankind needs the power of prayer more than ever before. Let me give you two reasons to prove my ideas.

Praying is concentrating. Do we really have to consult a psychologist to tell us how important it is to forget our past and present worries and to focus our ideas on something else? The expanding workload and responsibilities of our professional activities, the necessity to keep or improve the standards of living for our families, the compelling need for fulfilling civic duties, and last but not least our easy overindulgence in the diversified field of present entertainment, leave us less and less time for self-evaluation and self-reflection, in short for concentrating on our ego, our shortcomings, and our failures. I sincerely believe we should devote more time to self-analysis, thus taking a first step in the direction toward improved morale and greater ethics in this world.

Praying is hoping. Who would raise the slightest doubt that hope is one of the greatest factors of success which gives us courage, strength, and energy to accomplish the most difficult tasks? Whenever we are discouraged and ready to give up, hope will mobilize new energies, help us cross the barrier of our own inadequacy, and finally contribute to success.

A great number of other reasons should be added to this list to give a complete picture of the beneficial effects and results of praying, the need for which is as old as mankind itself.

More important though than all personal benefits which we receive from praying, let us not forget to pray for our friends, neighbors, and even enemies, and above all for the honor of God who created the great universe in which we are about to explore more and more scientific facts in deepest reverential awe.

PRAYER IS POWER

By Ralph Leroy Nafziger

Bakery Industrialist

❦

"Ask, and it shall be given you; seek, and ye shall find; knock, and it shall be opened unto you"

"For everyone that asketh receiveth; and he that seeketh findeth; and to him that knocketh it shall be opened."—
Matt. 7:7-8

"Therefore I say unto you, what things soever ye desire, when ye pray, believe that ye receive them, and ye shall have them."—
Mark 11:24

What a man dares to do, he does. What he thinks he can do, he can. Upon this philosophy is based our American way of life, with its freedom for a man to do what he can, or thinks he can, do.

Thus have free Americans built great industries, become successful attorneys and doctors, and otherwise helped themselves to the good life.

Prayer is more—much more—than a supplication for divine aid in little things to satisfy petty desires or the needs of the moment.

Prayer, to me, is a silent communion from which comes confidence and inner strength. It is an enabling and ennobling act of the spirit whereby with a combination of humility and courage, realization and imagination, we undertake to bridge the span between dreams and accomplishments.

295

Prayer is a combination of two things. One is the very seeking, the will to strive. As Matthew said, "Seek, and ye shall find."

The second, equally essential ingredient is confidence, or faith. Mark worded it, "When ye pray, believe that ye receive them, and ye shall have them."

Just two crucial times when prayer has worked for me will emphasize the strength of my belief.

The first, when I was in college, was the time I was called home because my father's little bakery had become bankrupt. The easy and logical solution would have been to settle the matter and resume my study of architecture. My decision was to build a business from this bankruptcy, on the foundation of faith with those creditors who otherwise would have taken a loss. With fortitude, determination, and prayer, a trinity upon which great enterprises are built, a great baking business was founded.

The second occasion came with the great crash of '29. It obliterated me. An easy alternative would have been to renege on my spoken word. But the course which commanded me was to honor spoken commitments at whatever cost, and then start again with nothing—except the determination that is born in confidence and prayer.

The lesson is ageless. Look not for help outside yourself. Look not to the government, or family, or elsewhere, for handouts of any kind. What is built on dependency is built on sand. Shift for yourself, with the divine help that is vouchsafed every man.

"Seek, and ye shall find . . . when ye pray, believe that ye receive them, and ye shall have them."

PRAYERS: FOR EACH HIS OWN

By Mildred Seydell

Publisher and Editor of *Seydell Quarterly*

Several years ago there was a popular song called **To Each His Own.** This title expresses my idea concerning prayer. Prayers that suit other people are sometimes distasteful to me. For instance, there are prayers that bargain—saying to God if You do this I'll do that or prayers that instruct God—telling Him what He should, or should not do.

A prayer that brings one in the closest communion with God, nearest the source of Divine Love, is the prayer best suited for the one who prays.

Such a prayer for me is short, silent and simple. Always it begins: **Thy Will Be Done.** Knowing that when I accept to be in harmony with **All Goodness** I am making my life count. I am inspired and strengthened. I no longer depend upon my own intelligence, but through prayer I connect with the one universal, all intelligent mind, God.

The prayer I make is short, but incessant, from waking hours to sleeping ones. Beginning all activities with a prayer followed by deep meditation on what I want to accomplish. I never pray for **things** believing that God knows my needs better than I, and that He will graciously supply them. And so I give thanks for my blessings and open my heart and mind to receive instructions, which come to me through inspiration when I am truly humble and ready to obey, having attained this estate through silent prayers of faith.

I have found that when one prays to be able to do God's will rather than to have one's own personal desires satisfied prayer is answered gloriously! And though perhaps denied the things one has ardently wished for, one is given instead a peace and joy beyond the imagination of any selfish mind.

297

A PATTERN FOR BECOMING

By Dr. Evelyn Millis Duvall

Author and Family Life Educator

Prayer is not a posture; it is a perspective. A multitude of details harass a busy life unless there are intervals when the spirit can look up and see the mass of minutia in proper proportion.

When I feel under pressure, I find release in stopping where I am and tuning my spirit in on the eternal verities. By stepping back and trying to see how God looks at the situation of the moment, I gather the courage to resist the less worthy for the nobler direction. It is in seeking the God's-eye view of life that prayer has its greatest meaning for me.

Prayer to me is the recurrent receptivity that makes true creativity and nobility seem possible. In moments of earnest seeking the good life, I am close to the great souls of all time who have stretched upward and outward. This to me is the fellowship of kindred spirits that provides the only valid answer to the question of loneliness. This is the real sense of brotherhood of man that keeps me close to the heart of all men everywhere under the fatherhood of God. Without such possibilities for regularly getting a deep sense of belonging, life would be petty. With prayerful sensitivity to others' similar strivings, I feel akin to them, and close to God our Father.

Prayer is so much more than petition. At its best it is a pattern for becoming. There are times, of course, when a troubled heart calls out to God for help. As a little child comes to its parents for solace and guidance, I need those great resources outside myself. Like a child, too, I look to the Master Life for the model of being what I would wish to become.

THE VALUE AND EFFICIENCY OF PRAYER

By Nolan D.C. Lewis, M.D.

Director of Research, New Jersey Neuro-psychiatric Institute

Prayer in some form is an element in all modern and in most ancient religions. It constitutes a petition to establish a spiritual communion with God, His representative or some object of worship. By means of prayer expressions of supplication, thanksgiving, praise, adoration and confession as well as requests for what is needed for biological survival are made with the hope that they will be acceptable.

Prayers may be made by a person in solitude or as a member of a group in a public place of worship. They may be spoken as words or expressed silently as thoughts. They may be spontaneously created or read from a prayer book with an attitude of reverence. They may become degraded from the spiritual to the mechanical as they are in some oriental religions, or as they are expressed by gesture or by extreme brevity. They may be combined with many other forms of worship.

Prayer is known to be of particular value in its reflex effect on the feelings of the worshiper, but this influence is usually not considered to constitute its whole value. In theory how can prayer influence the divine will? How can a belief in the power of prayer be reconciled with the various views of divine decrees? Several questions of this nature indicate the difficulties of understanding the relationship between the human mind and the supreme creator in the universe. However, regardless of the nature of theological formulations or of the speculations of others less qualified concerning the inconsistencies, the need for prayer and its power have to be acknowledged on the basis of demonstration. At the very least man is convinced that he thus becomes associated with his Maker.

It is conceded by most authorities that prayer to be acceptable must be for things in keeping with God's will as it is revealed in His word and that prayer for mere temporal or earthly good as well as that for moral support must be made in submission to the Will. However, it is usually assumed that the will of God has been made to encompass these desires.

Since prayer is a human phenomenon and is of human interest and expression, it reveals psychological characteristics. Something happens in the human pattern of life, which seeks fulfillment of wishes and cravings and it is at such a point that autosuggestion, the well-known psychological mechanism and principle asserts itself. The effect of autosuggestion is in direct proportion to the decrease of deliberate effort. Surrendering to the Almighty is the necessary attitude for the most effective operation of autosuggestion.

Prayer engenders reflective autosuggestion which when sustained over a period of time tends to bring about a desired change in mental outlook. The sensation of being possessed by the presence of a power greater than oneself invites a feeling of something positive and worthful which exerts a therapeutic strengthening effect. Prayer of this kind creates the condition under which autosuggestion can function in solving problems and producing tranquility.

Some persons prefer to pray in solitude, while others attending a public service in which several are joined in a common attitude of trust, hope and confidence, derive their greatest benefit. Here in the group, one finds the condition most favorable for therapeutic autosuggestion and the impressions on the unconscious mind may have a lasting effect which may come to full fruition in circumstances of life and living quite remote from those found in the formal worship situation.

It must be understood that from any point of view (theological, philosophical or scientific), prayer and autosuggestion are not incompatible phenomena, and that the answers to prayer must come in ways that are natural through psychological laws and processes.

Prayer is frequently a request for something needed in an emergency as a relief from fear, anxiety and acute threats of death. Here it reveals psychologically the elements of an ideal relationship between a child and its father such as expressions of atonement for misbehavior, gratitude, respect, adoration, love, and forgiveness, as well as the plea for aid in a specific stress situation.

When one is in doubt, prayer has a reassuring effect and is highly supportive of mental health. The mental ventilation, catharsis and relaxation involved tends to ease the strains of inner conflict and to bring about a clearer perspective. The feeling of being cleansed and forgiven, the thanks for food and friends, and for being delivered from worry, the hopes and aspirations offered in prayer all tend to be stimulating in quality since the trust in a higher, stronger power makes one more sensitive to pleasant life experiences and sharpens the tendency to success.

Many personal problems are started on the way to solution through prayer by means of the insurgence of psychic energy in the unconscious mental process, as sincere people are apt to do something about the matters they pray about. They pray, but may work hard as well, for what they desire. This aids in the fulfillment of the wish. (E.g., people may pray for better crops and then till the soil more scientifically and daily life assumes a deeper meaning and a higher quality.) There is an old saying to the effect that "God feeds the little birds but does not throw it into the nest."

301

A PRAYER IS A TALK WITH GOD

By Mrs. Henry S. Blake

Homemaker and Presswoman

❀

Prayer is the greatest blessing and hope of mankind. It opens to each individual human life a source of help and courage and inspiration for successful living, regardless of race, creed or color. It enables us to understand the meaning of life and the purpose of God's Kingdom on earth and it helps us to realize that each life has a special work to do in our Creator's plans for the world.

At an early age I was taught to depend on myself as much as possible and to ask for help from others only when it was necessary. This became a habit with me not only in regard to my human family but in my relationship with my Heavenly Father as well.

I have had no great personal tragedy in my life to impress on me my dependence on God for help and guidance. I had many problems in my life but most of them were little ones and I struggled alone to solve them as I thought God wanted me to do. I know now that I needed divine guidance for these little vexatious problems as well as the bigger ones. How much easier my life would have been if I had asked my Maker to share my burdens with me instead of depending so much on my own efforts.

My greatest regret today is that I did not realize earlier in my life the wonderful blessing of prayer. It is true that I made a fair success in my efforts as a homemaker, wife and mother, during the years. My husband was outstanding for his quality of character and his contribution to our local community, our state and our country of the better things of life. Our three children are now grown to maturity and each is making a record for himself for Christian living. All these things are a big consolation to me now.

Now, since I have learned the value of prayer in my life, God is very real to me. I understand now the purpose of His kingdom in the world and I know I have a definite place in His plans for work to do to help carry on His plans for the human race. I know He needs my help as I need His. I no longer struggle alone with my problems as I once did for I know He sees and understands them all and is not only willing to help me and direct me in my efforts but is anxious to do so for His own sake as well as mine. How simple it is for Him with His great wisdom to know the answers to our many perplexities of life and to guide us along the way.

The sudden death of my husband two years ago was a crushing blow to me and our family for we had been very close to each other in sympathy and understanding. Inwardly I grieve for the loss of his companionship and my incentive for creative activities in my different fields of interest and endeavor no longer seems to exist. My friends, knowing how close to each other we were through the years of our marriage, marvel at my courage and fortitude and my adjustment to life without him. They do not know of the heartaches I have tried to hide behind a cheery smile. My family and friends and acquaintances have been marvelous to me in this time of sorrow and I know God has sent them to me to give me courage and comfort. I have carried on my work in the church and community as before although at times it has seemed almost impossible to go on. In times like that I try to forget my grief and disappointments and count my many blessings, always with a prayer in my heart for help.

Although my conception of God and His kingdom and the

purpose of our life in this world was once vague and uncertain, I now fully realize the meaning of it all. I believe prayer is the greatest blessing of the human race for it keeps us in tune with the Infinite and it brings joy and peace beyond understanding into our lives. We should make it a habit to talk to God about our blessings as well as our needs, and depend on him always for direction and help. When we do these things we can be sure of a successful life here on this earth. These are the reasons I believe in prayer with all my heart.

SINCERITY IS THE ESSENCE

By George E. Sokolsky

Columnist, Author and Lecturer

We all pray instinctively.

The man who shouts, "My God!" when he is drowning prays as eloquently as the clergyman who makes a rhetorical big deal out of the same thought.

But the essence of prayer is the sincerity of motive. Does one really hope that a Divine Power will intervene for righteousness, or is he seeking some special favor for himself?

If the prayer is only for benefits, it would seem to be motivated by the same considerations as a transaction in business. It is as though one were to say: "God! I'll pray to you, but you fix me up so that I get something out of it."

The sincere man wants no contract. He expects no reward. He prays to be in communion with God. He pours out his heart to God. He feels the mercy of God upon him.

This is true in all religions for the blessings of the Divine Power are upon those who seek them with pure heart and noble purpose.

THOUGHT BRIDGE TO THE INFINITE

By Dr. Paul A. Siple

Explorer and Geographer with Office of Research and
Development, U.S. Army

❦

Although I've not always understood other people's concepts of God nor their evaluations of prayer, I've never tried to convince anyone that my understanding is better, at least as long as they are content with their contact with the Infinite. My God is all that is beautiful and orderly in nature. The orderliness and energy of an atom—the symmetry of a crystal —the intricate, vital structures of living tissue; or the beauty of a sunset—of a flower—or of kindly eyes, is evidence of my God at every hand. The ugly, disorderly and chaotic things in the world are worthy only of destruction or modification.

It is only natural, therefore, that my concept of prayer is the willful orderliness of mind thinking pleasant and beautiful thoughts. A prayerful mind is one in tune with the orderliness and beauty of the universe. When one needs advice from the infinite source of power he can receive it only when his mind is an orderly part of the universe.

A chaotic, scatterbrained mind, full of selfishness and ugly thoughts, couldn't hope for an answer to prayer if it were sought, for it has no means of hearing the answer.

Thus I conclude that all good thoughts of an orderly mind which emanate with a depth of kindliness and beauty are born of prayer whether the one having the thoughts has consciously made a formal attempt to make a prayer contact with God or not. Human minds tend to grow distracted and the urge for survival makes people selfish and greedy for power over others. It is so easy to let one's mind ricochet from one tangent to another, and in the hurry of life there isn't time to think or pray unless one sets aside a period of contemplation.

It is a matter of historic and geographic record that most of the great philosophies and religions were born in pastoral, desert or mountain regions where men had time to think.

One of the valuable by-products of my polar expeditions was the time to think. Mile after mile skiing and breaking trail in front of dog teams or lying awake in one's warm sleeping bag while a blizzard prevents travel gives time to muse on the deeper purposes of life. Time and again I've discovered that when I relax and let my mind wander at will on problems at hand, the solutions come tumbling into my mind until I'm stirred into action to go back to work.

Although I've never addressed my mind in prayer to the subject of an invention, I've found that by putting my mind into a receptive and orderly mood that novel ideas come easily which wouldn't seem to arise at all when I tried to concentrate under normal pressure of work. I've noted equally that when I've allowed my mind to become fully preoccupied by selfish and worldly thoughts my mental productivity falls off to an extent noticeable to myself.

Often on occasions of approaching duress, I have felt hopelessly at a loss for a plan of action. However, by trusting to an orderly flow of thought I could relax and draw on a power that seemed like a prompter at hand suggesting just what I should say or do next. Although this is far from any conventional concept of prayer I use this example to illustrate how the tuning of one's mind draws an unsuspected source of power.

I'm only too well aware of my own imperfections to assume

306

that I can keep my mind orderly and preoccupied with kindly and beautiful thoughts adequately long at a time. I do sense in others, however, gradations of personalities which show greater and lesser success. Certainly degree of education, sense of piety or search for reward are not the marks of those who seem most frequently in tune with the Infinite.

Christ had such a perfectly tuned mind with the Infinite that he unquestionably spoke with the authority of God.

PRAYER AS COMMUNION

By Dr. Paul Scherer
Union Theological Seminary

Prayer to me is that communion with God which is the natural outcome of the restored relationship in Christ between God and the human soul. I am as wary of talking about techniques as I am in the case of all deep, genuine, and intimate relationships. I am even more wary of talking about "results." It seems to me that one cannot very well use such language, involving either techniques or results, with reference to that sharing of life with life between friends, or that which has been made possible in Christ between our very selves and God.

Every sincere desire of the heart may be and should be made known, as a child would make known his desires to a loving father, though always in the context of glad submission to a will more gracious than we could ask, and of the profound realization that while we stand alone before God in prayer we nevertheless stand in the fellowship of all those whom He loves.

WHAT PRAYER MEANS TO ME

By Dr. Gilson Colby Engel

Physician and Surgeon

❧

Prayer is the greatest asset of the surgeon. It is through prayer that he is given the capacity for learning, the dexterity so necessary, the courage and the understanding and love for his fellowman. In thirty-two years of surgical practice the power of prayer becomes more and more evident. Many times have I seen the effects of prayer accomplish what we have believed the impossible, the hopeless case recover, peace come to one in anguish and a happy countenance come to a patient about to enter the great Beyond.

The effects of prayer can bring a thin smile to lips which have been tensed by pain, a thank-you speaking from eyes that have been dimmed with tears, and peace of mind to a patient who was depressed and confused. Prayer is our strength and our salvation. Through it we learn the wondrous workings of God.

A prayer is, to me, not a formal procedure but rather an intimate conversation with my God. Many times it has been silent, short, with a bowed head at a bedside or at an operating table, asking for peace and recovery of a patient and that I shall be given the wisdom and skill to effect that recovery. Often when indecisions are present about a case, a prayer brings solution.

Too often our prayers are only ones asking God to grant our requests and too little do we worship God or give prayers of thanksgiving. There is not a day that passes in anyone's life, no matter how beset we might be with trials and tribulations, that we do not have something for which to be thankful. Let us not forget that the power of prayer, to commune with God, is one of the greatest blessings with which we have been endowed.

THE BEST PRAYER IS A QUIET ONE

By Hon. Sherman Adams

Former Assistant to President Eisenhower

The subject of prayer is close to each believer's heart. The privilege of intimate communion with the spirit of Almighty God is a most precious and awful responsibility.

To me, the best prayer is a quiet one which seeks to know the Divine Will and asks only for strength to live according to His purpose—with confidence and thanksgiving. In my present work one of the most helpful expressions of faith comes from the Book of Common Prayer:

"Almighty God, whose kingdom is everlasting and power infinite; Have mercy upon this whole land; and so rule the hearts of thy servants The President of the United States and all others in authority, that they, knowing whose ministers they are, may above all things seek thy honour and glory; and that we and all the People, duly considering whose authority they bear, may faithfully and obediently honour them, according to thy blessed Word and ordinance; through Jesus Christ our Lord, who with thee and the Holy Ghost liveth and reigneth ever, one God, world without end. Amen."

I submit this prayer to you in the hope that it will be as meaningful to your readers as it has been to me.

IN TUNE WITH THE INFINITE

By Cleveland E. Dodge

Financier and Vice-president of Phelps Dodge Corporation

❦

From the dawn of history, man has felt that there is some power in the universe greater than himself. Man in those early times needed some definite object to revere that could be seen and felt, such as an idol or the sun. Gradually as some peoples became more intellectual, they began to look up to a spiritual power that could not be seen with the eyes but whose presence could be experienced. In the Bible we have, of course, the best account of the growth of a belief in a spiritual God. By example and supreme faith, Christ perfected this belief.

For those who believe in a spiritual God and that God has a real purpose in the world, prayer is the most direct way to try to sense God's will. I have always liked the phrase "In tune with the Infinite." It seems to suggest that we are seeking the truth and adjusting our actions to the purpose of the universe.

For all of us who have been under shell-fire in war or other real danger, prayer comes naturally and helpfully. The feeling that there is some power greater than ourselves and that we are calling upon that power for help gives confidence and strength. Essentially this is attaining peace of mind through submission to a power greater than ourselves.

Regular prayer at church or in private helps us to remember that there is a God and to live by His truths interpreted by Christ. Prayer helps in giving direction and purpose to our lives and in creating the right attitudes toward other people. Prayer and the recognition of a supreme power act to deflate our egotism and offset selfishness. Also, if we pray for some worthy cause, it tends to make us do our share by keeping the matter in mind and working with confidence to attain it.

I also believe that there is some kind of mental telepathy and that prayer by one person can influence another. Prayer cannot be proved scientifically, but countless persons in all ages have experienced its benefits and felt its power.

PRAYER SHOWS US THE WAY

By Lester E. Cox
Springfield, Mo.

❀

Prayer gives us a very satisfying philosophy of life. It removes all doubts and confusion, making life calm and peaceful. Without prayer, life would become empty and meaningless.

Prayer gives us dignity. It keeps us mindful that God created us and gave us an immortal soul. Prayer keeps us humble. We are weak creatures dependent upon the spiritual help which prayer alone can give.

We cannot boast that we achieve anything alone. It is only because He gives us health and intelligence that we can achieve anything. By prayer we grow strong and can achieve anything that is His will.

Prayer gives us a balanced sense of values. Wealth, social standing, and worldly pleasures become passing things of little value. Prayer keeps us alert and in tune with our spiritual values.

Prayer shows us the way, and by prayer we obtain guidance while we are here, and also for the hereafter.

"SPOT PRAYERS"

By William H. Barnhardt

President, American Textile Corporation

❦

Prayer is a medium God has created for the transfer of Spirit power. We do not understand prayer; we only know that "more miracles are wrought by prayer than the world ever dreamed of."

Prayer is like picking up a telephone and making a direct communication with Almighty God, only the physical telephone equipment and lines are not necessary. Years ago, before the invention of radio or television, it was hard for most of us to believe that it would be possible to transfer voices or pictures thousands of miles, instantly, yet today radio and television sets are in daily use in all our homes. We do not understand these means of communication, but that does not keep us from using them regularly.

Wherever we are, day or night, we can instantly receive power from God by contacting him in prayer. I believe most of us have thought that it is necessary to be in a church or to be bowed down on our knees in order to pray. This has kept us from using "Spot Prayers" which can be made anytime anywhere—while we are driving our car, walking about, standing or sitting around, or when riding in airplanes or trains. Regardless of where we are or what we are doing, the Great Power of God is available to us always through the medium of "Spot Prayer." If we do not recognize this great fact and make use of it continually, then we are constantly void of this —the greatest of all powers which God has provided for man's soul and spirit. If we do not use this power, then we lose the benefits it can bring to our lives. One of God's laws is that unless we use our mental, physical or spiritual faculties we lose the power which God created for us to use, through these mediums.

SURPRISING SUCCESS
THROUGH SUPPLICATION

By Clifton W. Brannon

Southern Baptist Evangelist

❧

"For over nine years now the Holy Spirit has led me to challenge people almost daily to claim the promise of God's Word that challenges me. It is found in Jeremiah 33:3. It is outlined as follows:

A Simple Request—"Call unto me, . . .

A Sure Reply—"And I will answer thee. . .

A Shocking Revelation—"And show thee great and mighty things. . .

A Surprising Result—"Which thou knowest not."

God is faithful. He has done exceedingly abundantly above all one could ask or think. Mountains of hindrances have been moved. Great and mighty missions have been accomplished. Miraculous things one would never think could happen have come to pass.

Is it a soul to be saved? Believe this promise and remind God according to Isaiah 43:26 of His Will, I Timothy 2:4, and recite I John 5:14 on the ground of John 15:7, believing John 14:14, and that soul will be saved.

Is it a heart to be opened? Believe Acts 16:14, command God according to Isaiah 45:11, and believe he will open it.

Is it for protection of loved ones? Claim Psalm 91:10-11. Believe the Word—pray using God's Word—expect the answer according to His Word."

313

PRAYER IN SPORTS

By Andy Pafko

Milwaukee Braves

❦

Is there a place for prayer in sports? In answer to such a question I would say, "Yes!" and "No!" It all depends on how prayer is used and why it is used at athletic contests. Although prayer in the open, that is, praying in public athletic contests, is becoming more and more evident in recent years, the question is still debatable as to whether such praying has a place in sports. In my opinion there is always the danger that the fans may interpret such prayers as mere exhibition, or part of the entertainment. In that case prayer is being misused and even cheapened. At least it is very doubtful that the general public comes to any sports contests or athletic events from any religious motives. Hence any show, or exhibition of a religious act at such athletic events, in my opinion, is out of place.

And yet, I must admit that there is a place for prayer in sports. Here I have in mind especially the prayer of the individual player. Should the individual player pray? I believe he should, and if he is a consecrated Christian, I am convinced that he will pray. He will do so not for the purpose of making a show of prayer, but to be in communion with his Lord. He will pray not openly, but privately, secretly.

I have been taught that whatever a child of God, a Christian does, he should do to the glory of God and for the welfare of his fellowman. As a Christian I must not forget that even when I am on the playing field, and especially in the heat of the contest.

If prayer is to serve to the glory of God and the welfare of our fellowmen, then it follows that certain matters cannot be included in the prayer of a sportsman. He certainly cannot include in his prayer the desire to win by all means and by any form of strategy. Playing the game fairly is far more important than winning it by foul means. Also ruled out of such prayers would be any desire for personal praise and glory. Such things lead to pride and pride too often leads to the fall. And, of course, it is self-evident that any antagonistic, or vengeful spirit cannot be associated with prayer. Such a spirit is contrary to the Christian spirit and should not be entertained by the sportsman. Now, since a player is constantly exposed to such temptations he will pray to overcome them.

In my prayer my request is that I may conduct myself as is expected of a Christian. I realize that as a professional player I am in the public eye and I serve as an example to many persons, especially the youth of America, by what I do and say, and how I conduct myself on and off the playing field. In my prayer I ask my Lord and Savior Jesus Christ to cleanse my heart of any intentions of willfully harming or injuring my opponents in order to gain any advantage over them. Furthermore I ask the Lord to help me to do the best I can with the ability and the talents He has given me. And above all, I ask Him to keep me humble.

As I look back upon my baseball years, especially my years in the Majors, I can truthfully say that the Lord has heard my prayers and has helped me. For that I owe Him my sincerest gratitude and deepest devotion.

PRAYER IS MANY THINGS

By Dr. Robert Kazmayer

Publisher and Business Analyst

In prayer there is forgiveness for our yesterdays, guidance for today and assurance for our tomorrows.

In the midst of bewildering days by prayer we approach an altar where our lives are steadied by a strength not our own and where our hearts are warmed by a surety that reason cannot follow because it passeth all understanding.

In prayer there is the lifting of our spirits as the flight of wings, the lifting up of our hearts as the lark that at dawn soars and sings its happiness at heaven's gate.

In prayer we meet all the dauntless souls who despite persecution, postponement and bitter cost have followed the gleam of brighter and better days.

In prayer we join in communion with the seers and prophets of the past who have gone ahead of the crowd to climb the beckoning hilltops of humanity's highest hopes.

Prayer is a listening as well as a speaking. By prayer we keep step in the ranks of all those who do justly, love mercy and who walk humbly with their God.

And whenever there is darkness prayer is the vision of the high white stars that lead on o'er moor and fen and crag and torrent, till the night is done and the gates of the morning open into the light of eternal day.

TO DO WHAT IS RIGHT

By *Cornelius Vanderbilt, Jr.*

Author, Lecturer, and Journalist

❦

I have found God through prayer out in the forest, on the high seas, far out on the desert, in crowded city canyons, in the House set aside for Him, **regardless of the faith.**

I travel a great deal in my literary business, and many problems arise. Often my own judgment is clouded. I am worried and upset. I ask Him for Guidance to do **the thing that is right.**

In my youth I attended church every Sunday in school and at home. Our pew in old Trinity Church in Newport, Rhode Island, was the same one in which George Washington and Lafayette had worshipped. My parents were very religious people, and I grew up with that kind of a background. I sang in the choir at St. Paul's School in Concord, New Hampshire; and I taught Sunday School for two years every Sunday morning in Old Norwalk, Conn; while attending a Tutoring School there, just before World War I started. Then I ran away from home and enlisted.

On the battlefields of France and Flanders I saw men die all about me, and I was frightened. I was deathly afraid the first time I had to go over the top; but I looked into the Heavens and I asked God to **make me do what was right.** I didn't want to kill, and I didn't have to kill, although I had been trained to kill. I was gassed and shell-shocked and sent home; but I know if I hadn't prayed I would not be alive now. In World War II I saw men die about me too, but I kept on praying and although my heart went back on me and I spent long months on a hospital bed at Walter Reed Hospital, I am still alive today.

Regardless of the faith if God is with you our prayers are always answered. I know. It has happened to me time and time again. I never ask for anything specific nowadays—but I do ask for guidance to do what is right.

SEEK GUIDANCE THROUGH PRAYER

By Paul Martin

Member, House of Commons, Canadian Parliament, and
Former Minister of National Health and Welfare

❧

During my long career in public service and throughout my private life, I have always depended upon guidance through prayer. The decisions of national importance which must be reached by a member of a Government are often beyond human ability alone and I firmly believe that a sincere public servant must seek guidance from a higher authority.

Prayer has always been a part of my everyday life. "Ask and ye shall receive" is not an idle promise, but we must be prepared to "receive" according to God's wisdom and not according to personal desires. Within our human limitations we do not always pray for what is best. "Thy will be done" must be implicit in our prayers and we must be prepared to accept the answer as being God's will.

I believe that through prayer I have been granted the strength and endurance to bear the burdens of life which are our common lot. I believe that no prayer is unheard or unanswered.

If we sincerely seek knowledge of the Divine Will, through prayer, we will surely be granted the wisdom and shown the way to use our talents to fulfill our destiny.

318

THE SECRET OF SUCCESS

By Kathryn Cravens

Author, Foreign Correspondent, Poet

❦

"What is the secret of your success?"

I have traveled around the world asking that question. The roster of success stories I have collected looks like an enormous edition of "Who's Who." Most of the entries climbed from poverty to riches or fame. But I found other kinds of success, much of it unheralded and unsung.

I focussed on a few people, born rich, whose wealth was a handicap rather than an aid to achievement. They fought the temptation to loaf through their lives and waste them. A force drove them to carve the patterns of their important careers.

But I have interviewed failures, too. And I think I have learned something about what it is that makes two citizens of the same world, equipped with the same purpose and the same opportunities wind up in middle age miles apart on the road.

Adolph Hitler and Benito Mussolini were arrogant with success as dictators when I talked with them. They had reached the pinnacle positions in their countries. And they ended the greatest failures I have ever known.

During their last moments of failure, Hitler and Mussolini cried out in the depths of their terror. A fleeing Premier of Italy was assassinated and then strung up by his feet in grotesque fashion on a street in Milan. People who had once adored Mussolini stepped up to his dangling body and spat on it.

Within a short time Hitler committed suicide. He almost shot his head off in a subterranean hideout far below the Reichchancellery in Berlin. As Allied bombardment crescendoed to a new peak of fury the body of Der Fuehrer was carried up out of the smelly darkness into the bomb-littered courtyard. Cans of gasoline were poured over him and then set on fire. The stench of burning flesh rose into the air outside the smoke-blackened ruins of the Reichchancellery. It had once been a gleaming monument to a desire for an empire that would reign a thousand years. It became the tombstone of a mad dream.

What were the elements that made these two men fail when others leaders of their countries succeeded? It has been my privilege to know four of our Presidents: Herbert Hoover, Franklin D. Roosevelt, Harry Truman and Dwight D. Eisenhower. These men kept their faith in God. They remembered to pray to a Higher Being. I have heard them ask God to help them make the right decisions in order that they might be guided to better serve their fellow man, their country and their God. The power of prayer gave them the strength to face the tomorrows before them. Because Hitler and Mussolini chose to ignore and forget God they ended among the "dregs" of humanity.

Two of the most successful people I have ever known were my own mother and father. And, yet, when they died, they left their seven children few worldly goods. Ours was a more priceless heritage—faith in God, love for our fellow man, ambition to improve our individual lives and a burning desire to leave the world better than we found it.

Father was a country doctor. Mother was the village postmistress. We lived in a tiny town that is not even a dot on the average United States map. The place is called Burkett and it is located in the sparsely settled region of Central West

Texas. Most of the 150 people who live there are hard-working and very proud about their town because for most of them life begins and ends there.

Burkett had no bank, newspaper, movie theater or drugstore. There was a general drygoods store, my mother's post-office, Father's office, where a skeleton was hidden behind a curtain, a blacksmith shop and a chili "joint." These were all one-room frame buildings. The public school, also one room, was out of town a mile away.

The heart of Burkett's social life centered around the church. There were three of them—Methodist, Baptist and Church of Christ. We belonged to the latter. But everybody joined in the special events of each church, regardless of membership. In the summer time protracted meetings were held underneath a crudely built tabernacle. Sometimes a hen laid an egg in the straw next to the pulpit or a cow wandered in to nibble at a small tree near the edge of the tabernacle but the preaching went right on.

There was one song the congregation always sang: "What A Friend We Have In Jesus."

> "What a Friend we have in Jesus
> All our sins and griefs to bear
> What a privilege to carry
> Everything to God in prayer.
>
> Oh, what peace we often forfeit
> Oh, what needless pain we bear
> All because we do not carry
> Everything to God in prayer."

I used to go home from church after hearing that song and pray that a railroad would come through our town. I would tell God that it was the most wonderful gift in the world that he could send us. Sometimes at night, I would run to the window and look out at the star-swept sky and pray again for the train to come steaming down the hill behind our house.

But no train ever chugged into Burkett. Probably none ever will.

One night after dinner, we gathered, as usual, before our fireplace in our parlor, prim with music boxes, plush albums and white lace curtains. I shocked my family by suddenly declaring that I was through with God. That Christ lied when he said in Matthew 21-22: "Verily I say unto you, if ye have faith . . . whatsover ye shall ask in prayer, believing, ye shall receive." Hadn't I believed? And hadn't I prayed for a train again and again?

That night I learned a lesson that I have never forgotten. My parents explained that prayer must be accompanied by active effort. That if the people in Burkett really wanted a train they would have to get busy and do something about it. That perhaps when I grew up I could work toward that end. Praying wasn't enough. There had to be action by someone else beside God.

"You must never give up your Lord," Mother said. "You won't always have your parents. There will be moments when you will need to talk to someone. If you keep close to a Higher Being, you will never be alone." And I have never been alone since that night.

My parents practiced religion. They went to church where they took an active part, thanked the Lord three times a day for the bountiful food on our table, they worked night and day for their children and for the community in which we lived.

Father refused to send bills to most of the people because they were poor. And he would drive twenty miles in bitterly cold weather in a buggy to visit a sick person whom he knew would never be able to pay even a penny for his call. Mother agreed that it was their Christian duty to take care of their neighbors. She tried to make up part of the financial loss by selling sidelines in the postoffice. Opposite her little grilled window and the pigeon hole boxes were shelves filled with millinery, a few toys, notions and cotton sacks. There was always a large freezer of ice cream for sale. And Mother was the only photographer within twenty miles.

But it didn't matter whether people came into the postoffice to buy or not. For years Mother sat on a high stool behind the little grilled window, sorting letters, talking to unhappy people, while rocking an old wooden cradle with her foot.

Mother wrote letters for people who couldn't write; read letters for people who couldn't read. And she comforted those whose friends and relatives no longer bothered to write.

There was always someone knocking on our door, day and night. The mentally troubled as well as the physically sick. My parents gave them help and encouraged them to understand that adversity and crises are common to people in every country in the world. The important thing was to accept problems and difficulties with courage. And to remember to ·"carry everything to God in prayer." He would help them withstand the burden of adversity and the hurt of sorrow.

Father died suddenly one autumn day on his way to see a patient. I was not yet ten years old. Mother was left with seven children. She came through incredible situations because of the resources upon which she drew. Somehow she managed to send us to college and she lived long enough to see us placed in important niches in the world far removed from the place of our birth.

None of us forgot that if we wanted to "get ahead" in the world the important thing was to pray and then put those prayers into action. To my mind that is the triumphant secret of success.

LEARN TO LOVE GOD THROUGH PRAYER

By Norman Soreng Wright
Organist and Composer

❧

Do I believe in prayer? Yes, indeed. Wholeheartedly. Prayer has been a part of my life for as long as I can remember. Naturally the form has changed many times. My early prayers were repetitions of prayers taught me by my parents or by my teachers in Sunday school. They were said with little or no understanding but did, at least, form the habit of prayer. Later I began to pray spontaneously, beseeching God for help and asking for things that I wanted. In time the realization of the selfishness of my praying came to me and I began to say prayers which were largely a matter of praise. For years I went to sleep at night with those prayers on my lips and in my heart. Though I was asking nothing for myself I found that those prayers bore fruit. My sleep was (and still is to this day) deep and peaceful. In concentrating on spiritual truths the cares and worries of the day were forgotten.

From this I moved into what I now choose to call Meditation. At the end of each day, having started with my usual repetition of prayers, I would find myself wondering: "What is God?" "Who am I?" and "Where am I going?" This search for communication with God became so insistent that I found myself grasping every opportunity to meditate. This has continued to the present day. I find great happiness, wherever I may be, in meditating on that Supreme Power which we call God. Problems have a way of solving themselves after such meditation; the mind is clearer, and all things are in sharper focus.

Today if there be any asking in my praying it is in the words of the well-known hymn, "Teach me to love Thee as I ought to love."

THE STRANGE TOUCH

By Kurt Singer

News Commentator

❦

I will never forget the night when my grandfather prayed with me, asking that I would pass a high school examination. I failed the test because no prayer on earth could make up for my deficiencies and negligence in study.

I will never forget the hundreds of Estonian women praying in an Eastern Orthodox village church. They kissed the floor and tasted the sacred wine from the same silver spoon. Many fell ill afterwards from what we would today call virus.

Nor can I forget the agitator who put up a huge table in the Circus Busch in Berlin. Thousands of Communists attended the meeting, and each one, after paying two marks, added his name to the growing list of those who officially rejected the religions of their forefathers and thereby joined the long ranks of atheists and free-thinkers. Each promised never to pray again.

I will never forget the anti-religious museums in the Communist countries where prayers are not only ridiculed but children in their first formulative years of schooling are shown gruesome paintings of priests torturing innocent people during the dark days of the Middle Ages. The instructors and guides constantly repeat statements that prayers are a kind of drug that opiate the minds of people living in the non-Communist world.

I cannot forget the fervent prayer Pastor Martin Niemöller gave in his Dahlem church outside of Berlin while the hollow sound of the heels of the Stormtrooper came ever nearer. He was arrested and compelled to spend eight years of his life within the dark and deadly walls of a concentration camp. But even in such a religiously arid environment, Pastor Niemöller organized prayers that were universal, in that they transcended secular beliefs and applied to all religions.

And in such a way, I have watched chaplains administering the last rites for the dead of the wars, offering prayers for the departed souls with no question as to the church of their affiliation—Protestant, Catholic, Jewish, Shinto or Hindu.

In Nazareth where He had lived I watched prayers being offered by both Jews and Moslems to the same Maker, although each was delivered in a different language and in a different fashion.

I have seen people all over the world praying together—in places where children have never known the taste of milk, in lonely corners of the earth where leprosy and yaws have destroyed human bodies and missionaries are only now finding their way through the infected jungle country.

Today millions of Russians pray in the sanctity of their homes and carefully hide their precious icons and Holy pictures when their simple devout ceremonies are over. They pray in spite of forty years of propaganda that teaches against the existence of God.

These experiences have lead me to one belief: the significance of prayer lies not in the surroundings, the elaborate churches, the scented altars, the temple bells but in the fact of prayer itself. Prayer is only, according to Buddhist scripture, framed by walls.

The prayer room of the United Nations Building in New York has tried to symbolize the fact that the searching spirit is more important than the splendor of the surroundings. In the center of the meditation room is a block of iron ore, untouched by artistry or symbols, the work of Nature itself.

It glimmers in a single shaft of light. It is an empty altar—empty, not because there is no God, but because there is a God who can be worshiped in so many ways. This is the altar to the God of all nations, colors and creeds.

Perhaps the world needs more meditation rooms where men and women can come together, without pettiness or split-hair tenets, to each find his place with God and with himself.

Newspapermen are hard-boiled. They pride themselves on skins like that of a rhinoceros and solid floodgates set up against tears. But few can shut from his mind when, at the end of World War II, General Douglas MacArthur returned to liberate the Philippine Islands which he had, long and arduous months before, been forced to leave.

Six reporters stood in his tent waiting for the victorious statement that would be cabled around the world. General MacArthur was neither savage about his enemies nor was he flamboyant in his success. He was tired, worn out. He felt the hot climate and the sweat poured from his lean frame and trickled down the front of his open shirt. Outside, the dead had not yet been buried.

Finally, MacArthur broke the silence: "I have nothing to say, but I want to kneel down. Join me if you wish, for we Christians have almost forgotten how to go on our knees in prayer. I want to ask the Almighty Lord to make this the last war, for any future war may be the end of the white man."

Perhaps the most sincere prayer I ever gave, and my most unforgettable one, was in a small church in El Paso, Texas. I closed my eyes and asked to be given strength and the wisdom to find myself—to be the sort of gentle husband I wanted to be, a man who was strong, honest and would not fail in his love for his wife and children, a human being who would not betray his own ideal and beliefs—ever.

In that moment, I felt some new hope, strength and assurance. I was touched by something far larger and profound than I. There was something unknown and indescribable. I like to call it a touch from my Maker, whose son I am.

This strange touch is still with me. I pray I will never lose it.

THE HIGHEST FORM OF PRAYER
By Edward G. Robinson
Actor and Motion Picture Star

Prayer, being as personal an experience as one may have, probably has as many variations of meanings as there are human beings. It is certain to be influenced by our concept of Deity, concept of ourselves, and the understanding of the relationship between God, the Creator, and Man. The fact that Man is the only creature who has the capacity to engage in this experience is significant; the fact that prayer has been a dominant factor in the history of Man is also meaningful. There is a compulsion to seek a power greater than ourselves when under stress, and Wisdom, a faculty of the soul, then guides us to the activity of prayer.

Simply defined, prayer is recognition of and communication with God.

Motivation to prayer is also varied. Some pray merely for things; others for success, health, peace, etc., and there is nothing wrong with this. Some pray because they feel it is a religious duty, and little can be said for that. The highest form of prayer, I believe, is the prayer of worship and thanksgiving to the Creator who is undeniably beneficent, loving and giving. I do believe in prayer.

THE VALUE, EFFICACY,
AND CONDITIONS OF PRAYER

By E. Schuyler English, Litt.D.

Editor, *The Pilgrim Bible*

❖

Prayer is the second half of man's means of communication with God. Two thousand years ago God spoke to mankind by His Son; now He speaks to man through His Word, the Holy Bible. Man's only way of speaking to God is by prayer.

The author recently lost his beloved wife. A relationship that was as perfect as human association can be, was interrupted for a while by God's sovereign will. For the departed one it is "far better" to be with Christ. Yet often he who has been left behind has longed that he might communicate with his beloved, to express to her his abiding love and to hear from her something of her experiences in the life beyond.

Another has gone before, God's only begotten Son who is one with the Father; and it is possible, through prayer, to speak to Him, as one learns about Him in the Scriptures.

Through prayer man can enter into the very presence of God. His approach is not to a throne of judgment but to a throne of grace, God's unmerited favor. There one tells the Almighty of his love, offers his worship to Him, confesses his sins, and seeks help for the day and guidance for the morrow.

And God answers prayer—not always exactly in line with the petitions, but always in accordance with His will and for man's good. Did God not answer prayer, He would not be true to His promises, as exemplified by the statement of our blessed Lord: "If ye shall ask anything in My name, I will do it." James tells us that "the effectual and fervent prayer of a righteous man availeth much."

But there are conditions to praying. Man must approach the Father in His way: prayer must be (1) in Christ's name (Jn. 16:23), that is, through the merit of the Son of God; (2) with every known sin confessed (Ps. 66:18); (3) while living in obedience to God's revealed will (I Jn. 3:22); and (4) in faith, believing that God will do what He has promised (I Jn. 5:14-15). God will not hear the prayers of those who do not trust Him, who do not believe in His Son Jesus Christ as their Lord and Saviour. But He will hear and answer those who confess His name.

Whatever one's position and condition in life may be, he can take time to pray. And he ought to do so. Prayer is to the spiritual life what food is to the physical life. As the day begins with food for the body, so it should commence with food for the soul. It can be nothing but gain to start and end every day with prayer.

LAUNCH OUR PRAYERS

By General Arthur G. Trudeau

Chief of Research and Development, U. S. Army

❁

Despite the extreme importance of exploring Space to its furthermost limits, and of sending up satellites that can begin to do our exploring, even more important is this 20th Century's challenge to believing men and women — a challenge for us to launch our prayers, which can and do go higher and further than satellite or rocket or space ship can ever reach, namely to the waiting heart of our Creator, if we ever expect to solve these problems about the peace of our world, which man clearly does not seem able to accomplish on his own.

PRAYER REMOVES FEAR

By Elmer W. Sherwood

President, Sherwood Associates, Public Relations Counselors

The value and efficacy of prayer have had a profound effect upon my life, which perhaps I can best express by relating the following experience:

During the Argonne Offensive in World War I, before the French town of Sommerance, I was a scout on signal detail of the Rainbow Division. The night of October 29, 1918, Fritz put on a whale of a bombardment, and some might wonder how we escaped to tell the story.

I was ordered to trace and repair our communication lines. I climbed out of my fox hole and darted into the inferno. Flashes of artillery fire at intervals lighted the blackness of the night. Explosions of enemy shells everywhere, the screams of the big ones flying overhead, and the bursts of bombs added to the thunderous uproar, so that I could not have heard my own voice had I dared to speak out, but I knew the Lord could hear me.

I thought of the prayer, Wits End Corner . . . "Are you standing at Wits End Corner, where Jesus loves to come? You are just at the very spot. Does all the world seem against you?"

Then came to me our Saviour's words: "Let not your heart be troubled, neither let it be afraid." And I was no longer afraid.

Sometimes I feel today as if I might be living on borrowed time, and each day I count my blessings and thank our Creator for his deliverance.

PRAYER, A WAY OF LIFE

By Dr. Cloyd H. Marvin

President, The George Washington University

❦

It is a layman's privilege to write of prayer from his experience. This I gladly do, for without the Bible in my desk and a book of prayers, my responsibilities could not be met. My first prayer for the day is one of thankfulness that I may pray to God without ceasing.

In prayer we have the most natural expression of the highest impulse of our souls; through prayer we establish the meaning of life; through prayer we are able to relate our lives to God's purpose; and through prayer we can remove from our hearts all that does not represent His love.

Christ taught us that prayer is an experience with God. If this were not true, we would never have learned to pray. In the prayer that Christ gave to His disciples, He pointed out adoration, reverence, and communion, and also petition, confession, and dedication. Such prayer results in humility, wisdom, power, and faith.

Prayer is acknowledgement of human need. It usually expresses concern about some of the most complex reactions in our reasonings and emotions. The attempt to establish a relationship with the Father can be accomplished only through the acknowledgement of our need to be associated with Him. This association not only orients us with "final cause," but it helps us interpret life in terms of human helpfulness. In these terms prayer is contact of spirit with spirit, the speaking of mind with mind, and the functioning of will with will. It makes our lives purposeful in that they may more nearly represent God's way. Prayer becomes a way of life.

Christ through example taught us that God's blessings are ever available. It helps to think of His blessings as being constant and permeating all things. To illustrate, in a not too comparable way, the earth receives cosmic rays. They come from where we do not fully know, but they permeate all space and are ever present to condition our universe that it may be responsive to the forces that make it what it is. God's spirit is ever present, and we are privileged to dedicate our lives to receiving the strength that comes from His knowledge, the purpose that comes from His will, and the understanding that comes from His love.

In our meditations we are given power to understand those things which overwhelm and confuse us. We realize within ourselves qualities of physical strength, of mind, and of spirit that otherwise would remain dormant. When we pray, our very lives become an integral part of God's plan.

Through prayer, through the Bible, and through service, we come to know of His love for us and, more, to appreciate the significance of our love for Him. So it is futile not to pray for guidance that through prayer and the understanding of His word our lives can become a part of His being. With prayer influencing our physical well-being, our manner of thinking, and our spiritual interpretations of life, our lives will be more purposeful. Confusion and darkness of mind give way to happy simplicity and enlightenment. Thus, we come to realize the dynamic character of prayer through which hope and courage are strengthened and understanding and steadfastness come into our lives. When we pray, we draw ourselves nearer to God's way and reflect His love.

THIS I BELIEVE

By Oral Roberts

Evangelist

❦

I love to pray. It is through prayer that I can make direct contact with God. By calling upon a Power higher than myself, I am relieved of excess burdens. Through prayer I give expression to my finer desires. Sometimes my most effectual prayer is not expressed in words but in the deep longings of my heart. It is at such times that I become intimately acquainted with God.

When I pray, I believe that God is, that He is good, that He is big, that He is available and that He is near.

I believe it is right to pray to be healed. Christ, in His healthy humanity, came against sickness and disease. Christ was so concerned that sick people be healed that He charged His disciples to heal the sick, and cast out devils.

He promised that the prayer of faith should save the sick. He said, "They shall lay hands on the sick and they shall recover."

Health is life, and Christ said, "I am come that they might have life and that they might have it more abundantly."

If it is right to be healed, it is right to pray to be healed.

I believe it is right to pray for ourselves. Jesus prayed for Himself in the Garden of Gethsemane. In the Lord's prayer, he taught His disciples to include in their prayer, "Give **us** this day **our** daily bread, and lead **us** not into temptation, but deliver **us** from evil. . . ."

The law of self-preservation is the first law of Nature and it demands that we include ourselves in our prayers. Through prayer for ourselves we can become better persons, better witnesses for Christ, more perfectly integrated personalities.

I believe that God is bigger than your need and wiser than your problem. He is too good to do wrong, too wise to make a mistake.

I believe God can hear my individual voice. Christ said, "The very hairs upon your head are numbered." He said that God sees the fall of even a worthless sparrow. He asks, "Are ye not better than the sparrows?"

Jesus called people by their first names. He recognized them as individuals and answered their prayers. I feel I am known to God as Oral Roberts. He knows my name, where I live and what I have to do.

I believe when prayer is offered sincerely, when faith is made a single act and sent out to God, one must have patience. There are **instant** answers and there are **delayed** answers. Delayed answers usually mean that certain changes must be effected, either by God or by yourself.

I have found that when I pray I must have some conviction about its being right for me to pray about this particular thing. The desire for it must be strong. I must make my believing a definite act of faith and release it. Then, I must not allow myself to become alarmed at the enormity of the thing I have asked for. I must keep my prayer on deposit and not recall it.

I believe there is no distance in prayer. Prayer is the most wonderful thing I have ever known.

IN THE ATMOSPHERE OF PRAYER

By Henry F. Henrichs

Publisher, *Sunshine Magazine*

❀

When I was a mere lad in knee trousers, I had my desires and longings for the things of youthful fancy. In the vision of a pair of new skates, or a bicycle, or a new suit of clothes just like my neighbor playmate, Fred Robertson, had, I would approach my father at times with hands in my pockets and a tremble in my voice. Though my father was kind and understanding, I remembered all too well the oft unfilled wood box near my father's favorite chair behind the old wood stove, which he had charged me to keep well filled, and the many times I had "forgotten" to do the chores for Father whenever my chum Fred across the fence had given me the inviting "H-o-o! h-o-o!" (in plain English, "Come over")—and the "sociable" chap that I was, I went, regardless.

But in my excitement before my father, I would keep up a gainful prattle, and in some sort of a running, incoherent way ask him for the thing I wanted. It is no wonder that often my father did not answer—because I did not give him a chance. Once, I remember so well, after I had asked my father in every way I knew for a new baseball cap, he was about to speak, but I dashed away to escape his reprimand. Months later I caught myself in the thought that perhaps my father was going to say, "Why, of course, son, you may have a new cap, and a mitt besides!" But I gave him no chance to tell me.

My trouble was, I failed to create an atmosphere for the answer that I craved from my father. Had I but waited in quiet patience for a few moments, giving Father a little time to consider my request and worthiness, I might have had his blessings, even though my request be denied. But how often, despite my manifested ill faith in my father that he would listen, did he grant my wish, to my great joy!

How do we present our petitions to our Heavenly Father? We are in haste. We think of the words from our lips instead of the impulse from our heart. We tell Him of our wants. We ask Him to bless us—for what? We prattle like children to their parents, and seldom stop to hear what the answer is, what our Heavenly Father has to say to us.

Someone has said that it is the ten minutes after prayer that matters—ten minutes of waiting on the Lord. This, to me, is the essence of prayer. In this ten minutes is created the atmosphere in which the answer may well come, with its blessing.

"Be still, and know that I am God." Be still after prayer and hear God. But we will not. We say our prayers—often from memory, often from reading—seldom from the heart. I do not know if God hears such prayers. Even so, before God can give an answer, we are up and away. Do we believe in prayer? Then let us create an atmosphere of prayer.

"I will hearken what the Lord will say concerning me," said the Psalmist. If God chose to grant wherefor we pray, many of us would not hear Him, for we would not be listening, nor would our hearts be open when He spoke. Instead of the many requests for blessings, might we not pray, "Lord, help us to wait before Thee," and in the waiting, in the atmosphere of prayer, may come floods of blessings.

And how and where can we most fervently create the atmosphere of prayer? Where can we draw nigh unto God and unburden our hearts? In the closet, perhaps, where dead walls have no ears? Verily, God is everywhere and He will know our bleeding behind impenetrable walls, if need be.*

There is a beautiful song that sings, "The place where I worship is the wide open spaces built by the hand of God." Indeed, in the wide open spaces one may see God in all His glory. There He reigns, and the atmosphere is surcharged with His presence.

In the wide expanse of earth and sky, where the meadows and the fields declare His handiwork and greatness, there the wayfarer may find the road back to God, and the faithful may find reassurance and peace. There, in the sacred silence of the dawn and the set of sun, one's trust in God is sealed, and one may speak with Him with perfect ease. There are no earless walls to confine the wings of prayer, and in such divine appointments one may hear God.

Or in the garden, where the miracles of beauty abound in celestial profusion, on every hand the touch of the Divine, God again becomes omnipresent. The wonders of His love are revealed in every petal and spear. Only the barren soul could fail to see God in the garden, and speak with Him.

Then one comes into hills and valleys and forests, where tall trees and mountain peaks point heavenward. Every branch and every leaf speaks God's language of Love to mankind. Here, too, one can kneel in blessed assurance that God is nigh, and in His gracious compassion answers prayer.

And when you come to the wide open, sacred places, open the flood gates of your soul in communion with God, and await

*When Jesus said, "When thou prayest, enter into thine inner chamber, and having shut the door, pray to thy Father who is in secret, and thy Father who seeth in secret shall recompense thee," he had reference to the futile prayers of the hypocrites "who love to stand and pray in the synagogues and in the corners of the streets, that they may be seen of men."

His answer, even unto ten minutes after the prayer. Here is the thought:

"Our Father, who art in Heaven and on Earth, hallowed be Thy name. Every flower that grows, every leaf that blows, reveals the power of Thy holy Name. In no other Name could the miracles of the ages be wrought. Truly, hallowed **is** Thy Name.

"Thy Kingdom come. Praise the Lord—Thy Kingdom has come into the hearts of the people around the Earth, and stands as a fortress against the wiles of sin.

"And help me, Lord, to do Thy will on Earth even as perfectly as it is done among the Saints in Heaven. Thou hast filled the lives of Thy people with divine abundance, and the fruits of the fields for their daily bread.

"Forgive me my transgressions as I have . . . O God, help me to speak in truth . . . help me to forgive as freely those who have sinned against me as Thou hast so oft forgiven me! I bow before Thee in contrition, dear Lord.

"And lead me not into temptation. There can be no temptation in Thy presence. But deliver me from evil as I depart into the world of men, where temptation abounds. Sustain me in Thy faith, my Father, and fill my heart with treasures which build more stately mansions; for Thine is the Kingdom, and the Power, and the Glory, forever."

Entreats Elsie Janis so simply: "Just tell me Lord, if I should stray, that I may pause along the way at any time of night or day, and talk with Thee."

WHAT IS PRAYER?

By Dr. Elmer Hess

Past President, The American Medical Association

❦

During a lull in the famous battle at Chateau Thierry during the First World War, a rough tough old regular sought me one night and asked if I would listen to his confession. He said he felt as if he were going to be killed the next day and that since there was no Catholic chaplain with the regiment he had selected me, the Battalion Surgeon, to hear his confession. I informed him that I was not a member of his faith but that I would be glad to do anything I could to help him. He told me a terrific story of his misdeeds and then said he felt better but he'd feel even better still if I would say the Lord's Prayer with him. We knelt and quietly repeated this great prayer together. He was killed the next day. Do I have to ask, "What did prayer do for him?"

Many years later, we had as dinner guests in our home a group of Catholic Nuns. My wife asked our 12-year-old daughter to say grace. Completely flabbergasted the child said, "Sisters, we'll have silent prayer." I'm sure the prayers were heard. One doesn't have to say words or kneel to express one's self to the "Infinite."

Many years ago, I was asked as a physician to pray with a lovely woman dying of cancer. She had been told that I was an Episcopalian as was she. I didn't tell her that I hadn't been to church for a long, long time. I simply asked for her prayer book and as I said the prayers she made the responses. Strangely enough as I started to read these famous old prayers, I found that they all came back to me and after I started, I no longer needed the prayer book. My childhood training had made an indelible impression upon me. That dear old lady never again asked for a sedative to relieve her pain for I had written orders that the nurses were to read the Bible and say morning and evening prayers with her. When asked why she didn't ask for a sedative to control her pain, she replied, "I want a clear mind when these good Christian women pray with me." In this case, prayer was the best medicine we could give this doomed soul for at that time our scientific skills were useless.

So I ask, "What is prayer?" Prayer isn't just the speaking of words. Prayer is more often the mental communication of the individual with the Creator. It cannot be defined any more than one can define conscience. It's the still small voice inside of the human being that raises him above the level of the animal and makes of him a strong, helpful individual, created in the image of the Creator. It is an expression of the desire in the hearts of men to create the brotherhood of man under the Fatherhood of God.

PRAYER IS DAILY REDEDICATION

By Harry F. Byrd

U.S. Senator from Virginia

I cannot imagine this world without prayer. It is the medium through which we commune with our God. It is the language of love, kindness, forgiveness, self-surrender, and eternity. It is a daily rededication to the ideal. It restores peace and courage. It reassures us that good will overcome evil.

WHAT WOULD WE DO WITHOUT PRAYER?

By Grace Noll Crowell

Author and Poet

❦

Thank God for the privilege of prayer! I cannot conceive of going through life with its countless problems, its insistent demands, its joys and its sorrows, without that gracious privilege.

When we pray we come to One altogether loving and wise, altogether patient with our faults and our failures. We can be assured that he understands our every need, and that he hears and heeds each sincere utterance, each cry for guidance and strength. What would we do without that blessed contact, the assurance it gives to our faith?

I believe he is pleased at any word of praise, any expression of gratitude we may make, and that he rejoices at any word of adoration we may lift skyward.

It is blessed to know that even the humblest among us need not hesitate to come to him because we may feel we are not eloquent in prayer. Many may all but be inarticulate at times, yet there are none who cannot cry out the two brief and all important words: **"Our Father,"** when we need him in any time of distress, or in an hour of rejoicing when we long to voice our thanks. We may be certain that at our call he stoops and listens, and he answers in his own wise and certain way.

There are few of us who do not need to grasp hold of some certain promise out of his Holy Word, and cling to it through times when the storms of life are beating heavy about us, claiming it as answered prayer, which he means for us to do. We repeat it back to God, calling it, as it were, to his remembrance, and we find new courage and strength for the day in that reiterated promise.

Personally I find certain words set down in the Scriptures that are like a voice speaking to me sincerely and earnestly. It is God's voice speaking across the centuries and I am grateful to him. Here is one answer to my pleading. "Fear not," he says, "for I am with thee. Be not dismayed for I am thy God, I will help thee, I will strengthen thee, yea, I will uphold thee with the right hand of my righteousness."

This is an answer to prayer as truly as if he were speaking to me face to face today—a wise answer, a good answer, a sustaining power to hold me in my need.

Indeed, what would we do without him? We do not have to face that dark prospect. He will not fail us, and we can thank him for prayer, and for its most vital meaning in our lives. Let us pray.

MY STEADFAST BELIEF

By Elsa Maxwell

Author and Party Hostess

❁

Yes, indeed, I do believe in the power of Prayer. I'm sure the prayers of thousands of friends and well-wishers saved my life in my recent illness.

Among my many blessings, I count the greatest to be my steadfast belief in a God who watches over his children.

"Prayer is the soul's sincere desire,
    Uttered or unexpressed.
The motion of a hidden fire
    That trembles in the breast."

A WAY INTO HIS PRESENCE

By Dr. Richard C. Raines

Bishop of the Methodist Church

❦

I believe in prayer because of what it has done to, in and through me.

When a junior in college I spent a summer school session living alone. I devoted the first hour of each day from 6:00 to 7:00 in the morning in Bible study and prayer. Christ became so real to me that I felt if I opened my eyes I would see Him. The trees, birds and flowers were beautiful in a new and different way. Many persons who had formerly seemed dull and uninteresting now came alive for me.

Continuing the regular daily discipline of Bible study and prayer during the next college year I found my life purpose being transformed. I had expected to be a lawyer. Gradually it became clear that I must become a minister.

God, through prayer, has knit in our home deeper and more satisfying ties than we could possibly have achieved by ourselves. In family devotions our children were led to experience the power of prayer.

God has answered my prayers. Sometimes he has said, "No," sometimes, "Wait," frequently, "Yes." Sometimes the answers have been strikingly unusual.

I pray for specific things believing that if they are according to His will God's answer will be yes. I pray for persons by name but never presuming to know what His will for them is or what their deepest need is; nor to tell God something he presumably does not know about them, or to awaken his love and concern.

Sometimes when I pray God does not seem close or listening. Then, I seek for the cause of my self-manufactured clouds that hide Him from me. But I persist in grateful prayer and in due season God is nearer and dearer than ever before. Prayer to me is not a method of getting God to change His mind or work my desire. Prayer is a way into His presence where His will is made known to me—power is given to undertake it and where my confession of sin, failure and worry, as well as my gratitude and joy, may be laid at his feet.

Prayer changes me from the prodigal leaving home demanding, "Father give me" to the prodigal chastened and returning to his Father and saying, "Father make me."

A DAILY CONFERENCE WITH GOD

By Eddie Peabody

The Banjo King

❦

My 38 years in show business, plus two world wars' of service, has been the life of one little fellow with his banjo named Eddie Peabody. I am still in show business trying in my way to bring some degree of happiness to the people.

I am proud to say that I contact and have my own daily conference with God through the channel of prayer. If we take the time to pray wherever we are, we will receive untold benefits in helping us to live a better life. I am alive today because of answered prayers.

DAILY PRACTICE IN PRAYER

By *Amy Vanderbilt*

Author of "Amy Vanderbilt's Complete Book of Etiquette,"
Syndicated Newspaper Columnist, Lecturer and TV Personality

❧

Because I believe in what my religion teaches and take comfort from my prayers as a daily exercise in spiritual devotion for both myself and my children, I have, as I grow, I hope, in grace and maturity, increasing emotional security. Of course, fears and anxieties sometimes beset me, but I now feel that I can face any difficulty life happens to hand me, and that God is there for help if I ask for it.

My religion means that I must try to abide by its precepts even at the cost of personal discomfort, that I must arrange my busy life for some spiritual communication each day. It means that I must accept, literally, Jesus' great commandment, "Love one another." This is less difficult than it seems to some of us, but it does take daily practice to find something to love at least in every one of God's other children, to put down feelings of irritation and criticism and tension in living and working with others. In Ecclesiastes it says, "Better is a handful with quietness, than both hands full with travail and vexation of spirit." What psychiatrist could tell us more than that?

What my religion gives me I try hard to pass on to others. It is easy to be gloomy and pessimistic and it is often hard to "count one's blessings." Thus, as a daily Bible reader, I take pleasure in seeking out the passages in the Bible that exhort me to be cheerful, and there are many. For example, the 100th Psalm—"Make a joyful noise unto the Lord. Serve the Lord with **gladness.**" Or, Ecclesiastes 3, which tells us that there is "a time to weep and a time to **laugh;** a time to mourn and a time to **dance.**" And, of course, the beautiful promise "Seek and ye shall find, ask and it shall be given to you."

I really do believe that we develop as individuals according to our compelling desires, whether or not we ask in formal prayers for the fulfillment of our deep needs.

I BELIEVE IN PRAYER

By Roger W. Babson

Founder, Babson Statistical Organization

I believe in sane and unselfish prayer. I, however, pray for guidance, courage and self-control; not for health, peace or prosperity. I pray that I may **do** the things and **live** the life which will bring about these desired results.

I never **directly** pray for members of my family or others distant; but I do pray that I may set them the example, may write them the right letters and say the words which will bring about the desired results.

I pray for peace, but always keep in mind that world peace means the elimination of tariffs, immigration restrictions and other handicaps to foreign nations—keeping in mind that the "letting down the bars" would hurt my business and mean a financial loss to me.

I pray for forgiveness, but remember that to be forgiven I must love my enemies and forgive my debtors. I have been cured of arthritis and ulcers by being kind to everyone and carrying no grudges.

Yes, I believe in prayer but not in the formal prayers made by the **preachers Sunday mornings.**

"BEFORE THE EVENING
SUN GOES DOWN"

By W. C. Handy

Musician and Composer

❦

I want to put my house in order, patch up my affairs, do my bit to lighten our burning worldly cares. Still that voice within me and settle ev'ry score. I want to spread my home-spun gospel to men of ev'ry creed. Lend a word of comfort to weary souls in need. Lead the way to Glory on that peaceful shore. I want to point out to God's Children, it pays off to be good, to help remold all nations into one big neighborhood. I want to earn my place in Heaven where rainbows never fade, mingle with the Angels, where joy is ready-made. Gain the right to join Him, up there forevermore, before — The Evening Sun Goes Down.

To take a few words from yesterday and frame them in words of today; to preserve spirituals of our own South and chant melodies from the Congo; to tell the story of the blues honestly and sincerely; to entertain or inform the reader and not parade a writer's ego. And finally, if my serenade of song and story should serve as a pillow for some composer's head, as yet perhaps unborn, to dream and build on our folk melodies in his tomorrows, I have not labored in vain. If, as my teacher predicted, "music brought me to the gutter," I confess it was there I got a glimpse of Heaven, for music can lift one to that state. If, as my father often said, "You are trotting down to Hell on a fast horse in a porcupine saddle," I rode with a song on my lips and its echo in my heart. If, as Gene Buck has so well said, "There is nothing finer on which to hang a memory than a song," I also hang a memory on these words from my mother's prayer which so aptly express my inmost feelings, "Lord, I thank Thee that we are living in a Christian land and a Bible country."

God Bless America.

EJACULATORY PRAYERS

By P. F. Henderson

Lawyer and Past President of the Bar Association of South Carolina

There are many kinds of prayers. There are public prayers, private prayers, prayers in the sanctuary, prayers in the closet, prayers of hope, prayers for relief from despair, prayers for divine guidance, prayers with beads and accessories, prayers before the family altar, prayers intercessory and prayers of Thanksgiving and many other prayers could be listed.

Then there are what I have for my own personal satisfaction called "ejaculatory prayers" and I may be coining an expression. While in no fashion they supercede other and more sedate prayers, these so-called ejaculatory prayers are to me most precious and useful. Daily, many times a day, hourly, momentarily they may be used.

We may, when we are at work, or at play, at home, in the street, in the store, at the desk, in the school cry out, (mentally and, of course, inaudibly) whenever the need arises, "Oh God, do guide me, help me" with whatever my plea is for,—for help, for guidance, for strength to resist temptation or for strength to act bravely and boldly, for momentary uplift, or for the sustaining hand of the Lord, now and always, in our daily walk and work. While this kind of prayer as I have said should not and does not and cannot supercede other prayers, to me it is sustaining as an ever-present aid in daily life.

349

I BELIEVE IN PRAYER

By Nathaniel Leverone
Industrialist and Civic Leader

I believe in prayer. It is my sincere belief that it is the only answer today to the bewildering problems which face our nation as well as the rest of the world.

All other plans to bring peace and understanding to a troubled world that have been tried since the dawn of history have failed because they were not based on the simple teachings of Christ and other great religious leaders, supported by positive prayer. What needless tragedies the world has suffered because of the lack of faith sustained by prayer.

In our own time we have seen Europe—the center of civilization and of the Christian religion; the educational, moral and spiritual stronghold of the world—divided into two opposing groups and waging the two most deadly and devastating wars the world has ever witnessed, two warring groups of Christian nations forgetting the teachings of the Man of Peace, bent on destroying each other, leaving once enlightend Europe in moral, spiritual and intellectual darkness.

Wars have never solved any problems, so when the last war ended, kindly, sympathetic, generous America attempted to restore peace and prosperity to a bitter and suffering world by making the largest gifts and loans of money, goods and services ever known, and tried to bring about agreements and treaties among the nations which would guarantee peace and which should have made the whole world hail America for its great efforts to aid humanity. Yet today America can truly say that it has no real dependable friends among the family of nations.

At home, we have tried to solve our many pressing problems by passing laws. In addition, we are not only caring for the physically and mentally unfit, but we have placed needless millions of people on federal, state and city payrolls. Also, slowly and surely we have been adopting the strange ideologies of the communists and socialists, telling our people—particularly our young people—that our government will always take care of them, provided they will give up much of their freedom.

As a result we are strangling all ambition in our future citizens from whom the great leaders of the future must come. We are destroying our incentive system which has inspired the people of this nation since the Mayflower landed at Plymouth in 1620 and the American incentive system started. After a short, futile attempt at communism, our forefathers decided that people would be rewarded according to the efforts they contributed. That has been the basis on which America has been built.

The reason we have made this remarkable progress and have become the leaders of the world is because we have always offered rewards for worthy achievement. Yet, for some reason, today there has been a wave of propaganda to lower all people to a common level—that all should be treated alike—that there should not be rewards in proportion to the service rendered. God in his infinite wisdom created all human beings entirely different—no two have ever been alike physically or mentally or in ambition or character or other human qualities. We all believe that all men are created equal before God and before the law but in no other way. In spite of that, many have gone so far as to propose that all receive the same recognition for work rendered; in fact, some have even proposed the abolishment of patents and copyrights, thus removing all incentive for great inventors, thinkers and writers.

Many of our public officials, preachers and other leaders are so bewildered and confused by the propaganda that has filled all our sources of information that many have lent support to these radical ideas.

I sincerely believe that prayer is the only method by which these men may be inspired with the vision to recognize the truth and the courage to place the welfare of the nation above that of any other nation or any minority pressure group to which they belong—whether they be racial, national, religious, business, labor, veteran or other groups.

So we have taken desperate measures to combat these dangerous trends. We have passed many laws, spent enormous amounts of money, placed useless or incompetent workers on payrolls—all in vain. Laws, promises and charitable donations have never solved a single racial, religious or moral problem. Let us then try prayer. That has been successful during many crises through which America has passed and can be depended on again now.

Let us not forget that America's great growth was due to the free enterprise system which was based on rewards for meritorious service. Christ himself offered the greatest possible reward. He promised those who believe in him and followed him should have everlasting life. Surely there is no greater reward.

Let us remember then to serve our fellow men through the power of prayer. The best way to serve God is by serving our fellow men. I agree heartily with that devout Quaker, a great believer in prayer, who was accustomed to say, "I expect to pass through this world but once. If there is any kindness I may show or any good thing I may do for my fellow men, let me not defer or neglect it for I shall not pass this way again."

A BASIS OF PERSONAL PRAYER

By Dr. Leonard Carmichael

Secretary of the Smithsonian Institution

❧

As an Episcopalian, when I think of prayer, I think of the Book of Common Prayer as used in the Church of England and in the world-wide family of Anglican churches.

The Prayer Book of the Episcopal Church today is fundamentally little changed from the great first Anglican Prayer Book of Edward the Sixth, which was published in 1549. Its sonorous English is largely a translation from the Latin Breviary and Missal of the historic Christian church.

The language of the King James version of the Bible and of the Book of Common Prayer for more than four centuries has done much to mold and also to ennoble the speech, the thought, and the religious attitudes of generations of the English-speaking people throughout the world.

My principal academic field of study has been psychology. From the standpoint of this subject, I cannot help believing that man's real needs as they can be expressed even in the most personal prayer change little from generation to generation. The Prayer Book formulates these fundamental human desires in its petitions, supplications, collects, litanies, and hymns of praise and thanksgiving. These great and historic verbal formularies are thus an epitome of racial wisdom about man's requirements both as an individual and as a member of society.

In the Book of Common Prayer a devout suppliant in this age does not feel that he is dealing with the sentiments of the past. Rather the magic of its words seems to give him an immediate opportunity to vocalize better than he could hope to do for himself his deepest, most sincere, and most secret longings and hopes. The non-Episcopalian may puzzle a little as to how such "written prayers from a book" may seem week after week to come from the heart of the worshipper and not become a mechanical exercise. To millions of Anglicans through many generations this book has provided in its pages the very essence of a personal and an immediate religious experience. One who uses it with a humble, lowly, penitent, and obedient heart may thus feel in a peculiarly direct way the opening of the very gates of what St. Augustine so truly called The City of God.

ON OUR KNEES IN PRAYER

By Frank G. Clement

Governor of Tennessee

While national defense is our duty and while we must be prepared to repel arrogant and godless forces at any time, the ultimate answer to physical force is not a greater physical force. It is instead a spiritual power and no national defense program and no preparedness plan is complete without the moral and spiritual benefits a God-fearing people can employ.

I believe that even the most reckless among us has no uncertainty as to the source of such spiritual power. If we are to create in the world this sustaining, this benign, this saving spirit—we must do it on our knees in prayer to Almighty God.

Never has the world needed Christian education, never has the world needed prayer, never has the world needed faith more than it does today.

PRAYER IS POWER

By Loretta Young

Star of The Loretta Young Show—NBC-TV

❦

I believe that prayers move like a beam of light toward Our Father and that He hears every single one. All the millions and millions—the trillions of them!

He Who watches the flight of the least of the sparrows hears, and answers, every prayer as it deserves. The self-seeking "gimme" prayers, the self-sacrificing prayers of the Saints, and all those in between.

I do not believe this—I **know** it is so.

When I was a child, I prayed as a child for the **things** I wanted—and I was a very "wanting" child. There was great love in our home but there was very little money and there were very few material possessions. I was just a baby when my father went away one day—and we never saw him again. Mamma didn't make a great fuss about her trials and troubles, nor burden us with sorrow because she was an abandoned wife and mother. She simply became both mother and father to us —gave to each and all of us kids the warmth of her love, the security of her devotion. We thrived upon both.

I was three when we moved from Salt Lake City to Hollywood and Mamma opened a boarding house. All of us girls got child-extra work in motion pictures, because Mamma's sister's husband was an assistant director. What we earned was very welcome at home and it all went into the family "kitty." Material need was a pretty stern disciplinarian in our household. But we were never in need of love, nor of Faith, and we were **never** without prayers.

I was taught, and I learned, to pray for what I wanted. It was almost automatic for me to pray for everything. I prayed for party dresses, for friends, and even for dates.

I prayed I'd be a motion picture star.

At fourteen I **was** a star, and I took all the blessings that went with being a star for granted.

The rewards of motion picture stardom are very great, but they depend upon the combined talents of many, many others. I was very young, very foolish. I gave myself all the credit for having earned all my rewards. As though only my talent, only my hard work had made them possible.

At sixteen I was super-confident headstrong. And I was accustomed to getting my own way—one way or another.

One day a Jesuit priest spoke to me. He didn't speak to me as a star. He spoke to a foolish young girl, rushing heedlessly along a dazzlingly bright road, blindly and indifferent to its many dangers.

"Don't you know, Loretta," he said, "that talent isn't given to us for the gratification of our own egos? Talent is given for the glory of God. Your talent places you in a position to be an example to others. You have no right to a selfish personal life. Whether you deserve it or not, Loretta, as a motion picture star, you are an example. Be a good example and you justify your talent as an actress. Be a bad example and you justify your talent as a fool. All of us have both those talents—in one degree or another. You **dare** not be a **bad** example. You **must** not be a fool."

That is why I began to think about the how and why of my prayers. Only in one simple prayer had I really been following my mother's example. Each night before I went to sleep, my last prayer was, "And please, dear God, make me a good girl." I discovered all my other prayers were for self-gratification or for material things.

That night I really prayed to lead the kind of life God

wanted me to lead. I prayed to know how to use whatever talent He had given me for the fulfillment of His purposes— not mine.

No one is ever too old, too young, too rich or too poor to pray. I believe in the power of prayer. I know that I owe all that I have to it. Every good thing I have ever accomplished, every good thing that has ever happened to me, is the result of prayer.

I know that prayer is power.

THE BIBLE AND PRAYER ARE INSEPARABLE

By Victor E. Anderson

Governor of Nebraska

The power of prayer, in my opinion, is the greatest influence in the world today. It is available to any human who has faith in God and seeks spiritual guidance.

We learn to pray from the teachings of the Bible which have stood the test of time and are the ultimate guide to the salvation of our world.

The very foundation of the American way of life, our Constitution, is based on God's law. Without this there would be no law for the rights of man.

In time of need we turn to God through prayer for guidance, and to the book of Psalms in the Bible for help and comfort.

Thus, I believe that the Bible and prayer are inseparable and that they hold hope for the future of the world and for eternal life.

357

MY DEEPER CONVICTION
ABOUT PRAYER

By Dr. Garland Evans Hopkins

Secretary General, The World Fellowship of Muslims and Christians

❦

I cannot remember when I did not believe in and practice prayer. Like so many of the best things of life, I have always taken for granted that prayer is the normal contact of man with God. I suspect, however, that until one day on Okinawa in September, 1945, I really did not understand what is possible through prayer. Until then, prayer was, for me, largely an exercise from which I received subjective benefit; and I was more than a little skeptical of the claims of those who believed it really **could** remove mountains, that prayer could produce an objective result.

The war had ended and I was engaged, under the authority of the American Military Government, in a study of the social, political and religious background of the Okinawans. As I went here and there, I met some of the leaders of the small Christian minority who had fled the war into remote villages and mountainsides. One of them, Toyama Seiken, asked me to help locate the Christian leaders and bring them together for a meeting to reorganize the Christian Church on the battle-scarred island. I agreed to help for such time as I might remain on the island. Several meetings were held, scouting expeditions sent out to discover others, worship services resumed here and there. We were progressing towards an island-wide organization and in re-establishing contacts with worldwide Christian organizations, but we were still just at the beginning of our endeavors when the blow fell.

Returning late one evening to my tent, I found a message asking me to come to the orderly room. Arriving there I was handed an order to proceed in two days to the Philippines for a long-overdue rotation home. The next morning I packed. In the afternoon I went to say goodbye to my Christian friends, particularly to Toyama-san. He and his colleagues received me graciously but were curiously unperturbed by my news. I was a bit upset because I had expected them to be very dismayed by my imminent departure.

"I don't understand why you are taking the news so calmly," I said to them. "I thought you would be very disturbed at hearing it."

"We are not disturbed," Toyama replied, "because we know you will not leave. We have been praying about this. You have not finished your work and we still need you. God has given us assurance you will stay until the job is done."

"Toyama-san," I said, "I have great faith in the effectiveness of the fervent prayers of righteous men. But I also have great faith in the orders of the U. S. Army. I am afraid this is it. I will leave tomorrow. So, let us say goodbye and Godspeed."

Toyama looked me straight in the eyes, a bit reproachfully, I thought, for my lack of faith.

"We will say Godspeed," he said, "but not goodbye. You will not leave."

I returned to my tent quite troubled. I thought how disillusioning it would be for my friends to find that Army orders took precedence over what they believed was God's answer to their prayers. There on my pillow I found another note directing me to come to the orderly room.

At the orderly room I was handed a teletype message: "Delete Hopkins, Garland E. 0-503125 from travel order . . ."

It was from XIII Air Force Headquarters at Clark Field, but it was unsigned and contained no citation of authority for the action ordered.

Anyway, my name was deleted and I was left, unassigned, on Okinawa, the last man of the XIII Air Force on the island.

I hastened to tell my Okinawan friends the news. They received it as calmly as on the previous occasion. "We were not worried," Toyamasan said. "We had our assurance."

After I had been picked up on the roster of the VII Air Force, I told my story to my new Commanding Officer and asked to be allowed to fly down to Clark Field to check it. He said he was as interested as I in finding out just what had happened and gave me the necessary orders.

Once at Clark Field I went to the Adjutant's Office and asked if I could find out why I alone had been left on Okinawa. "That's easy," the young first lieutenant said. "Corporal, get me Chaplain Hopkins' 201 file."

The file was produced and there was a copy of the teletype message, but still without any authorization noted.

"That is unusual," the lieutenant said. "Come back after lunch and we will have the data you want. Someone has snafu-ed!"

I went back after lunch, and again the next morning. But neither then nor since have I ever learned who issued those orders, or why.

"It beats me," fumed the adjutant. "I never knew this to happen before."

Two months later, one day in November when my Christian friends and I had finished a meeting of the newly formed

United Church of Christ on Okinawa, now in touch with and receiving support from the Mission Boards in New York, Mr. Toyama bowed low and addressed me, obviously on behalf of the assembled group.

"We have been talking it over and feel that the time has come for you to go. We believe you will leave us very soon. Your work here is finished."

From here and there neatly tied parcels suddenly appeared, my going-away presents.

"But, Toyama-san," I exclaimed, "I have no orders to leave and no idea when I'll go."

"It will be soon," he said.

Three days later my orders came and within a week I was en route home.

I believe in prayer. I always have. But since that experience on Okinawa, I believe with deeper conviction than ever before.

(Written exclusively for use in *We Believe in Prayer* and no reprints can be made except by permission of the author.)

PRAY WITHOUT CEASING

By Jane Pickens

Singer

❧

It is necessary to "pray without ceasing." And it is not difficult. The Bible tells us that man is made in the image and likeness of God. (Gen. I: 26, 27). It also tells us that God is Love, is Spirit and Truth, and that God is infinite. Then, it follows, that if man is made in that image and likeness, man also possesses these qualities infinitely and as he realizes them—quietly allows them to become a part of his consciousness—, they manifest themselves in his life. I John 4:6 "God is love; and he that dwelleth in love, dwelleth in God, and God in him."

To "pray without ceasing" means that one must examine one's thinking constantly and replace with good thoughts, those that are unworthy of the man created in God's likeness. This can become an habitual and happy pastime.

There are many "little foxes that spoil the vine," such as envy, jealousy, hate, falsehood, revenge, malice, judging, criticizing. When tempted with any of these things, turn to God immediately, with humility and selflessness, and silently stop and know—**realize**—that these qualities are not God-like and therefore cannot be a part of one's true selfhood. Then continue this process until these negative thoughts are replaced with the positive and healing **Love that is God.**

This type of thinking and praying can be enlarged to the world situation. Indeed, it is man's duty and privilege to take the world problems, as well as his personal problems, to the all-loving God for redemption, correction and healing. For example, instead of hating or fearing any of our so-called enemies—and ofttimes temporary enemies—they should be loved, because Love casteth out fear—and hate. All mankind is equally made in God's image and likeness. Loving one's neighbor as oneself is possible and understandable on this basis. Each negative thought can be reversed in the "twinkling of an eye" and replaced by a positive, loving one, a God-like one, when man is alert to his function and duty as God's child.

So the value of prayer is as infinite as God is infinite, but it is necessary to "pray without ceasing" in this simple, direct way, in order to prove man's oneness with God, which really means the world's oneness with God.

THE ECSTATIC JOY OF PRAYER

By Helen Traubel

Opera and Concert Singer

❁

I have been impelled since childhood by a strong and urgent **desire** for prayer—never in a conventional, formal or perhaps orthodox fashion. It always seemed to me that the **need** of prayer indicated a negative approach. I cannot for myself tolerate the use of prayer for material advantage or the "emergency" prayer. I instinctively feel a oneness with the universe as devised by our Creator. This, then, means the ecstatic **joy** of prayer—the **gratitude** for the privileges of a free and dignified life and a happy acceptance of the responsibilities and vicissitudes attendant with them. My prayer is a ferocious gratitude to the Almighty.

PRAYER IS A BRIDGE UNITING MANKIND TO GOD

By J. Edgar Hoover

Director, Federal Bureau of Investigation

❦

"In the Lord put I my trust . . ." Psalm 11

We have been propelled into a new age. The doors opening on the frontiers of space are being flung wide before us. The horizons appear to be unlimited and opportunities for advancing man's knowledge of God's universe are endless.

Are we going to measure up in meeting the responsibilities which have been so suddenly thrust upon us? Will we find ourselves pressing forward in frantic confusion, or have we the wisdom and the courage to turn to that Source from which our forefathers drew their strength?

The men who fixed the foundations and reared the vaulted rafters of this Republic had an indomitable, all-encompassing belief in God. The words they spoke breathed forth their faith. The documents they penned exuded faith. The government they created was based on faith, and the concept which held them to their task was spiritual and idealistic. Surely, they knew the power of prayer, for it was their belief in God which gave them strength to create a free America.

Our task is to keep America free.

In the face of the menace of materialism—father of both crime and communism—we must seek Divine help if we are to accomplish our task. The power of prayer does not lend itself to measure any more than does the strength of faith, but of this I am sure: the man who is lacking in faith and who has never sought help beyond himself is limiting his capacity to live, to create, and to be happy.

Who can explain the power of prayer? For some, it lends the strength to span the gap between that which we are and that which we might be. For some, it is the clarifying medium which separates truth from falsehood. For some, it is the force which disperses fear and confusion. For some, it is the current through which the soul receives surcease from sorrow and despair. For me, it is a kind of bridge. Our engineering miracles—the bridges of America—soar out across great barriers, uniting men, enabling us to reach out to each other, tying us to our fellow men in commerce and communication. Prayer, whether it be a hymn of praise or a simple plea for mercy, is the bridge which unites mankind to God.

Surely, as we move into that realm where His laws are precise and immutable—the realm of science—we need nothing so much as unity with Him. We need the power of prayer to guide us.

WHEN THE CHANNEL OPENS

By Monroe W. Smith

Founder and President, Youth Argosy, Inc.

My thoughts on prayer are not unusual. I believe prayers are always answered—sometimes with powerful, positive response and sometimes with a mighty "No!" I don't always want to accept the latter! But I pray for God's will to be done, and for my own will to **want** His will. Then the channel really opens.

THE EFFECTS OF PRAYER

By Dr. Gerald Kennedy

Bishop of the Methodist Church in the Los Angeles Area

❦

Prayer means much to me. My day cannot be properly begun unless I find the quiet moments when I sit quietly at my desk and concentrate on God. I center my thought on the great reservoir of Power which God promises and I ask Him that the day be lived in that consciousness. He never lets me down. When I pray, the day goes better, I keep my temper better, and I do not get so tired. I do a better job. The best use of prayer is to listen rather than speak, and for this we have the scriptural assurance that He knows our needs and we shall not be blessed for our much speaking. Listen to the still, small voice and focus your whole life on the presence of God.

This is not easy. For one thing, you find your mind wandering and it takes discipline and practice to concentrate spiritually. But it gets better with practice and it can be learned. Also there are the doubts, and many a time a man has to pray the prayer of the father whose son the disciples could not hear: "I believe; help my unbelief." This is a Christian prayer and very often a man has to confess his doubts and ask God's help in dealing with them. Above all, never try to cover them up and act as if they do not exist.

One of the effects of prayer which frightens many away is that it makes a man look honestly at himself. This is no easy thing to endure, for every man has much within he knows is wrong. He has tried to pretend that it does not really matter and other people are doing it anyway. This pretense can be maintained if he stays on the surface, but when, in the privacy of his own soul, he approaches God, then the barriers fall and he looks honestly at himself, sometimes for the first time. Not many of us can stand to look into the terrible abyss which holds our sins, compromises, betrayals and lusts. No wonder we prefer to talk about prayer but hesitate to pray.

But when a man can persist and look at himself as God sees him, then he can be healed. It is like covering up a boil and being afraid to let anyone get close to it out of fear, and then finding courage to let a surgeon lance it, cleanse it, and heal it. There is no release like facing the worst about yourself and confessing it all to God with a sincere prayer for cleansing and the restoring of health. Then a man is free.

PRAYER ACKNOWLEDGES DEEP GRATEFULNESS

By Dr. Paul H. Nystrom

Professor Emeritus of Marketing, Columbia University

❦

I heartily believe in prayer to God, the great, eternal and ineffable Creator and Director of this universe of which we are but insignificant particles on a minor planet of one of the many solar systems.

My prayer acknowledges deep gratefulness for life and its opportunities to the unfathomable majesty of the Creator. I pray that I may play my part properly, where I have been placed, to the best of my ability, and with patience, compassion and justice towards my fellow men and that I may be granted increasing light and understanding in determining what is right and what is in accord with the great progress in the development of the experiment of human life.

TO MY SONS AND DAUGHTERS

By Dr. Fred Eastman

Author and Professor Emeritus of the Chicago Thelogical Seminary

❦

The older I grow the more I believe in the power of prayer. Not power to gain wealth or material success; but power to commune with God and to seek to understand His will for me; and power to help others in our common struggle for freedom, truth, and peace.

I've made my will bequeathing what material assets I have to your mother and to you when the bell tolls for us. But there's something more important in my life than such assets—something the lawyer and the probate court cannot convey to you. It's my experience with prayer. I'll sketch here only a small part of it.

When I was about six my parents, by precept and example, taught me to pray. We had family prayers every evening. Father read a chapter from the Bible, offered a prayer thanking God for the day's blessings, asking forgiveness for our misdeeds, and courage to meet what might befall us on the morrow.

Despite my parents' example my private prayers through most of my teens were of the "gimme" variety—"Please, God, gimme a new bike."

When I entered the College of Wooster that type of prayer soon gave place to something more adult. The student YMCA encouraged the habit of a "morning watch" in my room, a before-breakfast period of twenty minutes of Bible study, meditation and prayer. As a guide I used not only the Bible but the concise and forceful writings of Harry Emerson Fosdick on the meaning of prayer, faith, service, etc. The college also brought to the campus a series of widely known heroes of the faith from mission fields at home and abroad. They challenged us to join with them and help to transform the hells of earth into some semblance of the Kingdom of God.

Now came the biggest crisis I had yet faced. What should I do with my life: become a lawyer like my father and someday his partner, or consecrate my life to a more distinctive form of Christian ministry? For days I wrestled with that choice. Finally in an agonizing prayer I told the Lord that if He really wanted me I'd become one of His ministers. As I rose from that prayer I felt a sense of profound relief. The burden of my choice had been lifted. In many a crisis since then I've felt the same sense of relief as through prayer I let God take charge of the direction of my mind and heart. The old "gimme" prayers couldn't do that.

In the fifty years since those college days, twelve of them in editorial work in New York and twenty-six teaching religious literature and drama in the Chicago Theological Seminary, each has had its full quota of crises. As my tasks increased in size and importance the need for God's guidance became deeper.

I learned much from others who had traveled the prayer-route to the solution of their problems—Saint Francis, John Wesley, George Fox, Robert Louis Stevenson, Walter Rauschenbush, Gandhi, and Kagawa. Although quite different their prayers had in common these factors: self-abnegation, penitence, recognition of the greatness of God, outreach for His fellowship and guidance, acceptance of His will, and intercession for others.

Perhaps my greatest help from prayer came in the Spring of 1951 when, at 65, I suffered a nervous breakdown. It struck suddenly with no physical cause the doctors could locate. It left me fearful, weak and trembling. I tried to pray, but my prayers seemed to fall at my feet like birds that had lost their wings. Then my family and friends and students did for me what I could not do for myself. They prayed. Then I began to feel a resurgence of my own faith in prayer. I turned again to the great affirmations of faith in the Bible from Isaiah's "They that wait upon the Lord shall renew their strength" to Jesus' "Ask and it shall be given you; seek and ye shall find; knock and it shall be opened unto you;" reading them over and over in sleepless nights until quiet and calm gradually replaced fear and trembling, and banished the fears.

Now, in "retirement," your mother and I start each day with our "morning watch" giving thanks for you and our grandchildren and praying that you may continue to be a blessing to your parents, your children and your communities.

PRAYER GIVES PEACE OF MIND

By Roy Chapman Andrews

Zoologist and Explorer

❦

I wish I might tell you what prayer has meant to me but your letter comes just as I am leaving for the hospital for a very serious abdominal operation.

I can only say that I have complete peace of mind. Prayer has given it to me. Without the strength of prayer, I would be a poor thing indeed. Because of it, I have no fear. "God is my refuge and my strength."

A SIGNIFICANT WORD WITH GOD

By Carl F. H. Henry

Editor, *Christianity Today*

❦

A Gallup poll could hardly determine the nature and value of prayer. Fifty million atheists could be wrong, and conceivably fifty million Christians as well.

One person, however, must be right, for he is in himself the only medium of effective prayer. He gives us also the meaning, the message, the motivation and the method of effective prayer. Jesus Christ is the final and supreme revelation of God the Father to whom we pray. As the unique God-man he links the eternal and the temporal worlds in his person and in his purpose: he becomes for us in our praying, therefore, our link between the eternal and temporal worlds.

Effective prayer depends on what Jesus the God-man **did**. By his atoning death for sinners, he erased the embarrassing distance between fallen man and the holy God. That is why Jesus taught the disciples to pray "in my name."

Effective prayer depends on what Jesus the God-man **does**. Besides becoming the way to God for us by his death and resurrection, Jesus himself is now with God (John 13:1) to hear and to answer prayer: "And whatsoever ye shall ask in my name, **that will I do** that the Father may be glorified in the Son. If ye shall ask any thing in my name, **I will do it**" (14:13). To believe who Jesus is; to believe what he accomplished on Calvary; to believe where He is now and what He is doing, comprises the open door to reality in prayer. This knowledge is defined and expanded in the Bible. To "have a word with God" in prayer means personal knowledge of Jesus Christ the incarnate Word, fully revealed in the written Word, the Bible.

God the Holy Spirit, the author of this written Word, is also essential to prayer. He teaches us the meaning of his Book, he reveals us to ourselves in the light of the Bible, he enables us to seek and to pray in consistency with God's will. He formulates our prayers, interprets our thoughts to God, keeps us in momentary rightness of heart to pray. In prayer we commune with the Power of prayer. We pray to God the Father in the name of God the Son by the instruction and power of God the Holy Spirit. At varying stages of spiritual experience we may not always be aware of or practice this pattern of prayer. But without this totality, prayer may be ineffective, even unheard and unanswered.

To use a technical term, prayer is communication. More specifically, prayer for me is meaningful communication between myself (once a prodigal but now an accepted child) and my living heavenly Father.

This communication in prayer succeeds only under conditions stipulated by God but which he also has fully met for me. He has ordained them for his self-disclosure to me for my blessing, and for my self-realization in him for his glory.

When God and I fellowship in prayer, the spirit surges with both humility and boldness, sorrow and joy, weakness and strength, nothingness and fulness, hate and love, death and resurrection. Nowhere is there such commingling of antithetical forces.

ONE THING CAN SUSTAIN US

By George L. Murphy

Stage and Motion Picture Actor

❧

In these troubled times I can think of no more worthy objective than to rebuild the moral forces and strengths so necessary for the future of our nation.

I was raised in the Roman Catholic faith and from the beginning of my instruction I have had the importance and the power of prayer implanted in my mind and in my character.

During the past five years my family and I have had some extremely serious and trying situations relating to health and other problems which at times seemed almost insurmountable. I assure all who may be interested that I can attest to the positive power of prayer without which I doubt very much if my poor nervous system would have stayed in one piece.

It is a wonderful thing to have all the cultural and scientific answers for so many of the mysteries of life, but inevitably it seems to me we all come to a place where the one thing that can sustain us is our belief and faith in the Supreme Being and in the use of prayer in supplication for help in our troubles.

I do not doubt for one instant that were it possible for all men to have the blessing of faith and prayer, the troubles of our tired old world would disappear and the peaceful calmness of the ideal life would be ours merely for the asking.

With all honesty I sincerely believe in the full power of prayer.

PRAYER'S SUPREME EFFICIENCY

By Dr. Albert E. Day

Director of Spiritual Life, Wesley Theological Seminary

❦

I believe in prayer because I have witnessed its transforming results in my own life and in the lives of people to whom I have sought to minister for more than a half century.

We read many stories of men and women who through prayer have had their financial needs supplied, their vocational perplexities unravelled, their inner tensions relaxed, their diseases healed, their tottering homes rescued from the threat of divorce, their enemies changed into friends. I could add to those heartening tales from my own experience and from that long and intimate contact with the private lives of all types of people who have come to me for help when the going has been heavy and disaster seemed inevitable.

God has been the answer again and again when "other helpers fail and comforts flee." Prayer has not prompted His answer nor persuaded His unwillingness. He is always on the alert and always more ready to be God to us than we are to have Him. Prayer is not a stimulant to an indolent God. It is not the persuasion of a reluctant God. It is not sales talk that overcomes divine resistance. It is not a lawyer's pleas that softens the heart of a Divine Judge and secures remission of deserved penalty. Prayer is the opening of the door of our lives to One who is forever seeking entrance.

> He patiently waits at the door of our hearts,
> He seeks but the gift of our will,
> He comes with the bounty of heavenly grace
> Our emptiness richly to fill.

All that is wonderful beyond all exaggeration. I would not

diminish the wonder of it nor discourage any one who comes seeking or who responds to the seeking God with faith and love.

But my own greatest confidence in prayer arises out of those personal transformations which have taken our human dust and changed it into gold, our natural egocentricity and supplanted it with outgoing love, our earth-born timidity and in its stead begotten a spirit that could face overwhelming odds with a song, our absorptions with the gaudy but fleeting prizes of this world and dedicated our time and strength and talent to the values that will outlast the stars.

One illustration must suffice. It is the story of a saint. Not an old, gray and worn-out person whose saintliness might be suspected as the final effort of a person about to die and eager to pass muster at the gate of heaven. No, this is the silhouette of a young woman who is alive and eager and on tiptoe for whatever the coming years may bring to her. She is in a vocation that calls for unwearied patience, unremitting service night and day to the afflicted, unbounded love for those who often are very unlovable, genuine tenderness, unreserved loyalty to her associates and a contagious faith in God. I have known some blessed people during my long ministry but none more Christ-like than this vigorous servant of humanity. I have seen her in the most perplexing situations respond with a poise that was little less than amazing. Buffeted by the hard selfishness of angry humanity, she has radiated a love that was little less than miraculous. Jesus Christ seems to be her constant companion and guide. For Him she lives and with Him she meets the trials and turbulence of this age of anxiety. Her life is a witness to the every-dayness of the grace of God and its availability for "the weary weight of this unintelligible world."

What is the secret? There is only one possible answer—prayer! Every day she sets aside one uninterrupted hour for communion with God. And it is real communion! So vivid is her sense of The Presence that she often finds it hard to bring her prayer time to a close. No wonder she is so like Him!

This is the supreme efficiency of prayer. It is not a way to use God for our purposes but rather the way to become the kind of people whom God can use for His glorious purposes.

SERENITY THROUGH PRAYER

By Harry J. Anslinger
U.S. Commissioner of Narcotics

Earnest prayer solves perplexing problems. I was brought up by a saintly mother who gathered all the family together after dinner to read a verse from the Bible and to kneel in prayer.

Many years ago I was faced with a profound problem. I had overlooked prayer. The tension was burdensome. I was lying on the bed in my hotel room turning over and over possible solutions, knowing that a gruelling ordeal was in store in the morning. I was getting nowhere. My eyes rested on the Gideon Bible. I picked it up and prayed that the page on which I opened it would bring strength and surcease. It opened on the 37th Psalm and after reading it several times, coupled with prayer, I faced the situation serenely.

I knew it would have a lot to do with my future career. The faith and fortitude prayer gave me, as I engaged in the battle, enabled me to solve the problem quickly and I emerged with the knowledge that victory came through prayer. Ever since, in fair or stormy weather, I have found in prayer a great spiritual uplift which began at my mother's knee and has carried me safely through revolutions, hurricanes, treacherous shoals and numerous hidden dangers. Prayer gives you courage and serenity.

PRAYER IN A SPIRITUAL UNIVERSE

By Dr. Earl L. Douglass

Author and Clergyman

❁

Why should I pray?

First of all, because the Lord commands me to do so. His words are, "When ye pray, say. . . ." He required prayer of all His disciples. If we could not discern a single benefit from prayer, we, as Christians, would nevertheless be required to pray simply because we are commanded by Jesus to do so.

In the second place, I observe that men of power have always been men of prayer. This is revealed not only in sacred history, but in so-called secular history as well. Abraham Lincoln is a great example of the power of prayer; likewise, George Washington, and many other heroes who served noble causes.

Most striking of all, I find that Jesus Himself prayed. Certainly if there was anyone who could dispense with prayer, Jesus would appear to have been that person. He and His Father were in continual communion one with the other. He was the only begotten Son of God. His power was so great that He could still the waves and by His touch restore health to diseased and broken bodies. Furthermore, He had all wisdom. Yet, before He chose his apostles, He spent the entire night in prayer. As He confronted the cross, He sought out Gethsemane and there, prostrating Himself before God, He uttered the most agonized and powerful prayers that ever went forth from human lips. Almost His last words on the cross constituted a brief petition to God that He would forgive His enemies.

If Jesus needed the daily support, inspiration, guidance, and ministration of prayer, how much more do I and my fellow men need it! It is plain to anyone reading the Bible that God never does for any individual anything that individual can do for himself. But man can go just so far and no farther. There is a line across which he cannot step. On the other side of that line are the issues of life's events, and these issues, let us keep well in mind, are always in the hands of God. Jesus urged men to plan carefully everything they desired to do, but they were to leave the issue of affairs in His hands.

Now in prayer we do precisely that. We praise God, we thank Him for His blessings, we ask His counsel, we express our desires—then we leave the issue of affairs in His hands. Prayer is really the bringing of life's events to Him and laying them at His feet.

Even Jesus needed prayer that this might be accomplished. How much more, therefore, do we need it.

Last of all, experience has taught me the value of prayer. One might just as well expect to keep his body healthy without food and drink as to keep his soul healthy without prayer and the study of God's word. Some people are more moody than others, but we all have periods of dejection; nothing lifts one out of dejection so firmly and satisfactorily as does prayer. The pathway before our feet is darkness; we pray and although we may not see far into the distance at least we see the next step plainly.

If any believing Christian will go back over his life and count the number of times the things he asked for have been definitely given him by the hand of God, he will be amazed. And what will amaze him most is that often when he asked for some definite thing God gently set his petition aside and gave him a much greater and more significant gift. The pray-er had asked for a little gift; God gave him a gift that partook of the glory of divine love and wisdom.

Yes, we must pray if we would live in a universe that is essentially spiritual in nature.

A NATION NEEDS TO PRAY

By Robert B. Anderson
Secretary of United States Treasury

❦

A nation needs to pray:
For things it has—for things it has not earned,
For gifts from men now dead, some dead
So long ago we never knew they lived.
Their hopes and dreams, their genius and their sweat
Now molded into wood and sculptured stone,
Iron and steel and countless things we cannot sense
But by awareness of an ordered scheme
That had to come from minds and plans and hopes
And struggle to reality.

A nation needs to pray:
For what will come out of a time unknowingly beyond,
Obscured by present tasks and inabilities,
Scarcely glimpsed by imagination,
Yet struggled toward and with a certainty
Beyond our reach except for fragments,
Parts of patterns, tossed into our paths
That lead us to believe we view the whole;
And viewing, pray that we may be
Spared confusion, and avoid futility;
That we may dream of the inaccessible,
And touch the possible.

A nation needs to pray:
That in humility we see that greatness
Is not measured by industrial grandeur,
Or destiny achieved by things we touch,
By things produced, nor things consumed,
Nor things we set afloat upon the sea,
Nor send into the air,
Nor delving down, gouged out of earth;
Nor is it known by tower set on tower
Groping for a finite place in infinity
Nor by any other things
That man may proudly say
Were made by mind or hand.·

All these we take, or make
In gratitude—with thanks

For what was added to us by the past,
Or by our contemporaries,
Out of substance that was part of earth
As we, before we became articulate.

These things we do that men
May eat and sleep—may work and rest,
And have a separateness.
And yet when all is done, we still shall seek
To yet define that which is humanity,
That quality that makes of mass,
And flesh, and good and bad,
A nation: That needs to pray.

How many things divide us!
Color, creed,
A different faith or tongue, geography;
The customs and the habits of our land,
A heritage as much a part of us as flesh and bone;
Yet all the time we seek to find the things
That will unite us; some universality
That spans our differences.
We labor to produce by rule and plan,
By treaty and documents, what we fail
In practice and in precept to lay down.

From out of all that troubles us,
Toward solutions that clarify and not confound us
Where shall we seek the answer?
How shall peace be made a practice and not a principle?
How make justice a world reality?
How minimize the frailties of man's rule
And live by the rule of law?

How shall we reckon with the forces of energy,
When for the first time in man's history,
We have in sight the possibility of
Freeing man to exert his own creativeness,
Rather than to toil under the dictatorship
Of need and want?

With such enchanting possibilities
Have we the means and the ability to
Avoid the use of energy to destroy?

No other question has this urgency;
No other men have faced the fearful choice

That history, pausing, places in our hands.
Yet first must come our own assured defense,
Not merely of our land and of our ways,
Not merely to protect our lives or what we hold as dear,
But in the knowledge that our free world holds
The sanctuary of the hope of man,
For freedom on this earth,
For the avoidance of world dictatorship,
Against the forward drive of ruthless power,
Of godless men, denying human worth.

So for all its awesomeness,
For all its destructiveness,
There is a moral purpose for the bomb;
There is a reason for its terror,
There is a need that will exist
Until we find the yet obscured
Concern of man for man.

Time might provide the leaven for us all,
But we do not have the time to wait;
Too closely press the possibilities of destruction;
Too cumulative are the consequences of continued waste;
Too fragile are the qualities of mortality

With all these imponderables,
Beyond the scope of mind and hand,
Our greatest need is:
For a wisdom that transcends our own;
For a devotion that insures
There is no instant of neglect
For that, wherein is held
The fate of all This nation
Needs to pray.

How overpowering to contemplate
Man talks with God.

So may it be that we, and all the host
Who follow on, find here the solace,
And the way through man's recurring doubts,
To peace, and what endures in souls,
That make of us the children of immortal heritage;
And here come to believe that earth
Will know its destiny, and man his purpose,
When each shall pray
"Thy will be done."

PRAYER IS A GUIDANCE

By Janet Leigh
Actress and Motion Picture Star

❦

For me, prayer is a living thing. I like to think that I am praying with every thought and movement of the day. I once read a line in a religious book that has stayed with me throughout the years: "Life is the showing forth of the very self of God." I have never been able to get over the wonderful feeling that this gave me. To think that everything I do in a day, no matter how big, no matter how small, can be a prayer or an expression of God.

Prayer for me can never be a once-a-day formality—and then put it aside until tomorrow at the same time. I like the informality of prayer because I like to keep it with me all day.

I hope I can adequately answer the question some day that is bound to be asked by my little girl, "Why do you pray, Mommie?", or "Why should I pray?" It will be a hard answer to give simply and concisely. I don't want to frighten her with a deep philosophical explanation—or a lengthy one. I just want her to know and feel the happiness that comes from prayer, and I will only be able to tell her how I feel, and I feel good! I feel close to someone, I feel that I am never alone. Even if I am putting books away or cleaning house or filming, my short little messages or thoughts are like road signs along a highway. It's not that someone is driving me along the highway but, like the signs, prayer is a guidance and a guidance not necessarily to great deeds of great importance, but a guidance to perhaps help me keep my temper, a kind word instead of a harsh word, maybe a thought of love instead of a thought of hate. Simple little thoughts, but these are the simple things that make up our lives—and, for me, prayer has helped to make mine a happier and fuller one. Thank God.

PRAYER IN THE LONELINESS
OF RESPONSIBILITY

By Dr. Richard L. Kozelka

Dean, School of Business Administration
University of Minnesota

❦

There are at least two familiar kinds of loneliness in which prayer is of assistance. One is the loneliness of a forest or prairie or a mountain, far from another human being. Another is the loneliness of a big city, surrounded by strangers. A third is the loneliness of responsibility.

The burden of decision-making, particularly when it affects the lives of many people, places the administrator or executive in a more lonesome position, the greater is his responsibility. He may consult and confer and study, but he is alone in the final decison.

Prayer, in the form of a "still, small voice," is sometimes looked to for the correct decision, as an inspiration direct from God. This is an abdication of responsibility, to expect God to make the decisions. But prayer can help to establish the conditions of calm, detached judgment in which the best decision can be made on the basis of facts and experience.

After the decision is made, the administrator is still in need of prayer to sustain him through the consequences. If he is in error, (and who can claim no failures?) he may be terribly alone. Then prayer can restore his confidence, carry him through the criticism of his peers and the disappointments of his subordinates, and give him the humility to learn from his failures. If his decision is correct, prayer can curb his pride and turn him sympathetically to those adversely affected by his action. Even if he is right, a storm of criticism may make it hard to stand firm by one's best judgment. Prayer can undergird the courage necessary to support a lonesome, unpopular, but necessary decision. The burden of responsibility cannot be removed by prayer, but it can be made bearable.

THE VALUE OF PRAYER

By John Murray Robey
Publicist with U.S. Information Agency

To me, prayer is a refuge, a relief and a help. Ever since my early boyhood days, when I was first taught my catechism by a very gracious lady, I have frequently and regularly sought solitude where I might offer prayers of thanks and appeals for guidance and help—in favorable or unfavorable circumstances. This practice has proved more than rewarding throughout my college and business life.

It was of immediate help during the years our four children were young and during the course of their development into splendid manhood and womanhood. We still give thanks to God for their fine characters, their welfare and their excellent successes.

In the past thirty-five years in various responsible positions in my professional field, I have come face to face with many trying situations where Faith and Prayer have been of inestimable value in solving problems and choosing the right path. Faith and Prayer are redeeming. Faith and Prayer are helpful when the prayers are for the right and truth. Faith and Prayer are everlasting bulwarks on the road that is life.

PRAYER: A WAY OF LIFE

By Royal Dixon

Author, Naturalist, Lecturer

❦

The ability to pray is a gift of God. It will lead one into wondrous paths, which are filled with great privileges and opportunities that are inherent in the natures of the sons of God. It was He who created the marvellous universe; and every plant, bird, animal or insect, must in some way have access to its source. He is a loving Father, who reminds us to "Consider the lilies how they grow; they toil not neither do they spin . . ." " Go to the ant. . ." "The cattle on a thousand hills are His. . ." He is mindful of all His creatures.

As a child, I was taught to pray at my mother's bedside; and was told always to go directly to God, the source, who reveals to man his oneness with the source. God is spirit; and they that worship Him must worship Him in spirit and in truth; then only can man realize that this amazing universe is fully equipped with the answer to every need of body and soul, which can be met here and now. Jesus portrayed to man the greatness of God; He said: "In my Father's house are many mansions. . ."

Often as a child, I stood in awe at the rising of the sun, and realized that the Lord must have spent billions of years to give us that day! We owned just three books: the Bible, Pilgrim's Progress, and Emerson's Essays. Here I got my first inklings of the wonders of the material universe, and the services it renders to the human soul. Small wonder that Christ was born in a manger, near the animals; and that the first to see the Star of Bethlehem were the shepherds who were guarding the sheep!

I found great admiration and beauty in roaming through the woods, and began to accept Nature as another great book, second only to the Bible. To me it was God's living earthly Bible, where every man is nourished by the grandeur of earth, sky, and ocean. Much travel and experience taught me the marvels of land, sky, and sea. I learned the principles God used in creating and realized the one great **law,** which is always operative. It comes to all who are spiritually attuned to Him. He is perfect, therefore His creation is perfect. It was all "very good" with Him; and Jesus said: 'The kingdom of heaven is at hand." It is everywhere, all around us, within us, "closer than breathing, nearer than hands and feet." Just to the degree that we accept this faith, we become painless, sickless, and sinless. The nature of God and the nature of man are one. This is not a philosophy but a fact, as is realized by all whose lives are dedicated to Him.

Through prayer—a way of life—prosperity and health are assured; and there is only one great thing needed, which all the prophets of the past have declared unto us—**vision** and **understanding** to be gained by searching the Scriptures. Only the praying man learns the will of God—that no man should be sick or afflicted, that prayer brings freedom, opens the door to God, assures man's victory over all evil, brings at-one-ment with God, reveals man's Godship, keeps contact with the great source, and unfolds the unity of the universe. Through it man proves his own spiritual powers, his identity with God, the glories of the Divine, the sanity of this marvellous universe, and the one powerful, all-inclusive law: **mind reproduces in body and circumstances anything upon which it dwells.**

LEARNING HOW TO PRAY

By Dr. Charles R. Sattgast

President, State College, Bemidji, Minnesota

❦

There seem to be at least two general philosophies concerning prayer. One considers prayer as a psychological preparation. The other is the belief that an individual, through prayer, may actually align himself in harmony with and draw strength from the great creative power of the universe which most people call God. If one were to analyze the thinking of the millions of people who pray, it is quite likely that most of them could be placed on one of the two above categories. It is my belief that both theories complement each other so that in addition to preparing oneself psychologically to bear the extra burden or undertaking a strange problem that at the same time an alignment with the creative power may be effected which will actually bring about changes.

In recent years there have been articles on prayer of a nature that would suggest prayer by a salesman to help him make a sale or prayer by an athlete for victory in an athletic contest. It has always been difficult for me to see how God could care whether or not the customer should buy the prayed about article or which side would win an athletic contest. On the other hand it is conceivable, even though God does not enter into making a sale, that the salesman through prayer build up his courage to better meet a client of whom he is somewhat frightened and as a result do better in his sales technique. It is also conceivable that in praying for victory in an athletic event the team members who pray may use this as a part of the psychological build-up for confidence necessary to meet an opponent. Prayer of these types may actually get results, but in my mind, so could a good pep rally. The basic question here is not related to results obtained through prayer but rather whether prayer for personal gain is a worthy goal.

If prayer is to be a real force it should be an alignment of the individual, or a group of individuals, with the power of God. This would put meaning into the statement. "Prayer changes things." If prayer changes things, a national day of prayer for peace or something similar to the Methodist 24-hour per day 365 days per year prayer, which is a continuous prayer for peace could, and I believe will, influence the minds of the ones who will decide on peace or war and so change the current flow of events. It is no more difficult to believe that the great creative power which can balance the numerous stars in the heavens or give the enormous energy to the atom could not at the same time provide the power to change men's thinking and so change the course of human events. If God answers prayer on this level, I can with ease believe that prayer on smaller issues can and will be answered also. Our problem would therefore become a matter of learning how to pray. To this Jesus taught us to say, "Thy Will Be Done."

When one prays it is more likely that both the alignment with the spiritual power of the universe and the personal psychological preparation operate to the same end and in harmony one with the other. The individual or the group of individuals who through prayer have the ability of aligning themselves with the creative spiritual power would without doubt also place themselves in a psychological mood for the acceptance, forbearance or intensive exertion necessary to help bring about the desired purpose. Prayer should therefore be a concrete means of bringing an individual closer to God, and at the same time better preparing him to undertake a new task or situation.

388

PRAYER LIFTS US UP

By Eugene Dewey Flaherty

Vice-president, American President Lines

❦

We renew our faith by prayer. It is precisely because we believe in God that we address our petitions to Him. Our belief in his power over all things leads us to request His aid and guidance in all good things.

We enlarge in goodness by prayer. Implicit in our faith in God is the belief that He is all good and can countenance no wrong. We know that He will reject any appeal based on wrong and which might lead to evil. When we pray we evidence our own goodness and right intentions.

We gain courage by prayer. When we ask for God's help, our faith tells us that we add to our own puny efforts the blessings of the Almighty and His assistance in our needs. With such mighty sponsorship, we go forward with courage to the realization of our hopes and aspirations.

We acquire confidence and contentment by prayer. We know there is nothing more uncertain than reliance on unaided self. But with God on our side we cannot fail. What a powerful feeling of confidence we gain when prayer lifts us up by His hand! And in this complex and confused world of ours, what can lead to greater contentment than our trusting reliance on His infinite kindness and mercy.

Prayer is love. We ask God for his aid with loving assurance that His own infinite love for us will not withhold the comfort we seek.

STUDY YOURSELF—
AND THEN PRAY

By Will Rose

Editor and Author

President, Board of Trustees, Edinboro College

❦

Are you in poor health? Is your marriage headed for the rocks? Are your children obstinate and ungrateful? Are you running into debt? Is your job in danger? Are you working too long and too hard? Is the family edgy? For these and many other everyday problems, study yourself and the way you think and do things, and then try intelligent prayer.

Don't just hope it may help. Be confident that it will.

People who have not discovered that Christian prayer can be a beneficial force in their lives are basically ignorant and insensitive.

These are the folks who scoff at prayer, until they find themselves in dire emergency. When they find themselvs in great danger, or pain, or sorrow, the most stupid and callous will turn to prayer, but even then their plea is likely to be strictly selfish, and contrary to all scientific reason.

Often it doesn't bring them any escape or relief.

They do not understand what prayer is, nor do they know how to use it in their daily lives.

Prayer is for miracles, they think.

Prayer may be for miracles — depending on the nature of the miracles — but prayer certainly is for the consecutive, little things that pop up moment by moment in our thoughts and conduct, and in our associations. Prayer is for Divine help so that we may think what we **know** we ought to think, and do what we **know** we ought to do.

And there is a formula for the most effective prayer.

The formula is a progression. It opens with sincere faith in the omniscience and omnipotence of God, stated or implied; or, if one attributes to himself too much super-intelligence to believe in a Supreme Being, even he may gain the benefit of prayer by acknowledging a sincere faith in a central source of orderly knowledge and energy, whatever its form, or wherever it may be.

Submission should be followed by confession, confession by thankfulness, thankfulness by a pledge to supply our share of the effort, and the pledge by the plea.

And I think I have learned in addition by experience that prayers can be answered only within limits.

That's because God's responsibilities extend to everybody and to everything in the Universe—not just to individuals. Many of these responsibilities are unknown to us because we have not yet reached complete knowledge of the Universe, much less understanding of it. But one responsibility, it seems to me, is definitely known. God must keep the Universe in balance. To do this, God has established immutable laws— known as causes and effects—which apply to the spirits, the minds, and the bodies of individuals, and to the physical Universe. Therefore, it is beyond reason to ask God for something which we assume to be a blessing (but may not be), the granting of which requires God to ignore his laws involving cause and effect. If any mountains were ever moved by faith and prayer, they only appeared to be moved. Either that, or God was moving them anyway, and prayer was only coincidental. Otherwise, if the slightest physical change were made, our air and water would become as poison, the tides depending on the moon would drown the earth, the rays of the sun would burn us to a crisp, and, in all probability, the entire Universe would be destroyed. Certainly our own earth with its life would be.

Now this should be simple enough to be within the grasp of all of us beyond the ages of babies. But we ignore it. Heedless youth is too self-confident to feel the need of prayer. Middle age forgets about prayer in the pressures of life. Only the intelligent among life's veterans turn to prayer daily for guidance, strength and help.

And so human relations are in pretty much of a mess, on the average.

During forty years of newspaper work, I have observed a great deal of human suffering, wailing and gnashing of teeth —always due to ignorance or recklessness of individuals, or of their associates, or of group society. So universally do we ignore God's laws that we do not even pause to concentrate sufficiently in an effort to anticipate hazards and thus avoid them. The penalty looms, and we wonder why God is so cruel.

But—during the same forty years of newspaper work, I have observed a great deal of repair, triumph and peace— always due to humility, confession, self-effort, and a plea for God's help.

THE COMMON DENOMINATOR

By Albert H. Daggett

President, Gould National Batteries, Inc.

❦

Prayer—the common denominator of the human race.

PRAYER IS A POWER TO CULTIVATE

By Henry James Forman

Author, Editor and Lecturer

❀

Human beings have been praying for untold millenia, yet there are many even today who are skeptical as to its efficacy. It needs only a very little thought to realize that prayer means talking to one's own highest self.

The Quakers, one of the most inward-looking of all religious sects, hold that "there is something of God in every man." In other words, God, or Divine Spirit, or the Supreme Creative Intelligence, call it what you will, is not only to be thought of as remote, distant, in some far-off heaven, but as actually resident in and filling our own hearts, minds, every atom of our being. Prayer, to me, is a turning to that inner Being, that is closer to us than breathing, nearer than hands and feet.

Prayer, the most natural of human expressions, is also a mysterious force which, as yet, even the wisest among us scarcely comprehend. The late Dr. Alexis Carrel, great physician, notable physiologist, Nobel Prize scientist, described some of the effects of prayer as observed in the grotto of Lourdes. He tells of a woman hopelessly ravaged by cancer, scarcely able to stand, even though assisted by a nurse. When she saw the throng of other patients, crippled, twisted, the faces of some eaten away by lupus, she spontaneously began to pray for those misery-laden human beings. Almost immediately the nurse supporting her felt a tremor going through her patient and the woman was healed. Her far-advanced cancer was cured while she was praying for others.

Dr. Carrel, great scientist that he was, felt compelled to

conclude that prayer is a force of which as yet we know little or nothing. But since man has been using it for thousands of years, ignorantly for the most part, it is certain that as he advances he will try to gain more accurate knowledge of this great and God-given power.

Prayer has been described as the soul's sincere desire. Even more it seems to me to be the soul's sincerest expression, the sincerest it is capable of. We hear today of a marked religious revival, of much greater church attendance. That is very good. But even more necessary is a revival of belief in prayer, public prayer, and especially private prayer, a belief in the divinity that resides in ourselves and in every being around us. If we dream of universal peace, if we hope for an abatement of crime, delinquency and misery in our world, that is the direction our thinking must take.

THE THERAPY OF PRAYER

By John Sparkman
United States Senator from Alabama

God is our greatest psychiatrist. He offers us release from the tensions of modern living through the therapy of prayer.

Each passing day imposes upon mankind more demands in order for him to keep pace with the confusing world of everyday living. Prayer is a restful retreat from mankind's everyday skirmish with our maddening pace.

My walk of life is that of a United States Senator. I know of few tasks more demanding. It is an interesting, vigorous and challenging walk of life. It is a life of soul-searching in which one must do his best to make the right decisions. This soul-searching must be done through prayer.

It is comforting for me to know that there is always room for God along side me in my Senate chair.

394

THE PERSONAL ENCOUNTER WITH GOD

By Dr. Milton S. Eisenhower

President of The John Hopkins University

❦

In the Judaic-Christian heritage which forms the basis of our free Western civilization, the whole of this actual world is to be taken seriously as a community of persons in which the living God acts and to which men freely respond. Thus we recognize the power of prayer:

It is always possible to read and believe the Bible without discerning the great truth it contains. It is equally possible to know the historic truth regarding the documents that make up the Bible and yet fail to hear the voice of the Eternal in biblical history. As literature, the Bible deals with great and noble themes—God, man, life, death, and destiny—and the truths that are revealed in its books are not **argued** out, but **acted** out. As drama, the Bible is supremely interested in a personal encounter between man and God; it is not abstract, but instead tells about people in a manner so vivid and penetrating that in their characters are revealed what we know as "everlasting realities" or "eternal verities."

One distinguished theologian, Professor Walter Russell Bowie, has said of the biblical drama, that "when we have watched the figures that fill the great stage of the Bible, we know not only what life **was** but what life **is,** and what the facts are with which every man must deal—selfishness and unselfishness—cruelty and gentleness, cowardice and courage. All these are in the Bible . . . as forces that live and move in people who startle us by their likeness to ourselves. . . Through the composite faces of many men we see **man**—struggling, groping, sinning, and yet aspiring, lifting his eyes toward

God, and at length beholding God come amazingly more near to him than he had ever dared to dream." . . . The Bible brings us its conception of God as active in history. The Old Testament, from its beginnings through the whole of its great expansion of religious understanding, is unvarying in that it reveals a God who is operative in our actual world. The events of men and nations are not a meaningless whirl; they are the arena in which an everlasting purpose is at work . . .

In the New Testament, the idea of a God active in history comes to us through the gospel of Christ: the gospel of "the Kingdom of God." He taught His disciples to pray, "Thy Kingdom come, Thy will be done on earth." This message of the Bible was dramatically captured by Sir Winston Churchill recently when he said: "What ought we to do? Which way shall we turn to save our lives and the future of the world? It does not matter so much to old people. They are going soon anyway. But I find it poignant to look at youth in all its activities and ardor, and most of all to watch little children playing their merry games, and wonder what would lie before them **if God wearied of mankind.**"

The Bible brings us a message of the accountability of men to the ultimate authority of God. When men look to nothing higher than themselves, their life inevitably begins to move on a mean, drab level. It is only when they look up to a Divine purpose—a purpose high enough and strong enough to hold them true—that they can steer through the caprices of the moment toward a steady, supreme goal.

Woodrow Wilson, while governor of New Jersey, made this affirmation about the Bible and its message of moral accountability: "This book is the one supreme source of revelation, the revelation of the meaning of life, the nature of God, and the spiritual nature and need of men. It is a book which reveals every man to himself as a distinct moral agent, responsible not to men, not even to those men whom he has put over him in authority, but responsible through his own conscience to his Lord and Maker. Whenever a man sees this vision, he stands up a free man whatever may be the circumstances of his life." . . .

The Bible concerns God — the maker of this vast universe, of man, our world; God, Who has addressed His message to every soul and therefore makes a demand upon every man. The Bible is the place where God is encountered, where His message is spoken and His will proclaimed. It is the instrument by which, with abiding faith and through the communicative act of prayer, each of us may see again — as John saw in the midst of chaos — a new heaven and a new earth.

—*Adapted from a baccalaureate address at The Pennsylvania State University, June 10, 1955. By permission.*

MY FAVORITE PRAYER

By Adlai E. Stevenson

Former Governor of Illinois

❧

Lord make me an instrument of Thy peace; where there is hatred, let me sow love; where there is injury, pardon; where there is doubt, faith; where there is despair, hope; where there is darkness, light; and where there is sadness, joy.

O Divine Master, grant that I may not so much seek to be consoled as to console; to be understood, as to understand; to be loved, as to love; for it is in giving that we receive, it is in pardoning that we are pardoned, and it is in dying that we are born to eternal life.

St. Francis of Assisi

397

PRAYER IN DAILY LIFE

By M. W. Clement

Retired President, Pennsylvania Railroad Company

❦

Peace is freedom from fear, and freedom from fear comes to those who place their faith in a Supreme Being to whom they pray, and thus break the bondage of fear. Even a man of little faith, or no faith, when faced by great danger, automatically turns to God with an unspoken prayer on his lips and a flash of petition in his mind.

Prayer runs through all life from this extreme of occasional use to the other extreme—that of perpetual adoration by those whose lives are given up to prayer. Through the lives of most men, midway between those two extremes, there exists a privacy of prayer known only to themselves, which is helpful and soul satisfying at work or at home and which is powerful in their lives.

Sometimes, just a moment now and then, the problems of those dear to you come to your mind. As you reflect upon them, paralleling the thoughts through your mind, there often runs a prayer for them—a prayer for intercession that helps you calmly and clearly to come to a conclusion helpful to you and maybe helpful to them, calming and peaceful in its influence on your inner self.

As you move through life and things go right, and you are becoming too satisfied with yourself, perhaps maybe just a thought comes over you that makes you appreciate the Master of us all. Your mind turns to a prayer of thanksgiving, not spoken, not put in words, that gives you a feeling of sharing the credit with the God of all—something that in the end

398

brings more satisfaction and more happiness to you than you could have had without prayer.

Through your daily life, day or night, the most soul-satisfying prayers of all are those that are part confession, perhaps part intercession, and maybe thanksgiving.

No matter how busy one can be, there are moments of the mind when work stops and relaxation comes. If in those moments one reviews in his mind with the Deity those things left undone, the things that should be done, or the things done that should not have been done, out of that confession comes a relaxation of mind, body, and soul that only prayer could have brought; and one can go on more able than before. Self examination and confession, with perhaps a little petition, brings one a satisfaction that can remain all the day long. Just now and then in a moment of relaxation, or a moment of reflection, a thought that is a prayer helps in trials and tribulations, in storm or strife, in effervescence of pleasure, or in the sunshine we all love. There is no better stimulus than such a moment of communion.

THE SPEAKER'S PRAYER

By Murray Shields

Economist

❁

How wonderful it would be, in these difficult and dangerous times, if every individual privileged to make any public expression—written or spoken—would, before preparing it, get down on his knees and pray for divine guidance that what he is about to say will make some contribution to the achievement of peace, progress, and prosperity for this troubled world.

THE MIRACLE OF GOD

By James B. Carey

President, International Union of Electrical, Radio and
Machine Workers, AFL-CIO

❧

I believe in prayer and I believe in miracles. I believe in living our lives in the sight of God. For He is with us, with each one of us, always present, always observing, always understanding.

Prayer is the means by which we communicate with God and He communicates with us. Prayer is our personal, private exchange with God. It is the method by which we seek and receive the guidance, understanding, faith and power to sustain us in our daily lives.

The testing ground of prayer is in our own individual lives. Each one of us must prove it unto ourself and experience it ourself. No one can do it for us, for God recognizes each one of us individually and He judges us for what we are.

It is not enough, however, simply to believe. We must practice our beliefs. We must live our lives in keeping with the principles of God, so that there is no conflict between the individual and God. The deed must match the word.

Nor is it enough merely to accept the idea of prayer and to go through the motions of praying. To pray—to reach God and to communicate with Him—requires strong personal conviction on the part of the individual. Even more, it requires intense power of concentration by the individual.

I have talked with many people on the subject of faith, and I feel that this, the intense power of concentration that is necessary, is probably the greatest barrier between people and

God. I feel that when many people pray, they do not possess the intense power of concentration necessary to bring about a meaningful exchange with God. Some people are so distracted by earthly considerations that their thoughts wander from their prayers. As a result, there is no communication and those people become disillusioned, possibly eventually forsaking prayer entirely.

I do not believe the only place to pray is in church. Nor do I believe that a person must set aside a special time or place to pray each day. I believe a person can pray while he is at work on his job, in his office, on an airplane, or in the country on a drive with his family. This I do myself. Sometimes I find myself praying, alone with God, in situations which to the orthodox might seem strange. But to me this is very real. And it is in times such as these that my prayers are rewarded most fully, for in these difficult situations, when each hour seems to bring ever-mounting problems, God gives me the strength and the faith to cope with them.

I feel that if anyone who truly believes will persevere and work at his prayers, he can achieve a meaningful exchange with God. And when we have elevated our own physical lives, as well as our spiritual lives, then—through prayer—we can see the miracle of God and realize the miracles which only He can work.

But I do not believe it is possible to pray and achieve selfish or designing objectives. Indeed, I am sure it is not possible. For that is not prayer; that is self-seeking. How could God possibly, even if He were so inclined, respond to a selfish plea when some other mortal might be petitioning Him for the exact opposite?

I do not believe that we can expect God to improve or change the world or our lives in ways which are within our own power to change and improve. God did not endow man with the ability to think and create so that man could invoke God to solve problems which man himself created. These are man's responsibilities and man—with his God-given ability to think and create—must resolve them himself.

However, if we work at our faith and our prayer, God will respond and sustain us with the power to bring about the improvements we seek. If we improve ourselves and live in the true spirit of God, our prayers will be answered if it is the divine will. For then we will be imbued with His spirit and His understanding. This is the strength that can move mountains.

A young minister from North Carolina once addressed our Union's convention. His address was one of the most moving spiritual pronouncements on the relationship of man to God that I have ever heard. Like this young minister, I firmly believe that the highest form of service to God is ". . . to work for justice, to comfort the suffering and the oppressed, to practice brotherhood—indeed, to do battle with prejudice— to proclaim the dignity of man as a child of God, and to extend the ministry of the church beyond its four walls into the social, political and economic life of the people."

When we do that, through prayer we **know** God.

I BELIEVE IN PRAYER

By Russell M. Riggins

President, Texas Gas Corporation

❦

Prayer solves all problems.

PRAYER MAKES POSSIBLE
THE IMPOSSIBLE

By J. Manley Phelps

President, Phelps School of Speech

❦

Not all that seems impossible actually **is** impossible. In the words of one of our prominent philosophers: "The **difficult** is that which can be done at once. The **impossible** is that which takes a little longer."

A man of character, of indomitable courage, of inexorable will finds no place in his vocabulary for such words as **failure, defeat,** or **the impossible.**

If this be true of a finite person such as man—and it is— think how infinitely true it is when man has attuned himself with God, and has learned to trust Him through faith and prayer.

In Luke 18:27 Christ tells us that the things which are impossible with man are possible with God. Over and over again we are taught that with the help of God—through prayer —we can do or accomplish anything.

Here is a wonderful gift of divine help which God offers us! Yet how often we ignore it or fail to avail ourselves of it. We pray for God to help us; yet as we pray we doubt that He will. A prayer that is filled with doubt is ineffectual.

In Mark 11:24 we learn, "what things soever ye desire, when ye pray, believe that ye will receive them, and ye shall have them." If we pray with defeat in our minds and hearts we can expect no answer, for we are doubting God's love and His promises to us.

If we pray for strength to carry us through our trials and

tribulations but, at the same time, doubt that we will receive that strength, we lack the faith so vividly expressed in the words of Paul, "I can do all things through Christ which strengtheneth me."

We read and remember many of the miracles recorded in the Bible which were the fulfillment of prayer and the fervent faith that sustained that prayer.

Yet when modern miracles occur before our very eyes we frequently are not even conscious of them, "for now we see through a glass darkly."

Moreover, when we do become aware of them we often try to rationalize them or seek some scientific or material explanation. Especially is this true of those of us who consider ourselves so very, very sophisticated or intellectual.

When "the chips are down," however, there are myriads of human phenomena or experiences or behaviors which cannot be explained or understood by scientific formulas or cynical intellectualism. In the words of Hamlet, "There are more things in heaven and earth, Horatio, than are dreamt of in your philosophy."

Prayer **can** and **does** work modern miracles which science and logic can never explain.

The modern doctor realizes that he must work together with the man of God whether he be priest, minister, or rabbi. They both have an important function in helping and healing those who are physically or mentally ill. Many times the prayer of the man who has faith and trust in God takes over where the doctor leaves off.

Christ himself said: "Pray for one another that ye may be healed. The fervent prayer of a righteous man availeth much."

Prayer can sustain one not only where there is sickness of

che body or the mind, but it is obviously the one and the only thing that can bring comfort and surcease to the sickness of the soul.

Spiritual sickness, or sickness of the soul, can be cured by God alone when one who believes has the faith to talk to Him through prayer.

Every thinking man or woman **must** believe in the efficacy of prayer. All of us can remember scores of times in our lives when we or our loved ones have been saved, or blest, or inspired through prayer, and through faith and trust that God will hear our prayer. Yes, we **must** believe in prayer—you and I.

I know of many, many times when God has answered my prayer or the prayers of my loved ones.

I know that my lovely wife, Catherine Denny Phelps, and her distinguished brother, J. Howard Denny, are alive today because her prayers were so devout and her faith and trust in God so absolute that they could not fail to reach the heavenly throne.

I know that my sainted father, who prayed and sang hymns of praise to God even as he died, is now with Him in Paradise.

THE DEEPEST WISH

By Frank Lloyd Wright
Architect

❦

To believe in prayer is only to believe in the deepest wish of a human heart—and of course I believe in that.

405

PRAYER IS FOR EVERYONE

By Werner Janssen

Symphony Conductor

❦

Prayer is a lifting up of the mind and heart to God.

No one can understand prayer without praying.

And no man can pass sanely through life without praying.

Eventually, every man must come to God.

"The most beautiful and most profound emotion we can experience," wrote Albert Einstein, "is the intuition of the mystical. It is the power of all true science . . . to know that what is impenetrable to us really exists, manifesting itself as the highest wisdom and the most radiant beauty which our dull faculties can understand only in their most primitive form."

Monks in a choir chant psalms. But the psalms, in virtue of their inspiration, are a revelation of the same Divine Word. Yet prayer is not only for monks; prayer is for everyone.

Some of us may not care particularly what the archaeologists think of us a few thousand years hence—but none of us wants to be short-lived because of our work, or our loved ones, or our friends; and limited as is our little span, we shall have an urge (pretty vague in most of us) to make our civilization last and maybe make it a little better for our children and their children.

The great hope that in America we may do this lies in the stirring of our artistic consciousness. "The glory that was Greece and the grandeur that was Rome" declined into materialism. If we can emerge from the hand-to-mouth materialism of our age, as it surrounds us, into a flowering of the arts, we have taken the first step toward a spiritual awakening that may yet save the world.

Music, love, art: these are holy words because they stand for all that is purest in man's inspirations. They are gifts from God and proof that there is and can be a better world.

THE PRAYER OF OUR PEOPLE

By Dwight D. Eisenhower
President of the United States

Before all else, we seek, upon our common labor as a nation, the favor of Almighty God. And the hopes in our hearts fashion the deepest prayers of our people.

May we pursue the right—without self-righteousness.

May we know unity—without conformity.

May we grow in strength—without pride of self.

May we, in our dealings with all peoples of the earth, ever speak truth and serve justice.

May the light of freedom, coming to all darkened lands, flame brightly—until at last the darkness is no more.

May the turbulence of our age yield to a true time of peace, when men and nations shall share a life that honors the dignity of each, the brotherhood of all.

PRAYERS ARE ALWAYS ANSWERED

By *William Hillcourt*

Director of Program Resources, Boy Scouts of America

❦

When I was a child I did childish things—and it took me many years to outgrow them. Whenever I wanted something, I prayed—prayed real hard. When my prayer was answered, I felt good—real good—I knew that I was in favor with God. When my hopes were not realized, I felt bad—real bad—I was sure that God hadn't been listening, that he was angry at me for some reason.

Until, one day, I heard the story of the old priest who was asked:

"Father, are your prayers always answered?"

"Always, my son," answered the priest. "But often in the negative."

In looking back I have come to the realization that when my prayers were not answered, when my hopes were not fulfilled, there was a reason—and the reason ultimately worked to my advantage. Most of the time something even better happened. Often new and much larger opportunities opened up before me as a result of a prayer denied.

And more and more I came to understand that small, selfish things have no place in a prayer—that the welfare of others and the submission of personal desires must be part of every prayer, every hope, every ambition . . . that perhaps Saint

Francis of Assisi better than most other humans knew how to pray:

"Lord, make me an instrument of . . . Your **Peace**
Where there is hatred, let me sow . . . **Love**
Where there is injury . . . **Pardon**
Where there is doubt . . . **Faith**
Where there is despair . . . **Hope**
Where there is darkness . . . **Light**
Where there is sadness . . . **Joy**

"Divine Master,
Grant that I may not so much seek to be consoled,
    as to **Console**
To be understood, as to **Understand**
To be loved, as to **Love**
For
It is in **Giving** that we receive,
It is in **Pardoning** that we are pardoned,
It is in dying that we are born to **Eternal Life**."

CONFIDENCE THROUGH PRAYER

By K. L. Wilson

Commissioner of Athletics, Intercollegiate Conference

❧

I am a strong believer in the value of prayer. In my work, which is beset with many troubles, I frequently pray that God will grant me judgment, wisdom and tolerance in making my decisions, that He will grant me courage, humility and patience in helping me through a difficult day. It gives me a feeling of strength and confidence to renew my efforts to do a better job and live a better life as an individual and as an administrator.

WIRELESS TO GOD

By Carolyn Sherwin Bailey

Author

❦

An electric storm shatters our telephone and telegraph system. For a longer or shorter time we are cut off from these daily forms of communication with our fellow men. Crossed wires, a shattered pole, an accident to the central system handicap us. We celebrate civilized man's invention of these systems of talking things over with one another.

There are no accidents to interfere with the transmission of prayer, the oldest known form of communication, an instant's means of talking it over with God.

The local exchange sometimes irritates us in its slowness in getting us our connection. We are irritated by this delay. Our prayer is transmitted without the medium of an exchange. No human intervention is required in reaching God through prayer. No matter how scholarly phrased, simple or selfish our prayer, no consideration of a prayer's source, sender, its plea, it reaches our Father in Heaven.

The reply telegram is more or less dictated by the sender. Is our simile of prayer to modern forms of communication then invalid? Prayer, we know, is not always answered in kind. This may be due to the nature of our request. We are not ready for the well-being, the success, the good fortune we asked. Our prayers are frequently answered in an entirely different form. We are not ready for good fortune; adversity and the spiritual growth involved in meeting trouble are what we need.

Christ's prayer in the Garden of Gethsemane seemed unanswered. His answer came in the rise and growth of Christianity. It is carved in the stones of every church, every foot-
step crossing the threshold of a church. Practice our oldest,
quickest form of communication, prayer, with the knowledge
that, in some form or another, it will be answered.

THE REAL MEANING OF PRAYER

By Philip K. Wrigley

Business Executive

❦

I have always had some very definite convictions about the
value of prayer. It has always seemed to me that the majority
of us in this world only turn to prayer when we are in trouble,
need help desperately or want something to satisfy our particular desires of the moment, and as soon as the emergency or
need is over, we forget all about it until the next emergency
arises.

It is my belief, and I have always tried to practice it, that
this is the wrong way to proceed. A prayer of thanks for good
health or good fortune given in an atmosphere of relaxation
and happiness is much more acceptable and effective.

Probably the best parallel I can think of to explain my
thinking is to refer to the old Chinese custom of hiring a doctor to keep you well instead of waiting until you fall sick
before you call him in.

Communion through prayer with our Creator has significance for the individual only as it becomes a constant and
steady practice.

PRAYER—THE STEPPING STONE
TO HAPPINESS

By Dinah Shore

Radio and Television Star

❦

Not long ago, when I visited the Shriners' Hospital for Crippled Children in Houston, Texas, I was not merely struck — but utterly overcome — by the overflowing happiness of the handicapped youngsters who lived there. They represented in every sense a cross section of America. They were children of all races and creeds and many, and heartbreaking, forms of infirmity. But I was astonished at their remarkable indifference to, if not complete unawareness of their afflictions. They were children who obviously lived by the wonderful injunction of Irving Berlin's song, counting their blessings instead of their handicaps when they put their darling little heads on their pillows at night.

But where were their blessings? How was it that these children of adversity, unable through physical incapacity to share in the freedom and abandon usually served up so generously in childhood, seemed to feel they had so much to laugh and shout and sing about? I turned to the doctor who had been guiding me through the hospital.

"I'm just overwhelmed," I told him. "What do you do for these children that makes them so blessedly happy? Have you perfected some wonderful new miracle drug?"

The doctor laughed pleasantly.

"No," he shook his head. "It's not a wonderful new miracle drug — but a wonderful **old** miracle prescription."

He took out a prescription pad, hastily scrawled some

words, and handed me the piece of paper. It said: "RX—TLC."

I looked at him quizzically.

"Tender loving care," he replied, "the greatest medicine in the world."

You know something? I don't think I've ever known anything to embody more beautifully the spirit and fulfillment of prayer than the miracle of TLC at the Shriners' Hospital for Crippled Children in Houston.

For I am convinced that from the cradle on, the sum total of all human prayer is wrapped up in two yearnings — to be loved and to be needed. Sometimes, if we happen to be introspective, we find words to articulate these prayers. Probably more often they are spoken in the language of loneliness, in the universal search for the feeling of belonging.

Every last one of those handicapped children at the Shriners' Hospital has experienced the miracle of answered prayer. Some may be destined to recover from their infirmities. I suspect, unfortunately, that most are not. But their prayers have been answered with a gift of learning to live with imperfection. I can't help feeling that any person, child or adult, has realized the ultimate in answered prayer when he or she learns that a physical handicap, any weakness or inadequacy, is not necessarily an obstacle to happiness.

Quite the contrary, through the wisdom that comes with prayer it can be converted into a stepping stone to happiness.

YES, GOD LISTENS!

By *Richard C. Harlow*
Former Football Coach at Harvard

I am very grateful for the opportunity to express my sincere feelings about the power of prayer. My experience with praying boys comes mainly from observations of three distinct segments:—the average college student; the football player and the serviceman fighting for his country.

During the second World War it was my good fortune to serve a period where I was in intimate touch with some of the bravest men in the world—the United States submariners. I have seen these men from seamen up to admirals come back from war patrols when the Pacific beyond Midway was a Japanese lake. Often they had been subjected to the most trying of nerve stresses, having been continuously subjected to depth bombing for long periods of time. Often have they told me that every man was praying—sometimes even while fighting. Normally if there was a proclaimed atheist aboard, he always prayed most fervently! I never met, among the bravest, a submarine man who did not pray.

Among college boys it is the same story. Whenever in trouble (real or fancied) the college boy prays earnestly and meaningly.

In football I wouldn't give a plug nickel for a team that wasn't a praying team. Of the many teams of wonderful kids that I have coached—the ones that prayed the hardest, won the most.

There is something in prayer that lifts a poor halfback to the heights. Prayer made America great. When it stops—America is through.

Thank you for giving me the opportunity to express myself regarding prayer. It's a bridge between God and humanity. Only prayer can save America now!

"ASK, AND YE SHALL RECEIVE"

By Julius Klein

Major General, U.S. Army Reserve

Past Commander, Jewish War Veterans

❦

Contrary to a popular belief, the most frequent subject of conversation we hear from day to day is not the weather, but prayer. More references are made to it, in an endless variety of ways—respectfully, humorously, fearfully—in our daily thoughts and conversation, than any other topic.

We often speak of a fortunate occurrence as "the answer to a prayer;" or to a prize fighter or baseball pitcher who has "nothing but a prayer;" and we make similar applications of the word to many other daily routines.

In fact, we can also refute the familiar quotation that "everybody talks about the weather, but nobody does anything about it." We all do the only thing that can be done—we pray for relief from distressing weather conditions, and history records a great many instances in which the prayers of a community have brought dramatic relief from calamitous weather.

Prayer, then, is so much a part of us, that we often fail to realize its influence on us. Actually, it is the most "natural" thing we do.

It was one of the first gifts of God, and surely one of the greatest privileges we could possibly have. In our complete dependence on God, how utterly helpless we should be, if we had no recourse, no hope of achieving improvement in health or happiness, nothing but the acceptance of a burden through all our lives!

But, we live, instead, in the inspiration and comfort of His words: "Ask, and ye shall receive; seek, and ye shall find; knock, and it shall be opened to you."

We are not merely allowed to hope or wish for blessings we desire . . . we are invited, even **urged,** to bring our troubles to God. He **wants** us to come to Him, like a child to its father, which is our actual relationship to Him, and to seek the comfort and protection only He can give.

Through our prayers, we speak directly to God, by His own invitation, and we know that He is always waiting to hear our voices; even though, far too often, we seem to call on Him only with our complaints and pleadings, and all too seldom do we remember to tell Him of our gratitude and happiness.

Prayer is not restricted to any language. Often, it needs no words at all. Without it, we are left with nothing. With it, if we pray in good faith and with complete resignation to His will, many doors will be opened to us.

Prayer is the universal privilege of rich and poor, the blessed and oppressed, the mighty and the lowly. It is the greatest common denominator, the brightest hope of the world, our only strength against fear and despair.

Where else can we turn, but to Him? How else, except by fervent and unfaltering faith and prayer? There never was a time when we needed God more desperately, and if we do not come to Him through love and devotion, perhaps many of us will find him at last through fear.

Ours is the privilege of asking, and seeking, and knocking on His door, every day of our lives. Perhaps we fail to say "thank you," but God never denies us the right to return as often as we wish. It is hard to conceive of many gifts more precious than the right to pray, and the knowledge that God is always ready to hear us.

PRAYER SHOWS GOD'S WILL

By Dr. T. Otto Nall

Editor, *The New Christian Advocate*

❧

I believe in prayer because it changes things, changes other people, changes me. And yet, I hesitate to say "it" because prayer is nothing less than conversation with the heavenly Father, and it is He who makes the changes.

There was a time when I imagined that prayer could change God's attitude toward me, or these whom I hold dear, or the causes in which I have faith. I learned better. God does not need to be convinced, and He cannot be cajoled or conquered.

He knows all my arguments before I make them. He sees all sides of the situation, so there is no use in my calling attention to some matters He may have missed. No promises I may offer, no bargain that I propose will have any effect on Him, for He already knows what is the right answer, and He will not make the wrong one.

Why pray then? My conversation with God can have profound effects on circumstances, even situations that may not seem to be the subject of prayer at all.

For example, I may make a trip, and take part in a meeting where my vote counts one way or the other. I may make a decision that affects the lives of others. I may throw all my strength on the side of a debated matter, and lose. Prayer can give me new insights. Prayer can give me courage. Prayer can lead me to new information. Prayer can strengthen me when I am defeated, convincing me that it is not the battle but the war that counts. All this is another way of saying that prayer shows me what God's will is.

Prayer can change people—people who are my friends, people whom I have never seen and never expect to see, people who are my enemies. It is not obfuscation to say that there is a mystery about prayer that the discoveries of the mind cannot unravel. "More things are wrought by prayer than this world dreams of," and these miracles are not in the area of stopping cyclones and avalanches, but in the places that affect the motives of people. Thought transference, but dimly understood, is in accordance with the laws of the mind, and the power of one person's mind expressing God's will has its results on the minds of others. There is no doubt about it.

So, we can pray for people, and we can pray with people, whether they know it or not, actually whether they wish it or not. Who is there to say that Russian atheists are not affected by the prayers of God-fearing and God-loving Americans, just as Americans are influenced by the prayers of the Russian faithful?

More important still is the result that prayer has on the person who prays. Of course, it is possible to offer a selfish prayer—to pray that our side may win the game, instead of praying that we may play as good sportsmen whoever wins. It is possible to pray that somebody else, or a whole nation of somebodies, may come to harm. It is possible to pray narrowly, vindictively. But if prayer is conversation with God, the Father of all men, such selfish praying will not get much higher than the ceiling. God will not say "yes" to such requests. We may get our request, but it will not come through prayer.

Conversation is two-way. We do not request and wait for a response. We talk with God in prayer. We listen, too. And He speaks, and we come to know Him better, and we discover how silly our selfish prayers are. Then we reach the end-result of all praying—"not my will, but thine be done."

I BELIEVE IN PRAYER

By Billy Graham

Evangelist

❧

There are thousands of people that pray only when they are in times of great stress, danger and uncertainty. I have been in airplanes when the motor conked out and people started praying. We have flown through bad thunder storms when people who never thought to pray before were praying all around us. I have talked to soldiers who told me that they never prayed until they got in the midst of battle. It seems to be an instinct in man to pray in times of trouble.

Jesus said that men ought always to pray. I do not believe that the problems of our world will ever be settled until our national leaders bow their knees in prayer. If only our leaders could discover the strength and reliance upon Almighty God we could soon see the solution to the grave problems that face the nation.

Elijah prayed, and God sent fire from heaven to consume the offering of the rude altar he had built in the presence of God's enemies.

Daniel prayed, and the secret of God was made known to him through the saving of his companions.

Jesus prayed at the door of the tomb of Lazarus, and the one who had been dead for three days came forth.

The thief prayed, and Jesus assured him that "this day thou shalt be with me in Paradise."

Paul prayed, and hundreds of churches were born in Asia Minor and Europe.

Peter prayed, and Dorcas was raised to life to have added years of service for Jesus Christ.

John Knox prayed, and Bloody Mary said that she feared the prayers of John Knox more than she feared all the armies of England.

John Wesley prayed, and revival came to England, sparing her the horrors of the French Revolution.

Jonathan Edwards prayed, and revival came to Northampton when more than fifty thousand people joined the churches.

Jesus Christ died to make this communion and communication with the Father possible. He told us of the joy in Heaven when one sinner turns from sin to God, and from his heart breathes a simple prayer—"God be merciful to me, a sinner."

In this modern age in which we live we have learned to harness the power of the mighty Niagara and to turn its force to our use and our good. We have learned how to hold steam captive in boilers and release its tremendous power to turn our machines and pull our trains. We have learned how to contain gasoline vapors in a cylinder and explode them at the appointed second to move our fast automobiles and trucks along our highways. We have discovered the secret of how to release the energy that is latent in the atom, which is capable of destroying entire cities and civilizations.

But very few of us have learned how to fully develop the power of prayer. We have not yet learned that a man is more powerful on his knees than behind the most powerful guns we have ever developed. We have not learned that a nation is more powerful when it unites in earnest prayer to God than when its resources are channelled into defensive weapons. We have not discovered that the answer to our problems can be had through contact with Almighty God.

I have found that the greatest need of the foreign missionary is not more money, though there is always a need; it is not greater and better educational facilities, though that is a need; it is not bigger and better equipped hospitals, though there is certainly a need for more Christian hospitals; it is not even for new churches—the greatest need of the foreign missionary is prayer. If the average Christian back home realized how much his prayers meant to these valiant heroes of the faith, they would not cease to pray day and night for their representatives out there in foreign mission fields.

We are only able to move in our evangelistic work, through our film ministry, through television and radio, by prayer. If it were not for the prayers of thousands of God's people throughout the world, our ministry would completely fail.

Our Lord said: "And whatsoever ye shall ask in My Name, that will I do, that the Father may be glorified in the Son. . . If ye shall ask anything in My Name, I will do it."

God help us to pray! If we are to survive, we must have spiritual revival! If we are to have spiritual revival, we must have more earnest, effectual praying!

COMPLETE FAITH THROUGH PRAYER

By Jacqueline Cochran

The World's Leading Aviatrix

❦

Perhaps faith was inherent in my case. It was partly developed through the help of a traveling priest who visited our sawmill camp on occasion. I was a child then, but I sensed the light of God in this priest, and it shone on me. Even a child can thrill to the promise: "Ask, and it shall be given you; seek, and ye shall find; knock, and it shall be opened unto you."

Because I have a strong faith and believe in prayer, it does not mean that everything always comes out right for me. There have been turbulence and air pockets. In the early days of my more than 10,000 hours of flying, I must have had a hundred forced landings and a dozen crackups, but I walked away from all of them.

My first place of business was destroyed by a hurricane. Four of my planes were also destroyed. I have made air records which were never recognized because a near-sighted judge on the ground failed at the proper moment to see me flashing by at altitude. Recently, while flying just 200 feet above the ground at close to 700 miles an hour, I set a speed record only to find on landing that the electrical timing equipment on the ground had not functioned and my efforts had gone for naught.

Recently I became the first woman to pass the sonic barrier and to exceed the speed of sound. That meant a climb to an altitude of nearly 50,000 feet. Up there, even by day, the sky is dark blue, and the stars can be seen. Earthbound friends are left behind.

But up there I did not feel alone. Indeed, I felt closer to the portals of Heaven, and more aware of the presence of God. When your innermost self is being tested, there is no dependence on the material world below. You cannot see or hear those dear to you. But you find yourself in Hands more gentle and trustworthy than human hands can ever be. Their invisible influence filled my being, and I was fortified for the moment when I turned the nose of my plane over a direct, full-power dive for earth.

Those Hands never left me during the subsequent antics of the plane and fighting the turbulent shock waves of the barrier. The speed I attained was well in excess of 700 miles an hour.

I have found adventure in flying, in world travel, in business and even close at hand. There can be adventure in such a simple pastime as my helping the wild quail on our ranch lose their fear and come trustfully close to me.

Adventure is a state of mind—and spirit. It comes through faith—for with complete faith there is no fear of what faces one in life or death.

PRAYER IS LISTENING

By Dr. Frank N. D. Buchman

Initiator of Moral Re-Armament

❧

Fifty years ago I was asked by the Democratic State Chairman for Pennsylvania to go to State College, Pennsylvania, where there was crisis in the student morale. Studies were at a low ebb and even sport was in the doldrums. The night I arrived there were nineteen liquor parties and someone said it was so wet you could float a battleship.

Prayer was the habit of my life, morning and evening; so I prayed fervently about the situation which faced me. Then, getting up from my knees, I set to work to organize activities of many kinds which I felt would counteract the poor morale of the College.

I worked hard, very hard. I was busy eighteen to twenty hours a day. I was so busy that I had two telephones in my bedroom. Still I was dissatisfied with the results. There was a constant coming and going, but the changes in the lives of the men who came to see me were inadequate, and not revolutionary enough to become permanent.

I became discouraged. I prayed more and worried more. Then it occurred to me that what I was worrying about was my own lack of success. Perhaps I was more concerned with doing God's Will in my way than in doing God's Will in His way. Was I just like any ambitious business man who asked God to bless his plans but never took the trouble to find out what God's plan for his life might be?

So I decided on a radical procedure—to give that hour of the day from five to six in the morning when the telephones

424

were unlikely to ring, to listen for the Still Small Voice to inspire and direct and to cut across my personal plans and my preconceived ways of doing things and launch me out in faith on God's plan.

That first morning instead of doing all the talking to God I took time to listen to God. Many thoughts went through my mind, but one stood out because it disturbed all my well-organized patterns. It was the name of a man, a student of whom, frankly, I was somewhat afraid. He never came near any of my activities; he was popular, successful, charming and apparently not interested in what I was doing. Try as I could, I was unable to get that man out of my mind. I said, "God, if you want me to speak to that man, I will do it."

That very morning as I went downstairs, I was almost knocked over by him coming upstairs. He apologized; inwardly trembling I asked him if he would like to come in and see me sometime. "I've been wanting to for weeks," he said, "but I haven't had the courage." That night he came and poured out a story of great unhappiness. He found a faith that night and changed so greatly that the whole College knew of it. Within a few weeks he had done such an effective work among his friends that the tide had turned in the College. The work I had been so laboriously wearing myself out in doing, was accomplished by the man I had considered the least likely, and far more effectively than I could ever have done.

That lesson has never left me. In many countries as I have met with statesmen and leaders of industry and labor, the key for the difficulties they face has been to listen, and to obey. When Prime Minister Kishi tells us that the new understanding between Japan and Korea and Japan and the Philippines is due to Moral Re-Armament, I think of the Japanese Senator and the Korean former cabinet minister who learned to listen to God and found the answer to bitterness, making peace through apology and forgiveness. Then together with other leaders they listened and found the policy for their two nations.

When Chancellor Konrad Adenauer says that the present good relationships between France and Germany are due to Moral Re-Armament, I think of a Frenchwoman, Member of the French Parliament, whose life was embittered with hatred for Germany, but who listened to God and found freedom. Her change set her free to go with a number of her countrymen and bring the answer to city after city of Germany. Former President Robert Schuman says of her that she has done more for Franco-German relations than any other person and calls MRA "a philosophy of life applied in action, the beginning of a far-reaching transformation of society."

To receive guidance from God is as normal an experience for every man as eating or sleeping. "God gave a man two ears and one mouth. Why don't we listen twice as much as we speak?" Guidance is the nations' life-blood. Without it nations perish. Statesmen living this quality of life will make it possible for the Mind of God to become the mind of nations. Through lack of this quality in their statesmanship, nations sell their birthright. "Men must choose to be governed by God, or they condemn themselves to be ruled by tyrants," said William Penn.

I SAW IT HAPPEN

By *N. H. Nelson*

Treasurer, The Evangelical Lutheran Church

❀

I am writing about the incident in the upper room at the Atlantic Athletic Club in the spring of 1948, when I was associated with Mr. Herman Reinhardt in the Georgia Baptist Hospital campaign. To appreciate the incident which transpired there, it is necessary that I give something of the background.

The firm of Ward, Wells, Dreshman, now the firm of Ward, Dreshman, Reinhardt, had contracted to conduct a campaign in the city of Atlanta and other areas in the state of Georgia for the Georgia Baptist Hospital, where facilities were far below those necessary in meeting the requirements of the community. There had been a number of meetings in connection with the direction of this campaign in an effort to secure leadership in the various divisions of the proposed effort. The unwillingness of the community leadership to accept responsibility had become a burden upon the heart of Mr. Reinhardt, who had conducted many campaigns in the city of Atlanta for community purposes. The situation which he faced in Atlanta became very tense.

The meeting was called in the Athletic Club, and a number of the men of the Hospital Commission and others in positions of leadership in Atlanta were present. The late Mr. Chris Dreshman stopped in Atlanta on his return from Florida and sat in on this meeting. There was some very frank discussion as to the situation, and Mr. Dreshman was asked how he felt about it. He made the very frank statement that unless the leadership of Atlanta came up with some responsible leadership in the proposed campaign, it would be necessary that the firm withdraw its personnel. There were at that time five of the firm personnel, including the writer, on the scene. Mr. Harrison Jones, sales manager for Coca-Cola at that time, presided at the meeting. I am sure he sensed the tension that had been built up around this campaign, and particularly after Mr. Dreshman's very frank statement. In fact, from my position of vantage at the entrance corner of the room, I could observe the faces and attitudes of those present, and I sensed that matters had come to a crisis. As I watched Mr. Jones, I noticed that he looked at several of the men and finally turned to the Reverend Louie D. Newton, pastor of the Druid Hills Baptist Church, also president of the Southern Convention of the Baptist Church at that time, and asked that he lead the group in prayer.

On this occasion, his impassioned prayer took the whole group into the presence of his Lord, and at its conclusion there was an audible sigh from most of those present. Immediately a contractor from Decatur was on his feet and made the following statement: "Mr. Chairman and Dr. Newton. I find that after listening to Dr. Newton and reviewing my relationship to the Church and to the community, I can no longer resist. I had come prepared to make a substantial gift to this campaign. I have already made a substantial gift to my church in Decatur. But I find that I must accept responsibility to see that this campaign succeeds. I will accept the leadership of one of the divisions."

At the other side of the room two men were already on their feet, the head of a chain of restaurants in Atlanta and the president of a life insurance company, who said, "We, too, find that we must accept responsibility. While neither of us can do it alone, together we will accept the leadership of one of the divisions."

At the conclusion of their remarks, a fourth person rose in the middle of the room, a distinguished member of the First Baptist Church of Atlanta and carrying a great responsibility in connection with the extension division of the University. He said, "I, too, find that I can no longer resist and find that I must accept responsibility in this effort, in spite of the fact that I am carrying very heavy responsibilities at this time."

Now to some this may have seemed just another campaign experience. But to the writer it had all the implications of an upper room experience such as was experienced by the disciples in the beginnings of the Christian Church. They, too, had been frustrated and very tense and had realized that of their own knowledge, strength, and wisdom they could not accomplish the purposes outlined by the Master before He left them. You will remember that group had continued in prayer for ten days, and no doubt they had discovered that their own strength was inadequate, and so they had surrendered all to the Divine guidance that had been promised them. And then came the Pentecost experience recorded in the Book of Acts.

The scene in the upper room at Atlanta had much of this in it. I feel quite certain that the men who were present that day had come to realize the inadequacies of their own resources, and during Dr. Newton's impassioned prayer, they suddenly became conscious of their shortcomings and submitted their problem to a power higher than theirs.

In this experience and similar experiences, there is, to me at least, the evidence of what can happen in the Christian Church when men learn to know their own inadequacies and seek the wisdom of a power higher than their own. It happened in the Graham meetings in New York. In fact, it is happening all over the world where men and women are consecrated and attuned so that the Divine power can flow into their lives.

In speaking to various groups, particularly to the men of the Church, I have used an analogy to illustrate how this great power seems to work. All are familiar with the use of radio. Any observing person knows that a radio, a table model for instance, is ordinarily a metal or wooden case filled with wires and tubes. But when it is desired to use this instrument, which is only material things put together in an orderly fashion, it is tuned into the source of power by plugging it into a wall socket. Now the power is there, but the instrument is still dead. Until the instrument is attuned to the sending station, there is no life, it is static. But when attuned and power is permitted to flow into the instrument, it becomes dynamic and speaks, and brings a message from the sending station.

Human experience is not unlike this. Individuals ordinarily are quite static. They are ordinarily good people, showing consideration of others, and leading orderly lives. But when it comes to the things of the spirit it is another matter. It is only when they have surrendered themselves completely in realization of their inadequacies, and have turned in humility to the Creator of all things and asked for power that power comes, and they, too, become dynamic Christian personalities. What would happen in our Christian Churches were this power realized generally, as it has been in individual instances? Here lie immense possibilities if only more have faith.

PRAYER THROUGH FAITH

By Edward F. Flynn

Former Director of Public Relations, Great Northern Railroad

❦

The Holy Bible tells us:

"And all things whatsoever you shall ask in prayer, believing, you shall receive." Matthew 21:22.

"Be nothing solicitous; but in everything by prayer and supplication, with thanksgiving, let your petitions be made known to God." Philippians 4:6.

"Likewise the Spirit also helpeth our infirmity, for we know not what we should pray for as we ought; but the Spirit Himself asketh for us with unspeakable groanings." Romans 8:26.

"Evening and morning and at noon, I shall speak and declare and He shall hear my voice." Psalms 54:18.

"Pray without ceasing." I Thessalonians 5:17.

"I will therefore that men pray in every place, lifting up pure hands, without anger and contention." I Timothy 2:8.

Thus the Father in Heaven tells us to pray. But He also informs us that we should **believe** in our prayers, that we should have **faith,** and not merely offer up prayers with our lips only, and that we should give thanks for the good things we receive.

In these directives to pray and how to pray, all men pray who believe in God and his Holy Scriptures.

All men who pray, have experienced the truth of these inspired quotations, for we all have received from Him many blessings that we did not deserve. Most of us have asked for many things in prayer that perhaps we ourselves did not believe in; that is, we had no faith and no belief that we should be given those things for which we prayed. Perhaps they might be likened to castles in the air; perhaps that for which we prayed was not good for us, but in all things for which we prayed, believing, and which were for our eternal good, we were granted.

Most people think that they have faith in their religious belief, but their description of belief or faith, may not be the true meaning of that word. We cannot merely say "This I believe" and make of that belief our faith, unless that faith is deep and abiding. Faith is not as easily obtained as that.

The Standard Dictionary describes the kind of faith we are discussing as "The assent of the mind or understanding to the truth of what God has revealed; belief in the testimony of God as contained in the Scriptures. A divinely wrought, loving and hearty reliance upon God and His promise of salvation, through Christ or upon the Christian religion as revealing the grace of God in Christ; sometimes called justifying or saving faith; as we are saved through faith."

I have always prayed with faith, from the time that I attained the sense of reason until the present time. As a child I prayed with my family in the kitchen, kneeling at a kitchen chair, for the parlor was kept for special occasions, such as Sundays or holidays. I prayed at least twice a day, generally many times throughout my life.

SOLVING PROBLEMS THROUGH PRAYER

By Harry A. Bullis

Chairman of the Board, General Mills, Inc.

❧

My mother taught me early in life that a man cannot depend on himself alone — that he needs strength beyond his own to help him make the right decisions and carry them out. Perhaps that is why to me religion is such a vital and personal thing. Faith in God helps me to keep my mind flexible and tough. My experience over the years has been that if we hook up with God through prayer, His dynamic energy will flow through us.

I believe that man, by prayer and by frequent and regular periods of silence, can draw to himself some of the power and wisdom from God. I believe that God expresses Himself by means of us or through us in proportion to our conscious receptivity.

Whenever I have to make a vital decision, or solve some problem that will affect not only my own personal life but the lives of people who depend upon my judgment, I trust my own intelligence and experience only up to a point. Beyond that I am humble. I pray for guidance. Then I listen, convinced that God will in some way assist me to reach the correct solution.

Here is my formula for solving major problems:

First, I consider with great care and patience all the evidence that I have in connection with the problem.

Second, I then get the opinion of one, or a small number, of interested persons.

Third, I pray daily for guidance to solve this problem.

Fourth, having done these things, I wrap up the problem, put it on the shelf and try to forget about it.

Fifth, I watch for some sign of the voice of God during the next week or ten days. It usually comes out of a clear sky while I am talking with someone, taking a walk, or often when I am reading or relaxing.

Sixth, I follow what I believe to be God's prompting, and

Seventh, I dismiss from my mind every other possible solution to the problem.

Whenever I have had the courage to follow what I believed to be God's will, I have reached decisions that proved to be right. But when I lacked the necessary courage, I have failed.

My own experience over many active years convinces me that if men will humbly take their personal and business problems to God, and listen to Him receptively, then confusion and pessimism will give way to optimism, and this will lead them to the fulfillment of their dreams. Faith in God gives men faith also in themselves and their future.

PRAYER IS A SPIRITUAL TRANQUILIZER

By James N. MacLean

Lawyer, Lecturer, and Author

Prayer is a spiritual tranquilizer, a haven of repose and comfort for those who have faith in God, and who earnestly seek His help and guidance in matters that at the time cannot be solved. Prayer is a light upon the path of those who seek to do good and to have mercy. It unites us into one sacred band of men and brothers.

PRAYER GIVES "COSMIC" SECURITY

By Dr. Henry Smith Leiper

Formerly, Associate General Secretary, World Council of Churches

When I think of prayer I often recall a conversation forty years ago. It was with one of my wisest and most brilliant ministerial colleagues, a thoroughly dedicated person. We were discussing prayer. He remarked that while he found the practice of public prayer inspiring he could not justify its use intellectually. I replied that my experience was the reverse of his. In my postgraduate years I had moved from a sophomoric skepticism about its power to a firm belief in it. But I found the practice of prayer—and in particular public prayer—difficult and unsatisfying.

After four decades my faith in prayer is still firm. But faith in it is often more pronounced than is the satisfaction derived from it. I have long felt that true prayer is "the soul's sincere desire, unuttered or expressed." Therefore to utter a desire which is not inwardly real—as so often happens in pulpit prayers—is not spiritually an honest or integrated act. For God who knows what we desire even before we ask also knows what we do not deeply desire even if we say we do!

This is all by way of saying that belief in prayer and praying are not the same. When the practice of prayer was easiest for me I had no rational defense of the act. Achieving a satisfying philosophy of prayer did not necessarily increase my feeling of prayer's reality or make it easier for me to pray. Talking about God is not the same as talking to God. Speaking to God is not the same as hearing God speak. Prayer is a two-way process of communication between God and man. But the emphasis should be more on listening than upon speaking.

One of my difficulties came from hearing people talk as if prayer is a power to change God's will, or alter His purposes. If that were the case, the man who prays would appear to be wiser than God with purposes superior to His. While I am certain that prayer changes things and changes people, surely it does not change God. I know that prayer changes me. I trust it is for the better. I know it changes my life for the better. For I have found prayer a mighty force; a tremendous factor powerfully influencing life's greatest moments: in the choice of my life work; in the choice of life partners; in the facing of bereavement; in calming fear under wartime bombings; in the miraculous cure of supposedly fatal maladies in the inner circle of my family and my associates.

Never can I forget that when my son was suffering from the worst type of "black" or "galloping" cancer—and his doctor had predicted death in a few months—his friends and mine could do nothing for him but pray. Happily the operations performed by the very doctor who had given us no hope removed the malignancy, and my son was restored to vigorous life. When the moderator of my denomination some years ago was told his cancer was beyond hope of cure his calm remark to me was: "Jesus cured the lepers. He can cure me if it is His will." Apparently it was, and Dr. Ozora Davis lived for several years, completing books which he had felt led by God to undertake in return for his increased span of life.

No less a scientist and physician than Alexis Carrel once said to me: "Prayer can do incredible things. I have known it to heal wounds with incredible rapidity and even to cure cancer. It is not only worship; it is also a invisible emanation of man's worshiping spirit—the most powerful form of energy that one can generate." Significantly he added that prayer is more efficacious when it is the prayer of friends for one in need of healing, not in the first instance when it is prayer of a person for self-healing. Through prayer we share in the creative, outward-going love of God.

Yet that is not to say that it has no power within the life of the one who prays! In seven operations requiring complete anesthesia—in one case for six hours under the knife in a delicate spinal fusion—I have known no fear, no anxiety, nothing but the confidence that in all that really mattered to me God was to be utterly trusted as a loving Father. I do not fear death because in one sense I have already died seven times. In each case there would have been no further conscious experience had the anesthetic been given in lethal dose. In one case my pain before the operation was so intense that it caused me to lose consciousness. Death would not bring more than maddening pain and welcome loss of consciousness. That I have, as I say, already known.

Prayer gives to life things nothing else can give—and it takes away from the unknown future all menacing terror. For in a world where physical or temporal security is impossible, prayer has the power to give a sense of cosmic security which even enemy sputniks cannot disturb.

WHAT PRAYER MEANS TO ME

By Dr. Donald J. Cowling

Former President of Carleton College

❦

Prayer means to me primarily an attitude toward life. "Prayer is the soul's sincere desire, unuttered or expressed." It is a name for one's thoughts and aspirations that go Godward. It has to do with one's purpose to bring his life into harmony with the will of God.

IN HARMONY WITH GOD

By *Harvey M. King*

Director, Department of Architecture

Division of National Missions of The Methodist Church

❦

Prayer makes the difference in the spiritual realm between light and darkness, life and death. Without it I would lack the stabilizing influence and the motivating force so essential to one facing the perplexities of life. Prayer is the vitalizing link between man and God.

The truth of Lord Tennyson's utterance becomes increasingly significant to me with the passage of time: "More things are wrought by prayer than this world dreams of . . . For so the whole round earth is every way bound by gold chains about the feet of God." My need for prayer in all human relationships and endeavors is felt so keenly that it is difficult to understand the minds of those who attempt to carry on without it.

For a long time I have been concerned about **how** to pray, and have come to the conviction that the form of prayer or the finesse with which it is expressed is relatively of little importance so long as it is genuinely and sincerely a matter of the heart. I find prayer a boon to the soul whether it is prolonged, of short duration, or a single thought prayer flashed spontaneously to God many times during the busiest and most tense moments of the day.

Much of the value and efficacy of prayer lies beyond human comprehension which leaves it shrouded in mystery. And yet prayer works. It is vital and real. Both personal and testimonial evidences of it are so great and so numerous as to be indisputable. Heeding the admonition to be constant in prayer yields blessings of the highest order. To have an inner consciousness of prayer is to have an inner **resource** which is difficult to define.

I am convinced that God answers all prayers in some way in His own good season. Fortunately He has answered some of my premature ones by saying "wait," and some of my immature ones by saying "no." If He had done otherwise, it would have led to my ruination, and probably that of others who would have been carried along with me. Irrespective of the short-comings of our prayers we know always that our heavenly Father shows mercy and deals justly.

As a young man my greatest hurdle was **complete surrender** of self. I wanted to serve God and to be a benefactor to humanity, though I wanted to do it in my own way. The devious paths of procrastination led through twelve long years, because I did not want to be either a minister or a mis-sionary in other lands. Resistance to this kind of service became a burden to me.

Even after I had graduated from college and was devoting full time to the teaching of architecture, several half-hearted attempts were made to enroll in a theological seminary. Once I made application and was accepted for service with the Omi Mission in Japan which was supported largely by commissions from the practice of architecture under the direction of Merrell Vories—a missionary and an architect in his own right. At that time I was on inactive duty serving out the remainder of a four-year enlistment in the United States Navy. As a result I had difficulty in getting a passport, so I did not go. Truthfully I did not want to go.

One evening during our family devotions in the solitude of our little apartment on Huntington Avenue in Boston I cried unto God to accept my full surrender of body, mind and soul for the ministry, the foreign mission field, or any other type of service for which He wanted me, but to give me a conviction that would lead to action. The burden left me and has never returned. Unmistakably I knew then that God wanted more than half, more than nine-tenths of me. He wanted **all** of me.

I do not know that the various moves which were made during those twelve years would have been different if my complete surrender had come sooner. I **am** convinced that I would have had greater peace of mind. The impressive thing is that He seems never to have wanted me to be a preacher or a foreign missionary. The passage of time has revealed that to me. He did want me unequivocally to remove the cumbersome resistance to a complete surrender. So long as I harbored that resistance it was a hindrance to Him and to me. The surrender that came through prayer made the difference.

God becomes most real when we recognize our insufficiency and cast ourselves completely upon Him. When we seek His forgiveness, His unqualified guidance, and the benefits of His infinite wisdom and power we find in Him a sweet release, and the indescribable peace of mind that accompanies it. Though life is not easy we have the assurance that God will neither fail nor forsake us so long as we remain true to Him.

THE MOST MAGNIFICENT PROOF

By Prince Rainier III

Principality of Monaco

❧

More and more we are led to believe in so many discoveries invented by the human brain . . . more and more, in the political field man is told to put his trust, his hope, his belief in another Man, who, elected as the modern Saviour, will bring economic ease and wealth to all, for this man knows how to acquire universal peace!

Our belief, thus imposed upon and abused, generates deception, mistrust, disorder, and insecurity.

And yet, amidst the hardships of times, we still believe in God, His words and His works!

For most of us, this belief remains the basis of our thinking and of our living, often as a raft to cling to.

In moments of fear or despair, as in moments of joy, we turn to God, in our own uneasy way, with our own clumsy words, to beg Him to help us, to ask Him to have mercy on us, and . . . sometimes to thank Him.

The greatest, like the most humble, be they of any race, of any faith, are sure that they will be heard and are able to join in prayer.

Is this not then the most magnificent proof of the everlasting strength of this simple message to God: our prayer?

PRAYER IS CONSTANT

By Dr. Arthur Pound
Writer, Editor and Historian

❧

Prayer, with me and mine, is well-nigh constant, but more often silent than spoken. However, when by myself I find myself often invoking God in whispers, on a guess perhaps once an hour. Never before have I had occasion to search for the meaning of, or ever given heed to, the context of these random supplications.

But since receiving your letter I have found myself listening to my prayers rather attentively, an attitude hardly devotional and which I intend to let lapse at once. However, I did discover that these bubbling prayers of mine were mainly pleas for individual and personal aid, and the fact that they were usually granted leaves me now somewhat ashamed. If I can make the switch from selfish to unselfish pleas without interrupting the outward flow of informal communion, I shall henceforth seek my own welfare less and that of others more.

I dare say that my habitual but informal prayers stem from early association—family prayers and Bible reading, choir singing and cross-bearing in the Episcopalian manner, with the result that God and I always seemed to be on good speaking terms with one another, not in chatty equality, but in humble and reverential discourse of the mind to a patient and forgiving Master able and willing to forgive all in return for a reasonable repentance.

It appears also, although I had never noticed this until your letter, that at age 74 I do my praying directly to God the

Father instead of God the Son. In my youth, as I recollect, it was the other way around; and I wonder if this change in the approach to Deity is a phenomenon of aging, as the individual soul contritely prepares itself, consciously or unconsciously, for eternal judgment by the Most High.

WHEN THE WAY IS OPEN

By Luther A. Smith

Sovereign Grand Commander, The Supreme Council, 33°

A. & A. Scottish Rite of Freemasonry

Southern Jurisdiction, U.S.A.

To me prayer is not a matter of asking God for favors but it is the means by which I consciously feel His Presence in my life. He is the Spirit, the Power, and the Explanation of the Universe. I have a spirit, and God is the Father of my spirit, and He is therefore part of me and I of Him, and there is between us a mutuality of understanding. There is no problem or perplexity, no fear, and no frustration.

I open wide the windows of my soul, and the Divine Light flows quietly in, and I humbly thank God for the resulting confidence and courage that is mine. He has done all He can for me, the rest is with me, my intelligence, and my will. There is no emotion, no mystery, no formula or dogma about it.

When I fail or refuse to open the windows there is definite loss and damage to my power of mind and efficiency; but when by voluntary act I open the windows—that is prayer, and it is efficacious. God is always ready to come in when the way is open.

THE EFFICACY OF PRAYER

By *Honorable Joseph C. Grew*

Diplomat and Former U.S. Ambassador

❧

It is the Church that lays the foundation of our faith and that helps us to build on that foundation. Upon the robustness of that foundation depends the strength and utility of whatever superstructure we are to erect upon it, and in the strength and day-to-day utility of that superstructure lies our preparedness to meet the appalling challenge of destructive and subversive influences that permeate our world today.

Now how is that foundation forged? In many, many different ways according to individual experiences in day-to-day living. Thus one learns how to reach out to that tremendous reservoir of strength and power and guidance that lies ready for all of us to draw upon if only we understand how to use it.

I have seldom tackled a difficult job in life without first asking for the help without which I know very well that my own puny efforts would have resulted in failure. Indeed, it sometimes amazes me to look at something that I have produced, after reaching out for help, and saying to myself: "That's not **my** work. Never in the world could I have done that alone."

Those values are permanent and unchangeable. They are values available to us all. But men and nations, which are made up of men, who are striving earnestly for enduring world peace, must understand those values and must use them in their daily lives, if our world and its civilization are to be preserved. Therein lies preparedness—preparedness to meet whatever may come.

Doesn't it all boil down to just one thing, **the efficacy of prayer?** Isn't it all expressed in those very beautiful words, "Ask and ye shall receive; seek and ye shall find; knock and the door will be opened unto you?" In the aliveness and sureness of those promises, built upon unswerving faith, lies the solution of most of the problems of life.

FAILURE WITHOUT PRAYER

By Philip Lovejoy
Educational Administrator, Business Executive
Past General Secretary, Rotary International

❧

To me prayer is unselfish. It is intercession. It is thanksgiving. It is a spiritual relation between me and my Maker to whom I owe my very existence and continued development. It is a strengthening process in my daily life. It allows me to put myself in the hands of my Maker so that the results of my daily work may be a continued advancement of the Christian way of life.

Time and time again I have personally recognized the effects of prayer in my life and in the life of others with whom I come in contact.

Never do I begin a lecture these days (and there are 150 to 175 a year) without praying that guidance may be given me to produce results that may have a permanent effect for good not only in those with whom I am in immediate contact but through them to the multitudes of others whom they will contact. For that was Jesus' way, that each must multiply his message through a geometric progression of personal activity. Without prayer my life and my work would be a failure.

PRAYER MEANS EVERYTHING

By Roscoe Turner

Aviator and President, Turner Aeronautical Corp.

❦

Prayer is our only communication with God. Our Lord and Saviour, Jesus Christ, instructed his apostles to pray when he was with them. The Apostle Paul was very emphatic about asking all of his people to pray, and also to pray for him in his work.

I can tell you this, that through the power of prayer my life has been saved several times. The most outstanding one was in the London to Melbourne race when we were lost over Central India and practically out of gasoline. God gave us guidance so we could locate ourselves and when the wheels of the plane hit the airport, both engines died for the lack of gasoline.

In the case of prayer, I was on the brink of losing a lifetime's work in my business, and I had practically made up my mind that it was going to go, but I asked God to give me guidance, and with his help I was able to save it, which was almost a miracle. Today I can truthfully say that my business is in a very healthy condition and going strong.

From my experiences I know that the power of prayer is everything, and as I have said, there is no other way of communicating with God.

I don't mean to say that through prayer God will do it all, because that is not true, and it is so illustrated in the Bible where He passed out the talents and those who multiplied them, He complimented, and those who didn't, He took them away. He gives us the help if we will try to help ourselves; and if the prayer is not answered, then we do not deserve whatever we have asked for, or the assistance we have asked for. The power of prayer means everything.

Thank you for asking me to write this, and I hope it will help convince more people of the importance of prayer.

PRAYER FOR PATIENCE

By Henry M. Stanley

African Explorer

❦

To relate a little of the instances in my life wherein I have been grateful for the delicate monitions of an inner voice, recalling me, as it were, to "my true self," it would be difficult for me to underestimate their importance. I, for one, must not, dare not, say that prayers are inefficacious. Where I have been earnest, I have been answered.

In the conduct of the various expeditions into Africa, prayer for patience has enabled me to view my savage opponents in a humorous light; sometimes with infinite compassion for their madness. Without prayer for it, I doubt that I could have endured the flourish of the spears when they were but half a dozen paces off. On all my expeditions prayer made me stronger, morally and mentally, than any of my non-praying companions. It did not blind my eyes, or dull my mind, or close my ears; but, on the contrary, it gave me confidence. It did more; it gave me joy and pride in my work, and lifted me hopefully over the one thousand five hundred miles of forest tracks, eager to face the day's perils and fatigues.

447

UNEXPECTED BLESSINGS
THROUGH PRAYER

By Jessie Burrall Eubank

Religious Educator

❧

There are literally limitless spiritual resources instantly available to everyone of us at any given moment!

This is a strong statement but wholeheartedly I believe it. I have lived with and by it, and tested its truth in the myriad problems and vicissitudes of daily living. I have taught others to realize its truth and to use these resources until my belief has grown into an absolute conviction of its validity.

These spiritual resources include among many others, courage, wisdom, insight, love, a sense of joyous aliveness, and ability to achieve our highest aims. In fact, they include all the qualities of mind, heart, and soul that man needs in order to live freely, graciously, helpfully, as he grows and develops more and more into the pattern God meant for him.

They flow into us automatically all the time. Consciously or unconsciously we are using them moment by moment. This is just another way of saying that "In Him we live and move and have our being." (Acts 17:28).

Moreover, they are greatly increased in their flow, at certain times in our lives. At any moment when what we are thinking, saying, doing is in accord with the "Will of God" or the Law of God, so built into all his creation as to appear to be the very grain of the universe, the augmentation of these spiritual resources occurs within us.

What is this Will, this Law, this Grain? Must it not inhere in the "first and great commandment? Thou shalt love the

Lord thy God, thy neighbor, thine enemy. Rather all inclusive, isn't it? "Thou shalt Love."

Does this not mean that at all times in all places and all circumstances no thought, word or deed shall emanate from us except it be rooted in and empowered by active good will and eager desire to be of help, leading to a continuous generous **sharing** of our best thoughts, words, acts, with all about us?

In defining Love, one of our dictionaries uses the words "an **outgoing** of the personality." And more and more in the thinking and writing of many of our great leaders today, love is described as an actual **current** more powerful even than electricity, a current that at times can actually be felt in its outgoing and incoming.

Furthermore, in the increased understanding and practice of this love we find new depth and realities in **prayer.** Just as love can be a current, an animation so can be true prayer. It is communion with God. It **is** thanksgiving, and praise. It **is** petition in our deepest needs and longings; as well as "a very present help in trouble."

But also, as Dr. Alexis Carrel points out in the brief leaflet "Prayer is Power."*

"Prayer is not only worship," it is also an invisible emanation of man's worshiping spirit—the most powerful form of energy that one can generate. . . . Prayer is a force as real as terrestrial gravity. . . . Prayer like radium is a source of luminous, self-generating energy."

And so it is that the deeper study, understanding and ·practice of prayer, coupled with active motivation of Christlike love, in all aspects of our daily living, can and often does

*Published by the Forward "Movement," 412 Sycamore St., Cincinnati 2, Ohio.

culminate in surprising and unexpected blessings. It may well and often does lead us into an actual, personal recognition of the presence, the power, the **instant help** of God, in the inmost recesses of the soul. This naturally releases our loneliness and anxieties ever leading us out into more joyous and meaningful integration of interests and aims with others, better health of body, alertness of mind and even unto an assurance of continuing eternal aliveness in Christ.

THE PRIVILEGE OF PRAYER

By Sir Wilfred Grenfell

The privilege of prayer to me is one of the most cherished possessions, because faith and experience alike convince me that God himself sees and answers, and his answers I never venture to criticize. It is only my part to ask. It is entirely His to give or withhold, as He knows is best. If it were otherwise, I would not dare to pray at all. In the quiet of home, in the heat of life and strife, in the face of death, the privileges of speech with God is inestimable. I value it more because it calls for nothing that the wayfaring man, though a fool, cannot give — that is, the simplest expression to his simplest desire. When I can neither see, nor hear, nor speak, still I can pray so that God can hear. When I finally pass through the valley of the shadow of death, I expect to pass through it in conversation with Him.

I CRIED; HE ANSWERED

By Dr. S. Maxwell Coder

Dean, Moody Bible Institute

❧

In my student days I was badly in need of a new suit. My wife and I made this a matter of definite prayer. One day a perfect stranger got in touch with me and insisted on getting my measurements for a tailoring establishment with which he was connected. In two or three weeks I was walking around in the answer to our prayer, but I never learned who had paid for it.

On another occasion I needed $50.00 to cover my fare to the seminary, and I had not a single dollar on the evening before my departure. In answer to prayer, five different persons placed money in my hands between 10:30 that evening and 1:00 a.m. the next morning. It totalled exactly $50.00.

Scores of similar instances could be cited from my own student days, and I hear of innumerable stories like these from students at the Moody Bible Institute today. I may not need clothing now, to the same extent I once did, but whatever the need is, God still supplies it. Recently wisdom was needed on a very difficult problem. It almost seemed that light from heaven flooded my office on the day the answer came, and events afterward proved that James 1:5 is still true, "If any of you lack wisdom, let him ask of God, that giveth to all men liberally, and upbraideth not; and it shall be given him." It is wonderful to be able to say with the psalmist, "In the day when I cried thou answeredst me" (Ps. 138:3).

There is no reason why anyone should not know the wonder and joy of answered prayer. The secret of it is nothing

451

more than meeting the simple conditions set forth in the Word of God governing prayer. It is written in Proverbs 15:29, "The Lord is far from the wicked; but he heareth the prayer of the righteous." Who are these? "Christ is the end of the law for righteousness to every one that believeth" (Rom. 10:4).

Another condition has to do with the Bible itself. "He that turneth away his ear from hearing the law, even his prayer shall be abomination" (Prov. 28:9). We may not always like what the Bible requires of us, but the God of the Bible has been pleased to reveal the secrets of answered prayer, and we cannot expect Him to hear us if we ignore what He has written to us.

"If I regard iniquity in my heart, the Lord will not hear me" (Ps. 66:18). To regard iniquity is to cherish it, to cling to some loved sin. We cannot have our sin and at the same time have the help of a holy God. We must make our choice for one or the other. But when we honor God's Word, what exceeding great and precious promises are ours!

"Beloved, if our heart condemn us not, then have we confidence toward God. And whatsoever we ask, we receive of him, because we keep his commandments, and do those things that are pleasing in his sight. And this is his commandment, That we should believe on the name of his Son Jesus Christ, and love one another, as He gave us commandment" (I John 3:21-23).

PRAYER MEANS POWER

By Dr. Valeria Hopkins Parker, M.D.

Marriage Counselor

❦

My parents taught me to pray. Indeed they believed that I had been born to them as a result of their own prayers, two years after they had faced their first sorrow together in the death of their first-born, the older brother who died when three months old.

I was baptized in infancy. As soon as I was able to talk, I joined my parents at morning prayers and was taught to say a simple prayer at night when I was put to bed.

My first memory of family prayers is after two younger sisters had joined the circle. It was hard to keep quiet while my father read a passage from the scriptures. We peeked at each other while my father, and then my mother, prayed for "grace" and "faith" and when our respective turns came we asked for material things such as a new dress or a gold locket or a tricycle and yet our prayers were usually answered, for we had a "fairy grandmother" to whom my mother sent lists of things we wanted, and they appeared on Christmas or birthdays. My gold locket appeared one birthday—heart shaped with a real "chip diamond." Not one, but three tricycles appeared beside the tree one Christmas morning. They were in graduated sizes with silvered frames and red plush seats. The neighboring children were duly astonished and envious as I headed the procession of three little sisters and rode proudly "around the block!"

At the age of six, I had my first experience with death when our three-months-old baby brother whose birth had brought a new interest into our lives, died as the result of a childhood disease. I was old enough to be taken to see him lying still and white in his little cradle and later to attend the simple services in our living room where "our baby brother" lay in a strange white box. Our minister gave prayers of comfort and committed his spirit to God. I hardly knew what it meant. When I was eight years old my mother confided in me that we were to have another baby at Easter time. She cut out and basted together the first tiny garments he was to wear and taught me to sew them. One by one, they were placed in a lovely basket lined with pink and covered with white dotted swiss, with pink bows of ribbon. I prayed most fervently that the new baby would be a brother—and it was! There has always been a close bond between us. He was a tangible answer to my prayers! Now he is a grandfather and I a great grandmother. I look to him for certain advice. When I joined the church in my early teens after my first years of Sunday School and regular church attendance as one of four whose parents sat at either end of the pew, my prayers were more or less perfunctory.

High School, College and Medical College brought so many real experiences that "the other world" seemed very far away. My prayers at the time of my marriage and the birth of my two children were prayers of happiness, thanksgiving and the need of help in fulfilling my responsibilities as wife and mother. I first **really** prayed when our little son at the age of seven was taken in three short days with an infection before which medical skill was then powerless. I was dazed with grief and had no power of my own with which to plan ahead but my daughter of six had lost her playmate and greatly needed help as the nursery with its two white cribs was changed into a "little girl's room" with a new full-size brass bed. I prayed only to be shown what to do and given strength to do it. The answer came in most unexpected ways. I had to face personal tragedy and was taken into a rich full life involving the use of my medical background in useful fields, both here and abroad.

Now I am in that period of life which is one of special study by "experts" for medical science has kept a growing number of older persons alive and active but many of us have not been able to save enough to cover increasing needs. We met the needs of our own aging parents during the financial panic of the late 20's, borrowing on life insurance and selling our war bonds after our own salaries had been cut to the bone! We miss our children and our grandchildren as they move to other places. Now that I am alone, I have learned that worry cannot help those we love, nor can we advise them—but we **can** pray for them.

Again my prayer is for guidance, and strength to meet whatever lies ahead; that I may show my gratitude for my many blessings by helping those whose later years are full of pain, loneliness and self-pity and those who are young whose experiences lie ahead. For this, new opportunities, are opening each day. In my 80th year I am partially self-supporting. I firmly believe this to be the result of prayer. The way in which I learned this was to put it to the test. Prayer is our link with the power of God himself. It is available to all persons wherever they may be. No other power can compare with it. I wasted much of my own power in learning this.

❦

The act of praying is the very highest energy of which the human mind is capable. —Coleridge

PRAYER TIME

By Don McNeill

Founder of The Breakfast Club

❦

I'll never forget the morning in 1944 when I first asked Breakfast Clubbers:

> "All over the nation
> Each in his own words,
> Each in his own way,
> For a world united in peace—
> Bow your heads, let us pray!"

The studio audience of 500 followed the example set by the cast and the orchestra seated with me around the breakfast table, and for twenty seconds silently blended their thoughts with ours. For a fleeting moment I wondered about the reactions of the unseen audience, accustomed to our early morning foolishness. Part of my personal prayer was that everyone would participate.

I had reason to believe the result would be favorable. The Breakfast Club had been founded on inspiration, good music, audience interviews, clean family fun and nostalgic memories, at the time of day when a person's outlook would influence his daily efforts. Furthermore, I believed that prayer—the greatest single force in the world—was urgently needed at this moment while we were at war. Our Breakfast Club mothers, fathers and sweethearts, I reasoned, needed a vehicle through which they could spiritually unite with their boys and friends overseas as the last supreme efforts were being made to bring order out of chaos.

Family prayer, I believed, was the vehicle. The Breakfast

456

Club family had laughed, sung, marched and reminisced together. Why not pray together?

Reactions were mixed. Some thought prayer out of place on an entertainment program; others applauded it. Several told me it was a courageous thing to try. The manner in which people expressed hope that I would continue "Prayer Time" made me feel they didn't think it could last.

Frankly, I hadn't visualized "Prayer Time" as a permanent peace-time fixture of our show. I regarded it as a call to action on the home front. With the war ended, our prayer for peace might be superfluous, I figured.

But ninety per cent of the 100,000 Breakfast Clubbers who wrote us insisted that prayer belonged on the Breakfast Club program and it has become, through the years, an important, much-loved part of the show.

Prayer time means much to people of all faiths, races and position. But none is more appreciative of family prayers than the McNeills. My wife, Kay, and I had occasion to pray, as only desperate people can pray, back in September, 1947, when our eldest son was stricken with polio. For seven straight days we prayed at the bedside of Tommy, then twelve years old. On the seventh day, the doctor reported that he could move his leg, and we knew that Tommy would be all right.

The next morning I told our Breakfast Clubbers about the crisis we had been through and asked that they join me in thanking God. Not only did they join us in prayer, but they literally showered Tommy and his friends in the polio ward with 15,000 letters, cards and gifts.

Tommy thanked our Breakfast Clubbers: "I had everyone scared for awhile, even myself, but because of your millions of prayers God did me a swell favor. The polio bug zoomed in and out of me on a non-stop flight."

GOD GIVES STRENGTH FOR EVERY NEED

By Dr. Walter H. Judd

U. S. Congressman from Minnesota

❦

When I went to China in 1925 as a medical missionary, I had in my heart this promise of Christ:

> "Lo, I am with you always,
> Even unto the end of the world."

I was afraid maybe that it wouldn't be true, but it is. How can we do the things He asks of us? No man can in his own strength. But Christ promised, "Ye shall receive power." It is true.

In 1930, morning after morning, during the eight months when I was in a polite sort of captivity, and when the Communists who had just killed two English ladies were off only about a half-day's journey, nobody in the city took off his clothes at night during the light of the moon, because the Communists practically always travel at night and arrive at your door at dawn. I had my litle package of quinine for injection, money, and a flashlight always near at hand, in case I had to get away on a moment's notice. During those months, I would wake up every morning with the question as to what that day would bring forth. No one could foresee. I would pray this simple prayer. And there would come into my spirit, just as my bed supported my body, something that supported and held me steady, gave me confidence and assurance during the day:

> "O Master, let me walk with Thee
> In lowly paths of service free:
> Tell me Thy secret—"

You had it, O Christ! They came into your clinic and they touched the hem of your garment. Something happened to them. Here they will come into my clinic today, sixty to a hundred of them. Here is a tooth to pull; there an ulcer to dress; here a woman with a hard malaria; there a child with its abdomen full of worms; there a man with a cough and a suspected spot of tuberculosis to search out in his lungs. Will anything happen to these because they have been with me today?

> "Tell me Thy secret! help me bear
> The strain of toil, the fret of care."
> "Help me the slow of heart to move
> By some clear, winning word of love;"

Just a touch! That is all I have, just a touch. Only as I have Thee, O Christ, in my life and words can that touch mean anything to these.

> "Teach me the wayward feet to stay—"

including my own!

> "And guide them in the homeward way.
> Teach me Thy patience—"

O Christ, I want results. I demand them quickly. I have got to see the thing done in a hurry. **Teach me Thy patience!**

> "—still with Thee
> In closer, dearer company;
> In work that weeps faith sweet and strong—"

plain, good, hard work that gives an outlet to inner tensions.

> "In trust—"

Yes, trust—confident, unswerving trust, that never fears or wavers.

> "In trust that triumphs over wrong;
> In hope—"

Oh, yes, Hope! If it weren't for that, I would jump off a bridge China has no hope, except in Christ and neither has America. Any merely human program is doomed to failure.

> "In hope that sends a shining ray
> Far down the future's broad'ning way."

Maybe not in my lifetime, but it must come.

> "In peace—"

459

steady, certain peace—

"In peace that only Thou canst give.
With Thee, O Master—"

this day, I can't see tomorrow, but this day,

"With Thee, O Master, let me live."

And He does not fail. It works.

I can't explain it all. No, I can't explain how some of the food I ate tonight for supper becomes brain, some blood, some bone. There is no chemist or physiologist in the world who knows all that in detail. If there were he would be the greatest scientist the world has ever known. But I haven't stopped eating just because I can't explain it all! Even so, I cannot explain this. It is not in the realm of explanation, yet. It isn't in the realm of logical proof. It **is** in the realm of demonstration, and prayer works.

PRAYER SUSTAINS US

By Roberta Peters

Opera Singer

I feel that without prayer we have nothing in this world. Prayer leads us through all the difficult moments of our life, sustains us and gives us courage to continue. Prayer also sustains us through our happy moments. We thank God for this goodness and pray that we will always find His favor.

PRAYER FINDS GOD

By Jessica Dragonette

Concert, Radio, and Television Singer

❦

The different flags unfurled in the plaza of the United Nations building are evidence that the nations of the world wish to live together in peace.

On the horizon above there, however, the war clouds seem to gather.

We believe the idea the flags imply; but we have difficulty accepting the fact that "faith is the substance of things unseen"—

Only a miracle can change the prospect for poor fear-haggard man; and peace, that long dreamed of prize of the ages, must come to dwell in the individual breast before it can blaze into reality in the wide breadth of the world.

Mere man is slow to realize that this miracle can be achieved by prayer. For prayer is the only power in the universe that seems to overcome to so-called "laws of nature." Prayer then is our miracle wand!

First, a quieter miracle must take place! Man must discover, individually, that prayer fills us, not only with a steady flow of sustaining power, but also supplies that harmony of mind, body and spirit which gives the frail human being his unshakable strength.

Our lack of emphasis on this spiritual awareness has brought us to the brink of destruction.

For a long time now, we have marked the tendency to secularize everything and to accord to science the supreme authority for solving every human problem.

461

A climate for this error has been made possible by misguided education techniques, focusing on man's "without" rather than "within."

We have, in a manner of speaking, exiled God from our lives. As a result, we have been thrown off balance. Starved of that spiritual exercise so necessary to our complete well-being; we lack the inner radiance which kindles energy enough for physical buoyancy, intellectual vigor, moral stamina and the true understanding of human relationship.

Over and over again, we hear man ask: "How can we find God? How can we pray? We don't know how. And isn't prayer an archaic relic of bygone ages? How is prayer compatible with modern life?"

Prayer finds God as truly as the geiger counter finds uranium or the sextant fixes the position of the stars.

With the poet, I believe, that "however it may be with the temporal world, seared with trade, bleared, smeared with toil—the world is charged with the grandeur of God; it will flame out like the shining from shook foil!"

In an age conspicuous for the greatest developments in communication, one wonders why the lines to God have not been explored and opened up!

"The hairs of your head are numbered—" would imply a kind of invisible umbilical cord, attaching us to divine Providence through which sanctifying grace enters to sustain us— and which makes prayer possible. The most intimate, personal contact the human being can have with the Father and Redeemer of all; a raising of the heart and mind, a communication with the Supreme Being.

These are the road signs that give us direction: "Ask and ye shall receive. Seek and ye shall find. Knock and it shall be opened unto you."

Christians have the beautiful example of **how to pray** given by Jesus. The Lord's Prayer expresses the conviction that God is **our** Father, Whose kingdom is on earth as well as in Heaven. He is willing to listen to our petitions provided we love one another.

The more we pray in the proper attitude, the more spiritually attuned we become, the more receptive to the influx of blessings and the more capable of journeying toward the realm of grace.

However feeble our tongues and intentions, even the slightest impulse to prayer is pleasing to God, a regenerative influence goes to work instantly, to make us new. For when we pray, we are harnessing our lives to the Infinite source of all energy—that inexhaustible power that spins the universe! Thus linked with the Infinite, through prayer, we augment our puny finite!

The Bible tells us that while Samuel was praying, God appeared to him! For praying is the time when the soul within us, the deepest, innermost part of our being, sacredly, sincerely, quietly, speaks to God, expressing the wishes of our minds and hearts.

Everything we do, whether we know it or not, is a quest for God. So viewed, this Geophysical Year is another dimension of our search to commune with the Infinite, for prayer is extra planetary, extra temporal, a broadened gauge of time and eternity.

As we stand on the shores of space, scientists are busy unveiling mystery after mystery, while politician, tactician and diplomat worry about lines of demarcation.

To the prayerful, though, for whom the firmament manifests the glory and majesty of God, this problem of sovereignty is already solved! Earth and heaven are the Lord's, these realms, long since, familiar in prayer—"world without end. Amen!"

So we can pray anywhere, anytime; in the church, in the street, in the house, on the subway, on the bus, under the sea, in the air. With practice, our lives become a way of prayer and we hallow as we go, like a butterfly of life on the wings of eternity!

Centuries before Christ, a Chinese artist wrote:

> I would not paint a face, a rock, nor brooks, nor trees,
> Mere semblances of things but
> Something more than these.
>
> I would not play a tune upon the string or lute,
> Something that did not sing meanings that else were mute
> That art is best which to the soul's range gives no bound,
> Something besides the form
> Something beyond the sound.

Man must reclaim his birthright! His neglected soul must be made strong again. "Keep your heart with all diligence for from out of it flow the issues of life," says the book of Proverbs.

Prayer, the basis exercise of the spirit, must be cultivated. If this power is released and used, we can be "a light unto the nations," and there is hope that our prayers for peace in our days will surely answered, for we will have found God!

THE VERY SACRIFICE OF GOD

By Cardinal Mercier

Catholic Prelate

❧

Men long unaccustomed to prayer are turning again to God. Within the army, within the civil world, in public, and within the individual conscience there is prayer. Nor is that prayer today a word learned by rote, uttered lightly by the lip; it surges from the troubled heart, it takes the form at the feet of God of the very sacrifice of life.

THE REAL OBJECT OF PRAYER

By The Right Reverend James A. Pike

Bishop Coadjutor, Episcopal Diocese of California

❦

Prayer is not just an exercise for certain times in the week or day, nor should it be used only as an SOS in emergency. It should be just like breathing—a constant response to a life-giving God who is closer to us than our own breath. It should include the main elements of a fine relationship between a child and his parent.

Our admiration and respect for Him are to be constant—and unqualified. Hence our response to Him is called by a different name, reserved for Him alone—adoration. The **prayer of adoration** asks for nothing. It begins with a simple recognition that God **is** and passes on to meditation on His mysterious greatness, His utter integrity and reliability, His loving care. It reaffirms that He comes first. Adoration nourishes a vivid sense of God's presence, and so it puts a different face on everything in life that we experience. This type of prayer is of value to **us;** but more important than that is our first duty to God Who is to be adored, not simply "used." Such admiration is fundamental to our nature: if we lack it we are not whole persons, just as a man who grows up with no admiration or respect for his father is, at least in a measure, a psychically crippled person.

The **prayer of penitence** naturally follows that of adoration. As we think of His utter purity and His clarity of Objective we are bound to think of our own imperfections and mixed motivations. It is important to realize that examination of conscience is really a form of prayer. A general feeling of unworthiness is not particularly useful; in fact, it can be psychologically dangerous. But we should visualize in specific terms the way that we have "let God down" and in specific terms tell Him that we are sorry. It is only then that our prayer of penitence is sincere, only then that we really feel cleansed and know our relationship to Him to be restored, only then that we can hope to do much about our faults and begin to live up to the sonship for which He has destined us.

The **prayer of thanksgiving** quite naturally follows the prayer of penitence, through which we prepare ourselves for the most precious gift of all—our re-acceptance by God when we haven't been worthy of it. This type of prayer actually increases our joy because it makes us more sensitive to the good things of life and enhances our appreciation as we look on the spiritual and physical world in which we "move and have our being." The right motivation for this kind of prayer is to yield to God what is due Him for His own sake, for His own nature, and for His activity in the world.

The prayer of thinksgiving leads us to the **prayer of petition** in which we focus the direction of our action, as especially concerns ourselves. We should remember to pray not simply in terms of what we want, but in terms of how we can better serve Him. And in our **prayer of intercession** we call to mind the various claims upon us which take the form of remembering the needs of others. A good test of the sincerity of this kind of prayer is our willingness to **do** something about the things for which we pray. The Epistle of James scorns in wholesome sarcasm those who address the needy with the greeting, "Depart in peace, be ye warmed and filled"—but offer no help.

And in the form of prayer we so often neglect—**the prayer of silence**—we give God the Holy Spirit the opportunity to speak directly to us, in compunction for the past and in guidance for the future, even when rational analysis of relative

466

goods and evils reaches no clear conclusion His voice can speak to us unequivocally.

How much time in a day should be devoted to prayer and how much to action will vary, depending upon your personal situation. But there should be no day so crowded with activity that a definite time is not set aside for prayer. In the morning, for even five to ten minutes, you should acknowledge the presence and reality of God and form your intentions for the day. While riding a bus, or going up and down the stairs, or waiting for an appointment, you can turn to God in your heart and bring yourself into His Picture. Thus day-to-day life can take on an entirely new dimension as you are more and more conscious of living your moments out under God, for God, and **with** God. This is the real object of prayer—and the clue as to how to pray.

WE CANNOT HELP PRAYING

By Professor William James
Educator and Psychologist

We hear in these days of scientific enlightenment a great deal of discussion about the efficacy of prayer; and many reasons are given us why we should not pray, whilst others are given us why we should. But in all this very little is said of the reason why we do pray. The reason why we do pray is simply that we cannot help praying.

SOME THINGS PRAYER CAN DO

By Dr. Ralph W. Sockman

Minister, Christ Church New York City

When prayer calms and cleanses the mind, it thereby goes on to do a second service in the **healing of the body.** The close relationship between flesh and spirit is increasingly recognized by medical science. Doctors and ministers are holding many conferences to explore and develop new ways of co-operation.

There is no physical affliction without its mental accompaniment, and no mental attitude without its effect on the body. If prayer can help the mind, it will aid the body.

We can readily understand this effect in certain ailments. Prayer can shorten healing in sickness involving long convalescence because prayer keeps the whole system toned to health. It can help in certain operations by calming a fear-stricken and physically weak heart so that it can stand the strain of anaesthetic and shock. And, of course, in those bodily ills which are due to fears and repressions and complexes, prayer is the medicine for both mind and body.

The revived interest in this healing ministry of prayer promises much if handled by responsible and intelligent persons. The person who promises too much or the charlatan who exploits religion by reducing it to a mere healing art renders a disservice. But when, like the Great Physician of Nazareth, we put the body in its proper place as the servant of the spirit and then bring the power of the spirit to bear on the body, thoughtful persons are loath to set limits to the healing power of prayer.

And in physical afflictions which are not cured, prayer

may give a deeper healing. One person becomes embittered by his incurable ailment, another becomes ennobled. The difference is in the attitude, and prayer shapes attitudes. Saint Paul prayed repeatedly for the removal of his afflictions, his "thorn in the flesh" as he called it. It remained! But Paul said he got an answer from God which put fortitude into him. Listen to the divine message which Paul heard: "My grace is sufficient for you, for my power is made perfect in weakness." Prayer does not guarantee escape from pain but it does give insight, patience, fortitude and sympathy, and thereby does make some persons feel that they "are more than conquerors through him who loves us."

Convinced that prayer can calm and cleanse the mind, help in healing the body, and also give increased strength, but can prayer change things outside ourselves? Where are we to draw the line between changing things within us and around us? A changed attitude of mind changes the situation in which a person finds himself. Also, if we are to change our inner selves we sometimes have to alter our situations. Suppose I pray, "O Lord, deliver me from the curse of drink." But salvation from drink not only depends on my inner strength of will but also involves the number of persons who offer me a drink and the number of bars I pass on my way home from work.

Or suppose I pray, "O Lord, give me peace of mind." But if I am a decent person I cannot enjoy peace of mind if I neglect the poverty of my neighbor's children and the peace of my nation.

Hence, when we pray to be changed inside, I do not see how we can keep from praying for things outside.

PRAYERS ARE ANSWERED

By Dr. Louis P. Lochner

Newspaper Correspondent and Radio Commentator

❀

Early in my life an event occurred which so visibly impressed me with the power of prayer that the memory of it has given me confidence again and again to turn to God under normal but also especially desperate conditions. I was never disappointed. My prayers were heard. The event to which I refer is the following:

My favorite teacher at Bethlehem Lutheran School, Milwaukee, was gravely ill. Several previous intestinal operations had brought only temporary relief. Once again the surgeon's knife was to be applied. There seemed little hope that this time, with the deepest incision yet made in prospect, the source of trouble might be removed.

Our class had doubled up with a parallel class tutored by as devout a Christian as my favorite teacher was. When the hour for the surgical operation came, he asked all of us to kneel down with him and to pray fervently and earnestly that God would so guide the surgeon's hand as to spare us our teacher's life. Half an hour later, when presumably the patient was being stitched together again, we were on our knees for a second time, praying that no complication might set in and our teacher's recovery take its normal course.

More quickly than on previous occasions our teacher was in our midst again, this time for good. The earnest prayers of nine and ten-year-old children, led by an instructor who believed in his Bible and Jesus' admonition to appeal to our Heavenly Father in His name, had convincingly demonstrated the power of prayer.

MY EXPERIENCE WITH PRAYER

By Joy Elmer Morgan

President, Senior Citizens of America

❦

On the frontier of western Nebraska, where I grew up in the farm home of my grandfather, profanity was practiced as an art. There may have been a reason for this. The pigs and cows and horses and mules of that time and place were scrub stock. They could be most stubborn and exasperating. Then, too, there was much wind and one had to be understood in the teeth of it. The short forceful words of profanity seemed to suit the occasion. My grandfather and the hired men on the farm seemed to take a certain pride in being able to utter the longest and most picturesque string of oaths without repetition.

Every young boy wants to be a man and naturally imitates the ways of his elders. So I learned a goodly collection of swear words before I even went to school. These had no evil or sinister meaning to me. They were merely a part of the longing to grow up and be big. Just then my grandmother who was the religious side of the family began taking us to Sunday School and there the teacher taught us that God watched over us and knew everything we did or thought and that swearing was a sin; that we should ask God's help to keep oaths from our mouths. This I resolved devoutly to do. But the next morning when a mean cow broke through the fence and I was obliged to chase her through the briar patch in my bare feet, I fell into the usual vigorous language. Immediately, there came over me the deepest sense of failure and remorse and I got down on my knees there in the orchard and asked God's help and his forgiveness and again had the sense of belonging to a Being greater than myself. It was a lesson I have never forgotten.

Again later in life when I was very ill and feared one day that I would die and the next that I wouldn't, there finally came to me a sense that my life was not in my own hands, that others had gone through much harder trials than mine and had lived to be useful and that whatever came, I must accept it and do the best I could under the circumstances. As my faith deepened I began to improve and found my way back again to health and strength. Out of solitude and loneliness and fear came prayer and faith and new vision. It has happened again and again.

One summer as I watched a beautiful sunset in Glacier Park where I stood alone on a hillside, there came over me such a lifting sense of the glory and greatness of God's universe that I knew what the psalmist meant when he wrote:

> And let the beauty of the Lord our God be upon us:
> and establish thou the work of our hands upon us;
> yea, the work of our hands establish thou it.

Beauty and work have ever since been associated in my mind and my memory is filled with images of lovely things that I have known through the years. Often I have had this feeling as I have flown over the continent high above the clouds with the sun streaming down on a gleaming ocean of alabaster white.

More recently, as I have felt disturbed and concerned by the endless headlines of crime, tragedy and war and the reliance on force to gain man's ends, I have turned to God in prayer and have felt reassured that if man will only do his part, the ways of love will assert themselves in our relations between nations as they have increasingly come to do in relations between individuals.

472

PRAYER IS THE BASIS OF
PERSONAL SECURITY

By Fred Waring

Orchestra Conductor

❧

Prayer, in one or the other of its many forms, has always been a part of my life—so intensely personal that it does not yield itself easily to public expression. Yet I believe that some sort of prayer is man's ultimate basic of personal security in a world where such security is not easily attained.

In the frantic cycle of our work there is little time—and great need— for meditation and spiritual readjustment. Formal worship and formal prayer, alike, become increasingly remote from us. Yet there remains for each the spiritual closet into which he may enter and, "when he has shut the door, pray to his Father which is in secret."

The time, the place and the circumstance seem not to matter—and perhaps they should not matter. At least Emerson had a good word to say for prayer-on-the-run:

"It is not only when we audibly and in form address our petitions to the Deity that we pray. We pray without ceasing. Every secret wish is a prayer. Every house is a church, the corner of every street is a closet of devotion."

Yes, I believe in prayer—in communal prayer, in family prayer and in formal, personal prayer. But when Emerson's "corner of every street," nationally and internationally, becomes a closet of devotion, we shall have achieved a great miracle, indeed.

THE PLACE OF PRAYER IN A CHAIN REACTION OF TRANSFORMED LIVES

By Robert B. Doing

The Strait Gate Project

❦

"If my people, which are called by my name, shall humble themselves and pray, and seek my face, and turn from their wicked ways; then will I hear from heaven, and will forgive their sin, and will heal their land." (2 Chr. 7:14). How desperately our world needs the healing that God alone can give! As I write, the leaders of the world powers are jockeying for position in a proposed United Nations Security Council meeting, their language overtly hostile, even insulting. I read in this morning's newspaper that the Cairo radio, in the interests of Arab nationalism, is constantly sending out broadcasts of bitter hatred and denunciation against the western world, urging the assassination of mideast leaders who differ with the sponsors of the broadcasts.

The world is truly getting darker every day. There are more people being born into the world in a physical sense than are being born into the kingdom of God. The hundreds of millions of people behind the iron curtain are being told in government broadcasts that religion is part of a life that is now outmoded, and therefore must be eliminated.

What is required to offset this negative influence is an extension on a mathematical progression basis of a faith so vital that through it God can make men over into truly altruistic individuals who will in turn work with others to this same end. Transformed men and women will then work to transform social institutions along altruistic lines, finally accepting a whole new set of values which, when worked into our culture, will produce a world more nearly like the one

474

God would have it be. Such is the faith of Christ crucified, and our problem after having come to know Him, is to find the most effective way of passing on our knowledge. That way involves the chain reaction principle, or revival, or, if you prefer, a spiritual awakening.

There is in the universe a tendency to run down called entropy; a tendency for order to become disorder. The moment we are born we begin to die. In the business world we see an efficient procedure become less efficient as we direct our attention elsewhere. The efficiency is only revived as we inject new effort into it. A great artistic skill deteriorates unless it is constantly exercised receiving new injections of power from the will of the artist. In the spiritual realm our effectiveness dwindles to the point of backsliding unless we receive new surges of power from the Holy Spirit. A whole church or community will suffer a lowered spiritual potential without realizing it in many cases, because the people concerned are so busy with secondary activities. The antidote for this running down is revival, renewal, a spiritual awakening in which the Holy Spirit is working simultaneously in many hearts to create a climate favorable to spiritual advance.

A century ago Charles G. Finney wrote that revival of religion is as naturally the result of the use of the appropriate means for producing it as a crop is the result of the use of its appropriate means. When you prepare the soil, plant the seed, and assure an adequate supply of water you are not surprised when a crop results. You would be surprised if it didn't. Likewise where the truth is widely made available to men through witness and preaching, and when a genuine spirit of prayer moves upon these people, in that place you can expect a revival of religion. The truth is the supernatural birth, life, death, resurrection, ascension, exaltation, and promise of return of our Lord Jesus Christ. Prayer beyond anything ever before deemed necessary or desirable is the second factor that God, who is the Author of every spiritual awakening, will use to bring it about.

Reuben Torrey, who was used by God to spearhead spiritual awakenings in churches and communities around the world, said that the way of it is (1) to let a few Christians get thoroughly right with God themselves; (2) let them bind themselves together in a prayer group to pray for the awakening until the heavens open and God comes down; and (3) to put themselves at God's disposal for Him to use as He sees fit in winning others to Jesus Christ.

Prayer is an integral part of all three steps. Much prayer will help us see what is required of us to get thoroughly right with God ourselves. With God's help we will do what we see to be necessary, then get down to pray to God for an enducement of power for our witness, finally praying for those around us that they may be persuaded to take the same road of complete surrender to Jesus Christ. This road requires that they in turn seek to pass on to others through the same kind of preparation, prayer, and witness that which has transformed their own lives.

LIFE WITHOUT PRAYER IS SAD

By Zoe Akins

Author

It is sad to think of a life from which no prayer has ever ascended.

PRAYER IS POWER

By The Very Rev. Sturgis Lee Riddle, D.D.

Dean of the American Cathedral in Paris, France

❧

One summer in New York while on a preaching visit home, I stood by the hospital bed of a friend, the wife of an officer of my Cathedral in Paris. During a stay with her family in the States, she had been taken with a severe heart condition. I found her in an oxygen tent, apparently unconscious. I was told that there was little hope for her life. Her husband had been summoned from Paris. The end seemed only hours off. The chances of getting through to the flicker of life that was left, shrouded as it was in the cumbersome tent and in a veil of unconsciousness, seemed negligible.

But I have always believed that man's extremity is God's opportunity. I bowed my head. In silent prayer, I entrusted this life, apparently "in extremis," beyond human help, to the never-failing care and love of God—knowing, as the Prayer Book puts it, that He was doing for her "better things than we can desire or pray for." I left the hospital assured in prayer that whatever happened in life or in death, all would be well for my friend.

Soon afterwards, when I came again to the hospital, I found my friend laying hold of life again. Consciousness had returned. The body had begun to function anew. We were able to converse as usual. The nurses told me that recovery had set in from the moment of that silent invocation. Divine power had been brought to bear in a situation where human resources were not enough.

After some weeks of convalescence my friend returned to Paris where I had gone on ahead. She told me that the only thing she remembered from those days when her human life was at its lowest ebb was that prayer. Even in the silence and in the valley of the shadow she had been aware of it. The divine communication had been established. Life flowed back from the source of life. "They that wait upon the Lord shall renew their strength."

Her husband, a doctor, who in despair had had his beloved restored to him, said to me later: "That indeed was a miracle!" I preferred to think of it as a perfectly natural application of a spiritual principle available to all at any time. I thought of the words of Isaac Watts:

> "Great God! behold my reason lies
> Adoring: yet my love would rise
> On pinions not her own
> Faith shall direct her humble flight
> Through all the trackless seas of light,
> To Thee, the eternal Fair, the infinite Unknown."

In our modern world, science is opening up whole new exciting supplies of physical power, harnessing them to human need. Supplies of spiritual power are equally there, ordained of God, waiting to be applied to human need. Prayer is the key to bring them down to earth. Prayer is power.

❦

Without prayer I would have been a lunatic long ago.

—Mahatma Ghandi

AN EXPLORER LOOKS AT PRAYER

By Dr. Wendell Phillips

President, The American Foundation for the Study of Man, Inc.
and Economic Adviser to the Sultan of Oman.

❦

For a professional explorer conducting operations in Arabia an outward appearance of unswerving self-sufficiency is essential to success. The explorer may often be involved in situations calling upon all his resources of determination, sense of justice and diplomatic skill. It is not always easy, especially over sustained periods of time, to make consistently wise and workable judgments, especially if these be on behalf of people whose code of ethics may be radically different from one's own. This is one reason why, as an explorer, I am deeply conscious of the need for prayer, not only to add balance, continuity and spiritual fulfillment to a briskly paced life, but to provide the moral courage necessary to make difficult and delicate decisions.

In no other part of the world is one made more conscious of prayer than throughout the empire of Islam, "the religion of submission to the will of God." Prayer is one of the five basic tenets of Islam and the faithful, as ordained by the Koran, pray unashamedly and with constant regularity five times a day, at dawn, noon, afternoon, sunset and evening.

Christians rarely pray at such evenly spaced intervals. True, we worship together in church on Sundays and on special holidays, but what of the times in between? Unhappily, we tend to turn to private prayer only at times of crisis. Many of us, for example, have had wartime experiences when, under fire or at other equally trying moments, prayer seemed the last and only resort left to us. Or perhaps it was an occasion of great personal grief suffered, say, over the death of a loved one that last motivated us to pray in solitary. Prayer, however, is not meant to be restricted to periods of great stress but should be an integral part of daily life, to be used in time of joy as well as sorrow.

It seems paradoxical that prayer should be more faithfully practiced in so fatalistic a religion as Islam, one based so firmly on the concept of predestination. One would think that prayer would be of especial value to the Christian who, after all, has a freer hand in determining his own fate. Daily communication with God through prayer can serve to confirm the individual in his faith, to further his understanding of himself and others, to provide the self-confidence and direction so necessary and valuable to the person who is seeking to guide his own actions by Christian values.

Paleontology demonstrates how brief an individual span we are allotted in the total scheme of things and archaeology shows us that prayer has been a function of worship down through the centuries, since eras long predating the miracle of Calvary. As a scientist and as a human being I want this brief span to be as full and worthwhile as possible. Nothing can enrich life more than can daily communication with God, and there is no way to achieve this communication which surpasses that of prayer.

A STATE OF PRAYER

By Edwin Balmer

Author

❦

Prayer acknowledges the presence and power of a Divine Spirit. The acknowledgement may be exceedingly shallow and it may be so profound that it establishes "a state of prayer."

In those four words Dr. Alexis Carrel described the condition which, at times, evidently has effected cures so extraordinary and beyond explanation under commonly accepted physical laws that they have been called miraculous.

He warned that such cures were rare; to bring them about, the indispensible condition—and the only indispensible condition—was that some one near the afflicted person be "in a state of prayer."

So many other persons of unquestioned reliability attest to the power of prayer to effect cures that, even if I doubted Dr. Carrel's findings—which I do **not** doubt— I would be bound to believe in prayer.

Shortly after the discovery of the new "miracle" drugs, I met a doctor friend of mine who, I knew, was attending a child who had come down with cerebro-spinal meningitis.

I inquired about the child and the doctor told me, with no less than awe in his voice, that the little boy already had made a complete recovery and he meant **complete.** My friend added: "Even a year ago, that child would have been dead or left deaf or with some impairment, most likely." He told me what remedy he had used and said: "Edwin, it's an answer to a prayer."

He meant merely to describe to me how completely effec-

tive the new "miracle" drug was; I was sure he was not thinking of it literally as an answer to prayer; but wasn't it? And
what else is the Salk serum? Unnumbered millions prayed year
after year for their children to be saved from infantile paralysis;
and now they can be.

Daily, all the world witnesses that answer to prayers.

Any sincere prayer is far more than a mere petition; it is
also a challenge; and the challenge in it supplies much
of its power.

You pray for a lasting peace—for international antagonisms
to diminish, for the "cold war" to cease. Do you not, therefore,
feel in all reason and in honor bound to exert yourself in every
reasonable way to help establish a situation in the world which
promises peace?

It may mean—in our America where we fortunately live—
that you make sacrifices for the sake of less fortunate peoples,
since it is the destitution in other parts of the world which
causes the unrest that threatens peace.

If everybody prayed sincerely and honestly for peace and
accepted for himself the challenge in his prayer, peace would
be much nearer and more certain.

The challenge in prayer is another reason I believe in it.

"THE NEW IDOLATRY"

By David Lawrence
Editor, *The United States News*

❦

If another World War is not to become "inevitable," the measures short of war must be given even greater attention in the future than in the past. That is the real problem confronting civilized mankind today.

There remains a greater weapon than any of the rest—Moral Force.

The phrase may seem to some to be a weak instrumentality —idle words in a gale. But this is only because the world has not familiarized itself with the most effective device available to it to affect the action of human beings everywhere.

In time of travail, personal bereavement, or human disaster, we turn as individuals to a higher Being. We seek comfort and solace in the thought that God has a purpose or a plan, unfathomable though it may be to our finite minds.

Why, then, should we not re-examine ourselves and utter in unison as nations the prayers we have been accustomed to speak in our hours of sorrow and personal meditation?

Moral Force has before it dramatic opportunities in mass prayer.

Suppose that in every country of the world five minutes were set aside at noon each day for a week in which all work except absolute necessities were stopped while people bowed their heads and asked God to help free the world from the yoke of men who would exploit their fellow human beings? Suppose these mass prayers were not merely confined to pleas for the tragic victims of the dictator's wrath? Suppose, instead, the prayers were offered, too, for the dictators themselves?

For we have tried bloodshed and have brought forth only fear of more bloodshed.

We have tried nationalism and have brought forth only worse forms of nationalism.

We have tried brutality and we have only brought forth worse forms of human torture.

Is it not time to try something else?

Moral Force is, therefore, our best approach. But before it can be applied effectively a start must be made at home to regenerate the selfish and the proud, the self-centered and the intolerant—for there are in our midst persons who inwardly believe in the "new idolatry" and who would exchange their very souls for the fancied security of materialistic gain. These individuals little realize that in the whole course of human history, security is an illusion when it is founded on the wreckage of human liberty. Nothing is more ephemeral than the supposed stability of a nation which has lost its soul though it has gained a plethora of profits.

Christianity is a religion of sacrifice, of mutuality of interest. The peoples of Europe and the Americas are predominantly Christian. The Church has for two decades wondered why it had so often been subordinated, why its usefulness has seemed at times to be questioned if not nullified in a world of sin. The Church has been groping, too, even as you and I.

But does not the crisis of today afford the very opportunity which the Church has been waiting for—something that makes it possible to turn the rank and file and the leaders once more to the simple principles which have come to us through two thousand years of human experience? Who then are the captains and the generals in the new army of Moral Force which must be mobilized here and abroad? They are the militant spokesmen of the Church who have given their days and nights to the task of elevating the human spirit.

May they sound the bugles that will call human hearts to action.

May they teach us anew the language of prayer which we have forgotten in our era of creature comforts.

May they tell us in the homely terms of a simple faith how to ask Divine Providence to help us sacrifice and even suffer so that mankind may by its own regeneration destroy these new forms of idolatry and substitute therefor an unremitting worship of the merciful God before Whom must stand, when the final Day of Reckoning comes, all the mortal dictators of human destiny, the leaders and the led, the rich and the poor, the oppressors and the oppressed.

—Reprinted with permission of the author from **The United States News,** December 12, 1938.

PRAYER, THE PATH TO PARADISE

By Dr. Charles R. Joy

Writer and Foreign Relief Administrator

❧

A thousand years ago a Buddhist monk lived on the side of Mount Hiei in Japan who tried to bring his Buddhist faith to the common man. So he used to leave his monastery and descend to the city, where he danced through the streets with a tinkling bell hanging from his neck as he sang songs like this:

> "A far, far distant land
> Is Paradise,
> I've heard them say;
> But those who want to go
> Can reach there in a day."

I do not know how the old monk elaborated his central thesis, but I feel quite sure that he did not tell people that they would find paradise in some Buddhist temple. He might have told them that they could learn something about the way to paradise in a temple, but paradise has certainly no inseparable connection with a formal place of worship.

As a matter of fact, paradise can be found in many places, depending upon the need of our lives. If one is seeking heaven, it is important to know from what hell one is trying to escape. If one is sick a hospital can be heaven. If one is hungry a meal can be manna. If one is tired a bed can be bliss. Let us beware that we do not limit God, relegating our heaven to some far, far distant place, postponing it to some far, far distant time.

> "Daily with souls that cringe and plot,
> We Sinais climb and know it not."

486

If "heaven lies about us in our infancy," it lies about us all the time. The Kingdom of God is at hand. We have but to find the road that leads to it, and the gate that gives access to it.

Generations of discerning souls have taught us that prayer is one of the most certain paths to paradise, and when one approaches heaven by that pathway the gate opens of itself.

Jesus and his disciples, suffering under the shock of John's untimely death, and troubled, the gospel of Mark tells us, by many who were coming and going leaving them no leisure even so much as to eat, went into a desert place to rest a while. And there in the solitude they sought by prayer to restore their faith, to sense again the immediacy of things not seen, the reality of the invisible. From the desert they returned to preach once more that the kingdom of heaven was at hand. Through prayer they had regained their paradise.

Paradise may take many outward forms, but inwardly it is a state of serene content, of fulness of being, of oneness with God and his universe. As we shut out the many strident voices of our crowded lives, and open the door to God by prayer, we gain strength and courage and vision. We find ourselves at home in the lovely world of the spirit, at peace with one another, at peace with ourselves, at peace with the Infinite.

PRAYER IS THE ANSWER

By Harry Bruno

Public Relations Counsel

❦

The voice on the telephone that noon of May 7, 1915, said, "The Lusitania was torpedoed and sunk." The immediate shock was tremendous. My father and mother were on board. The next few days were even worse than the first. Then came the confirmation that they both were lost and my brother Frank and I were orphans.

Friends, in their kindly way, tried to help but my mental state was getting worse. One dear friend had the answer. He took me in his car out to the Connecticut countryside; stopped by a wayside stream and told me to get out and sit for an hour on its banks. He said he would return to pick me up. That hour was one of the most important in my life. I bent my head in prayer and after a short space of time, there came a great sense of peace. It was as if a loving hand was on my shoulder. When I opened my eyes, they rested upon hundreds and hundreds of violets—truly I was sitting upon a bed of these beautiful spring flowers. When my friend returned, he said I looked like a new man, and that was how I felt. In my mind was the determination to work hard and justify my parents' faith in me. Prayer had lifted me from the depths—it has been my strength ever since.

Twelve years later, and in the same month, but the 20th day instead of the 7th, again I had to pray harder that I had ever prayed before. I stood beside Brigadier General Charles A. Lindbergh and the "Spirit of St. Louis" at Roosevelt Field, L.I., N.Y. The time was about 5 a.m. on a damp, rainy morning. I was there with my late partner, Richard R. Blythe, as

Lindbergh's personal representatives. Suddenly, as the mechanics finished fueling the airplane, a watery sun rose, and its rays lit up the fragile aircraft, revealing that it rested upon a bed of violets. My mind went back to that other May day, and I silently prayed for the young aviator's success. At the take-off I drove my open roadster behind the lumbering "Spirit of St. Louis." Beside me was Abram Skidmore, Chief of the Nassau County Police, who was holding a fire extinguisher. The plane bounced once, and I prayed as I have never prayed before. Twice more the frail undercarriage hit the ground before the plane staggered into the air. As I brought my car to a jolting stop at the end of the runway, Chief Skidmore said, "Harry, I never before heard anyone pray so fervently and so loudly driving a car at 60 miles an hour."

When I returned to the cheering crowd at the takeoff point, I was asked by newspapermen whether I thought Lindbergh would get to Paris. My calm assurance that he would came from an inner feeling that my humble prayers and those of millions of others would go with him to a successful landing in Paris.

To me, prayer is food for the spirit and even more important than food for the body.

Let us pray.

AN INHERITANCE

By Dr. Daniel A. Poling

Editor, *Christian Herald*

❧

The only prayer we know as the road to Peace with Power is the prayer that claims the promise of Jesus Christ: "Whatsoever ye shall ask **in my name,** that will I do" and "If ye shall ask anything **in my name, I will do it.**"

The prayer never fails. That promise stands fast. And that prayer is first of all our inheritance. I received it from my parents as they received it from theirs. With my face buried in the calico that covered my mother's knees and with her worn, gentle hands on my head, I uttered the first prayers of childhood. The faith my father declared from the pulpit he nailed together became my faith.

The prayers of my parents and their faith have companioned me through the years. Memory becomes more vivid as times passes. The low and armless rocker behind the airtight wood stove in the Oregon sitting room where my mother comforted her children was an altar too. Always in the morning an open Bible lay upon it. There she had worshipped before other members of the family were astir. There she found the strength for her crowded day, and there she breathed deeply of the grace she breathed upon us all.

Once when I lay with a broken body in a Massachusetts hospital, her prayer came to me, claiming life and recovery for me. "I have the answer," she wired. "Psalm 91:15-16." And presently I read: "He shall call upon me and I will answer him, I will be with him in trouble: I will deliver him and honor him. With long life will I satisfy him and show him my salvation."

It was a command to recover. She had the answer. She knew and I believed. Crushed hips, fractured vertebrae and ribs, internal injuries—nothing for science to do but wait, and for ten days without hope, but she "had the answer."

The last time I saw her she came out of a coma to greet her reunited family. For the first time in years the six children and their father were all together and with her. I had flown across the continent to join the reunion, and on the late evening of the day when I must return I was alone with her.

As I knelt by her bed she said, "Put your face upon my hands for I cannot lift them to your head." And then as her lips brushed my hair, she whispered, "My son, if when you come again I am not here to greet you as always I have greeted you before, then, my son, you will know where to find me!" And with that sure knowledge I left her and flew into the East.

Prayer, the road to Peace with Power, is my inheritance.

But increasingly prayer to me is something more than an inheritance; it is **infinitely** more than an inheritance; it is my experience, my day-by-day experience. And as an experience, prayer must become an achievement if it is to be for all the vicissitudes and for every circumstance of life, the road to Peace with Power.

PRAYER WITHOUT ACTION IS FUTILE

By Mrs. Oscar A. Ahlgren

Past President, General Federation of Women's Clubs

❦

"The things that are impossible with men are possible with God"—Luke 18:27

Sputnicks overhead, alarming as they are, do not surprise me. After spending a month in Russia during the fall of 1956, I was aware of Russian superiority in education. Impressive as it was, that was not the most frightening observation. I found a dedicated people—dedicated to machines—dedicated to world domination. I found eight-year-olds being taught Arabic, Chinese, and other languages, as well as English, planning ahead to rule the world.

We in the United States know that man must have faith in something. We put our faith in God. The Communists are completely anti-God. They put their faith in machines. Therein lies the difference.

We believe that faith triumphs over wrong. We have faith that we can win over all obstacles because we believe in God. Through prayer we find the courage to meet all challenges victoriously. As we keep close to God in prayer His wisdom guides us for His Spirit is within us. We are then no longer afraid or confused. Through association with Him in prayer we are encouraged and strengthened. No matter how grave a situation may appear to our finite minds, the power of God is mighty to overcome all opposition. God is in all of us. He is in those who are separated from us by miles, by language, and by custom. He is in the men of all nations, of all religions, and of all colors—if they will but seek him.

Prayer has been a guiding force in my life. I come from a praying home. No matter how busy I am, I spend a few minutes each morning with God in prayer. I see the dome of St. Matthew's Cathedral in Washington from my window and the first thing I do in the morning is to gaze at it and repeat: "I begin this day in the name of the Father, Son, and the Holy Spirit." Then I turn to God in prayer. I talk to God as I would talk to a friend. He is my counselor and my guide.

For many years it has been the annual custom in the church of which I am a member (Plymouth Congregational of Whiting, Indiana) for the senior high school Sunday School class to take complete charge of a Sunday morning service. On one particular Sunday morning a tall, lanky, freckle-faced boy gave the benediction. I have never forgotten it. What did he say? Was it the usual benediction we were accustomed to hearing? This is what the boy said: "Now let us all go out and live the spirit of God as well as to talk about it. Amen."

A Chinese philospher once said: "Words without action is to climb a tree to catch a fish." Prayer without action is futile. Prayer should make us a channel through which power and energy flow into action.

Let the prayer of our hearts be: "Now let us all go out and live the spirit of God as well as to talk about it. Amen."

WHAT I MEAN BY PRAYER

By *Philip M. Klutznick*

President of B'nai B'rith

❧

.Prayer is the spokesman of faith and a measure of our humility. It is the verbalized link between man's soul and his spiritual awe of the Almighty, humbly declaring that destiny lies in hands greater than his own. The cleansing reality of prayer is that it softens the arrogance of the mighty and inspires hope among the troubled and fallen.

We petition God in prayer. But what might we ask of Him? In the Judaic approach to prayer, man does not beseech God to run his errands or solve his problems. Since, in my mortal weaknesses, I am without the infinite wisdom to judge what is ultimately good or wrong for me, dare I plead that He fulfill my common desires? The Hebrew sage, Rabbi Eleizer, admonished us: "When you are in peril do not ask God to change the laws of nature for you. Ask for something else. Say, 'Do Thy will in the heavens above . . . do what is good in Thy sight.'" Thus, in the petitional fervor of prayer, the committed Jew asks Divine inspiration for courage, strength and widsom so that, with serenity of soul, he can accept God's will.

In the same sense, prayer expresses praise and adoration. But the Talmud warns that this is not to impress God or flatter Him. It is, rather, a sensitive awareness of His wonderous talent of creation. Man is moved to psalms of praise for the holy source of life.

It is profoundly said that we Jews pray philosophy. **Sh'ma Yisroel Adonoy Elohaynu Adonoy Echod. "Hear, O Israel, the Lord our God, the Lord is One."** This thought is the core of all Judaic prayer. Yet it is not a supplicating prayer; it asks nothing. This single, terse sentence defines the religious philosophy of Jewish life. Here is man's simple, exultant profession of One Father to be served by the brotherhood of man.

I find in prayer the highest expression of Jewish thought. For, essentially, it is self-judgment. Prayer in the ancient tradition of my fathers—and as I believe in it—is to review my thoughts and actions within the confines of my mind and soul. It compels me to ask: Have I been silent when I should have spoken out? Have I been selfish instead of generous? Thoughtless rather than considerate? Hostile and not friendly? Out of this self-probing process flows the spiritual recognition of man's responsibility to man. For one who truly feels kinship with Him must rebel against the hurt or destruction of anyone created in His image.

The broadest considerations that confront our troubled universe are based on the spiritual strength of meaningful prayer. Those who believe . . . and who pray . . . are by their very nature more sensitive to the need for understanding and tranquility among the peoples of the world. A genuine belief in prayer carries with it the nourishing desire for man to rid himself of the distrusts and hatreds that corrode the mind and soul.

FAITH GAVE ME A NEW START AT 56

By J. C. Penney

Founder of the J. C. Penney Company, Inc.

❧

One night late in 1931, I was convinced I would never see another dawn. I wrote farewell letters to my family. Then I waited for the end—a failure at the age of 56.

I was in a sanitarium at Battle Creek, Michigan, a nervous and physical wreck, plagued by shingles, and certain I did not have a friend on earth. I believed the whole world was against me, including my wife and children.

As a result of the financial dislocations of the depression, I had watched the fruits of a lifetime of toil swept away in a few brief months—a fortune estimated at $40,000,000, including all of my stock in the J. C. Penney Company, an organization I had seen grow from a single small Wyoming store in 1902 to the world's largest department store chain, with modern merchandising centers in every state in the Union.

From being in a position to move mountains (I thought), I was overnight transformed into just another beaten man, in late middle age, flat broke and with no apparent future. As is not unusual in such crack-ups, I blamed everyone except myself. My failure seemed to weigh a ton on my shoulders.

Somehow that dreadful night passed. The next morning as I shuffled from my room I heard the sound of singing coming from the mezzanine. The song was a hymn. I will never forget the title. It was: "God Will Take Care Of You." I was drawn to the source of the song. A group of patients were holding a prayer meeting. Wearily I joined them.

I prayed for God to take care of me, and an amazing thing happened. Suddenly I knew that He would. A profound sense of inner release came over me. The heavy weight seemed lifted from my spirit. That moment marked a turning point in my life.

Perhaps the feeling of imminence of death was a sign that a new man was being born in me. Or maybe at long last I was learning how to pray, by truly submitting myself to the will of God.

It had never occurred to me that I did not know how to pray. I regarded myself as a religious man. My father, who supported his family with a farm near Hamilton, Missouri, had been a minister in the old-fashioned Primitive Baptist Church. He reared me in strict discipline of that faith. In all my dealings I had sought to follow the principle of the Golden Rule.

But I hadn't realized what had taken place in me. As I rose in wealth and power, dealing in millions of dollars and guiding the activities of thousands of men I had grown to depend entirely upon my own judgment. My spiritual life had been stored away in a separate compartment. God had very little hand in my everyday thinking. With this condition prevailing, in the matter of prayer I was as helpless as a man in deep water who doesn't know how to swim.

In any case, a remarkable change followed that session of prayer. I rapidly regained my mental and bodily health. Within a couple of months I was well enough to return to my family. We had been living on our sixty-five acre estate at White Plains, New York, in a manner commensurate with wealth that no longer existed. Together with my wife, I now had the strength to take the steps that were needed.

Our children, two daughters and a son, were sent to live with their grandmother in Phoenix, Arizona, until things got better. We discharged the servants and closed down the large house, except for the kitchen and one bedroom, creating an apartment my wife could manage alone. We laid up our expensive automobile.

The Penney Company offered to put me on a salary. It had always been one of my proudest boasts that I had never drawn a cent of pay for my services to the company. But with my stock holdings gone, such pride was out of the question. I had to get on a payroll if my family was to continue to eat. I gratefully accepted the offer and plunged into work.

The years that followed were not easy. But two of the banks with which I had done business agreed not to close out my holdings entirely. This gave me a small foothold for the long climb back. But I still had many inner obstacles to overcome. However, when things got too bad, I drew strength from a piece of paper I carried with me always. On it I had copied these words from the Ninety-first Psalm:

"He shall cover thee with his feathers, and under his wings shalt thou trust: his truth shall be thy shield and buckler."

And I prayed—developing the habit of spending fifteen to thirty minutes in prayer and meditation just before retiring so that my last thoughts before going to sleep were on God and my spiritual needs.

In time I got back on firm ground. I had much less in a material sense than before, but I had gained immeasurably in spiritual wealth, something that cannot be calculated in dollars and cents. I had finally turned to God for guidance in all the acts and decisions of my life.

I do not mean to give the impression that because of my awakening I have successfully applied Christian principles to all phases of my life. I have not followed Christ's teachings as well as I might. But I am earnestly trying to make up for what I failed to do. Last year I made more than two hundred speeches, stressing Christ's two fundamental commandments —to love God and to love your neighbor as yourself. I expect to continue with this work as long as God grants me the strength.

I picture the trouble that befell me as a parallel to the situation which we, the American people, face today. Too many of us are trying to live, grow, and accomplish without God's help. We feel powerful beyond the need of anything except the material. But, as this barren philosophy failed me, it will fail America as a whole. We must stop and realize that the seeds of our own failure—possibly even of our destruction —lie within us.

As I see it, the one great need for all Americans, whether facing personal difficulties or worried by the ominous war clouds of today, is to make God a part of our daily lives.

PRAYER IS COMMUNICATION
By Marshall M. Fredericks
Sculptor
❁

I believe that nothing exists except through the power of God, and as an expression of God, and man is undoubtedly the highest expression. Therefore, it seems only natural and right that we should endeavor to reflect the attributes of God to our greatest ability and to identify ourselves with Him.

To attain this relationship we must communicate, and prayer to me is the means of communication. Our constant attempt in whatever manner we wish, is to feel at one with Him and to express Him in our daily lives, in our relationship with others, in our thoughts and desires, in our work and in our entire being.

PRAY AS TRUE SOLDIERS FIGHT

By General Nathan F. Twining

Chairman of the Joint Chiefs of Staff

❧

Our shot-up B-17 Flying Fortress took off from Guadalcanal on a clear day in January, 1943, headed for Espiritu Santo, a South Pacific island 600 miles to the southeast. A bad front had blanketed the airfield at Santo making a landing impossible, so our pilot elected to try setting down at another field 150 miles away where the weather was not so bad. The storm whipped up so violently during this leg of the flight that a landing there was equally impossible, and we decided to head back for Santo, get as close as we could and attempt a water landing. We knew our gas would not take us all the way in to the field.

There was ample time to prepare for ditching; we were all familiar with the difficulty of making a night landing in heavy seas and with the need for rapid evacuation to our rubber life rafts. I am certain that every man aboard called on God, as he had never done before, for assistance and courage.

The pilot made a perfect landing. Fifteen men exited from the plane and swam to the inflated life rafts. Our rations were lost in the crash, but God's Providence spared our lives.

We drifted aimlessly in our small craft for six days and nights, drinking rain water, eating bits of food the men had in their pockets, or munching on raw albatross which we shot.

We did not know then that the Navy had called off its aerial search on the third day, nor did we know that Colonel (now General) Hank Everest had refused to give us up and had kept planes continually in the sky in hopes we would be spotted. They found us and radioed the Navy to send seaplanes. Our never-to-be-forgotten ordeal ended a few hours later when we landed safely at Espiritu Santo.

I have always felt very grateful to have been allowed to survive that accident. I prayed, as did the others in the rafts, with confidence in God that He would stay with us and eventually guide us to safety. He kept us calm and united in our plight and gave us the strength to carry on.

Prayer has always been a source of deep satisfaction to me. Through the years, in various positions of responsibility in the military service, I have been called on to make some extremely significant and difficult decisions. I admit to having been afforded good, sound advice prior to making up my mind; but, at the same time and in my own way, I can say with pride that I sought God's guidance — I looked to Him to give me direction. He has never failed me.

I firmly believe that every man, in his own way, must recognize the existence of a superior being and must pray to Him. We should pray as true soldiers fight — full of courage and full of high hopes. We must realize that we are definitely privileged to be on this earth and that our lives are in God's care. When we do these things, we will find true happiness.

THAT THE OUTWARD AND INWARD MAN BE AS ONE

By Dr. Milton R. Konvitz

Professor of Industrial and Labor Relations, and Professor of Law,

Cornell University

❂

When I was a junior in high school I found in a bookstore a secondhand copy of the **Meditations** of Marcus Aurelius. I had never heard of the book or of the author, but the title attracted me and I bought it. When I had the book at home I turned the pages and my eye caught the following passage:

> "One prays, 'Let me not lose my little child.'
> Pray thou rather, 'Let me not fear that loss.'
> Turn all thy supplications this way, and see
> What cometh to pass."

I have never forgotten the lesson of that passage; and as the years have passed on, its implications have become more meaningful to me.

For to pray that God—who is all-knowing, all-powerful, all-loving and all-just—should please be kind enough to do **my** bidding is to make him my servant and to make myself his master. To do this is prideful idolatry.

To pray that God should alter the course of nature on my account—that he should alter the direction of the wind, or send or withhold rain, or arrest the sun in its motion—is to misjudge my position in time and place and to confuse religion with magic.

To pray for specific things is to assume that we know more than God knows what is really good for us, and thus we may be asking him to harm us. Indeed, as Oscar Wilde remarked, it sometimes seems that when God wishes to punish us, he does so by answering our prayers!

When I pray, it is not that God should listen to me, but that I should hear him.

When I pray, it is not that I should give him of my strength to interfere with the sun and the moon and the stars, or that I should give him of my wisdom to direct the course of my life or of human history, but that I may have the strength and the wisdom to do **his** will: to follow in the path of truth, to do justice, to love kindness, to enjoy beautiful things, to seek knowledge and understanding, to endure with dignity human miseries for which there is no consolation, and to admit into every experience the "eternal note of sadness."

To pray thus is not to add words to a great distracting noise but to hear them as they come out of an infinite, eternal silence, and to feel that as they seek to reach God, in them God seeks to reach me.

The ultimate of prayer should be that my prayers should be built into my work, my acts, my experiences, so that, in some sense, they—my deeds—become my prayers into which my spirit flows and pours itself. This, I think, is what Socrates meant when he prayed to beloved Pan that the outward and inward man be as one.

PRAYER IS MORE THAN A WORD

By Everett McKinley Dirksen

U.S. Senator from Illinois

❦

As a young man active in Christian Endeavor, I remember with what gusto we sang such hymns as "Sweet Hour of Prayer" and "Take It To the Lord In Prayer." In those days perhaps it seemed only a word.

There may have been some reason for it. Youth, ego, a sense of self-sufficiency, good health, confidence, and well-defined ambitions made it seem unnecessary to ask the all-prevading God for a helping hand. It was simply a part of the I-can-do-it-myself creed of youth.

But in every life there comes moments when confidence in one's capacity to stand alone is shaken. Anxious days on a battle front when one is tempted to scold the Lord for letting men kill each other; the passing of a saintly mother just when she might have more completely escaped from the hard work and more richly enjoyed life; a personal affliction which threatened blindness; and equally anxious moments do raise the question to what source one can turn for answers for comfort and for peace of mind.

I recall sitting in a dug-out on the unquiet Western Front thumbing through a khaki-bound Bible. Why should one turn to a seemingly historic nobody named James, whose only claim to fame seemed to be a single letter broken into five chapters and addressed to the scattered twelve tribes? He called himself a "servant of God and of the Lord Jesus Christ." I was not too impressed as I read the first chapters of this letter. But in the last chapter was something which made me pause. "Is any

504

among you afflicted? Let him pray. . . . . . Is any sick among you? Let him call for the elders of the church and let them pray over him. . . . . . . The effectual fervent prayer of a righteous man availeth much." I have recited those words to myself many times. James spoke of **effectual** prayer. Instead of asking the Lord to come over into my corner, I thought the proper thing was to ask him to let me to get into his corner if it was to be effectual. James speaks of **fervent** prayer. If through conscience and faith it is not fervent, why should the Lord bother about it anyway?

James qualified it all by saying "of a righteous man." I was never sure I could claim righteousness. I believe I could say that my intentions were such. The question is, was that enough? I thought it was. Surely the Lord would not cast aside the prayers of a sinner if he earnestly sought the righteous course, even though he might often fail in the endeavor.

This then seemed like the formula and one can tie it all up in a simple little package by saying "Lord, I try to be righteous. Where I fail, give me a hand for another try. So often I need direction and hope. Do not send it on a platter. Just tell me how and where to find it and let the labor be mine. Just let the light shine a little so I can find your corner."

What else is there to say, except that it works?

PRAYER IS MORE THAN PRAYING

By Dr. Marcus Bach

School of Religion, University of Iowa

When a man prays, he unlocks a door. He enters his own chamber, the chamber of his heart. He closes the door behind him.

He says, "I am now going to explore the God-consciousness in me. It may be that I will not even know what to say. It may be that I will have no words at all, only thoughts and impressions, and hopes and fears, and faith and questioning, but this is my moment for communion and God-realization. I know that I shall find Him and that when I abandon my will to His will my prayer will have been said."

Prayer puts your true self in harmony with God. Those who think of prayer or of affirmations as some systematic trick or modern magic to make God a servitor miss the point. Prayers and affirmations are means to an end, and the end is a consecrated life.

Prayer is a yearning and a striving and a closing out of the world, until whatever you are praying for or about becomes a living reality in the world and the life within.

There are some people who should readily understand the technique of prayer. The musician should understand it because prayer is like committing some immortal composition into mind and heart. Only when you have been over-powered by it, can it over-power you.

An artist should understand what prayer is, for it is a deeply creative expression. It is something that tugs at your heart and will not let you rest until you have given it form.

A lover ought to understand prayer, for it is, as so often has been said, "the soul's sincere desire, uttered or unexpressed." If prayer is not a mystical experience, it is nothing.

A mother should understand prayer, for prayer is compassion. It is nothing if it is not compassion, selfless, solicitous and unconcealed compassion.

A doctor should know what prayer is when he holds life in his hands. A soldier should know what it is when, in that moment of conflict between his life and another's all life becomes suddenly holy. A miner should know what prayer is when he crouches inside the earth and hears nothing and sees nothing except the endless dark, and knows even while he stands there that in that dark is endless light.

The seaman, the traveler, the scientist, the businessman, the farmer, the laborer, the man who has more of this world's goods than he deserves and the man who has less than he deserves; each should know what prayer is because of that moment when he suddenly sees himself as he truly is, when he enters into the sanctuary of his soul and speaks to God— and listens as God speaks to him.

Prayer is more than praying. If you honestly ask, "What will prayer do for me?" there is but one honest answer, "Pray and see."

PRAYER IS POWER

By Dr. Alexis Carrel

Physician, Noted Physiologist, and Nobel Prize Scientist

Prayer is not only worship; it is also an invisible emanation of man's worshipping spirit—the most powerful form of energy that one can generate. The influence of prayer on the human mind and body is as demonstrable as that of secreting glands. Its results can be measured in terms of increased physical buoyancy, greater intellectual vigor, moral stamina, and a deeper understanding of the realities underlying human relationships.

If you make a habit of sincere prayer, your life will be very noticeably and profoundly altered. Prayer stamps with its indelible mark our actions and demeanor. A tranquillity of bearing, a facial and bodily repose, are observed in those whose inner lives are thus enriched. Within the depths of consciousness a flame kindles. And man sees himself. He discovers his selfishness, his silly pride, his fears, his greeds, his blunders. He develops a sense of moral obligation and intellectual humility. Thus begins a journey of the soul toward the realm of grace.

Prayer is a force as real as terrestrial gravity. As a physician, I have seen men, after all other therapy had failed, lifted out of disease and melancholy by the serene effort of prayer. It is the only power in the world that seems to overcome the so-called "laws of nature"; the occasions on which prayer has dramatically done this have been termed "miracles." But a constant, quieter miracle takes place hourly in the hearts of men and women who have discovered that prayer supplies them with a steady flow of sustaining power in their daily lives.

Too many people regard prayer as a formalized routine of words, a refuge for weaklings, or a childish petition for material things. We sadly undervalue prayer when we conceive it in these terms, just as we should underestimate rain by describing it as something that fills a birdbath in our garden. Properly understood, prayer is a mature activity indispensable to the fullest development of personality—the ultimate integration of man's highest faculties. Only in prayer do we achieve that complete and harmonious assembly of body, mind and spirit which gives the frail human reed its unshakable strength.

The words, "Ask and it shall be given to you," have been verified by the experience of humanity. True, prayer may not restore the dead child to life or bring relief from physical pain. But prayer, like radium, is a source of luminous self-generating energy.

How does prayer fortify us with so much dynamic power? To answer this question (admittedly outside the jurisdiction of science) I must point out that all prayers have one thing in common. The triumphant hosannas of a great oratorio, or the humble supplication of an Iroquois hunter begging for luck in the chase, demonstrate the same truth: that human beings seek to augment their finite energy by addressing themselves to the Infinite Source of all energy. When we pray, we link ourselves with the inexhaustible motive power that spins the universe. We ask that a part of this power be apportioned to our needs. Even in asking, our human deficiencies are filled and we arise strengthened and repaired.

But we must never summon God merely for the gratification of our whims. We derive most power from prayer when we use it, not as a petition, but as a supplication that we may become more like Him. Prayer should be regarded as practice of the Presence of God. An old peasant was seated alone in the last pew of the village church. "What are you waiting for?" he was asked; and he answered, "I am looking at Him and He is looking at me." Man prays not only that God should remember him, but also that he should remember God.

How can prayer be defined? Prayer is the effort of man to reach God, to commune with an invisible being, creator of all things, supreme wisdom, truth, beauty, and strength, father and redeemer of each man. This goal of prayer always remains hidden to intelligence. For both language and thought fail when we attempt to describe God.

We do know, however, that whenever we address God in fervent prayer we change both soul and body for the better. It could not happen that any man or woman could pray for a single moment without some good result. "No man ever prayed," said Emerson, "without learning something."

One can pray everywhere. In the streets, the subway, the office, the shop, the school, as well as in the solitude of one's room or among the crowd in a church. There is no prescribed posture, time or place.

"Think of God more often than you breathe," said Epictetus the Stoic. In order really to mold personality, prayer must become a habit. It is meaningless to pray in the morning and to live like a barbarian the remainder of the day. True prayer is a way of life; the truest life is literally a way of prayer.

The best prayers are like improvisations of gifted lovers, always about the same thing yet never twice the same. We cannot all be as creative in prayer as Saint Theresa or Bernard of Clairvaux, both of whom poured their adoration into words of mystical beauty. Fortunately, we do not need their eloquence; our slightest impulse to prayer is recognized by God. Even if we are pitifully dumb, or if our tongues are overlaid with vanity of deceit, our meager syllables of praise are accept-

510

able to Him, and He showers us with strengthening manifestations of His love.

Today, as never before, prayer is a binding necessity in the lives of men and nations. The lack of emphasis on the religious sense has brought the world to the edge of destruction. Our deepest source of power and perfection has been left miserably undeveloped. Prayer, the basic exercise of the spirit, must be actively practiced in our private lives. The neglected soul of man must be made strong enough to assert itself once more. For if the power of prayer is again released and used in the lives of common men and women; if the spirit declares its aims clearly and boldly, there is hope that our prayers for a better world will be answered.

PRAYER CHANGES THINGS

By Dr. L. L. Carpenter

Editor, *Biblical Recorder*

❦

In an intimate talk with his disciples Jesus said, "If ye shall ask any thing in my name, that will I do" (John 14:14, ASV). This is a wonderful statement and has much meaning for every true Christian. This promise of Jesus gives assurance as to the answer to prayer. Of course, the prayer must be in keeping with that which is right and good and according to the will of God. But this passage and other parallel passages in the New Testament give assurance as to the answer to prayer.

It is often said that prayer changes things. Prayer changes the one who prays. It brings him into harmony with the will and purpose of God. God hears us when we pray, and many times he answers our prayers in more ways and better than we can dream.

Perhaps the most vital and creative thing a Christian ever does, occurs when he enters into communion and fellowship with God through prayer. A Christian is a child of God, and when he prays he is actually talking to Almighty God, his heavenly Father, who made heaven and earth. And in turn God speaks to him. One can hardly conceive how vital and important this prayer experience is in the life of even the average Christian.

Someone has written these striking and meaningful lines:

Whosoever draws near to God, one step through
    doubtings dim,
God will advance a mile in blazing light to him.

Every one of us should follow the Scriptural injunction: "Pray without ceasing," and then we would know in our won experience that prayer changes things and we would enter into fellowship with God and follow more faithfully every day His will.

GOD ANSWERS PRAYER

By Dr. Robert J. McCracken

Minister, The Riverside Church, New York

❀

People have prayed for recovery from sickness and been restored to health. They have prayed for deliverance from danger and a way of escape has been opened up. They have asked God for a blessing on their labors and have been convinced that they did not ask in vain. The evidence that prayer is definitely and directly answered is too strong and too age-long summarily to be set aside.

I cite the testimony of Mary Slessor, missionary to Calabar: "My life is one long, daily, hourly record of answered prayer. For physical health, for mental overstrain, for guidance given marvellously, for errors and dangers averted, for enmity to the Gospel subdued, for food provided at the exact hour needed, for everything that goes to make up life and my poor service, I can testify with a full and often wonder-stricken awe that I believe God answers prayer."

To this may be added the considered judgment of Sir Wilfred Grenfell of Labrador: "The privilege of prayer to me is one of the most cherished possessions, because faith and experience alike convince me that God Himself sees and answers, and His answers I never venture to criticize. It is only my part to ask."

PRAYER UNITES

By Dr. Carl E. Lund-Quist

Executive Secretary, The Lutheran World Federation

❀

Prayer unites Christians. This I can attest after watching world-wide developments in the last thirteen years. The discovery of the fact that Christian unity is a living thing—through prayer—has been one of the great satisfactions for me in this post-war era. As people and congregations get to know one another they are prompted to pray for their brethren wherever they may be.

In several congregations on the Island of Sumatra in Indonesia I discovered an interesting fact. There congregations were formed of recently converted Batak people with a spiritual vitality that was expressed in overwhelming attendance, lively singing and loyalty to the church in the face of strong persecution. But they were most interested in the situation of the German East Zone congregations under the present government. Not only were they interested, but they were praying for these people. Prayer by the congregations in Sumatra for the congregations in Leipzig was a form of unity that was as real as anything in life.

The same experience has been true in other parts of the world. Congregations in Madagascar have prayed for congregations in Holland; people in South Africa are praying for the church in Finland; Czechoslovakian Christians pray for Christians in India. In this mutual intercession I see God at work helping them to a unity that would not otherwise exist.

In the 1957 world Assembly of Lutherans in Minneapolis one could see the results of this prayer unity. Leaders and representatives of churches in Asia, Africa, South America and behind the Iron Curtain became figures of flesh and blood for our American churches. The prayers of thousands for these men in these many years made it possible to experience unity in a remarkable way. The unity of prayer has another result, namely that when we pray we also share. Prayer and sharing have resulted in international bonds that raise church funds for global tasks lifted to a completely new level from government funds.

In contacting congregations, pastors and church leaders I have discovered the vital power of prayer in the daily existence of people. Many pastors have said that life would be intolerable if it were not for the knowledge that people are praying for them. The complexities, the constant fear, the human mistrust that is so cleverly sown among people would be too hard to bear if these people would think that they were neglected in prayer. Prayer unites churches in a real sense—black and white, East and West, those living under Communism and Capitalism. I will long remember the last visit with Bishop Ordass of Hungary (one of the truly great men of our time). When we parted in November, 1957 I asked him what we could do. He simply said, "Pray for us."

PRAYER, ITS POWER AND MEANING

By Felton G. Clark

President, Southern University, Baton Rouge

❦

I believe in prayer. I believe that it is a power—a dynamic, cosmic, germinal influence; a prime mover, a causal force which has effect. Steinmetz, the great electrical engineer and scientific genuis of General Electric, when asked just before his death, what should be the next subject of scientific investigation, answered "Prayer." The answer of this man who was interested in all concepts of power implied that prayer as a power can have far more effect than man's mind can contemplate.

I believe that prayer serves the individual good. It serves the individual soul of man. My own experience is a witness to this. Life has brought many moments of choice between values—many moments of decision—to keep on or to quit; to fight or turn the other cheek; to withdraw or advance; to live or die. Life has brought moments of doubt, especially when self has been measured against the challenge of a seemingly insurmountable task against all odds. Life has even brought despair, growing out of illness and aloneness—the aloneless which all human beings face at times. In these moments I have resorted to prayer. The answer has always come: The power to make the choice which is not only helpful to me but to others; the power to endure—to live more abundantly, to walk the second mile—to thread the growing edge where in the darkness there seemed no firm footing; the power to do good to those who misuse me; to love my enemies. Prayer has taught me that even my sufferings and limitations can be a blessing leading to goodness, truth and beauty. Prayer provides that moment when I literally throw myself in utter dependence and reliance upon God, forgetting self, like a child. The answer comes, sooner or later, through a person, an idea, a thing, or a feeling of comfort. He provides the source of guidance, illumination and light. I believe He is available to every individual as a source of guidance and goodness.

Finally I believe that aside from its personal meaning and source of power, prayer is more important in its group or social meaning. It serves man but it also serves humanity. One should pray as much for his brother as for himself. I have tried this. It is the source of power—the dynamic—the motivation of improved human relations—that through prayer man can transcend the limits of individual, racial and national egotism to accept his brother as brother and wish him good. Jesus gave us the perfect example of prayer when He prayed:

Our Father, (Not my father)
Give us this day our daily bread—(not give me my daily bread)
Forgive us our trespasses (not mine only)
But deliver us from evil (not me only)
For thine is the Kingdom and the Power and the Glory.

We share in God's glory and power only as we know that He is and in prayer seek His will for us and strive to do it.

THE PRAYER AND THE
ANSWER ARE ONE

By Upton Sinclair

Author and Novelist

An enemy has dogged my footsteps, sitting like a hungry
wolf on my doorstep through my forty writing years; that
is insomnia. I have never been willing to use drugs, tea or
coffee to wake me up, or tobacco or narcotics to put me to
sleep. And since I won't use drugs, I have to pray.

One thing you learn, in fighting insomnia, never worry;
I have found it better not to think about sleep at all. Think
about what you are saying; believe what you are saying,
every word. Don't stop to argue; silence the skeptic who
lurks within, and tell yourself as follows:

"God is here, and God is now. God is alive, and God is real.
God is all, and God is love. God is my Father, and God is my
Friend. God is keeping me, and God is helping me. God gives
me power, and God gives me peace. God comforts me, and
God heals me. God enfolds me, God surrounds me. God covers
me with a living blanket. That blanket has power to drive
away all other thoughts. It protects me and keeps me safe.
Under its shelter God and I are alone. God watches over me.
God helps me. God heals me. God teaches me. God guides
me. God gives me peace . . . . "

And so on. It doesn't matter which of these things you say.
It doesn't matter how many times you repeat any of them.
The point is that you keep your mind full of images and ideas
of a power greater than yourself, a power which has the necessary strength, the necessary knowledge, to take care of you and

do for you what you need. "Now I lay me down to sleep" is an expression of the mood in which to approach autosuggestion for sleep. Hymns are good; they supply both words and music to hold your attention.

It is a fact that there is a power that keeps you when you sleep, it causes your heart to beat, your lungs to breathe, your tissues to renew themselves. Your job is to trust that power, put yourself consciously and continuously into its hands, cast out fear, make yourself "as a little child."

My God is a still, small voice in my heart. My God is something that is with me when I sit alone, and wonder, and question the mystery. My God says: "I am here, and I am now."

My God says: "Speak to Me, and I will answer; not in sounds, but in stirrings of your soul; in courage, hope, energy, the stuff of life." My God says: "Ask, and it shall be given you. Seek, and ye shall find. Knock, and it shall be opened unto you."

My God is the process of my being; nothing strange, but that which goes on all the time. I ask: "Can I pray?" and He answers: "You are praying. The prayer and the answer are one."

PRAYER IS A FORCE

By Dr. Benjamin P. Browne

Executive Director, The Board of Education and Publication,

The American Baptist Publication Society

❦

"Prayer is either a farce or a force," said a famous preacher. To me prayer is a force. By this I mean that having employed prayer as a habit of long years and having tested prayer through a variety of experiences I have found it validated for me by its spiritual benefits and blessings as well as all its practical results. Sincere prayer in quietude or in the worshipping congregation brings fresh and sometimes priceless insights, often suggests the solution to vexing problems, elevates the mind to new and creative ideas, steadies the will to do the hard right rather than the easy wrong, softens the stubborn spirit to penitence toward God and to a readiness to forgive others, quickens the impulse to acts of kindness, recalls the mind to duties long neglected, stabs the spirit with awareness of another world, supplies new energy and renewed incentive to righteousness, harmonizes the soul with the will of God, and undergirds the entire being with the joy of Christian service and the glamour of the good life.

These daily needs are met by daily prayer, and we are helped to keep going on, "chins up," amid the pathos and tragedy of life. Often we fight our way through the darkness by the earnest outpouring of our heartfelt prayers. Nor can we discount the physical and mental healing power of prayer when we have witnessed its power to give risen life to those in the grip and shadow of death. Moreover, prayer brings us into the presence of Christ in a face to face communion where the fellowship is more than any fellowship on earth.

Surely all poking of fun at prayer is scurrilously ignorant in a day when the scientist listens to the music of the spheres and the radio broadcasts around the world the human heartbeat.

On May 26, 1958 a famous New York heart specialist, Dr. Arthur Briskier, broadcast recordings of the heartbeats of his cardiac patients to physicians in Paris and Rome, the first intercontinental broadcast of human heartbeats. Well, is it then too difficult to believe that God hears prayers that sincerely rise from the human heart? Cannot the great physician also hear the heartbeats of the praying believers?

Aren't all the giant radar screens now listening to the signals of the stars? Our sensitive scientific listening devices get signals from worlds 270,000,000 light years out in space beyond our planet Earth. Prayer is but finally the faith that God signals back to human souls attuned to him and listening for His word of insight, direction, and help.

Let those who will, doubt, but let those who have known and tested prayer in experiences continue to pray always as men ought to pray. Jesus did not say, "If ye pray," but "When ye pray," knowing that prayer is inescapable.

SIMPLE FAITH CAN
MOVE MOUNTAINS

By Earl Warren

Chief Justice of the United States

In this land of liberty our governmental affairs have always been guided by men and women of religious faith—not people of one church but of all churches. During that period, with absolute freedom of worship, our nation has grown strong spiritually until today it is a beacon light of hope for oppressed people everywhere in the world.

I believe no one can read the history of our country without realizing that the Good Book and the Spirit of the Savior have from the beginning been our guiding geniuses.

Our people at the time of the Revolution were religious people—they read the Bible. They believed it. They wanted always to be free to read it and to belong to the church of their choice. When the Constitution did not guarantee that right in specific words, they insisted immediately on a Bill of Rights that would do so. I believe that the entire Bill of Rights came into being because of the knowledge our forefathers had of the Bible and their belief in it. Freedom of belief, of expression, of assembly, of petition;—the dignity of the individual, the sanctity of the home, equal justice under law, and the reservation of powers to the people. These things are the very essence of Christianity. They have characterized all our institutions. They have shaped our national life. They have given us our vision for the future.

I like to believe we are living today in the spirit of the Christian religion. I like also to believe that as long as we do so, no great harm can come to our country, and that the spirit which fortifies our individual wills will strengthen our nation, and make it both spiritually and materially strong and useful, not only to ourselves, but to mankind.

What we are doing for our neighbors throughout the world in these turbulent times should be an assurance to people everywhere that we are, not only a great nation, but a Christian nation which has for its foremost objective: "Peace on earth, Good Will to Men."

Traditionally we have chosen men to lead our country who have that spirit. Only a year ago we saw our President stand on the steps of the Capitol, and within the hearing of his countrymen from coast to coast, offer his personal prayer for Divine guidance and for the goodness as well as the greatness of our country. I am sure it heartened every American.

This is the kind of simple faith that can move mountains. And before these perplexing days in which we are living pass, it may be necessary to move mountains. It is good, therefore, to keep the faith together.

—Excerpts from an address delivered at the Annual Christian Action Conference, Feb. 4, 1954.

THREE PRAYERS

By Sophie Kerr

Author and Former Editor of *Woman's Home Companion*

❧

To those men and women who possess faith and reverence but are not members of any definite religious group, there sometimes comes an overpowering need of expression of their spirit in prayer, yet they do not know what to say and they grope blindly for adequate words to bring them peace and strength. For such seeking souls there are three great short prayers, all very old, all honored by long tradition, treasured infinitely by those who know them.

The first of these prayers is the greatest of the three, the oldest, and the most appealing; it is the answer to all questions, all situations, all exigencies, all times. It is, of course, the familiar "Our Father" which most children learn when they are too young to grasp its full meaning, but which they will say again and again with deepening understanding as they grow older. Because this prayer was first taught by Jesus Christ Himself it has no equal and never will have. A day that begins with "Our Father" and ends with "Our Father" is inevitably bettered, inevitably graced.

The second prayer which I feel the inarticulate should learn (it will please the articulate also) is the little prayer of Saint Teresa of Avila which begins: "Let nothing disturb thee, nothing affright thee. All things are passing. God never changeth." It is beautiful in its original Spanish but the English translation is good and easy to learn. It is not so much a real prayer as an affirmation of confidence in divine power and majesty. For a long time I have carried with me in my handbag a written copy of Saint Teresa's prayer and often I give it away and have to write another for myself. Saint Teresa was a glowing, positive woman, energetic, practical, in many ways contemporary, so she speaks to us with exactly the warm comfort we need. Everyone who learns Saint Teresa's prayer will find a friend there.

The third wonderful prayer—quite different from the others—is the Prayer of Saint Chrysostom from the Protestant Episcopal Book of Common Prayer, morning or evening service. In this prayer God is asked for the fulfillment of the "desires and petitions" of His servants, with the humble qualification "as may be most expedient for them." Chrysostom was a highly educated Greek and his prayer expresses perfectly the reaction of his nature and his talents to prayer. He is honest with himself and honest with God—he asks only that humanity may be given what God knows is "most expedient." Though Chrysostom was born **circa** 347, he too speaks as a modern.

Those who wish to pray but have found no fitting words will, I believe, do well to learn by heart the three prayers I have cited here. And perhaps they might say along with them the petition of King Solomon who prayed for an understanding heart!

BY PRAYER I FIND STRENGTH

By Dr. Leonard D. Heaton

Major General, United States Army, Commanding
Walter Reed Army Medical Center, Washington, D. C.

and

George D. Heaton, D.D., Charlotte, N. C.

❦

What do I believe about prayer? It is as difficult to answer adequately this question as to answer, "What do I believe about love, or justice, or friendship?" However difficult, I shall try in these few words to express my belief.

I believe in prayer because I believe in God and in man. What I believe about prayer is determined by my convictions about God and man. Prayer cannot be for me an end in itself, nor can it be a strategy to avoid or alter reality. Prayer is a description of the relationship which exists between a man and his God, and is therefore obviously conditioned by what he thinks of God and himself.

The God in whom I believe is no more interested in me than He is interested in all men, and I could never think of prayer as a means to gain preferred treatment. His interest is in us all.

God is creative, and I never associate with Him any destructive action.

God is love, and it is impossible for Him to act in a pattern of ill will or hatred.

God is good, and it is inconceivable that I should try, or think I need to try, to alter His behavior toward me or my patients.

God is truth, and He is constantly energizing us to pursue the truth. As a physician, part of this search for truth means to me the conquest of disease.

The God in whom I believe wants man to conquer polio; He does not use the disease to punish man. God wants man to find the answer to cancer. I do not believe in a God whose will is to afflict people with cancer.

Because I believe in such a God, and because I believe man's fulfillment is in identification with God, prayer becomes the way whereby my life is more responsive to Him.

By prayer I find strength—not only for the specific act of surgery, but also for life's total experiences. Through prayer I can see the course more clearly and can pursue it more energetically. By prayer I confront life's variations more heartily, and think of my companions more tolerantly and compassionately.

Prayer does make a great difference—not in God, but in me. I would not have it otherwise.

My weakness and regret are—although I know and believe prayer to be all of this—I have explored so slightly the unlimited potentials of power in the experience.

I MUST BELIEVE IN PRAYER

By Costen J. Harrell

Bishop in the Methodist Church

❧

I believe in prayer because I believe in God. We know that God is the source of every material and spiritual blessing. He is perfect in power and wisdom and love. All things are under his control, and from him no secrets are hid. It would be most unreasonable to suppose that God does not hear the call of a person in need and answer him. We who are mortal men are moved by another's appeal. We take his need on our hearts and reach out hands of compassion to give him succor. If God could not or would not do what good men in their smaller spheres are doing every day he would be less than man, and not God at all. That is unthinkable!

The only perfect Man who ever lived found in prayer sustenance for his faith and strength for every day. In the story of his life we find him alone, early in the morning before the day's work had begun, conversing with God—and in a desert place, and by the sea, and in a garden, and amid the pressures of the crowd, and in the agony of death on Calvery. He prayed without ceasing, as Paul urges us all to do; that is, he lived always consciously in the Father's presence, and in everything looked to him for direction and support. What was necessary for the Redeemer must be necessary for the redeemed.

The best and noblest men and women who have walked life's way have, like the Son of God, relied on the power of prayer. By it they have obtained forgiveness and a good conscience, a balm for sorrow, wisdom for living, direction for the way, and a continuing sense of the presence and approval of God. Said Wilfred Grenfell, whose labors in Labrador the world will not soon forget, "Faith and experience alike convince me that God himself sees and answers, and his answer I never venture to criticize." And another who lived many centuries ago, and whose labors still bless mankind, speaks out of a storm-tossed career, "For nothing, nothing is more powerful than prayer when fervent and genuine."

When I review the years of my own life I cannot doubt the oft-proved power of prayer. I do not attempt to explain the mystery—how the infinite God hears the prayer of a lone person and comes to his aid. I am sure that our petitions do not change God's beneficent purposes: but I know they do release them. I cannot recall an instance when in answer to fervent prayer God did not grant my request or do for me something that proved to be much better.

Prayer is conversation between mortal man and God the Father Almighty. Man calls and God responds. And after we speak to him we must be silent if we would hear his answer. For many say, "Hear, Lord, for thy servant speaketh!" And so few, "Speak, Lord, for thy servant heareth!"

❋

I have been driven many times to my knees by the overwhelming conviction that I had nowhere else to go. My own wisdom and that of all around me seemed insufficient for the day.   —Abraham Lincoln

TRUE PRAYER

By Dr. Bob Jones, Jr.

President, Bob Jones University

❦

Prayer is not wishful thinking, idle dreaming, or mental suggestion. Prayer is a man communing with God as a child communes with his father. The Bible tells us that "As many as received him, to them gave he power to become the sons of God, even to them that believe on his name." So to become the child of God with a right to pray and expect an answer, a man must be born again by faith in Jesus Christ, the Son of God.

Our Lord promised "Whatsoever ye shall ask in my name, that will I do, that the Father may be glorified in the Son." Perhaps an unsaved man can pray, but God does not promise to hear and answer the unsaved man.

For the born-again man or woman prayer is asking, seeking, knocking, with the assurance that he shall receive, he shall find, and the door shall be opened. "Ask, and it shall be given you; seek, and ye shall find; knock, and it shall be opened unto you" (Matthew 7:7). Asking presupposes the power of giving. No man asks another for something which he knows he is unable to grant. One does not ask riches of a poor man or food of a man who is hungry. No wise man asks a favor of one who is powerless to grant his request. Asking of God, we are making our request to the One who has power "to do exceeding abundantly above all that we ask or think" (Ephesians 3:20). The man who rightly asks is the man who asks in faith, believing that God is able to grant and that God is willing to grant.

530

The matter of prayer goes beyond asking, however. We are told to seek, and promised that in seeking we shall find. God sometimes expects us to seek for the answer to our prayer. We may even say He expects us to help Him to answer it. I have known young men who were studying for the ministry to pray the Lord to send them money to meet the needs of their educational expenses when they were too lazy to go out and make the effort to raise the money. It is good to ask the Lord to send, but it is better sometimes to pray, "Lord, direct me in my search and send me where I will find the thing which I desire." Some folks pray for a deepening of their spiritual life, yet never seek to find deeper spiritual life in earnest communion with the Lord and in study of His Word. Some pray for patience but never seek the tribulation which worketh patience.

True prayer goes still further. "To him that knocketh it shall be opened" (Matthew 7:8), is the promise. Some people are not willing to knock and wait for the door to swing wide. They try to tear it open themselves or break it down. God in His own good time will remove the obstacles. When He is ready the door will open. Perfect prayer harnesses itself to the will of God. Perfect faith waits for the answer to come in His own way at His own time.

❦

Prayer is and remains the native and deepest impulse of the soul of man.   —Thomas Carlyle

PRAYER IS RELIGION IN ACTION

By *Sherwood Eddy*

Ex-Secretary for Asia, YMCA

❧

For sixty-two years I have been working in thirty countries as an evangelist, beginning in India in 1896. Like many others, I have found that prayer is "religion in action," the Christian's "vital breath," and that if we ask according to God's will prayer is answered.

At the Edinburgh Missionary Conference in 1910 Azariah and myself, two young secretaries of the YMCA, "agreed" to pray that our divided churches should be united. For thirty-seven years we both prayed and he worked, winning first the Bishop of Madras, Henry Whitehead, and last the Archbishop of Canterbury, William Temple, who saw the plan of union through the Lambeth Conference of the Anglican bishops of the world. Then a decade ago in the cathedral of Madras there met the representatives of one million Christians: the Anglicans, Presbyterians, Methodists and Congregationalists to form the United Church of South India in which I worked on my recent visit to India in twenty-six cities for five months. Other divided churches can be united by prayer as these were. "We have not because we ask not."

As a second answer to prayer, when John R. Mott at the Edinburgh Missionary Conference in 1910 asked me to become Secretary for Asia of the YMCA I saw I would need a private secretary to send my report letters to all the wealthy men in America whom I hoped to call upon. Just once I claimed the promise in I John 5:14 "if we ask anything according to his will" and never repeated that prayer. At the first conference I attended in America in Lake Forest near Chicago I was introduced to Madam McCormick who offered to drive me to the conference in her car. As a complete stranger without a hint from me, for it was far from my mind, she proposed to give me a private secretary and pay his salary and expenses round the world of $5000 a year, which she continued throughout her life for many years. At her death her daughter Mrs. Emmons Blaine, unsolicited, asked the privilege of continuing the support of this secretary in her mother's name.

These are only two of an endless series of answered prayers by which I live. For years I have lived on two promises which have carried me round the world several times: Philippians 4:19: "My God will supply all your own needs from his wealth in glory in Christ Jesus" and John 4:14: "Anyone who drinks the water I shall give him (and **keeps** drinking as the Greek implies) will never thirst any more" to the endless reaches of eternity.

"We have not because we ask not." Our spiritual life is sustained by prayer, is measured by prayer. "Ask and it shall be given you." Prayer is the lost secret of the spiritual life.

WHY WE NEED TO PRAY

By Dr. John Heuss

Rector of Trinity Parish, New York City

❧

> ". . . so much the more went there a fame abroad
> of him: and great multitudes came together to
> hear, and to be healed. . . . And he withdrew
> himself into the wilderness, and prayed."
>
> Luke 5:15-16

When you first read these words, they startle you! For anyone to get up and leave just when he is getting results is not what we ordinarily expect. Why, in the name of all that is sensible, did Jesus withdraw just when multitudes began to flock to Him?

It wasn't that He was shy! Making friends everywhere was second nature to Him. It certainly wasn't that He disliked crowds! Time and time again He spoke to throngs of people. Nor was it that He was moody and temperamental! No more steady tempered man has ever lived. Neither did this happen only once. You read over and over again in the Gospels how Christ deliberately sought solitude.

What was His reason for doing so? The reason was a truth so elemental that we wonder how we constantly overlook it. He needed to pray. Without prayer He could not live. He needed prayer more than He needed food. He needed prayer more than He needed human friendship. He needed prayer more than He needed money. He needed prayer more than He needed anything.

And so do you and I. Everyone thinks otherwise. They believe they need dozens of things more than they need to pray. Whether we know we need to pray or not makes no difference at all. Just as everyone needs fresh air, a balanced diet, reasonable rest, and moderate exercise, so do our bodies and our souls require prayer. We can exist for a time, of course, with our breathing polluted, eating quantities of starch, and overworking. But your insurance company will tell you what will happen. You will reduce your chances to live a long life by ten to twenty years. You can also stay alive for awhile without praying. But you will live longer if you pray.

Let us see why we need to pray—why prayer is not an option in life. We shall start with the purely practical reasons.

In the first place, prayer calms us down.

About five years ago, I boarded the night flight on United Airlines to fly from Seattle to New York. It is always a remarkable experience to fly over the jagged peaks of the Rocky Mountains. It is especially unforgettable in the winter time when a full moon and the northern lights create a fairyland of "make-believe." Early in the morning we started to make our first landing in Minneapolis. The memory of the night's beauty was blotted out quickly when the stewardess announced that the landing gear was not working and that the plane's wheels would not go down. Stark fright filled everybody's heart! I began to pray. I prayed for safety. I prayed for my family. I prayed for everybody in the airplane. I knew that, most of all, I should pray for courage to face death. Frankly, I was terrified. Slowly the miracle took place within me. My fear subsided. I grew calm. My hands stopped shaking. A power greater than my own had taken possession of my emotions. While I still did not want to die, I was no longer afraid.

I do not know whether God answered all the prayers that were said by everyone in that airplane. But I do know that He gave me confidence and calmness. After an hour of endless low flights over the airport, the wheels did come down, and we landed safely.

Yet, it is not only in moments of great danger that we need to be calm. Modern life goes at a furious pace. Especially is this true in New York City. The noise and speed of street traffic tighten up our nervous systems. Crowded subways and buses rub our patience raw. The day never has enough hours to accomplish all we plan to do. Newspaper headlines feature disturbing clashes between men and nations. Radio, television, and movies blare at us with screaming crooners, music that is all savage beat and no melody, or dramatize violence and sudden death. By the time you have lived from Monday to Friday at a pace like this, you are exhausted. It is no wonder that there is so much drinking. It is no wonder that there is such a mad desire to find a numbing forgetfulness. The human constitution was never intended to be submitted to such tortures.

How can we escape the destructive consequences of the life we have to lead? The most sensible way to do it is to make room for quiet withdrawal and daily prayer. It takes only fifteen minutes on your knees in your bedroom or in a nearby church to quiet down your whole system which has been ravaged by the frustrations and irritations of a normal working day. Try prayer, and see how differently you will feel.

The second reason we need to pray is to get life back into focus. Many situations conspire daily to throw the outlook of the steadiest man out of perspective. Sometimes, things get out of focus because we have to deal with annoying people. Often some unforeseen, troublesome development comes up and throws off the whole day's schedule. We are frequently irritated with our own failures. Things get out of focus most disastrously when we do outrageous things, and disguise our real motives under a mask of self-righteousness.

536

I don't know whether you have had the doubtful pleasure of seeing the type of three-dimensional movie for which each spectator must wear an odd set of colored glasses. The usher gives you the weird contraption as he shows you to your seat. Naturally, your first reaction is to say to yourself, "Why do I have to put on these silly things?" So you look at the screen and squint your eyes. But no matter how hard you squint, the picture stays irritatingly out of focus. Finally, you look sheepishly around to see what your neighbors are doing. There they sit—all dressed up in their fantastic goggles, looking like something out of interplanetary space. You reflect sadly on what a strange world the twentieth century has become. At last you put on your glasses. What you see on the screen for the next three hours may not be worth seeing, but it finally is in focus. You try to forget you are a philosopher, and relax to enjoy the show.

This modern parable describes how prayer restores perspective. We go to the movies in the first place because we know that we need something. Our minds have taken all they can stand for the time being. We want some kind of release from tension. We want to relax. We may not recognize it, but what we really need is not the sedative of entertainment. What our spirit is crying out to do is to pray.

When we get settled in the theater, everything on the screen is blurred. This is exactly what we first experience when we get on our knees to pray. It is hard to concentrate. God seems far away. Our emotions are all mixed up. Nothing seems to be quite clear. So we begin with something we know by heart like the Lord's Prayer. And, miraculously, the very act of praying is like putting on a pair of glasses which corrects our vision. Slowly, confusions straighten out. An unbelievable sense of relaxation creeps over our mind and body. Our spirits are refreshed. Confidence is restored. Our attitude toward people becomes kindly once again. Our sense of humor returns. We feel good all over. At last we get up off our knees, ready to take our part in the passing show of life and enjoy it once again. This time what we see is well worth looking at. What miracle has taken place? The greatest miracle you and I will ever experience has happened. Life has gotten back into focus once more.

PRAYER

Lord, what a change within us one short hour
    Spent in Thy presence will prevail to make—
    What heavy burdens from our bosoms take,
What parched grounds refresh, as with a shower!
We kneel, and all around us seems to lower;
    We rise, and all, the distant and the near,
    Stand forth in sunny outline, brave and clear;
We kneel how weak, we rise how full of power!
Why, therefore, should we do ourselves this wrong,
Or others—that we are not always strong;
That we are ever overborne with care;
    That we should ever weak or heartless be,
Anxious or troubled, when with us is prayer,
And joy, and strength, and courage, are with Thee?

—R. C. Trench. Prayer Poems, Compiled by O. V. and Helen Armstrong. Pub. by Abingdon-Cokesbury, p. 119.

Up to this point, I have described why we need to pray in order to get two practical things. We need to calm down and we need to get a fresh viewpoint. But we have a third need that is much deeper than either of these. I suppose you could say that it is a theological reason. Let me be blunt about it. **We need to pray in order to express our dependence upon God.**

This need makes us pray, but it is not primarily concerned about getting back anything tangible. It is like the feeling we sometimes had when we were children. We would wake up in the night, frightened by something. We would call out for our father or our mother. When they answered, the sound of their voices, reassuring us that their protecting love was close at hand, was all we really wanted. To be able to call out and be sure that someone heard made us feel secure and safe again.

Why is it that this need to find the presence of God comes so often to us as grown-up people? It is because deep down beneath all our masquerades of self-sufficiency, each one of us knows in his own heart that he is dependent upon some power greater than his own. To make contact with that power is the most important reason why men pray. I suppose the best illustration of this need to pray is that it is like the feeling all of us have at the end of a long winter. When we want to get out in the warm sunshine and just let it pour down upon us. We don't ask for anything in particular. We just want to be exposed to the warmth of the sun's strengthening rays. After we have been out, we feel refreshed and clean.

Do you remember what happens when iron filings are brought under the unseen influence of a magnet? The power of the magnet on the filings causes them to rearrange themselves. Now remember something else. The iron filings always rearrange themselves in a pattern which is harmonious with the forces of the magnetic field. This is exactly what our souls are longing to have happen, and this does happen when we expose our lives to the presence of God in prayer. Reaching out to find God by praying rearranges our lives after His harmonious pattern. We are changed and not only on the surface. We are changed deep within our innermost being.

As soon as we acknowledge the supremacy of God by praying, and by the same act acknowledge our own insufficiency, we establish a relationship with Him. The existence of this relationship is what the human heart needs and wants more than any other thing.

If we had only a sense of our own inadequacy and nothing more, life would indeed be a tragedy. Where prayer leads us from self-despair to trust in God's grace, it brings courage, strength and deep peace. Our need to find God just for Himself alone, is the most powerful reason why we pray.

> What is prayer but listening in—
> Attuning
> Mind and heart to hear
> A still small voice beyond life's sin,
> Assured that God is ever near?

—WHAT IS PRAYER? — Vs. 1 by Marie Barton. Pub. by Abingdon-Cokesbury in "Prayer Poems" compiled by O. V. and Helen Armstrong.

If you have never really prayed, do not deprive yourself longer of the benefits it brings. You were created with a built-in need to pray. To pray is as natural as to eat, and sleep, and breathe. Prayer is just as necessary as each of these for health of body and of soul.

—Reprinted by permission of Seabury Press, Greenwich, Conn.

For many years it has been my practice in traveling among the nations to make a study of the sources of the spiritual movements which are doing most to vitalize and transform individuals and communities. At times it has been difficult to discover the hidden spring, but invariably where I have had time and patience to do so, I have found it in an intercessory prayer-life of great reality.   —Dr. John R. Mott

A GREAT INTANGIBLE OF THE SPIRIT

By Oveta Culp Hobby

President, The Houston Post, and former Commandant
of the W. A. A. C. during World War II

❦

No human expression is quite so personal, quite so unique-
ly of oneself as prayer. Only a person of rare closeness to God,
and of rare ability to express himself, can convey to another
person anything of the experience of private prayer.

And even then, words can but outline or sketch a great
intangible of the spirit.

It often seems to me that no one can really prove the power
of prayer—because always the charge of coincidence can be
brought. The power of prayer is something we know by inner
conviction, not by proof, however decisive it may seem to be.

Yet who can doubt it who has ever prayed?

Prayer offers many solaces.

Simply to put oneself deliberately into the position and attitude and mood of prayer is automatically to take one step in
the right direction.

Nobody can genuinely pray without achieving in that first
instant some better attitude than he had, some better perspective, some greater ability to see the problem at hand in a new,
more just light.

In the simple act of praying, we gain new growth in mind
and spirit.

Whether or not we gain more from prayer than a righting
of our own attitude depends, I think, on one's ability to listen.

Many of us are so filled with things we want to say to God, or ask of God, that we fail to listen for His answer.

Solitude grows more and more difficult as the world whirls faster and faster upon its axis. But there can be no true prayer unless one learns how to remain absolutely silent—silent of thought as well as of lip. Unless one can learn how to push all thoughts out of mind, to empty the mind, in hopes that into that receptive void may come the word or will of God.

A great bishop once told me that there are days when he finds it impossible to do this. But that every day he practices. Every day he spends some time, alone on his knees, determinedly attempting to listen to God. And though the answer comes only now and again, the moment when it does come is a precious and wonderful experience.

A VISION OF PERFECT JUSTICE

By Harold E. Hegstrom

Warden, Federal Correctional Institution, Danbury, Conn.

God is an inexhaustable source of power for everyone who through prayer calls upon Him. Man is a lonely creature, shut off from actual contact with his kind, even the nearest and dearest. Nowhere is this most true than to the man or woman imprisoned for violation of society's laws. Prayer is defined as the lifting of our hearts and minds to God to adore, praise and thank Him, and to ask blessings for ourselves and others. It is man's tribute to God, his Spiritual Father. But, aside from paying rightful tribute to God, prayer is a powerful weapon for us as individuals.

542

To those unfortunates, products of the social disorganization which exists today, exiled from all and everything, which the rational being holds dear, to pray is often all that they can do. Perhaps their prayer is purely selfish, for all those personal and family wants peculiar to their situation, but as it has been succinctly stated, "who rises from prayer a better man, his prayer is answered."

Prayer enables man to look behind suffering and injustice and learn submission to the greater Wisdom of God, with a vision of perfect justice in eternity. "Blessed are those who weep." God has never said that suffering does not hurt, but He has declared that those who mourn have in His eyes a special right to the consolations of His Divine Mercy, available each moment of life to those who "ask and it will be given."

To the imprisoned, the desolate and abandoned then prayer has a unique and special meaning, and consequently a unique and special demand on the consolations of Christ.

When from the depths of our soul we shall have submitted ourselves to our whole duty, when dismal surroundings, lusterless spheres of life, dreary monotonous days are no longer obstacles to our prayer, then, we can begin to pray and we shall always find the Merciful Comfort of God unceasingly.

This is to me the Power of Prayer, the ability of man to reach out and petition the Merciful and loving Creator and secure therefrom the inspiration and strength to overcome the daily vicissitudes of living. This has been exemplified to me on myriad occasions by men during their prison life. They entered the walls bitter and disillusioned, overcome by the thoughts of years of imprisonment in the future, frantically seeking human means to alleviate their despair, finally and almost involuntarily turning to their Creator, from whom they had alienated themselves perhaps for many years, and finding in that "Fortress," the refuge and haven to face their future with equanimity.

DO I BELIEVE IN PRAYER?

By Dr. Daniel Starch
Psychologist and Business Consultant

✺

A serviceman back from the Solomon Islands said to me, no matter how tough their manner or how coarse their language, when the shells flew and the bombs exploded, the men prayed. Whether accustomed to pray or not, many people we know, when in a tight spot or deeply worried, pray. They turn outward to find help, to find an anchor outside themselves. The forces of nature are so overwhelming and their mysteries so hidden despite the proud discoveries of science, that in times of trouble, man feels alone, inadequate and helpless. Prayer is an effort to communicate with something outside greater than himself.

Do I believe in prayer? Do I think it does any good? First let me ask, what do you mean by prayer? If you mean begging for something, whether right or wrong, whether good for you or not, my answer is, NO. I don't believe in that kind of prayer. In the long run, I don't believe it accomplishes anything. Such egoism is almost certain to disappoint the petitioner. Very different is prayer when directed for something good and right and especially for guidance in seeking what is right and good under the circumstances. In that sense, prayer can have powerful subjective as well as objective effects. What are these effects?

First of all, when deeply shaken and worried, prayer will help you get hold of yourself, will help you collect your thoughts and emotions, keep you from becoming hysterical and help you get a clearer perspective of yourself and your situation.

Next, prayer will help you find out what to do, what is

the good and right thing to do, will help you avoid doing the selfish, the wrong, the harmful thing, and that can never be overvalued. Notice that the model Lord's prayer, right from the beginning, emphasizes, **"Thy** will be done."

Third, prayer will help you take courage to follow through in the confidence that you are doing the right in the best way you can. Many who practice prayer can recall many illustrations from their own experience.

But, what about prayer when you are not in a tight spot? That is the time to cultivate the practice of prayer. Then you will naturally and receptively turn to prayer when you do get into a tough place, but more than that, it leads you to periodic self-analysis to cut yourself down to proper perspective and to appreciate the good and right achieved.

It may be asked, isn't this, however, a kind of milk toast, "fuddy duddy" way of living? No, not at all. Businessmen, of all people, making important decisions need every day to pray for two things, insight to see the right and courage to do the right. What is right isn't always a clean cut yes or no. Insight, analysis and courage are needed. When you penetrate their inner decison center, you will find many more top executives like the soldiers in battle turning to prayer for clearer perspective and guidance, than you would guess from external appearances.

Nearly five centuries before Christ, Socrates in humility and serenity offered this prayer:

> "Give me beauty in the inward soul; and may the inward and the outer man be as one. May I reckon wisdom to be wealth, and may I have so much gold as a temperate man and only he can bear and carry — This prayer, I think, is enough for me."

If I may be permitted a personal comment, I find the attitude and daily expression of thankfulness and forward-looking expectancy most uplifting and rewarding. Expectancy of success increases probability of success. I do not mean passive expectancy merely as a mystical something. I mean dynamic expectancy that leads you to direct your attitude and effort toward achieving betterment. I seldom fall asleep without some expression of gratitude, either of my own, or by recalling from memory, some of the many fine phrases from Biblical and other literary sources — gratitude to the all-pervading, orderly, compassionate spirit, the Great Spirit we call God, and it takes this form: We give thanks thou Great Spirit for well-being, for loving-kindness of friends, for opportunities around us. Give us light to see the right and courage to do the right. May we "do justly, love mercy and walk humbly."

Is prayer answered? Yes. George Meredith puts it this way: "Who rises from prayer a better man, his prayer is answered."

PRAYER AS A FOUNTAIN OF FAITH AND A SOURCE OF MORAL POWER

By Dr. John J. Tigert

President Emeritus, University of Florida

❀

Prayer is the solitary vehicle of communication from man to God, the spiritual channel from the finite and the natural to the Infinite and Supernatural. Without faith in an eternal, omnipotent, beneficent Being no one but a hypocrite would pray; and without continuous thanksgiving, praise and supplication through prayer, no man could be expected to retain faith in God. This is why I believe in prayer.

As a boy, like many others of the last generation, my mother taught me to pray on my knees. Though the particular mode of prayer may be immaterial, yet the spiritual essence of suppliant dependence upon the Deity may be best invoked by reverent attitudes, such as kneeling or bowing. Without the element of reverence, prayer would be a mere mockery.

I doubt whether the Deity interrupts the course of natural events in answer to specific requests in prayer, as many believe; but undoubtedly, there are Divinely inspired acts in the lives of all who have faith in God and who worship Him in honest and earnest prayer. Certainly, all who pray are strengthened in their faith, reverence, and religious devotions by this process.

My firm belief in prayer stems easily from my philosophy which I taught in four institutions. Philosophy and psychology have been my life-long fields of concentration. I am an idealist. Plato, among the ancients, and Kant, among the moderns, best express my beliefs. The mind or soul of man is **sui generis**. Man is immortal.

Man is not merely a glorified animal. No elaboration of physical and biological processes can explain his powers of abstract reasoning or his freedom of action in the realm of morals,—as some moderns attempt to do. The lower animals live in a sensuous plane. No amount of asseveration can prove man to be a mere animal. Truth and absurdity are both irrefutable.

As man possesses a soul so he must lean upon God and this he does by prayer. As St. Paul says, "We walk by faith not by sight."

During my early life, it was customary for families to pray together each day. I think that this was responsible for a higher social standard of life. The cessation of family prayer, in some measure, has had a direct effect upon the lowering of standards of living in recent years. It may even account for the acknowledged increase in crime and immorality among youth.

IT'S WORTH A CONTINUING TRY

By Lee H. Bristol, Sr.

Chairman of the Board, Bristol-Myers Company

❦

Whether it be the record high statistics on church membership today or the bookstores full of religious themes or maybe just the unselfconscious way Church may be mentioned at a dinner party these days, I think all of us are conscious of the remarkable revival of religious interest in America today.

But I suspect it is a curious fact that even among us churchgoers, with all the distractions of these days, most of us fail to make as much use of the tremendous power of prayer as we might.

I believe in prayer, because I know it works. I saw how prayer changed the hearts of people who were opposed to a meditation room at the U. N., so that such a room now exists and the General Assembly is opened with silent prayer. I know how prayer changed the whole climate of a deadlocked labor dispute and helped provide an atmosphere where minds could meet. And I know how prayer — right now as I write these words — is giving a young couple with a doomed child the grace to cope with their heartbreaking problem.

For prayer to be real, one wants of course to resolve to be absolutely honest, because only then will our prayers mean something to us and consequently something to God. If my mind starts wandering during prayers, I shall want to tell God and ask His help.

Some find it helpful to choose a regular time for prayer, but this does not mean that we shall neglect those important little "flash prayers" during the rest of the day. I know of a friend who keeps a notebook to keep a prayer list not only of friends or relatives but also of particular groups he likes to remember on different days.

Instead of merely prayers of petition and intercession, certainly the committed Christian will want to remember prayers of praise, prayers for forgiveness, and thanksgiving as well. The more specific I make these prayers, the more I find they mean to me.

By these few words on prayer, I do not wish to pose as any expert. I have made no spectacular progress. I know that as a pray-er I am still very much a beginner. But I believe in prayer. I believe in the way prayer enables one to grow. And I shall continue to try through prayer somehow to come closer to God's highest hopes for my life. Is this not, after all, the true calling of any Christian?

"THY WILL BE DONE"

By Thomas J. Hamilton
Director of Athletics and Physical Education,
University of Pittsburgh

❦

Prayer is not a one-way street which provides a way to let God know what we want, but it is the trail blazer, when properly used, which opens up a broad highway for return benefits to travel from God to us. In prayer we should seek to know what is God's will, and for the strength, wisdom and guidance to carry out our part in His plan. I cannot believe that God will grant each of us the small desires we strive for in our daily tasks, but when we earnestly endeavor by prayer to find out God's will, the more we communicate, the clearer our course of action is revealed to us.

Like a wise father, I am sure that often He must say "No" to personal requests, but by communing with Him often, and being ready to bend to His will, our daily decisions will be more in harmony with the right way, and our questions and conflicts become less.

I have the tendency to wait until trouble or an emergency arises, and when obviously my powers cannot cope with the situation, to pray for help and guidance. Then I am always sorry for my past laxity in prayer for I believe I would recognize His way of telling me if I had a closer relationship.

Having been a Navy aircraft pilot for twenty years, it could only have been God's will that brought me through several times in airplane emergencies when others perished. I am sure that my prayers had no more reason to be answered than the other fellows', but these incidents have illustrated to me how insignificant our own power is, and how dependent we are for the blessings we enjoy.

Sometimes I see some basketball players cross themselves as they prepare to shoot a foul attempt, and I am tremendously amused. God cannot possibly grant favor on all such requests, but I suppose since there is an expressed desire to keep in close relationship which probably helps when other and bigger issues become apparent.

My sentiment is expressed in a part of the last prayer given by the late Dr. Zebarney Thorne Phillips as Chaplain of the Senate:

"Endue us with courage sufficient to face each fateful task with a devotion unsoiled by thought of self, but ennobled by that large loyalty to God and country that shall compel us to dare our utmost for the betterment of our world, content to leave with Thee all consequences."

GOD UNDERSTANDS MY PRAYERS

By Jimmie Fidler

Radio News Commentator

❧

It is inconceivable that there could be anyone who does not believe in prayer, but I suspect that a great many people (such as I) who love God, find it difficult to pray to Him.

I find it very hard to keep my prayers completely unselfish, and I believe prayers should be unselfish. I believe that when I ask the Lord for something for myself, it should be something that, through me, may benefit others.

For example, during a very bad business era of my life, my financial affairs were in precarious shape. A small push or two in the wrong direction might have meant bankruptcy, and bankruptcy for a man with a family of six is disaster indeed.

During this period I was able to pray with deep feeling. True, I was praying for a way out of my financial difficulties, but I sought the way not for myself but in order that I could get my estate into a solvent condition to assure the care of my loved ones in the event something ill might befall me.

This prayer has been answered, and I am sincere when I say that I believe God understood that it was not a selfish prayer. I was not concerned with a new suit, or a new car, or a gay vacation trip for myself. I only wanted assured protection for those who love and depend upon me for the needs of life.

In my nightly supplications to God, I always include The Lord's Prayer, but I have altered it slightly from the wording we hear and repeat in our Houses of Worship. I have changed the line, "Give us this day" to "Give us each day." And I have altered another line from "Lead us not into temptation" to "Guard us from temptation."

The changes make good sense, in my mind. The second change is obvious: God would not "lead us into temptation." But it is sensible to believe that he would, if sincerely asked to do so, "Guard us from temptation," or in other words, "give us the moral strength to resist temptation."

Yes, I often find it difficult to pray because so many things pop into my head that I might ask for in my own behalf, and I must constantly struggle that I do not allow my prayers to become greedy appeals designed to satisfy my mortal desires, rather than my moral necessities.

WHERE IS THE POWER?

By Dr. Donald Grey Barnhouse

Editor-in-Chief, *Eternity Magazine*

❀

I am not so sure that I believe in "the power of prayer," but I do believe in the power of the Lord who answers prayer. Many people do not know that there are more verses in the Bible where God promises not to answer prayer than there are verses in which He promises to answer prayer. How shocking is the first impact of His declaration through Solomon: "Because I have called and you refused to listen, have stretched out My hand and no one has heeded, and you have ignored all My counsel and would have none of my reproof, I also will laugh at your calamity, I will mock when panic strikes you like a storm, and your calamity comes like a whirlwind, when distress and anguish come upon you. Then they will call upon Me, but I will not answer; they will seek Me diligently but will not find Me, because they hated knowledge and did not choose the fear of the Lord . . . " (Proverbs 1:24-29).

To say, "I believe in prayer," is as naive as saying, "I believe in cashing checks." There are more rules for getting a true prayer really answered than there are rules for getting a check cashed. There must be a deposit in the bank in one case and there must be true faith in the Lord Jesus Christ in the other case. To attempt to pray to the true God, the God and Father of our Lord Jesus Christ, without coming in the name of the Lord Jesus is as wicked as signing a check when there is no account.

Jesus Christ did not say, "I am one of many equally good ways; I am a phase of truth; I am an aspect of life." He did say, "I am THE way, THE truth and THE life," and added, ".no man cometh unto the Father but by Me" (John 14:6). When the rules are met then God pours out all blessings on those who come to Him in prayer. There is real power. There is comfort in time of need; strength in time of weakness; forgiveness when we have sinned; consolation in time of bereavement; joy in time of sorrow.

When one has accepted God's terms of approach through the redemption that is provided by Christ there is immediate access to Him, and all the promises of God become certified to us. Then we come as a child to the Father, but always through the Son; then we know that the power is not in talking to Him but in being so related to Him that He can work for us and in us without violating His holiness and His righteousness. Herein lies the power of God, that is made available to us through the Lord Jesus Christ, in whom and through whom we have constant access to the Father.

FAITH MUST PRECEDE PRAYER

By Charles Malik

Minister of Foreign Affairs, Republic of Lebanon

❀

You speak of "Proving the value and efficacy of prayer in various walks of life." If God really exists and if we get nearer to Him through prayer, then I have no doubt that such prayer is efficacious in our lives. It has been so in my life on many occasions. Even if one cannot point to definite physical interference in the course of events through prayer, faith must make us believe that the Creator of the world can make a difference to His creation after He has created it. Thus faith in God and the love of God are more important than any magical results that we may prove we have obtained through prayer.

The important thing is to get closer to the source of our being and to rest in His tender embrace. That is the greatest value and the greatest efficacy of prayer. When I contemplate the Cross in truth and in brokenness my soul gets completely transformed, able to receive everything and to understand everything. This, rather than any external result, is the greatest value and the greatest efficacy of prayer. My sins, my worries, my distractions, my needs, my sufferings, my stupidities, my utter failures, my basic rebellious humanity—yes, these and many other things about me are indeed overwhelmingly crushing for my soul. Shall I therefore tell God: look here, You either cure me of these things or I cease believing in and loving you?

In prayer I confess my sins to God and ask Him to have pity upon me. The privilege of being able to do so in sincerity and in truth is the greatest thing about prayer. He is there and

He makes it possible for us to know that He is there and to approach Him with a contrite spirit. That is the greatest thing about prayer. Thus prayer is first and foremost the necessary concomitant of faith. The moment I cease to believe, I equally cease to pray. And so long as I have faith I shall continue to pray regardless of value, regardless of results and regardless of efficacy. Is it not enough that God exists and that He manifests Himself to us through the Church and through the sufferings of our life? To know Him and to get closer to Him through all this is enough for me. Glory therefore be to the Father, to the Son and to the Holy Ghost, now and forevermore. Amen.

WE ARE NOT ALONE

By Richard L. Evans
"The Spoken Word" heard over the
Columbia Broadcasting System

❁

Some men live blessedly long, and richly round out a fulness of years. Some are taken sooner. But no matter how long we are allowed to live in this life, we are all faced with some uncertainties, and we are none of us free from some troubles, some sorrows, some problems and disappointments. We are all faced with actual or possible illness or accident, with misfortune or failure, or the fear of failure, and with the troubles of the times. We are sometimes subject to discouragement and depression of spirit. We are all sometimes subject to loss of loved ones — and to a long list of other unwanted intrusions upon our peace and plans and purposes. If we think there are those who are free from all such realities and reverses, it is likely because we don't know enough about them — because we don't know what is hidden in their hearts.

But fortunately in facing life, we need not be left alone. Fortunately there are the help and comfort and counsel of friends and family and others; and fortunately there is help beyond the help of human hands. When, for our troubled hearts and perplexed thoughts and weary searchings, and stubborn ailments and gnawing anxieties we need higher help, there is the sustaining, strengthening power of prayer. It would be terrible to feel alone in life; it would be terrible to face any serious situation without the privilege of approaching Him in whose image men were made and who is mindful of the men He made.

In every problem of every passing day, in the laboratory and the shop, in the factory and the field, and in the family circle, in the classroom, in the sickroom, in the halls of government and in humble homes, in all our activities and in all extremities, the power of prayer is (or can be) a guiding, enlightening, and lifting force; a source of wisdom beyond the wisdom of the world; a source of the truth for which men are ever further reaching; a sweet and healing influence; a source of comfort, of protection, and of the peace that passeth understanding.

Prayer is an approach to Him who gave us life and whose endless power and purpose give us settled assurance that life and time and truth are limitless and everlasting, and that despite all discouragement, all problems, and all perplexities we we are not left alone in life.

Reprinted by permission of Harper & Brothers, publishers of "Tonic for Our Times," by Richard L. Evans.

"PRAYER IS THE SOUL'S SINCERE DESIRE". . .

By Dorothy Clarke Wilson

Author of Religious Plays and Novels

❧

This morning, for the first time in many days, I had a real prayer experience. I did not get down on my knees. I sat at my desk. The worship material I used was not the Bible. It was not a book of daily devotion. It was not even a volume of inspiring poetry. It was my checkbook.

God and I discussed many things together. He reminded me (through a letter I had recently received) of a week spent some years ago at a great Christian university in the Middle East, and it was suddenly my "soul's sincere desire" that that university should be given power to help meet the needs of that troubled area. I **desired** it so **sincerely** that I wrote the university a check.

God nudged me then to look in my desk drawer where the India Anti-Tb. Christmas stamps were still lying, unused and unpaid for. After attending to that, we considered some of the needs he had shown me in India last year: undernourished children in danger of losing their rations of dried milk from Church World Service; blind villagers who could have their cataracts removed if somebody in America would send enough money for an Eye Camp. I had spoken to God many times about these needs, begged him to do something about them. I had called it prayer. Now suddenly I really began to pray . . . with my checkbook.

Yes, I believe in prayer. But not as a means of teasing or cajoling or arguing God into changing the laws governing his creation, the laws of his own being. These laws are as inexorable in human relationships as in Physics and Chemistry. When men perform in certain ways, certain results are bound to follow. Disease, health, crime, decency, war, peace—these things are not acts of God. They are the results of either living or not living in accordance with his laws. Though every person in the world were to "pray" for peace at a particular moment, unless the act created new attitudes, decisions, actions which were in accordance with the laws of peace, the prayer would not be fulfilled.

Prayer changes things, yes, but only as it changes people. God does not change. He is always endeavoring to create goodness, health, peace. The communion with God attained in prayer is the best, perhaps the only way to so thoroughly understand the laws of his being that we will act in accordance with them. It may be also that there are powers of the human mind as yet undreamed of, that the very act of "praying" or "desiring sincerely" for or with other persons can create a stronger mutual purpose which may bring those desires to fulfillment.

But it matters tremendously what kind of God we pray to.

Traveling in the East during the last months, I have seen many people praying. I saw a villager pray to a painted image of the small-pox goddess. I saw a little boy clasping his hands before the carving of a snake. I saw a priest bow to a black stone lingam. I saw an educated young Hindu perform worship before a wall niche containing the image of an elephant. One day just at noon I saw a group of professional men prostrating themselves on the ground with their faces turned toward Mecca.

"Oh, but we pray to the true God!" We protest in shocked piety.

Do we? If "prayer is the soul's sincere desire, uttered or unexpressed," do we not pray daily to gods exactly like painted

558

stones and elephants, gods who can avert calamity, satisfy our whims, grant us prosperity? I do. I pray daily, if unconsciously, to gods far worse than those worshiped by my most ignorant Indian friends. I **desire** things, fame, entertainment, ease, good food, money . . . **desire** them so **sincerely** that I spend most of my days bringing my prayers to fulfillment.

Even when we pray consciously, it is not often to God. It's to an early Old Testament diety who can be cajoled into forgiving, who might make an exception to his laws in our case if we teased hard enough, who fights wars, who loves our country better than those we call our enemies. Not to One who is in his very being the Law of Love the Father of all men.

Yes, I believe in prayer. It **can** change things.

PRAYER IS A PARTNERSHIP

By Dr. Felix Morley

Writer and Former Editor of *Washington Post*

❧

During World War II a group of American flyers were discussing how best to break the cigarette habit, to which all but one of those present admitted addiction. "How did you do it, Jim?", the others asked.

Jim, a friend of mine, was and still is a quiet, soft-spoken fellow. His combat record was second to none, but you would never learn that from him.

"There's only one sure way," he answered slowly. "Just pray to God, night and morning, to help you break the habit.

Then you'll be ashamed to fail in your share of the partnership you've set up."

Jim put his finger on the intrinsic value of prayer. It is essentially a rallying of one's own resources the better to confront not only exceptional trouble, but also the daily irritations and vexations. It is a form of self-discipline which, with sufficient practice, will provide true security amid the hazards of life. Test it among your friends and you will find that those who confront disaster most valiantly are also those who pray most regularly.

Whether there is a divine answer to prayer, direct or indirect, may be a matter of debate. But there can be no question that the man or woman who daily invokes spiritual aid is helped thereby. By this silent self-communion the individual is fortified; resolution for any worthy purpose is confirmed; troubles fall into healthier and less disturbing perspective. That, certainly, has been my experience.

Prayer is a purifying process. It is an occasion for reflecting on our own shortcomings, thereby becoming more tolerant towards those of others. It gives us greater ability to endure discomfort and pain. It renews courage and energy for the appointed task. By reverently asking God to help us, we help ourselves. Perhaps the only sin beyond human capacity is to ask divine assistance towards a personal end which one knows in one's heart to be unworthy.

Civilized life would be degraded, if not impossible, without the virtues of Faith, Hope and Charity. All of these virtues are strengthened by regular prayer, and tend to wither away without it. Therefore the devotional act, properly visualized, is a necessity for continued progress. The man or woman who has learned to pray, regardless of social or economic status, is for that reason—and not just by coincidence— a good and worthy citizen.

A DYNAMIC FOR RIGHT LIVING

By Dr. Clemens M. Granskou

President, St. Olaf College

❧

In the summer of 1952 we participated in a Spiritual Life Conference in west Berlin. The young people gathered at this conference were an interesting crowd. Most of them had come from the Russian sector—principally east Berlin. The general themes around which the discussion resolved were:

> the reason for living
> the power of faith
> the insecurity and uncertainty of the times.

They talked rather freely about their own future, about family and marriage, religion and morals, about the sense of Christian vocation. Plenty of ideas were expressed. Many people talked. No one faced the future with any degree of confidence.

Perhaps the most thought-provoking response to the discussion came from the Swedish bishop, Dr. Anders Nygren, using as his text Revelation 2:9, **"I know thy tribulation and thy poverty, but thou art rich."** The bishop reminded his hearers that the world is divided into two halves. Not the imaginary line like the equator which divides the world into the northern and southern hemisphere. The line dividing east Germany from west Germany was really no imaginary line. It was felt by all. The young people in the audience had experienced the tragedy which divided Germany, and also the world into two distinct parts. **"However, we must not dwell on this side of the line,"** said the Bishop from Lund. **"There is another side of the picture—'but thou art rich.'"**

Few people would call this motley crowd rich. Most of them had lost their homes. Their future was uncertain. Their parents had been killed or were in prison or exile. Whatever wealth they had accumulated had been taken from them or had simply evaporated. But they were told, **"there are few spots in the world where the potentialities of the gospel are so great. As Christian young people you have been driven together by a deep sense of responsibility and an indomitable faith."**

This poses a piercingly penetrating question for all of us who are concerned about life's meaning, purpose and destiny. How are we to bring the gospel of God's grace to those who have experienced death more than life? How is this gospel to become a living reality to those who have lost the sense of eternity, as they have also lost the fear of death? For as men lose the fear of death, another fear takes its place. It is the fear of life itself.

"You are rich," insisted Dr. Nygren, **"because there are few spots in the world where the dangers confronting people offer such unique opportunities to make a determining choice; there are few spots in the world which offer such challenges for individual and social creativity. The words of the evangelist spoken centuries ago on the island of Patmos are applicable to the present situation! 'Behold I set before you an open door, which no one is able to shut.'"**

There was a prayer session before the conference adjourned. What did they pray for?—the comforts of civilization, and an escape from the bitter realities of life? No! They prayed for courage in the face of hard decisions and strength to proclaim the truth of God with fearless courage. It was like being transported back into the book of Acts where the disciples were gathered in the upper room after their release from prison. They were forbidden to witness in the name of Jesus. But this

562

is the burden of their prayer: **"And now Lord, look upon their threatenings: and grant unto thy servants to speak thy word with all boldness."** Acts 4:29.

The conclusion of the matter is simple, but inescapable. The testimony of Scripture and of experience down through the centuries is that the Lord has refused to yield His world to its selfishness, greed, hatred, and brutality. He has not left this world of ours without a witness of His power. And we, whose lives are hid with Christ in God, find each morning new reasons for hope, new meanings for each day's activity, and new goals for existence.

PRAYERS AND FAITH
SAVED MY LIFE

By Kate Smith

Singer and Motion Picture Actress

My family had taken a house for the summer on Colonial Beach, Va., not far from my native city of Washington. One day two little girls with whom I had become friendly invited me to go canoeing with them on the Potomac River.

The day was warm and clear. The river lay serene and very blue—reflecting the cloudless sky above. Chattering excitedly, we climbed into the canoe, and all three began to paddle. Soon we were so busy exchanging girlish confidences that we didn't notice we had reached the part of the river which empties into Chesapeake Bay where there are strong currents.

Suddenly it dawned on us that we were much too far from shore and moving faster than we should. The blue in the sky had changed to a pale dull grey. We grew frightened. "We'd better turn back," one of the girls said. "Paddle towards shore, Kate." I tried to follow instructions and turn the canoe around. I remember my feelings as I stammered, "I can't do it."

The wind grew stronger. We tried to scream for help, but fear paralyzed our voices. Without warning the canoe suddenly flipped over, pitching the three of us into the cold water of the Potomac. Not one of us was a good swimmer, and even a good swimmer could not have survived those raging currents.

"Hold on to the canoe," I yelled. "Don't let go." Numbed by the sudden cold, sputtering and desperate—we held on. Finally we found our voices and screamed for help. But we were too far from shore for anyone to hear us. For the first time in our short lives I thought: "We can't help ourselves. We are going to die." It was a staggering thought for a little girl. Then I remembered the wise words of my parents—that there would be a time when I could not help myself but God was always available to help. Did I believe that? Yes, I cried to myself, I must believe it. I prayed with frantic intentness. Then came doubt. Maybe He wouldn't answer—perhaps He had forgotten us. Maybe He was too busy with much more important matters than to save three little girls. We couldn't hold on much longer.

Suddenly an on-coming fishing boat appeared out of nowhere and spotted us chattering with cold. We were lifted out of the icy water and brought back to shore. My prayers were answered.

GUIDANCE THROUGH PRAYER

By Frank E. Burkhalter

Former Professor of Journalism, Baylor University

❦

Proper prayer will help any Christian make a success of whatever line of life work he has been led by God to adopt.

This conviction is predicated upon two premises: The numerous definite promises in the Bible that God will answer prayer, and my personal experience in putting those promises to the test.

Space will permit the listing of only three of the passages dealing with answered prayer, but they are adequate for my purpose:

1. "Call unto me, and I will answer thee, and shew thee great and mighty things, which thou knowest not" (Jer. 33:3).

2. "But my God shall supply all your need according to his riches in glory by Christ Jesus" (Phil. 4:19).

3. "If ye have faith as a grain of mustard seed, ye shall say unto this mountain, Remove hence to yonder place; and it shall remove; and nothing shall be impossible unto you" (Matt. 17:20).

These and all other Bible promises are absolutely dependable, being guaranteed by God himself. They are sufficiently comprehensive to embrace every individual need.

Here is my test of these promises: I was reared on a farm by poor but devout parents. While my father and mother sympathized fully with my desire for a college education, they were unable to provide as much as one dollar toward the attainment of that goal. I was even compelled to forego high school so I might help my family get back on its feet after a disastrous fire had wiped out their life savings.

However, my sympathetic Sunday School teacher, knowing my hunger for an education, proposed to defray all my expenses through both prep school and college, stipulating that he would not permit me to repay any portion of his investment in me, after I had finished college.

Naturally, this generous offer made a tremendous appeal to me, but when I made my decision a matter of prayer, I received a definite impression that I should reject it. After I had been led to decline my teacher's proposition I promised God if he would help me obtain an education by my own efforts I would seek to serve other boys just as my friend had encouraged and inspired me.

Heaven heard this prayer, too, and opened up ways whereby I was able to finish prep school and earn degrees from two outstanding universities.

In fulfilling my promise to God I have been privileged to serve worthy boys through Boys Clubs for 46 years. Also I have had the joy of teaching 16-year-old boys in Sunday School for 41 years. So, as my teacher definitely influenced my life, God has enabled me to make an impress for good upon several thousand youths.

During the 50-year interval since my graduation from college several opportunities for professional advancement have come to me. Before accepting any of these new positions I sought the Lord's guidance through prayer, and the answers he gave me always proved to be the right ones.

Some of these posts involved large responsibilities, but

trusting God for guidance and strength, I have been able to discharge them.

I have found encouragement to tackle both professional and personal problems in the stimulating sentiments voiced in the first stanza of the late B. B. McKinney's hymn "Let Go and Let God:"

Are there any rivers that seem to you uncrossable?
Are there any mountains you can not tunnel through?
God specializes in things that seem impossible.
He knows a thousand ways to make a way for you.

PRAYER BRINGS SERENITY

By Estes Kefauver
U.S. Senator from Tennessee

❦

The importance of prayer is that is opens up the mind and soul to the highest impulses. At times of doubt, weariness, frustration, and defeat prayer can induce calm, point out right directions, allay fears, and renew courage. There is no doubt that prayer can do these things. It can do more; in an increasingly crowded, noisy, bustling and anxious world, it can provide, even if only for a few moments, the solitude which communion with the Highest brings. If the act of praying brought nothing more to us than serenity, it would be enough.

Does prayer bring all things? I think not. Except that prayer might quicken determination—which of course it can —I doubt that prayer and prayer alone brings answers to selfish ambitions, I doubt that prayer and prayer alone would bring material things asked for selfishly. It is when we pray for wisdom to know the right, when we pray for courage to face defeat, that is the prayer most surely answered.

On some occasions in the years which I have spent in the Congress, issues have arisen for which popular clamor and support, sometimes in my own State, was on the side which I felt in the long view would result in injustice. The easy way is to vote with the majority, no matter how ephemeral or temporary that majority might be. It is instances like these in which prayer gives help that nothing else can give. It gives free reign to conscience. It provides courage to do the right. It allows that precious thing called integrity to work.

No one can go through life without dark hours of self doubt. They are the blackest hours of a man's life. When defeat or misfortune or sorrow come it is one thing if they can be blamed on someone else or on blind fate. It is when self-blame arises that we lose courage and hope and that is when the power of prayer shows itself most truly. If it opens the eyes of the soul to the truth, if it gives us the determination and thereby the power to reach the truth and act accordingly, prayer does for us what no other agency can.

Whether we fall on our knees in the old and humble way, it does not matter. We can pray anywhere and at any time. Whenever man prays, whether it is in a crowd or in his loneliness, he makes a temple for himself in which his thoughts and purposes can soar to the Highest.

GIVING THANKS TO GOD

By Thomas Casilear Cole

Portrait Painter

❁

The need to communicate with his Maker was born in man. It is older than religion and is a natural part of his being. I cannot imagine a world without prayer.

Our country was founded by prayer. The brave men and women who first colonized these shores were armed with courage by the strength of their religious faith and conviction. Our history from the discovery of America to the first English settlements, the growth of the thirteen colonies into a strong nation, and the pioneering and development of the West, is a chronicle of man's trust in God. The founders left us a heritage of Thanksgiving to God.

In medieval Europe, her art, born of the Church, was devoted to worship of God and Christ, and adoration of the saints. During the fervently religious period of the Renaissance her great inspired art flourished in a spontaneous outpouring of sacred works. Magnificent cathedrals of unsurpassed architecture reached upward to the skies. Adorned with exquisite stained-glass windows and great masterpieces of paintings and sculpture, these constituted an exalted expression of worship, an enduring symbol of prayer and thanksgiving.

Among the earliest forms of Christian prayer set to music were the profoundly beautiful Gregorian Chants of the Middle Ages. Later were sung the devout hymns, many of which borrowed their tunes from popular street songs in England. Some of the greatest works of the 18th and 19th century composers were those inspired by religion, as were their exalted hosannas and anthems of praise to Almighty God.

The deeply religious and melodious Negro Spirituals are unique in the intimacy of their feeling for God and Jesus. They are a beautiful and powerful contribution to the prayers of the world.

I believe the form of prayer is important only as it best fulfills the need of the individual. It is the spirit which gives meaning to prayer. Some people pray only in church, others only at times of great stress or bereavement, or at the point of death, and some others not at all. It is a great pity that so many deprive themselves of the privilege of prayer which is always available, and in the right spirit is invaluable.

A poet or painter or any creative and true artist must love beauty. Therefore, he must love the Master Creator. He should render thanks. A creative artist often feels insecure in his power to create. Many times he is lacking in the spirit to do his best work or even to produce at all. Prayer will help him. An artist is an idealist, who must put all his heart and soul into his work, with "the utmost for the highest." To achieve a true work of art he must feel constant affinity with the Creator.

Giving thanks to God for the infinite beauties of the Universal Creation, as well as for personal blessings is very natural and right to do. I feel deep gratitude for the gift of life itself, for being allowed to share in the wonders of this world, and for the capacity for joy and appreciation contained all in the senses and in the mind.

Consider the joy of color in its incredible and inexhaustible beauty, the pattern and colors of the myriad of stars in the majestic everchanging skies, the glory of sunrise and sunset, the loveliness of every growing thing, of trees and birds and flowers, the grandeur of the mountains and the sea, and above all the incomparable and subtle beauty of the human face and form, of God's supreme creation of beauty.

His gifts are boundless and unending. Consider the music of the roaring surf and rippling waters, of wind in the leaves, the orchestra of insects, the songs of birds and call of animals, the voice of man, the laughter of children, the serene silence of desert and forest. Consider the wonder of the changing seasons and the miracle of spring. Then, too, the potentialities of the human mind, and the great works of man's genius. In these, God who speaks also through Man, has endowed the world with added gifts for our pleasure and welfare.

Everyone who loves life, or children, his fellow man, or his dog; everyone who loves nature and beauty and art, loves God. Everyone who loves God should thank Him devoutly for the multitude of his blessings.

SNATCH A MOMENT FOR PRAYER

By Dr. Thomas S. Kepler

The Graduate School of Theology, Oberlin College

Certainly in an atomic age we are forced to think of this universe as filled with power! Fifteen pounds of atomic energy will run all the machinery in the United States for one year. A boxcar full of atomic energy will supply energy for a thousand years to the entire world for its heat, light, and machinery. Is there not some analogy that God as power can be drawn upon by those who worship correctly? If so, then "prayer is power."

How often should a man pray? The answer depends largely upon what a person expects from prayer and from religion.

In my student days at Marburg University there was a placard in my room, "Noten Bringt Beten" (Need causes one to pray). If prayer is simply a nervous outreach when things are not going well, then no set schedule can be prescribed for praying. Augustine saw a higher motive for praying: "When I seek Thee, my God, I seek a blessed life." This seems to be the motive for all great saints in prayer—they wanted to become blessed, like their Master; and the more they prayed, the more they felt their lives moving toward the blessed life. Bernard of Clairvaux, a master in the art of prayer, said, "I would rather pray than sleep!"

In my study the book which I cherish the most is a large pulpit-sized red leathered Bible, published in 1861, with a record in it of the marriage of my grandfather and grandmother on April 20, 1844. This was the old "family Bible," from which my grandfather, an Iowa farmer, would read each morning as his family of ten children and his wife gathered for family worship, before the day's long labor in the fields began. They would often arise shortly after four in the morning, and work until dark at night; but there was always time to begin the day with prayer and reading from the Bible. Have we lost this practice in American life today—and do we miss it?

How often should a man pray? William L. Stidger wrote an article fifteen years ago entitled "Rest Where You Are," in which he pointed out that in our tense times we ought to snatch a moment for prayer as often as possible—as we stop for the red traffic light, as we await an interview in the office, as we pause a moment at the desk or in the home. Through the accumulation of these "snatch prayers" throughout the day, moments "to rest where we are," we learn the value of prayer.

—From **A Journey Into Faith** by Thomas S. Kepler. Copyright 1954 by Pierce & Washabaugh. By permission of Abingdon Press.

THROUGH PRAYER COMES
GROWTH AND JOY

By Marjorie M. Melton

Vice-president, James Melton Enterprises, Inc.

❦

Yes, I believe in prayer. I believe that through prayer comes growth and joy in all phases of life. When a human being acknowledges, in his heart, a Higher Power he has gone the first step on the long road to happiness and self-fulfillment. But the recognition is not enough; the **contact** is vital. And contact with the Higher Power that is the source of Love, Good, Hope, is only attained through prayer.

Call that Higher Power God, or Love, or Jehovah, or Lord Almighty, but **call** Him. Pray. Ask for strength, for guidance, for the great wisdom that pours from this Source of Truth like a broad shining river, yours to touch, to be refreshed.

To pray sincerely is to touch the cornerstone of humility; and until a man has stripped himself of all vanity, pretenses of greatness, conceit and lordliness, he is "as sounding brass" —empty. Then and not until then does the human mind approach reality which is the Law of God and His Love.

When a man can deny his vanity and turn his mind and heart to God, then is he approaching the beginning of greatness. When he can say "Lord, my Father who art in Heaven, grant me Thy grace, Thy wisdom, Thy compassion. Give unto me tolerance, temperance and deliver me from temptation"—then truly has he achieved humility, which is the recognition of God's truth supreme above the weakness and errors of the flesh. Man is fallible. The power of Perfect Love, of Godliness, is infallible.

573

This knowledge was given to me in an indelible and convincing manner. My husband was to sing on a broadcast some years ago, The Lord's Prayer, as set to music by Alfred Hay Malotte. In rehearsal he carefully explored the technical aspects of the majestic score; and then in performance, it seemed to me that he soared above the earth as the complete reverence of the words lifted me beyond myself. Whenever I hear this, I experience the same glorious transportation. This, to me, is prayer; the complete absence of self, the complete Presence of God.

PRAYER IS ALWAYS AVAILABLE

By George Grim

Minneapolis Tribune Columnist and TV Commentator

❦

Prayer is something that should be intensely personal. It is the supreme moment of proof of our faith. It is the time for believing what you cannot see, being certain of something you cannot touch. Sadly, prayer is often a spiritual parachute. You keep it packed up and ready in case of emergency. Should that come, you pull the rip cord and out billows a prayer, skyward. The fact that such prayer can come to your rescue proves more about the prayer than about its sudden user.

That line about there being no atheists in foxholes is just that sort of crash-basis praying. When you suddenly get in real, deep trouble, you find prayer simple and convenient. And, let's face it, almost too available.

Our tensed-up today leaves little time for quiet meditation. There's noise from morning until night—and sometimes into the night itself. There's less time for being alone. In fact, most of us dread being alone. Pop into the house and nobody is there. What happens? Crank on the radio, light up the TV, telephone somebody, put a record on the phonograph. Create a distraction quickly. We have a fear of being left to our own resources. There are so many gadgets, we keep telling ourselves. All can help us.

But along comes that moment of trouble, and we are suddenly left alone. Then we look for that exit marked prayer. Gadgets fail. The power can go off. But prayer's always available. More's the pity that it isn't used every day. Without an emergency.

When things are going really right, how many people say a prayer that begins with thankfulness, compared to the prayer that begins with the word "help?"

As youngsters, most of us said our nightly prayers. These childish prayers have a sense of wonder to them. The youngster thinks of those whom he loves and asks a blessing for them. Rarely is this a prayer of crisis, a plea for immediate help. All of us could do with more of that.

A bit of silence—not for a public minute in a city—but for a private time in one's own heart and mind . . . this would mean far more. The assurance of oneness with the source of greatest strength, solace, and inspiration, should come every day. In the midst of great happiness as well as in the depths of crushing crisis.

Let's try not to parcel out a time for prayer or a time for being kind. Our life comes each minute, every day. Each heartbeat is a challenge—and a source of prayerful thanks.

PRAYER IS NOT RATIONED

By Earl Red Blaik

Football Coach, United States Military Academy

❦

If you were to ask my mother the value of prayer she, in her 92 years of Christian living, would cite over a half century of devotion to a Presbyterian faith which she and my late Father, an immigrant Scotsman, knew was the foundation of their years of happiness. To them daily prayer was as natural as the need of food. Spiritual impoverishment could be tolerated less than physical hunger.

The dedication of a daily hour to contemplation and prayer may be partially lost in these days when the mind has little respite from the continuous reminders that our civilization courts chaos.

It may seem strange, however, that in face of these major world problems stoically accepted, there comes to all men days of great individual difficulty as personal events of seemingly overwhelming pressure cannot be answered without guidance, and such guidance is only found in prayer.

Strength through prayer is the foundation of confidence when the pressure of great spectator sports all but overcomes the minds of players. It is far more common than not, to see college teams get an added source of power and confidence as they pause for a short prayer before play; a prayer such as Coach Ray Eliot's is the one used by the hundreds of youngsters who play on the Pop Warner Midget Teams:

> "As we gather here today
>   We take a moment, Lord, to pray;
> That You will guide us in our play
>   And show us how to go Thy way;
> Make us honest, fair and true
>   In this game and all we do."

576

Prayer is not rationed as a commodity is in war or reserved for those bleak days of sickness and trouble. Prayer is the means of spiritual growth which compounded will give the individual the mental strength to surmount daily problems and provide the needed peace of mind.

We meticulously prepare for changing conditions which are met on the football field of play. Confidence, which destroys anxiety, is based on faith, and is a top requisite for the competing champion. All the training of his great physical attributes are of little value to the champion without a faith in himself gained only through prayer and contemplation.

Prayer may be a personal matter, but for the ordinary soul daily meditation with the following prayer given by Chaplain Clayton Wheat to the Corps of Cadets when I was a cadet, will stengthen your belief in the power of prayer.

Cadet Prayer

O God, our Father, Thou Searcher of Men's hearts, help us draw near to Thee in sincerity and truth. May our religion be filled with gladness and may our worship of Thee be natural.

Strengthen and increase our admiration for honest dealing and clean thinking, and suffer not our hatred of hypocrisy and pretense ever to diminish. Encourage us in our endeavor to live above the common level of life. Make us to choose the harder right instead of the easier wrong, and never to be content with a half-truth when the whole can be won. Endow us with courage that is born of loyalty to all that is noble and worthy, that scorns to compromise with vice and injustice and knows no fear when truth and right are in jeopardy. Guard us against flippancy and irreverence in the sacred things of life. Grant us new ties of friendship and new opportunities of service. Kindle our hearts in fellowship with those of a cheerful countenance, and soften our hearts with sympathy for those who sorrow and suffer. Help us to maintain the honor of the Corps untarnished and unsullied and to show forth our duty to Thee and to our country. All of which we ask in the name of the Great Friend and Master of men. —Amen.

PRAYER AND ACTION

By True D. Morse

Under Secretary of Agriculture and President,
Commodity Credit Corporation

❁

The strength and guidance that comes through prayer must be put into action. There is so much to be done — and too few prepared, ready and willing to aggressively work at the job of seeing that —"Thy will be done on earth as it is in Heaven."

In 1948, it was my privilege to serve as Chairman of the first Lay Section ever set up in a Convention of what is now the National Council of Churches. The Council accepted our report which contained such statements as,

"... the primary work of the church is not done on Sunday or at the church.

"The work of the church is done seven days in the week in the homes, in business, and wherever church people work." This I firmly believe.

Lay people make up 99 per cent of the Church. We must look to them, under sound leadership, to accomplish all that must be done if the Lord's Prayer is translated into life and action, "Thy kingdom come, Thy will be done on earth . . ."

For most people, the great and most effective opportunity to serve Christ as Lord is in our everyday activities.

We need to be regularly in church — to associate with church people, and to receive inspiration and direction from our spiritual leaders.

We need the quiet and meditation of prayer.

We need spiritual leadership; the church; and prayer — to be solidly anchored and effective in the rough and tumble of everyday living. We can not "go it alone" — we must have strength and capacity that only come from God.

As I write this (January, 1958) I have completed five years in Washington, as a United States official. I am increasingly impressed with the great need for men of character and of solid Christian faith to serve in government.

The Honorable Howard Pyle, Administrative Assistant to President Eisenhower, and former Governor of Arizona, says,

"Of all the fields open for individual endeavor, I have long since come to the conclusion that the two most challenging, most necessary, and most urgent are religion and government. If there is failure in either of these categories, no other science or profession can save us."

I believe that too. Good government "of the people" is dependent on Christian faith and action "by the people." That means all of us who have the right to vote and live and work in our great land. It is world leadership too.

PRAYER HELPS TO CLARIFY NEEDS

By Melvin H. Baker

Chairman of the Board, National Gypsum Company

It has been said that God helps those who help themselves, but before helping one's self there must first be a clear understanding of what is to be done. I believe that prayer helps to clarify what we want.

Praying is a humble way to acknowledge God and to reinforce our faith in all that is good and right. From faith comes confidence that life has a purpose other than mere selfish gains. Material gains are essential if we would fulfill our duty to society but, if had at the expense of others, we have missed the teachings of Jesus when he said, "Do unto others as you would have them do unto you."

God is the Creator of all things, and it follows that men who work together for creative purposes fulfill His will and their own goals as well. I believe that prayer helps us to better understand the great issues of our time. Perhaps this quotation from a prayer I recently read will illustrate this purpose:

> "Forgive us our evil thoughts, mellow our hates and prejudices. We are grateful to Thee for your guidance in the wisdom of our forefathers who laid the groundwork for this great country in which men are free to worship, work and plan as their conscience dictates. Above all, teach the people of the world how to live together that we may have Peace."

I believe that if all would subjugate greed for power with this prayer, we would have peace, prosperity and a higher order of civilization.

I have always felt that faith is important to any great achievement—faith in God and faith in one's self. We in business may think of it as character, willingness to work and knowledge of what we are doing. However, too often the issues become confusing to where we cannot make up our mind. Then is when we find the answer by reducing the issues to their simple form with that something that compels action —Faith that we are right.

WHEN THE TENSION IS ON

By Frank Gifford
All-American Football Player, Voted "Most Valuable Player" in National League, 1956

❦

To handle the tension that comes before every football game, I've worked out a formula. Although quite simple, it is every bit as important to me as making sure my shoulder pads fit securely.

I find myself a quiet corner in either the locker room or the training quarters, and take just a few minutes for a silent prayer. The prayer itself, rather than being a request to perform well, is one of thankfulness that I have been given the physical ability to take part in something I sincerely love to do.

When I was in high school and later in college, I used to be somewhat embarrassed, and would always look for a place in which to offer my prayer as far away from my teammates as possible. Then I discovered that other players were also wandering off to some quiet spot for the same purpose.

One of the highlights of my football career was being invited to play in the 1954 All-Pro Game (similar to baseball's All-Star game) in the Los Angeles Coliseum. I'll never forget an incident that happened before the game.

Players and coaches had finished pre-game discussions, when Abe Gibron and Lou Groza, two stars of the Cleveland Browns, stood up and asked the entire team if they would mind waiting just a moment.

"It's a custom with us to have a moment of prayer together before each game," said Groza.

With that, each of those 250-pound goliaths dropped on one knee and bowed his head.

When one of the referees entered the locker room to tell us we were holding up the game, our whole ball club was kneeling for two minutes of prayer. I have often wondered what he thought then, and later, as we meshed together perfectly to beat the Western All-Stars by a wide margin that day.

You spectators, if you have field glasses, watch the pre-game huddles of professional, college, or high school games and notice the many players whose eyes are closed and lips moving. I notice it before every game the New York Giants play.

More and more athletes realize today that not only is body conditioning necessary, but also the spiritual conditioning of their minds. In football, as in life, you get knocked down and suffer losses from which you must recover. This takes good physical equipment and the proper mental outlook.

When I first joined the New York Giants back in 1952, I felt I could never be anything but a defensive back, that I could not run, pass or kick well enough to make the team.

I told this to the Giant coach who took me at my word, figuring that if I had no confidence in my offensive skill, he certainly wouldn't. So for several years I played a defensive halfback only.

Then during one of my pre-game prayers, it occurred to me that it was primarily a lack of faith that limited me to one role in football. So I asked God, not to make me a good runner or passer, but simply to help me to use all of the abilities which He had given me in a maximum way.

This prayer changed my attitude. The new attitude was followed by action. I began using workouts to practice running, kicking, passing. Soon the chance came for me to play offensive halfback in a game, and I was able to make the grade.

If I have learned anything about prayer it is this: When the game is close and I have a chance to score the winning touchdown in the last minute of play, an emergency call to God won't get it for me. What will, is determined by how well I have prepared myself physically and mentally over a period of months.

In other words, I don't see how one can expect miracles from an emergency prayer if he hasn't bothered to develop a closeness to God when things were going all right. Just as a football player could never amount to anything without physically conditioning himself, so too am I convinced that our prayers will not be effective unless we spiritually condition ourselves through life.

Reprinted by permission. Copyright 1957 by Guideposts Association, Inc. Guideposts is an inspirational monthly magazine for all faiths published at Carmel, N. Y. $2.00 a year.

THE SIGNATURE OF THE SOUL

By Margaret Culkin Banning

Author

❦

It has always seemed to me that prayer is so completely personal that it can be called the signature of the soul. Even if habits of worship are regulated by teaching or creed, even when words of supplication are spoken in concert, prayer itself will bear the mark of each individual. That can be imitated but never exactly duplicated.

The negligent-appearing man, so relaxed in his pew, may be deep in contemplative prayer. The apparently pious one, bent almost double as he prays, may be trying to drive a bargain with God, to trade good behavior for a personal favor. There is no necessary attitude for prayer. There is no recipe for prayer which can insure success. There is no prescription which can give the right amount of prayer for each person. Some live constantly in a state of prayer. Some schedule the time for it and always keep their appointments. Some pray only occasionally. No one knows which prayers have the most value. The only certain thing is that everyone needs prayer. The lives of those who never have that aspiration of wonder, gratitude and hope which we call prayer are truly frustrated.

Many years ago, in a time of desperate anxiety over the life of a child, I said over and over again a prayer which I had been told had always been answered. The child died. It didn't work, I thought bitterly, and for some time I was so sterile of soul that I could not pray. Then I found that without prayer I was confused to the point of breakdown. In my own way I brought my suffering to God, and even my explanations and arguments were prayers to Him. I began to realize that I had used that prayer "which didn't work" as a kind of charm or spell, and that, in the way I had made use of it, it was not a prayer at all.

Supplication must enter into many prayers, of course. But you can not take the excerpts out of the Lord's Prayer which suit you best and leave the rest of the context. You may and should ask for your daily bread but you must also be willing that God's will be done, if that particular prayer is to be completed. The Lord's Prayer is inclusive, and once that is mastered philosophically, the values of all prayers become more clear. For example, it is not possible to pray while you are bitter and resentful, except for release from such moods so that you may be able to pray.

If you can and do pray, you need no psychiatrist to help you. For prayer does what the psychiatrist tries to help you to do. It searches your actions and memories with perfect freedom, it deals with the secrets in your life that only you know. You reveal those secrets to God, sometimes without so much as a spoken word, and gain relief, pardon, and the sense of no longer carrying a burden in loneliness.

Prayer has always given people the deepest confidence which is available to human beings. It has been responsible for the greatest ventures. The one who prays can cast off fear. Whenever I board a plane I close my eyes and say a short prayer at the take-off. It often makes my seat mate say, "Lady, are you feeling badly already?" But I do not feel badly. In one instant I can offer gratitude for all the benefits of my life, wish with all my heart that I had done better, and accept any outcome. With that prayer said, I am ready for any flight and danger.

Prayer is the best cure for loneliness. In times of bereavement even the kindness of your friends can not reach your loss or offer real companionship. It is only in prayer that I can seem to establish contact with those I love and can no longer touch or see. But prayer can make contact when the senses can not, and I have often thought it proves immortality. Without some ability to pray and the hope of sustaining it, I would not care to live. For I would not be useful. I would always be at the mercy of despair, the most desolate state as well as the deepest mental sin. Prayer is hope. It is the secret desire of every man to feel—for himself and in his own way— that humanity is indestructible.

HOW PRAYER BALANCED A BUDGET

By Dr. L. R. Lunden
Comptroller, Treasurer, and Professor, University of Minnesota

❧

I thought at one time that I had known every anxiety of preparing a balanced budget for an institution of higher education. This was in a publicly supported one, and it was all a part of my job. Suddenly I found myself elected to the Board of Trustees of a church-related college and because of my background was named to the budget committee on the occasion of my first meeting. The financial outlook was dismal, and at the end of a long discussion the committee voted to bring to the Trustees a budget that was sadly out of balance. Because of my unfamiliarity with the local situation, I refrained from comment during this part of the discussion.

The unhappy budget was presented with no helpful hints as to how it might be balanced. The Chairman, a most devout Christian, asked the members of the Board to stand and join in prayer to the end that in some manner God would point out a way for a balance to be struck.

At that moment I asked to be heard. I said, rightly or wrongly, that it was not incumbent on God to balance that budget. Rather it was up to the trustees as stewards of His property to exercise every ingenuity at their command to bring the budget into balance and that the prayer should be for God to grant to us the wisdom and the courage to bring the budget into balance. I joined fervently in this prayer, and I am glad to say that this prayer was granted.

Since then I have returned to the primary responsibilities of my position among which is the preparation of a budget and the securing of public funds to effect a balance which is so important to the ongoing of a great institution. I have been helped in this by prayer. Not prayer that I would acquit myself creditably before official bodies but rather that the integrity of the institution that I represented would be maintained and that the thousands of faculty, staff, and students whose well-being depended upon the effectiveness of my presentation would be preserved.

I have never asked God to help me do a good job for myself. I have, through prayer, asked God to help me do a good job for those who depend upon my efforts. In approaching God with such a prayer I have examined my motives and the justice of my request. I feel that God is a partner in my work and that through prayer I have an infallible line of communication for help and guidance.

INTERCESSORY PRAYERS
BRING RESULTS

By Dr. Oliver J. Hart

Episcopal Bishop of Pennsylvania

❖

All effective prayer begins with the recognition that God is the creator and sustainer of all things. Once I went to Summerville, South Carolina, in the spring and as I looked at the beauty of the azaleas and dogwood and yellow jasmine, I thought, "What a poor world this would be if we did not have Someone to thank for such beauty."

Amidst the terrific pressures of life today I find serenity and courage in the realization that God is running the universe and we can base our lives on that sure foundation. We cannot force God's hand by a trick. We cannot outwit God by an occasional obedience. We must commit ourselves unreservedly to Him and then we can pray, "Our Father." Very often what we call our unanswered prayers are really our unfulfilled desires. One thing, at least, I have learned, i.e., to thank God that some of my prayers were **not** answered. Sometimes we glibly ask God for spiritual blessings which we really do not want. We have to learn to mean what we say in our prayers.

I have experienced and seen wonderful results from intercessory prayer. I do not know how it works. I know that it **does.** So often in life the best thing that we can do for those for whom we care is to hold them up to the goodness and love of God. Our prayer may not be answered in the way in which we desired but it **will** be answered. A man once said to me, "Help us to get rid of our pastor. He can't preach." I replied, "How hard do you pray for him? I know that he is sincere and earnest. You can help to make him a good preacher." Sometime later I met this man and he said to me, "I didn't put much stock in what you told me about praying for my pastor but I tried it and it really worked." Of course, his prayer had made a change in the man's attitude towards his pastor but I believe that it also helped the pastor himself.

I know that I have been helped by the prayers of my people —those on the earth and those in the world beyond this. I am convinced that we do not have to live on a dead level. If we pray sincerely, God will give us the power to be more unselfish in our thinking, and more effective in our service to other people.

THE ROOTS OF FAITH

By Strom Thurmond

U.S. Senator from South Carolina

Because I believe in God, I believe also in prayer. I do not see how a man can have one belief without the other.

A tree does not live very long if it cannot put out roots. These roots enable it to gain sustenance from the soil. Prayers are the roots of religious faith. Faith without prayer soon withers like a tree that has been severed from its roots. Prayer is the means by which we maintain communication with the Creator and derive spiritual sustenance.

One of my favorite verses in the Bible is Mark 9:23: "All things are possible to him that believeth."

I suggest, however, that this verse of Scripture implies that the believer must be one who prays, praying being an essential part of believing. Through prayer, the believer learns that while "all things are possible," all things are not desirable in the sight of God.

One may pray for a specific objective, and the prayer, no matter how earnest, may be denied. The supplicator does not get everything he wants, but he achieves something that is infinitely more important. He finds out what God wants.

In the Congress of the United States, regular prayer meetings are held, with one active prayer group on the House side and another in the Senate. Our Senate group meets every Wednesday morning for alternate periods of prayer and meditation. The leader's spiritual message is often followed by a general discussion of the importance of divine guidance for the country's lawmakers. Prayers are then offered for the legislative day, for colleagues, and for the country. I understand that twelve such prayer groups, their members coming from various branches and agencies of the government, meet in Washington.

While this is not the sort of thing that can be set down in the law books, I maintain that the practice of prayer is an important part of the legislative process. Truly, "all things are possible" when men of good-will share their great responsibilities with the Almighty!

Prayer takes many forms. I would not presume to advocate one form to the exclusion of others. For my own part, however, I find special solace in the kind of silent prayer that goes by the name of meditation. For prayer is not only beseeching, it is also listening, and quiet meditation is a way of listening to God.

"Faith is the substance of things hoped for, the evidence of things not seen." And prayer can invest faith with increasing substance, and bring new evidence from our God.

WHY I BELIEVE IN PRAYER

By E. B. Germany

President, Lone Star Steel Company

❀

So many instances in my life point to the real efficacy of personal prayer that I find it difficult to select any one phase of my prayer life to put down in this statement.

No important decision seems complete until it has been presented to God for His direction. Prayers for wisdom and guidance are my most common petitions. On many occasions when I am confused, prayer for calmness and direction have cleared my thinking and calmed my nerves. The greatest feelings of inspiration and real joy, however, come when I am traveling down a highway alone when I contemplate the goodness of our Lord as reflected in the lives of good men and women I know. On these occasions my prayers of gratitude, simple and spontaneous, flow in grateful praise and thanksgiving until I am completely humbled and shamed for my own weaknesses, omissions and sins.

I know God travels with me everywhere I go. I really felt His presence one afternoon when a dark, ominous cloud and heavy rain almost shut off all light just as I was crossing a railroad track. Suddenly a dozen high tension power lines and other telephone and telegraph wires fell across my car, both front and back. The live electric wires were burning the paint and exposed metal all around me and my motor died. I knew I was in serious trouble. Now, I clearly remember that I prayed, not for safety or escape, but for a wise decision. I know God gave me a calm head and reminded me the safest thing to do was sit and wait. I felt as though He were there with me in the car and panic left me.

Soon the storm ceased, electricians removed the hot wires and I went on to my office safely because God stilled my panic and gave me the wisdom to sit still and wait.

The longer I live the more conscious I am that in this busy era it is well to "Be still and know" that He is God.

PRAYER BRINGS INNER CONTENTMENT

By Albert H. Edwards

Formerly Vice-president, National Container Corporation, now retired

❦

No matter what is done for us, we should convey our thanks either in deeds, spoken words or writing. It takes so little to say "thank you" and yet it means so much. If this be true between man and man, then surely it should be true between man and God.

As we view the break of dawn, the setting sun, the bursting blossoms, the falling leaves, the growth of vegetation, animal life, and the human being, we must be awed by the wonders which God has created for us to enjoy.

I feel thankful and grateful to our Lord for everything around me, for the opportunity he has given me to live and to enjoy life.

A prayer of thanks is on my lips as I awake, as I deal with people, and as I sink into slumber at night.

Prayer gives me a great satisfaction. As I pray I am in communion with God. I also pray for his continued aid in all my doings, that I may always distinguish right from wrong. I pray that I may ever act justly in all my dealings.

God is ever watching over us during our lives, in sickness and in health. We must give thought to our safety and we shall be helped by our Father in heaven. As it is said, God helps him who helps himself.

A good meal is even better when we have thanked God for all his wondrous works, and have asked his blessing for that of which we are about to partake.

I gain satisfaction and contentment in giving praise to the Lord in unison with others, and believe that faith has a real restraining influence on those who would stray from the straight and narrow path.

It delights my soul to say prayers of thanks for the health and welfare of dear ones with tots who are so anxious to be lead into the right paths if their parents would only lead them.

How much better our world would be if everyone of us believed in prayer. Children would travel the road of rightousness and avoid juvenile delinquency if the parents and all adults would just set the proper example.

I know that prayer has helped me in many tight situations. God has answered by giving me strength when I needed it, by instilling the proper reasoning and thoughts in my mind when I felt helpless, by giving me the virtue of patience to listen to others. Meekness, humility and sincerity have brought about understanding and agreement, where there might have been only chaos.

Every human who seeks true contentment, will find it through prayer far faster than without it.

THE ETERNAL MIND

By Dr. Frank Hanft

School of Law, University of North Carolina

❧

Prayer should be part of our lives, like eating or sleeping. But is not habitual prayer likely to be only a stilted repetition of words? In church we may repeat the Lord's prayer, but although our tongues utter the proper words, our minds often are not on what we are saying. We hear our own voices say, "Hallowed be Thy name," but there may be no accompanying thought, no desire in our minds that His name be hallowed. Does this mean that our prayers are vain and insincere?

I think not. Of course we should not encourage the practice of letting our minds wander while we pray. But it is well that we pray regularly even though, being human, our minds do wander sometimes. There will come times when we will mean every word of our prayers. Life brings us tragedies, heartaches, moments of despair, crushing feelings of guilt, decisions which seem beyond our power to make. At such times our prayers come from our very souls, and our minds do not wander. Our whole thought is centered in our petitions to God, and we are unconscious of anything else. And it is well that meanwhile turning to God has become part of our way of daily life.

Is it not presumptuous to ask God for anything, since He is supreme goodness, and already knows what is good for our well being? On the contrary, throughout the Bible it is made clear that God desires that we pray. Part of God's purpose in wanting us to pray may be to cleanse our desires. Who among us has prayed, "Lord, help me cheat my neighbor?" Or, "Help me to corrupt my child, make him immoral, and implant in him all the conceit and vanity which have been mine?"

Of course not all prayers are petitions to God. Prayers are of many kinds. There are prayers of confession, of meditation, of praise to God. Then, too, there are prayers of thanksgiving. A man may be so lost in the beauty of a sunset sky that he forgets himself, and for the moment is not aware of whether he is warm or cold, young or old, standing up or sitting down; his mind loses itself in the beauty of the sky; for the moment the beauty has absorbed him and the sky is in him and he in it. Such an experience, incidentally, by analogy gives us a glimmer of understanding of Christ's teaching that He was in the Father and the Father in Him. After such a complete experience of beauty, one which only God can give, what is more natural than to thank God for it? Our thanks to a friend who takes us to a wonderfully beautiful show are enthusiastic and overflowing. God takes us to wonderfully beautiful shows every day of our lives if our eyes be open.

But does prayer really reach any ears but man's ears, any mind but man's mind? We pray, we speak words, our talking is real talking. But how many of us have heard God say anything? Is not prayer a monologue? What rational basis is there for thinking God answers, when silence invariably settles down when our own voices have finished praying?

In our day a new psychology is shedding a partial light on the truth we have long known to be there. Pioneers like Professor Rhine of Duke University are demonstrating that it is possible for thought to be communicated from one mind to another without any physical means whatever. No voice need speak, no telegraph keys need click; only the mind need think. Another mind may pick up the thought instantaneously. Since God in one aspect of His personality is infinite and the eternal mind, it is entirely in accord with what we now know that the eternal mind can receive our thoughts and communicate answers to our minds without spoken words. When inner assurance comes in response to our heartfelt prayers God may be answering us more directly than if a super-human tongue spoke words vibrating physically in ears of flesh. Men beyond number have, in other days and in our own, felt answers to their prayers although they have heard no words.

"IN REMEMBRANCE OF ME"

By Dr. Fredrik A. Schiotz

President, The Evangelical Lutheran Church

❧

There are few topics which engage the attention of people about which it is so easy to theorize as it is about prayer. But I am rescued from this temptation by the requirement for this statement, namely, as I understand it, that it be anchored in experience.

The daily prayers of appointed periods of personal or family worship vary for me from a quality of routine and compulsion to one of spontaneity and satisfaction. But I yield to the sense of compulsion even as I accept the necessity of regular eating.

It is the unscheduled private moments of prayer that seem to leave the greatest residue of blessing. Jesus' injunction in Luke 18:1 ". . . men ought always to pray, and not to faint" (or in the RSV "and not to lose heart") has served me as a muezzin call many times. When fear, worry, or frustration short circuits power prayer re-establishes contact.

If I meet someone whom I find it difficult to like, this mood changes when I pray for the person. Reaction response is then harnessed to a deeper level of life and thought. I find this transformation experience equally true when I pray for the man I could so easily enjoy hating.

All of us encounter moments of exhilaration: the solution of a knotty problem, the completion of an exacting piece of work, the honest gratitude of someone whom you have helped, the joy of stimulating companionship. Such exhilaration has to be expressed. Beyond what we may say to people, the unseen whispered ejaculation of thanksgiving to God keeps the soul on a straight course and robs pride of opportunity to do its debilitating work.

Group prayer is usually spoken prayer. But private prayer means most to me when it is an experience of listening, directed by the promises of God's Word. Archbishop William Temple put it well when he said, "If I have five minutes to devote to prayer and devote four minutes fifty-five seconds to remembering the presence of God, leaving but five seconds for speaking to Him, that is not a bad proposition."

In the remembrance of God, His wholeness (holiness) convicts me of my lack and self-centeredness (sin); but the same remembrance wipes out the guilt feeling in His forgiveness, leaving me with peace. In this act of remembrance, I am reassured that I do not walk or work alone: the Paraclete is at my side and I may count myself a co-laborer with God.

When Jesus instituted the Lord's Supper, He concluded by saying, "This do in remembrance of me." In this injunction I believe He also gave us a basic orientation for all prayer.

THE TRANSFORMING POWER
OF PRAYER

By Wilber M. Brucker

Secretary of the Army

❦

In my life prayer has been, and will always be, a simple matter of of talking with God, in an effort to identify myself constantly with Him, knowing that His all-prevailing presence and power will make my life infinitely more meaningful.

When I prepared to assume the grave responsibilities of the office of Secretary of the Army, my first request was that the Army Chief of Chaplains be present and invoke on my behalf, the Lord's benediction. I knew I could not successfully meet the challenge unless God's presence was made manifest at that moment in the act of prayer. I also asked that the 91st Psalm be read, because I was reared in a home where religion was considered as important as air and food, and the faith which the psalmist so eloquently expresses,—"I will say of the Lord, He is my refuge and my fortress: my God; in him will I trust,"—was the foundation upon which my life was built from early childhood.

Throughout the history of our military forces, prayer has played a most important role. Ours has always been a "praying Army," from the time its first Commander-in-Chief, General George Washington, knelt in the snow at Valley Forge in a dark hour, and besought God's blessing on his country's cause. Today our Army is still praying, as the individual soldier seeks comfort and guidance from his Maker, following the injunction of the great Apostle Paul; "Be anxious for nothing, but in everything by prayer and supplication with thanksgiving let your requests be made known unto God."

I have seen soldiers praying in worship at our Army chapels. I have seen them with heads bowed in prayer in many other places, both at home and overseas. In the rigorous cold of the Arctic, in the steaming heat of the tropics—wherever American troops are stationed—soldiers pray in concert or in solitude for the spiritual stamina they needed to perform their duties.

In the act of prayer we show our faith in God, our all-loving Father, Who knows our needs and will respond, out of His infinite love, in the way that is best for us. Our silent or spoken prayer to Him gives us strength to do His will, and to persevere in life's struggle. It is the means by which we gain the spiritual power to meet the demands of our time. Through the transforming power of prayer we bring ourselves and others to that better life and wider understanding which advance the work of God's kingdom on earth.

Answered Prayer

He asked for strength that he might achieve; he was made weak that he might obey..

He asked for health that he might do greater things; he was given infirmity that he might do better things.

He asked for riches that he might be happy; he was given poverty that he might be wise.

He asked for power that he might have the praise of men; he was given weakness that he might feel the need of God.

He asked for all things that he might enjoy life; he was given Life that he might enjoy all things.

He has received nothing that he asked for, all that he hoped for. His prayer is answered. He is most blest.

—Author unknown.

PRAYER BRINGS PEACE

By Mrs. George T. Gerlinger

Clubwoman, Author and Humanitarian

※

From the time I was a very little girl I believed strongly in prayer. At a time when I was seven or eight years old and living on our big cattle ranch in Arizona part of the time and part of the time in a mining town about thirty-five miles distant, our chief recreation was riding our saddle horses and driving in our various conveyances, often gathering up some young friends and with one of the ranch hands going on picnics in the nearby hills. These excursions usually occurred on Saturdays and I remember praying very earnestly that it would not rain so we could have our usual Saturday picnics. For seven long years my prayers were answered! Not a drop of rain fell in that part of Arizona and southern California, so we had picnics as usual for awhile, but soon we no longer had horses or surries, but were ruined financially by the seven-year drought when the cattle that had not died were hurriedly moved off the ranch, but sold for practically nothing because of the absence of fresh grass and the ranch land was worthless.

When I saw what was happening because I had prayed so earnestly that no rain would fall — and it did not fall for seven years — I felt a dreadful sense of responsibility that it was my prayers that had caused this terrible calamity to us and to all our neighbors. We had to send every day to Los Angeles for very large jars of drinking water. Otherwise, we could not have survived. So during all my days of childhood I prayed earnestly for special favors to me and it never occurred to me there was anything wrong about it. So as I went on into the University of California and had several opportunities to

600

join various women's sororities I stood up under the stress of rushing, together with a young friend of mine who was going to be a Y.W.C.A. secretary. I had my heart set, even from my young childhood, to be a missionary to the Chinese.

After six weeks of intensive rushing that had narrowed down to two of the groups of girls who were so attractive and their standards were high, it was impossible for me to make my decision and my roommate, who was looking forward to being a Y.W.C.A. secretary, said to me one evening, "I cannot make up my mind between these two groups and I am going to put it up to you to make the decision." I said, "I am just as puzzled as you are, but I will ask God to give me guidance in this matter." When I wakened in the morning it was perfectly clear which of the two groups I was going to join, and my roommate said she would go with me.

At that time I could not see why it was so important, but it was apparently God's will. About three years later I realized that what had determined the matter was what God probably had in store for me, and that was to marry a man from Oregon who came down to spend the Christmas holidays with the same family in San Francisco that I was visiting that Christmas time. Had I joined the other group I would not have met my cherished future husband.

Almost immediately he talked me out of being a missionary to the Chinese and said that I could probably hunt up a lot of things to do in Oregon that would be in the nature of missionary work. I married him and had forty-five years of great happiness as his wife and with our children. There were various things that came along for me to do and I have tried to measure up to many things which a dedicated public servant could do.

At every step in my life where a decision had to be made

and I felt incapable of determining it myself, I asked for guidance and it was always given to me. My dear husband who was a very earnest Christian always said that our daily prayers should be for grace to meet whatever comes to us in the way that Christians should meet life.

So my firm faith in the efficacy of prayer has brought peace and happiness throughout my long life.

PRAYER FOR GREATER STRENGTH

By Dr. Sanford Bates
Consultant in Public Administration

❦

The prayers that help are those in which we ask for more courage for ourselves, more devotion to principles of right action, more tolerance of others, more generosity of substance and of spirit.

These are the prayers that are likely to be answered, rather than prayers that ask for some material things to which we may not be entitled.

Instead of praying for riches, we will pray for the perseverance, and self-denial and steadfastness that bring us riches— riches in spirit, if not in dollars.

Instead of praying for good health, we will pray for the power to live the kind of life that brings health, health of mind if not of body.

Instead of praying for rain, we will pray for the patience and fortitude to keep cheerful and resourceful in times of deprivation as in times of plenty.

Prayers for the sort of advantage we have not earned will

probably not be answered—but the mere fact of prayer for greater strength within ourselves ofttimes carries its own response.

In our radio or television set, the response is there although we cannot hear or see it until we have "tuned in." Prayer may be our tuning in process, the method whereby we tap the great reservoir of eternal support. The universe in its infinite regularity, dependability and general beneficence is kind and good to those who seek to receive from it that which is kind and good.

Prayer is not the ecclesiastical version of the three wishes bestowed by a fairy godmother. Prayer is not selfish but unselfish. Prayer is the effort to get into right and helpful relations with the infinite and kindly force which governs the universe and which most of us call God.

The story is well told of an energetic farmer who purchased an old run-down farm in Vermont, neglected and overrun with weeds, the buildings falling into decay. The parish parson suggested that together they pray for the help of Almighty God in restoring the property—which they did.

A year later, the parson called again and exclaimed in surprise over the neat, well-painted buildings, the trim lawns and flowering shrubs. "Well," said the parson, "our prayers are answered. You and Almighty God have done a wonderful piece of work." "Yes," said the owner, "and you remember how it looked when God had it alone."

Prayers are for the strength which can come from religion and the Great Source of strength, but the answer lies within ourselves.

THE TEST OF PRAYER

By *Robert Wood Johnson*

Chairman of the Board, Johnson & Johnson

❦

As I believe in God, Who created the world and directs mankind and every individual who seeks His aid, I certainly believe in prayer. Jesus Christ gave us the model prayer in "Our Father," and told us to pray continually.

In prayer we lift up our minds and hearts to Him, Who is all powerful, all knowing, and Who is Providence itself. Such an act may be explicit—as when we use some form of prayer— or it may be an implicit or subconscious prayer, a kind of habit we can acquire which makes us do what we have to do with all our heart and mind, giving God service thereby and serving others. Such service, done in God's name, is a high form of prayer and is recognized by God as an act of love done to Himself. "Inasmuch as you did it to the least of my brethren you did it under Me." All work, therefore, done for the wider and wider application of Christian moral standards in social and industrial relations is in God's sight also a prayer.

Such a daylong prayer, shown in service, not only helps others and is perhaps the most sure way of building a true happy society, but it also has a direct influence on one's own conscious thoughts and unconscious actions. It makes one ready and responsive to the challenge of the moment, ready too to undertake whatever one feels by duty or charity called upon to do. What is more, such prayer preserves the mind from self-deceit, from giving honorable names to what in fact may be sheer self-interest or dishonest dealing.

Prayer is a way of living with God, as in a happy family each member is benefited by the others and is quietly conscious of their affection. It makes one steadfast in adversity and modest when successful, since it insures that we possess ideals which are not dependent on actual good or bad fortune. It gives his soul an inner strength, and at the same time inspires a man to ask God for help for all that he may need in his work, whatever it be, so that he may live a full life and complete what God has created him to be and to do.

Appeals for help from God are neither silly nor selfish. They are guaranteed by the words of Christ, "Ask, and you shall receive;" and though what we receive may not be what we expect, it is always what in the long run works out to the betterment of ourselves and the world. "We propose and God disposes." He disposes of our efforts, our work and our prayers.

Our prayers should be balanced with offers of thanks. With this we should pledge our offer of service to God and our neighbors. It is not for us always to ask, but also to give. The test of a prayerful life is whether, at the end of each day, one can offer the labor of it to God, for God to appraise it and to say, "Well done, thou good and faithful servant" and friend.

PRAYER IS MANY THINGS
By Dr. G. Paul Butler

Book and Religious Editor, The New York Mirror, and Editor of the Annual Volumes of Best Sermons

❀

Prayer is many things to different people. For some it is asking for something from the Ruler of the Universe—a favor, ability, children, life, health, beauty. And God has the power to give all these things.

Men of all races pray. The way they pray has varied from century to century and nation to nation. One man turns toward a special city; the Christian feels that his God is everywhere and goes with him at all times.

But prayer to others is a means of getting themselves in the mood to know and do God's way. My friend Chaplain Carpenter of the Air Force had a way with such prayer. It is important to know the will of God. The Bible points the way to know God's will—prayer confirms that way for each man or woman.

Prayer is many things—but most of all it is communication with God. True prayer is not getting something, but giving, not asking, but communing.

In need, man cries out for rain, for help, for love, for victory, for strength, for bread, for deliverance, for understanding, for wisdom.

True prayer is like love—it is being one with the Heavenly Father.

It is being one with Christ the Savior and Elder Brother, For a child, it may be the beginning of worship; for adults, it is growing up in the Way of God.

Prayer is bringing the mind and heart into harmony with God.

And prayer can be a true thanksgiving for things received by individuals or nations.

Public prayer is getting the spirit of all the people in a church or a nation in harmony with God, ready to do His will when or if they know it, and seeking His way if they do not know it.

"Secret Prayer" is what man really wants, what he says to his God in the innermost secrets of his heart; it is the real man or woman speaking to the Creator—Father of the Universe, the Christian speaking to his Christ and Savior.

Prayer is asking, seeking, finding—but it is also doing, one must knock on the door of faith, achievement, salvation, if the door is to be opened to you.

IN TIME OF TROUBLE

By Bolitha J. Laws

Chief Judge, U.S. District Court for the District of Columbia

❦

No doubt most people believe in prayer and in the usual course of their lives many customarily engage in daily prayers. Such prayers often are routine and without any specific appeal. But every person at some stage in his life will find need to turn in earnest appeal to Almighty God to provide help in time of hard stress. The human being is inadequate to meet many major problems. He is not sufficient unto himself. He may go through periods, perhaps years, when all is well with him. He may climb the ladder of fame. He may achieve fortune. He and those dear to him may enjoy good health. When problems have arisen, human help has been found to be sufficient to supply his needs. When he has turned to counsellor, physician, neighbor or friend, his needs have been filled.

But times inevitably come in the span of every life when momentous events will arise which are not within human powers to solve. One may strive valiantly to meet the crises caused by these events. At such times, he may seek aid from others more skilled than himself, but he finds no solution. In the stress of these occasions, his sole recourse is to the great Power beyond the earth, the mighty God, the everlasting Father. Here is his refuge and strength, his help in trouble.

It is a glorious privilege to be able to direct one's appeals to the hills from whence cometh help. This privilege will not avail unless the appeals not only are sincere and fervent but are in accord with the will of God and His purpose to promote righteousness. There is ready access to God by the man who has prayed at other seasons, has offered his thanks in times of favor and happiness, and has held to constant trust in the Almighty. Saints who have prayed through long seasons have received miraculous answers to prayers. But the one who prays for the first time will not be denied response if his appeal is sincere and his purpose measures to the pattern of the will of his Father in Heaven. God is a merciful Father and is understanding. Thus all persons have within them the privilege to turn earnestly to God for help and to have faith in obtaining a response which will quiet their unrests and their worries. This access to the Omnipotent is the greatest privilege of human life, for here is hope of peace and comfort when shadows creep and human help fails.

If there were to be taken from me any privilege I enjoy in life which I should beg to save beyond all others, it is the privilege to turn to my Creator in prayer in time of trouble.

WORK IS PRAYER
"LABOUR EST ORARE"

By J. George Frederick

Author and President, The Business Bourse, International

❦

I take the pragmatic view about prayer—and in my opinion and experience, this is the truly fundamental American attitude; the great outstanding characteristic of our modern western era, distinguishing it from others—even from the Continental one.

This attitude represents the distillation of all our western thinking and development, and I believe it goes like an arrow to the heart of the **real** "religion" of modern times. I have certainly no criticism of those who wish to cling emotionally to old religious forms and orthodoxies. But I am afraid that the "beat" of modern western life, experience and philosophy antiquates them, because they tend seriously to impair the great psychological core of truth in prayer, which is **prelude to action.** We want action in this world; the orthodoxies have mostly degraded **this** world in favor of some other world; a paralyzing philosophy.

No wonder the Romans, unChristian as they were, coupled work with prayer for even they, men of action, could not dodge the fact that the two are twins.

The humanist, who is the modern American, I think, is no believer in miracles or waiting for the end of this world, and has a complete distaste and mistrust of prayerfully asking Heaven to intervene for his personal benefit and profit. It represents a philosophy he cannot square with the finest feelings he knows, or the noblest standards of character. He hates weakness and is conditioned by western history to self-reliance. (That is no doubt why we are having a sturdy reaction against a "conforming" tendency now noticeable in American life). We definitely do not like spinelessness and laying our burdens on someone else's shoulders, and thus the older orthodox notion of prayer, as call on God to take over, is not really American in spirit, nor at all sound in the best religious philosophy.

We are using our newer, deeper knowledge of the human spirit; and also our greater modern spirit of independence and confidence in trial and error in our psychiatrically revised concept of prayer. The pragmatic philosophy is like that which Emerson put forth: "Let us do that of which we are most afraid." No wonder that this Emerson philosophy—which is what activated Clarence Day, Franklin Roosevelt and others, in their great hour of trial—is as typically American as corn-on-the-cob. It is the essence of modern prayer, to face courageously to that very thing of which we are most in terror. We are always, humanly, afraid of the very difficult, risky, dangerous, unknown task—but that is always in forward looking America, what our work is. Our very concept of work, we know is different from others—we see it as a challenge, a test, an opportunity for going faster forward, a step into the unknown, a new accomplishment, a thrilling experiment, a breaking out of the old shell into a newer life and return for our effort, a chance to measure our skill and our spirit of progress. We definitely like the new better than the old, and our prayer, our work, is ever to struggle forward.

Our American prayer therefore is **a form, a part of action.** We may use the old form and "ask God" but we are—and rightly so—really asking **ourselves** for help. We are "briefing" our spirits, bestirring our vagrant impulses, challenging our flagging energies, **ordering** our hesitant emotions to come to heel and **do.** Our "God help me" of today is not the medieval expectation of a Man with a Beard to step down from the Infinite to mend our little broken fence, all because we ask Him. It is, on the contrary, a challenge from our "Super-ego" to measure up to the best in us; measure up even more than we ever dreamed possible, if the matter is double serious, even tragic. We know we must somehow meet the challenge before us, and in our prayers in extremity we may even mystically challenge that part of us that we have realized is God-like and mysteriously stronger than we know; for we understand that "this is it"—that we are up for very grave trial.

Prayer, in our modern humanistic western view is therefore no old orthodox fuddy-duddy remnant, but a living psychiatric value which works. It is a proof that mind and spirit are supreme—that they can perform a real wizardy of help by calling out all of the still unfathomed resource that is in the human spirit when it stands up to its challengers and goes to work. Labour est orara.

MY PRAYER

By H. R. Baukhage
News Commentator

Almost every year, during the twenty years when I was broadcasting, I recited my mother's prayer:

My Prayer

Health, hope and working zeal,
A life no over long,
A Faith to make my purpose real,
A Love to make it strong.

There are several definitions of prayer. I cannot support unreservedly "that part of a petition which specifies the request or desire" unless that request or desire goes beyond purely selfish concern. A "solemn address to be Supreme Being" can result in renewed Faith and can strengthen Love, without which all else is futile.

PRAYER NECESSARY TO SUSTAIN LIFE

By Lillian Gish
Motion Picture Actress

Having had a wonderful mother, I was taught to say prayers before I can remember. So now it is like breathing—natural and necessary to sustain life in this beautiful world.

THE GREATEST SOURCE
OF MORAL POWER

By General Thomas S. Power

Commander-in-Chief, Strategic Air Command

✿

There is a great deal of talk today about the need for superior weapons in order to insure the survival of our way of life. But important as these weapons are, we must never forget that the character and quality of the men who handle these weapons are just as important.

The Soviets' all-out efforts to achieve their avowed goal of world domination are posing a grave threat to the free world, not only because of their ever growing military might but, even more so, because of their often demonstrated utter lack of morals and scruples in using any means at their disposal to attain their ends.

To counter this threat, we need both superior military and moral strength. I am confident that the same American ingenuity, which has made our country the most prosperous in the world, will always give us the military strength we need. And I am equally confident that the American's love for freedom and justice, which have made our country the bulwark of democracy, will always give us the moral strength to successfully fight for our convictions.

As we match weapon for weapon, we match fanaticism with dedication. And there is no doubt in my mind that the fanaticism of a godless society can never equal the dedication which stems from the devotion, loyalty and faith of a free people. It is this dedication to their vital mission which is giving the men of the Strategic Air Command the moral strength to perform their arduous duties in maintaining the most powerful deterrent to aggression the world has ever known.

Indeed, selfless dedication to our ideals and to the defense of these ideals is the very backbone of our military strength and the principal assurance that our solemn cause will prevail over the evil forces of communism. For those who threaten our cause have nothing to motivate them but the fanatic ambitions of their dictators, while our men are inspired by their faith in God and the knowledge that they can always draw renewed strength from the greatest source of moral power there is—their prayers.

"PRAYER WITHOUT CEASING"
By Dr. Edwin H. Rian
President, Jamestown College

❦

The Apostle Paul exhorts the Thessalonians to "pray without ceasing."

This seems psychologically impossible, because no man can pray constantly. On the other hand, everyone does pray "without ceasing," and in doing so reveals the innermost secret of his life. This is a fact because one's greatest desire is his greatest prayer, and this prayer he makes "without ceasing." Every ability and effort of a man's life are dedicated to this accomplishment.

This is one of the most significant meanings of prayer to me, because it lays bare my life—is it noble, Godlike, or is it mean and self-centered?

RESOURCES OF FAITH AND PRAYER

By Brooks Hays

Former U.S. Congressman from Arkansas
President, Southern Baptist Convention

❦

While I believe strongly in the practice of prayer in political matters, I question the use of prayer for victory for oneself or a favorite. I prefer the example of one of the country's great pugilists who was once asked if he prayed for victory in the ring. His reply was, "Would that be fair? With God on my side the other fellow wouldn't have much chance, would he?"

It is in the individual determination of great policy decisions and political judgments that religious guidance has chief significance. My political course has been full of frustration, yet I believe that God has made His strength and His counsel available in the major decisions. I have not sought to determine through prayer a course of expediency and success but rather to find in the use of spiritual resources the answer to the question that stirs the hearts of more public men than perhaps the people know, namely, "What is right?"

Even we hardened political workers are entitled to an occasional retreat to the household of faith. When I am privileged to be out of range of political shafts in the cloisters of faith, I have an opportunity in fellowship and in prayer to gain strength for the dilemmas that politics inevitably provides.

There have been other situations in which I felt the need of falling back finally upon the resources of faith. One of them came soon after I was elected to Congress. It involved legislation of a highly controversial character and there was considerable feeling about it in my District. I listened attentively to the debate because I was anxious to cast the right vote. I was convinced finally that I should vote against the pending bill. Several of my closest friends used phone calls to urge me to support it. One of them who had been prominent in my campaign was a friend to whom I felt such a strong obligation that it caused me real pain to have to say "No" to him. It was a matter about which he held a strong conviction and I knew that it might mean the severance of our political ties, though not our friendship. His protests made me realize that I might have to pay with defeat for my own convictions. But I recalled that many others in places of governmental responsibility had faced even greater tests and had subordinated personal interests. Their examples encouraged me.

There was the incident, for example, involving my friend from a populous state who stood almost alone against his colleagues because he thought they were wrong. As he leaned against the back rail in the House Chamber as the roll call began, I asked "How are you voting?" He said, "I don't know—I just know how I ought to vote, and how I vote will prove whether or not I am fit to be a member of this House." I was proud of him when I heard him vote against his political interest. More of that occurs, perhaps, than our people realize. My friend's reward for his courageous vote will not come in providential interference with his state's election but in the satisfactions of an honest heart and a consciousness of God's approval.

In the situation confronting me in this early congressional experience it was extremely difficult for me to vote against what I knew to be the prevailing opinion in my District. I wanted to remain in Congress, so the pressures were both political **and** personal. Most of my closest friends—those who had taken greatest interest in my campaign—were for an "aye" vote. I was unconvinced by the arguments, and voted "no." Again I had help in prayer. Sitting by an old friend in the

House Chamber who remained silent as the roll was called, because perhaps he knew of the conflicts troubling me, I asked God to help me—to give me inner peace that comes from doing what one knows he should do. Millions had done it before and would do it again. I received the assurance that an answered prayer provides. I walked from the Capitol with calmness and peace. From this experience I have had my most convincing proof that the Eternal God is indeed our refuge, and underneath us are the Everlasting Arms.

PRAYER IS PRICELESS

By Walter J. Kohler, Jr.

Former Governor of Wisconsin

❦

The power of prayer is as deep, as abiding, as eternal as mankind.

It rests on humanity's belief that life has significance, purpose, and meaning.

It rests, too, on the conviction that there exists a Being who is wise, just, powerful, compassionate and understanding far beyond our comprehension—a Being of love and kindness, who having created all must therefore know and understand all.

The power of prayer is as miraculous, mysterious and infinite as the universe. It can assuage grief, ease pain, revive courage, renew strength.

It can restore determination, overcome fatigue, create patience, dissipate fear.

It is priceless—and costless.

It is immeasurable.

And it is everywhere, all the time.